**Oryx Sourcebook Series
in Business and Management**

Hotel and Restaurant Industries
An Information Sourcebook

by Judith M. Nixon
Consumer & Family Sciences Librarian
Purdue University Libraries, West Lafayette, IN

ORYX PRESS
1988

94-0783

The rare Arabian Oryx is believed to have inspired the myth of the unicorn. This desert antelope became virtually extinct in the early 1960s. At that time several groups of international conservationists arranged to have 9 animals sent to the Phoenix Zoo to be the nucleus of a captive breeding herd. Today the Oryx population is nearly 800, and over 400 have been returned to reserves in the Middle East.

Copyright © 1988 by
The Oryx Press
2214 North Central at Encanto
Phoenix, AZ 85004-1483

Published simultaneously in Canada

Printed and Bound in the United States of America

∞ The paper used in this publication meets the minimum requirements of American National Standard for Information Science—Permanence of Paper for Printed Library Materials, ANSI Z39.48, 1984.

Library of Congress Cataloging-in-Publication Data

Nixon, Judith M.
  Hotel and restaurant industries : an information sourcebook / by Judith M. Nixon.
    p. cm. — (Oryx sourcebook series in business and management ; 17)
    Includes index.
    ISBN 0-89774-376-8
    1. Hotels, taverns, etc.—Bibliography.   2. Restaurants, lunch rooms, etc.—Bibliography.   3. Food service—Bibliography.
  I. Title. II. Series.
  Z6250.N59   1988
  [TX911]
  016.3384'7647'94—dc19   88-15413

Contents

Introduction

Hospitality is an expanding and developing industry. The sales of food consumed away from home have quadrupled in the last fifteen years, and employment in hotels and restaurants has nearly doubled since 1970. Foodservice is one of the fastest growing job categories in the United States. In addition, we have seen an increase in college-level programs that offer degrees in Hotel and Restaurant Management. In 1922, Cornell University offered the first degree-level course in hotel administration; today there are over 500 schools offering courses related to the hotel and restaurant industry. Each of these schools is building a collection of books and journals and teaching students how to research problems in the industry.

Yet there has been no current bibliography to assist in this collection development. In 1984, the National Restaurant Association published a bibliography called *The Foodservice Library*, but it covers only the restaurant industry and is already becoming a bit dated. The subject catalog cards of the Cornell Hotel Administration Library were photographically reduced and reproduced in two oversized volumes in 1979 and published as the *Subject Catalog of the Library School of Hotel Administration, Cornell University*, by G. K. Hall. This catalog is useful for retrospective research but not helpful for current books.

New Hotel and Restaurant Industries (HRI) schools frequently call our library for a list of currently acquired materials to help them start a collection. To meet this need, I have reviewed and annotated over a thousand of the the most important books and journals available in the United States related to the hospitality industry. Emphasis has been placed on material published in the 1980s; but earlier works are included if they have historic value or are still useful. The bibliographic information for each title is included. In cases where the publisher or place of publication was not listed on the book, the abbreviations s.n. (sine nomine) and s.l. (sine loco) have been used.

This bibliography is based primarily on the Consumer & Family Sciences Library at Purdue University in West Lafayette, Indiana, which has been specializing in restaurant and hotel materials for many years and has accumulated an excellent collection. To expand the bibliography, *Books in Print*, trade journals, and publishers' announcements were searched for additional titles. Many of the books not available at Purdue were purchased or obtained on Interlibrary Loan. Every title included in this book has been carefully examined and annotated for this volume.

This book concludes with two appendices. The first provides a list of state and national/international associations. The second appendix is a list of colleges offering hotel, restaurant, and foodservice programs. It is my sincere hope that this bibliography will increase access to material in the industry and be of assistance to restaurateurs, hoteliers, foodservice managers, and all the librarians who serve them.

Core Library Collection

BOOKS

1. American Hotel Association Directory Corp. *OAG Travel Planner, Hotel & Motel Red Book.* Oak Brook, IL: Official Airline Guides, Inc. 1886–. (Quarterly)

> This directory lists all members in the American Hotel and Motel Association plus nonmembers who apply for a listing. As such, it is very comprehensive and includes over 12,000 hotels and motels across the U.S. and Canada. The main section is arranged by state; the address, telephone, credit cards accepted, and rates are given for each hotel. In addition, each hotel is categorized by location, such as airport, expressway, downtown, resort or suburban, and meal plan. Special sections list airport hotels, meeting hotels, resort and condominiums, and international hotels.

2. Bohnet, Gerald V., ed. *The Travel and Tourism Index.* Laie, HI: Business Division, Brigham Young University—Hawaii Campus. 1984–. (Quarterly)

> This is a new index published by Brigham Young University, Hawaii Campus. It indexes periodicals, newsletters, and bulletins related to the travel field. It does include some very important journals not indexed elsewhere and, therefore, is a good supplement to them.

3. Bowes, Anna De Planter. *Bowes and Church's Food Values of Portions Commonly Used.* 14th ed. Revised by Jean A. T. Pennington and Helen Nichols Church. Philadelphia, PA: Lippincott, 1985. 257 p.

> Designed as a quick reference for the nutritional value of foods. The main table, "Nutrient Contents of Food," lists almost every common food and beverage by name, description, brand name, and serving portion. Items are arranged in general categories (i.e., meats, etc.). Each entry has twenty-nine headings, ten more than the last edition. Water and cholesterol content and a number of new vitamin and mineral entries are now included. Amino acids are now in a supplementary table at the back of the book where other substances of nutritional concern, such as caffeine, are also found. There is a straight alphabetical index by food item.

4. Chesler, Bernice. *Bed & Breakfast Coast to Coast.* Lexington, MA: Stephen Greene Press, 1986. 416 p.

> This directory lists over 200 B&B reservation services that can place travelers in bed and breakfast accommodations. Arranged by state, each entry includes name of the reservation service, address, telephone number and hours, type of accommodations available, other services (such as airport pick-up), settings of B&Bs, descriptions of hosts, breakfast and reservation policies, and rates.

5. Coffman, C. DeWitt. *Hospitality for Sale: Techniques of Promoting Business for Hospitality Establishments.* East Lansing, MI: Educational Institute of the American Hotel & Motel Association, 1980. 339 p.

> This is a textbook on marketing techniques for the hotel and motel industry. The goal is very specific—to plan and carry out sales programs in the restaurant and lodging industries. It is divided into five parts: "Pre-sale" (planning), "Selling Instruments" (advertising,

publicity, and public relations), "Sales Agents" (use of outside organizations), "Act of Selling," and "Post-Sale" (evaluation.)

6. Coltman, Michael M. *Hospitality Management Accounting.* 3d ed. New York: Van Nostrand Reinhold Co., 1987. 449 p.

> A basic textbook on accounting systems appropriate for hotels, restaurants, resorts, clubs, and volume feeding operations. The second edition incorporates changes reflected in the *Uniform System of Accounts for Hotels* (1977). This new third edition includes new chapters on feasibility studies and financial goals and information systems. Also additional information on pricing and budgeting have been added. Topics include financial statement analysis, ratio analysis, cost control, and cost management. Glossary appended.

7. *Composition of Foods.* Agricultural Handbook, no. 8. Washington, DC: U.S. Dept. of Agriculture, Human Nutrition Information Service, 1976–. (Loose-leaf)

> Since 1896, the U.S. Department of Agriculture has compiled nutrition composition tables. This new edition is a major revision which will greatly expand the access to the information available on food composition. Instead of a slim, one volume book, it is being issued in the following parts: "Dairy and Egg Products"; "Spices and Herbs"; "Baby Foods"; "Fats and Oils"; "Poultry Products"; "Soups, Sauces and Gravies"; "Sausages and Luncheon Meats"; "Breakfast Cereal"; "Fruits and Fruit Juices"; "Pork Products"; "Vegetables and Vegetable Products"; "Nut and Seed Products"; "Beef Products"; "Beverages"; and "Legumes and Legume Products." Other sections will be published in the future.

8. The Consortium of Hospitality Research Information Services. *Lodging and Restaurant Index.* Edited by Judith M. Nixon. West Lafayette, IN: The Restaurant, Hotel, and Institutional Management Institute, Purdue University, 1985–. (Quarterly)

> This is the most comprehensive periodical index available in the hospitality industries. It indexes twenty-nine journals under subject headings developed especially for the industry. Each entry includes title, author, and bibliographic citation. Important articles are starred. The consortium plans to expand the scope in future years by adding additional titles and possibly other media.

9. Council on Hotel, Restaurant, Institutional Education. *U.S. and International Directory of Schools.* Washington, DC, 1972–. (Annual)

> Arranged alphabetically by state, this is a directory of schools that offer degrees in hospitality. It includes schools that are not members of the Council on Hotel, Restaurant, and Institutional Education as well as those that are members. The book is arranged by state or country. Within each state, schools are arranged by level (baccalaureate degree granting colleges, community and junior colleges, secondary schools). Each entry includes school, department name, address, telephone, contact person, degrees, and a brief description of the program. Some overseas schools are included.

10. Cournoyer, Norman G., and Marshall, Anthony G. *Hotel, Restaurant & Travel Law.* 2d ed. North Scituate, MA: Breton Publishers, 1983. 675 p.

> This book's purpose is to educate hoteliers and restaurateurs about legal problems and how they can be avoided. It covers the laws and regulations in labor relations, safety rules, and product liability as well as local, state, and federal regulations specifically related to the industry. The case method approach is used with the intent of training future managers to consider the legal aspects of their decisions.

11. CSG Information Services. *Directory of Chain Restaurant Operators.* Chicago: Lebhar-Friedman, Inc. (Annual)

> This directory contains detailed information on 3,000 chain restaurants. In addition to the directory information, it gives sales, number of stores, and various other useful financial facts.

12. Culinary Institute of America. *Culinary Learning Resources Catalog.* Hyde Park, NY, 1985? (Loose-leaf)
The Culinary Institute of America produces a wide variety of audiovisual materials to teach cooking and foodservice techniques. This catalog is a selected list of programs that can be purchased, previewed, or leased from them. Each entry includes a description of the program, time, instructor, and order number. In addition to cooking topics, there are programs on table service, and sanitation. Most programs are video tapes, some are also available in slide-tape format.

13. Culinary Institute of America, and Editors of Institutions Magazine. *The Professional Chef.* 4th ed. Edited by LeRoi Al Folsom. Boston: CBI Publishing Co., 1974. 470 p.
First published in 1962, this is the most comprehensive study of professional cooking available. It includes information on equipment, formulas, techniques, and recipes from many nations. Most recipes are for fifty portions. The introductory chapters cover chefs, foodservice occupations, sanitation, safety, cost, and converting recipes. The bulk of the book is quantity recipes.

14. Daschler, John P., and Ninemeier, Jack D.*Supervision in the Hospitality Industry.* East Lansing, MI: Educational Institute of the American Hotel & Motel Association, 1984. 332 p.
This is an application of basic supervisory principles to hospitality operations. Part one gives background information and explains the responsibilities of the supervisor and his or her role in various aspects of the operation. Part two covers the supervisor in personnel administration including training, evaluation, and salary administration. Part three discusses communications, motivational techniques, the disciplinary process, and related skills. Part four includes working with unions, labor control systems, and management development.

15. Dittmer, Paul, and Griffin, Gerald G. *Principles of Food, Beverage, & Labor Cost Controls for Hotels and Restaurants.* 3d ed. New York: Van Nostrand Reinhold Co., 1984. 352 p.
This college text is designed as an introduction to the process of cost and sales control. Principles are applied to purchasing, receiving, storing, issuing, and preparing of food and beverages. Labor control is also covered. Learning objectives are clearly stated at the beginning of each chapter and problems and exercises are provided at the end.

16. Dun & Bradstreet Credit Services. *The Restaurant Industry: A Strategic and Financial Analysis of Full Service and Fast Food Restaurants.* 2d ed. Strategic Industry Study. New York, 1985. 436 p.
A detailed study of the present and future trends of the industry based on key business ratios and industry norms from Dun's Financial Profiles and demographic and marketing information from Donnelley Marketing Information Services. National and regional analyses are provided. Continuing and newly emerging trends are discussed in detail. Extensive statistical charts and graphs are included.

17. Ellis, Raymond C., Jr., and The Security Committee of American Hotel & Motel Association. *Security and Loss Prevention Management.* East Lansing, MI: Educational Institute of the American Hotel & Motel Association, 1986. 285 p.
This text is designed to help in the development of a security program and also to inform employees about security concerns. The nine chapters address various security issues such as security programs, equipment, procedures covering guest concerns, responsibilities for guests' assets and funds, emergency management, and safety. A guide to OSHA regulations is included. Appendices include sample room postings and some court cases.

18. Emerson, Robert L. *Fast Food: The Endless Shakeout.* rev. ed. New York: Chain Store Publishing Corp., 1982. 345 p.

Emerson is a securities analyst, so his book offers an outsider's view of the chain restaurant industry. He looks at why some chains have succeeded where others have failed, the keys to consumer acceptance of fast food, and how to manage and control rapid growth of a chain. Interviews with chain executives from McDonald's, Wendy's, Pizza Hut, Kentucky Fried, and Burger King discuss strategic decisions, past mistakes, and future prospects.

19. Ensminger, Audrey H., et al. *Foods & Nutrition Encyclopedia.* Clovis, CA: Pegus Press, 1983. 2 vols. 2,415 p.

This two-volume encyclopedia covers virtually everything about food and nutrition for consumers and professionals. Over 2,800 entries covering historical topics, brief definitions of terms, and full encyclopedia-type entries on many foods, nutrition, and health topics. Black-and-white illustrations and charts are included. A full "Food Composition Table" is included in volume one.

20. Epstein, Becky Sue, and Klein, Hilary Dole. *Substituting Ingredients: A Cooking Reference Book.* Charlotte, NC: East Woods Press, 1986. 127 p.

This book lists over 350 ingredients that can be used as substitutes in recipes. The called-for item is followed in each section by a list of possible substitutes. Chapters include baking ingredients; condiments; dairy products; fruits and nuts; general cooking; herbs, spices, and flavorings; meat, fish, and poultry; and vegetables. There also are chapters on measurement equivalents, formulas for homemade cleaners, and instructions on how to compensate for putting in too much of some ingredient.

21. Fay, Clifford T., Jr.; Rhodes, Richard C.; and Rosenblatt, Robert L. *Managerial Accounting for the Hospitality Service Industries.* 2d ed. Dubuque, IA: W. C. Brown Co., 1976. 596 p.

A text on the use of practical accounting techniques in the hospitality industry. The authors, who are members of the accounting firm of Harris, Kerr, Forster, and Company, emphasize the role of accounting in managerial decision making. Chapters cover most aspects of basic accounting as it relates to the industry, including such subjects as financial statements and uniform systems, cost-volume-profit analysis, cost accounting, responsibility accounting in the hospitality service industries, capital budgeting, and income tax planning and decisions.

22. Fay, Clifford T., Jr., et al. *Basic Financial Accounting for the Hospitality Industry.* East Lansing, MI: Educational Institute of the American Hotel & Motel Association, 1982. 237 p.

This is an introductory text designed to replace *Basic Bookkeeping for the Hospitality Industry.* More emphasis and detail are given here to major financial statements, and a chapter on equities has been added. Organization and format have been revised. All basic aspects of accounting as it applies to the hospitality field are covered including front office, sales and payroll accounting as well as other aspects like fixed assets and inventory.

23. Forrest, Lewis C., and Ninemeier, Jack D. *Training for the Hospitality Industry: Techniques to Improve Job Performance.* East Lansing, MI: Educational Institute of the American Hotel & Motel Association, 1983. 354 p.

Training is a problem in the lodging and foodservice industries because they are very labor-intensive fields that utilize large numbers of unskilled or semiskilled workers. This results in low productivity and high turnover rates. To combat these problems, Forrest outlines a framework for training including recruiting and selecting employees, initial training, assessing when job performance can be improved by training, or other work-improvement approaches.

24. Frank, Robyn C., ed. *Directory of Food and Nutrition Information Services and Resources.* Phoenix, AZ: Oryx Press, 1984. 287 p.
   This book is a gold mine of information on the food industry; it is both a directory and a bibliography. Included are organizations and universities, databases, software, journals, abstracts and indexes, and a list of key reference materials.

25. Gisslen, Wayne. *Professional Baking.* New York: Wiley, 1985. 346 p.
   Originally designed as a text for students, this book is also aimed at amateurs who wish to learn professional techniques. Basic theory and principles as well as proper procedures for professional baking are explained. The approximately 400 recipes have been selected to reinforce the techniques explained in each chapter. All basic baking categories are covered including breads, doughnuts, pies, pastries, cakes, cookies, and other desserts as well as icings, sauces, and decorating techniques.

26. Gisslen, Wayne. *Professional Cooking.* New York: Wiley, 1983. 680 p.
   This is one of the best textbooks teaching basic cooking skills for any type of foodservice operation. It has a dual goal of understanding and performing, and it includes over 800 recipes applying procedures and techniques presented. Illustrated with drawings, photographs, and color plates.

27. Gomes, Albert J. *Hospitality in Transition: A Retrospective and Prospective Look at the U.S. Lodging Industry.* Houston, TX: Pannell, Kerr, Forster, Houston Administrative Office, 1985. 166 p.
   A clear and scholarly review of the hotel and motel industry's history, composition, and its impact on the economy in general. Many statistical charts are included.

28. Goodwin, John R. *Hotel Law: Principles and Cases.* Columbus, OH: Publishing Horizons, 1987. 693 p.
   A college-level textbook, this examines the laws and regulations in the travel and hotel industries and emphasizes management principles that are necessary to comply with the laws. It is arranged by business topics in the industry. Topics covered include sales contracts, agents and contractors, employee relations, credit cards, business organization, ownership and management of property, duties and rights of innkeepers and guests, legal liability, reservations and check-in, guests' property and injuries, restaurant and bar law, travel agent law, and carrier law.

29. Griffith, Clyde L. *The Legal Problem Solver for Foodservice Operators.* 3d rev. ed. Washington, DC: National Restaurant Association, 1983. (Loose-leaf)
   A National Restaurant Association publication which covers basic legal information in nonlegal language on such topics as minimum wage, working hours, tips, overtime, hiring, record keeping, tax problems, and using the polygraph among others. Supplements tabulate wage, hour, and child labor laws by state.

30. Grossman, Harold J. *Grossman's Guide to Wines, Beers, and Spirits.* 7th rev. ed. Revised by Harriet Lembeck. New York: Scribner, 1983. 638 p.
   Grossman's is one of the major text and reference books in the field. Updated periodically, it has excellent information on wines from all over the world as well as beers, distilled spirits, and liqueurs. Information is included on how various alcoholic beverages are made and how they should be served. There are also chapters on bar operation, merchandising, beverage control, and beverage laws.

31. Hart, Christopher, and Troy, David. *Strategic Hotel/Motel Marketing.* rev. ed. East Lansing, MI: Educational Institute of the American Hotel & Motel Association, 1986. 319 p.
   This is a text on marketing principles and planning. It covers basic concepts, analysis, advertising, and other tools of marketing, as well as the marketing plan and growth strategies. Case studies and present and future trends are included.

32. Hartland, Robert W. *Responding to Unionization Efforts: A Guide to Assist Foodservice Owners and Managers in Overcoming Unionization Attempts.* Washington, DC: National Restaurant Association, 1984. 31 p.

This is a pamphlet designed to help management overcome unionization attempts. Stage one covers positive relationships with employees as well as "no solicitation" rules and proper security of employee lists. Stage two gives early warning signs. Stage three tells how to mobilize management, gather data about the union, and get your position heard. Stage four discusses how to deal with union representatives.

33. Horwath & Horwath International. *Worldwide Lodging Industry.* New York, 1975–. (Annual)

This work compiles statistics from all over the world on various aspects of the lodging industry. It begins with an overall analysis of the present state of the worldwide industry. The data are then presented for the five regions: Africa, Europe, Asia and Australia, North America, and Latin America. The statistics on over a dozen subjects are presented for each region including market data, comparison of sales and profitability, occupancy, and food and beverage statistics. Each area includes a short section giving the highlights of the survey for that region, a general profile of the typical contributor, and currency conversion tables.

34. *Hotel & Travel Index.* New Jersey: News America Publishing, Inc. 1951–. (Quarterly)

Published quarterly this is the most comprehensive and up-to-date directory of hotels available. It includes listings of hotels, motels, and resorts worldwide; over 36,000 hotels are listed. Arrangement is geographical by country, state, and city. Entries are very concise and include number of rooms, rates, appointed hotel representatives, manager, address, telephone, 800 number, cable number, a code denoting automated airline reservation system, and codes for credit cards accepted. Many advertisements are included which have additional information. Over 250 city maps are also included.

35. Hotel Law Publishing Service. *Hotel & Motel Laws.* Canoga Park, CA, 1977–. (Loose-leaf)

This is a legal loose-leaf service which covers federal and state statutes related to the operation of hotels and motels in the U.S. Administrative regulations and judicial opinions are cited but not reproduced in the set. Replacement and supplemental pages are regularly mailed to subscribers to keep the set current.

36. Jefferies, Jack P. *Understanding Hotel/Motel Law.* East Lansing, MI: Educational Institute of the American Hotel & Motel Association, 1983. 310 p.

This book deals in lay terms with basic legal principles that affect the lodging industry. Special emphasis is given to federal regulations including OSHA regulations and the National Labor Relations Act. The book covers the hotel guest and employees, laws relating to general operations, taxes, antitrust laws, franchises, convention and group contracts. Appendices include a glossary of legal terms and illustrative cases.

37. Kasavana, Michael L. *Computer Systems for Foodservice Operations.* New York: Van Nostrand Reinhold Co., 1984. 259 p.

A book intended to help incorporate the computer into foodservice management, it explains computer terminology, point-of-sale systems, control systems, and accounting-based systems for the foodservice area. Electronic cash register configurations, automated precheck systems, precost systems, menu engineering, and beverage control through computerization are among the topics included. Diagrams, summaries, and lists of key concepts in each chapter facilitate understanding for the nonexpert.

38. Kazarian, Edward A. *Foodservice Facilities Planning.* 2d ed. Westport, CT: AVI Publishing Co., 1983. 308 p.

This textbook covers facility design for all types of foodservices from fast food restaurants to hospitals. The major emphasis is on the planning process including the feasibility study and planning for functional use and for atmosphere. Space requirements for workers and equipment and layouts are also included.

39. Keister, Douglas C. *How to Use the Uniform System of Accounts for Hotels and Restaurants.* 2d rev. ed. Washington, DC: National Restaurant Association, 1983. 50 p.
Designed to supplement basic accounting texts, this book is written specifically about hotel and restaurant accounting. It is intended to amplify topics presented in *The Uniform System of Accounts for Restaurants* (National Restaurant Association, 5th rev. ed., 1983) and *The Uniform System of Accounts for Hotels* (American Hotel & Motel Association, 7th rev. ed., 1977). Chapters cover accounting terms, posting, journals, cash, accounting, inventories, accrued expenses, and nearly sixty other topics. Separate practice sets are included for hotels and restaurants.

40. Kleinman, Rhonda H., and Kleinman, Allan M., comps. *The International Cookery Index.* Neal-Schuman Cookery Index Series, no. 1. New York: Neal-Schuman Publishers, Inc., 1987. 230 p.
This is an index to over 25,000 recipes from fifty-one English-language cookbooks that contain recipes from around the world. All books indexed are currently in print and available in the U.S. The index provides access by name of well-known dishes (i.e., sauerbraten), major ingredients, preparations (i.e., jellied or pickled), and nationality or cuisine. Under each nationality entry there is a list of major books on that cuisine.

41. Knight, John Barton. *Knight's Foodservice Dictionary.* Edited by Charles A. Salter. New York: Van Nostrand Reinhold Co., 1987. 393 p.
This comprehensive dictionary gives short, concise definitions of basic ingredients and preparation methods, accounting and cost control terms, equipment, management and marketing concepts, nutrition, sanitation, and safety terms. Some foreign terms are included also. Cross-references to related terms are printed in bold type.

42. Kotschevar, Lendal Henry. *Management by Menu.* 2d ed. Dubuque, IA: W. C. Brown; Chicago: National Institute for the Foodservice Industry, 1987. 364 p.
Like the first edition, this updated edition presents the menu as the central theme controlling most other foodservice functions. It is still the only book that ties the menu in with management principles. Among other subjects, it covers menu planning, analysis, pricing, and merchandising.

43. Kotschevar, Lendal Henry. *Quantity Food Purchasing.* 2d ed. New York: Wiley, 1975. 684 p.
This is the most well-known textbook and reference handbook in food purchasing. Emphasizing the product information needed to purchase food, it is divided into chapters based on food categories, i.e., fruits and vegetables, dairy products. Each food is then described; various kinds are compared; and sizes, qualities, and seasons are listed. Alcoholic beverages and some nonfood supplies such as linen and tableware are also included.

44. Kotschevar, Lendal Henry, and Terrell, Margaret E. *Foodservice Planning: Layout and Equipment.* 3d ed. New York: Macmillan, 1986. 543 p.
A textbook dealing with the overall arrangement and layout of foodservices and equipment. Section one on planning, discusses the design of the facilities, layout characteristics, and space allocation. Section two is on functional areas of food facilities such as receiving and storage. Section three is on supporting factors such as lighting and energy. Section four is on equipment selection.

45. Langdon, Philip. *Orange Roofs, Golden Arches: The Architecture of American Chain Restaurants.* New York: Alfred A. Knopf, 1986. 223 p.
Langdon provides a look at the history and development of chain restaurant architecture in the U.S. He traces the decor and design from the origins of chain restaurants to the present. The author's thesis is that these restaurants embody the spirit of their times. Chapters include origins of the chain restaurant industry, standardizing the image, drive-ins, Googie-style coffee shops, and design since 1975.

46. Laventhol & Horwath. *Uniform System of Accounts for Restaurants: Adopted and Recommended by the National Restaurant Association.* 5th rev. ed. Washington, DC: National Restaurant Association, 1983. 159 p.

> The purpose of the uniform system is to give restaurants a common language for their accounting statements. Part one outlines the classification of income and expense items. It covers profit and loss statements and balance sheet accounts. Part two contains examples of the system using various types of restaurants, i.e., large, small, drive-in, hotel, and club. Part three has forms for keeping detailed records. Part four contains forms and explanations for record keeping in a small restaurant.

47. *Leisure, Recreation and Tourism Abstracts.* Farnham Royal, England: International and World Leisure and Recreation Association, 1981–. (Quarterly)

> This quarterly publication indexes and abstracts (or summarizes) journal articles from around the world related to tourism. It continues *Rural Recreation and Tourism Abstracts* (1976–1981). The abstracts in each issue are arranged by a broad subject classification. Author and detailed subject indexes are in the back of each issue. (Available online through Dialog as part of CAB Abstracts or on BRS.)

48. Lichine, Alexis, et al. *Alexis Lichine's New Encyclopedia of Wines & Spirits.* 5th rev. ed. New York: Alfred A. Knopf, 1987. 771 p.

> This is a comprehensive encyclopedia covering wines and spirits, regions, vineyards, and wine terminology. Entries vary from single sentences to several pages. Brief chapters are included in the front of the book on the history of wine, serving wine, starting a cellar, and related topics.

49. Longreé, Karla, and Armbruster, Gertrude. *Quantity Food Sanitation.* 4th ed. New York: Wiley, 1987. 452 p.

> This is a detailed guide to the prevention of foodborne illness with proper sanitation. Early chapters give basics on spoilage and microorganisms and other agents of foodborne illness. Several chapters deal with reservoirs of microorganisms causing gastroenteritic outbreaks. Others deal with procurement and proper storage, sources of contamination within the foodservice establishment, and multiplication of bacterial contaminants in ingredients. There are also chapters on control of contaminants and the education of personnel. This edition has a special section on microwaves and discusses their effect on microbial life.

50. Lundberg, Donald E. *The Tourist Business.* 5th ed. New York: Van Nostrand Reinhold Co., 1985. 252 p.

> Now in its fifth edition, this book stands as a benchmark in the field. It covers all the various businesses that comprise the tourism industry: travel agencies, tour operators, hotels, restaurants, airlines, rental car agencies, tourist attractions. How these interrelate and affect one another is the focus of the book. It also addresses the social and economic impacts of tourism and addresses the strategies for developing a tourist attraction. Case studies of Club Med, Disney World, and the Rockresorts are used to illustrate marketing strategies. Special attention is given to travel agency business.

51. McDermott, Albert L., and Glasgow, Frederick J. *Federal Wage & Hour Standards for the Hotel-Motel and Restaurant Industries.* Washington, DC: American Hotel & Motel Association, 1981–. (Loose-leaf)

> Increased minimum wage requirements, overtime penalty pay, and record-keeping requirements of the federal labor laws and regulations have an important impact on the hospitality industry. Failure to comply can result in litigation and substantial liability. McDermott explains how these problems can be minimized by adapting appropriate management and personnel policies. This book discusses how the Federal Fair Labor Standards Act (FLSA) and its various amendments, the Equal Pay Act, the Age Discrimination in Employment Act, and the Federal Wage Garnishment Law, apply to hotels, motels, and restaurants.

52. Mengelatte, Pierre; Bickel, Walter; and Abelanet, Albin. *Buffets and Receptions.* 4th ed. Edited by Michael Small and Mabel Quin. London: Virtue, 1983. 1,221 p.
>This is the most complete and elaborate book on buffets available. Originally published in French, it is intended to accompany *Modern French Culinary Art* by Pellaprat. Part one, "Functions," gives guidelines on various forms of parties. Part two, "Customs and Traditions," covers eating habits from other countries. These sections are followed by the main part of the book which is a collection of recipes from chefs around the world. Illustrated with full color plates. The fourth edition varies only slightly from earlier editions; it actually is more a reprint than a new edition.

53. Miller, Jack E. *Menu Pricing and Strategy.* 2d ed. New York: Van Nostrand Reinhold Co., 1987. 170 p.
>This new edition provides a choice of strategies for menu pricing and development. Calculations for figuring breakeven points, minimum sales points, and the like are fully explained. It shows how to design menus for different types of restaurants and determine prices. Various menu marketing techniques such as coupons are covered. It also includes sample menus and a menu self-evaluation. Provides both text and discussion of the "U. S. Government Guidelines for Accuracy in Menu Language."

54. Montagné, Prosper. *The New Larousse Gastronomique: The Encyclopedia of Food, Wine & Cookery.* Edited by Charlotte Turgeon. Translated by Marion Hunter. New York: Crown Publishers, 1977. 1,064 p.
>This is the most comprehensive encyclopedia available. It covers the history of food, cooking, and eating habits in concise articles arranged in alphabetical order. Many of the entries include recipes, so it can serve as an extensive cookbook as well as an encyclopedia of food facts. Numerous color and black-and-white photographs and diagrams are included.

55. Myers, James R. *Commercial Kitchens.* 6th ed. Edited by James R. Modlin and Harry C. Anderson. Arlington, VA: American Gas Association, 1979. 349 p.
>Published by the American Gas Association, this book discusses the effective use of commercial kitchens. Emphasis is naturally on the advantages of gas appliances though others are discussed. There are good chapters on foodservice layouts and kitchen design as well as comparisons of gas to other fuels in terms of cost and efficiency. The main part of the book provides detailed descriptions of most types of gas appliances for commercial kitchens.

56. National Institute for the Foodservice Industry. *Applied Foodservice Sanitation.* 3d ed. A NIFI Textbook. Dubuque, IA: W. C. Brown Co., 1985. 299 p.
>This updated edition of the National Institute for the Foodservice Industry's sanitation management text includes changes in Federal Drug Administration standards and new equipment. Chapters cover sanitation and health, purchasing, storage, and preparation, as well as cleaning, facilities and equipment, pest control, employee training, and sanitation management. A chapter is included on sanitation and safety regulations and standards.

57. National Institute for the Foodservice Industry and National Restaurant Association, comps. *Junior/Community College and Culinary School Programs in Hotel, Restaurant, and Institutional Management in the United States.* Chicago, 1984. 40 p.
>A pamphlet by the National Restaurant Association and the National Institute for the Foodservice Industry giving addresses and phone numbers of schools throughout the country with Hotel, Restaurant, and Institutional Management programs. The entries are for nonbaccalaureate, postsecondary programs in hospitality management and commercial cooking.

58. National Institute for the Foodservice Industry and National Restaurant Association, comps. *Senior College Programs in Hotel, Restaurant, and Institutional Management in the United States.* Chicago, 1984. 16 p.

A pamphlet by the National Restaurant Association and the National Institute for the Foodservice Industry giving addresses and phone numbers of schools throughout the country with Hotel, Restaurant, and Institutional Management programs. Entries for schools that emphasize dietetics rather than commercial foodservice are flagged with a "D." An "M" indicates that postgraduate degrees are offered.

59. National Restaurant Association. *Conducting a Feasibility Study for a New Restaurant: A Do-It-Yourself Handbook.* Washington, DC, 1983. 130 p.

This is a step-by-step guide to using marketing techniques in determining the success of a proposed restaurant. The guide divides the process into five major steps: "Researching Your Market Area," "Surveying Potential Competitors," "Analyzing the Selected Site," "Developing a Restaurant Concept," and "Constructing a Pro Forma Financial Statement."

60. National Restaurant Association. *Foodservice Library: A Comprehensive Catalog of Foodservice Publications.* Washington, DC, 1984. 108 p.

Over 500 books and audiovisual materials are listed in this bibliography. Each entry includes bibliographic information, ISBN, price, short description, and a list of chapters. National Restaurant Association publications are omitted because they are listed in a separate publications list. Indexes to authors and titles are included.

61. National Restaurant Association. *Market Research for the Restaurateur: A Do-It-Yourself Handbook for Market Research.* Washington, DC, 1981. 118 p.

The National Restaurant Association provides a do-it-yourself guide to market research. It is intended to assist owners and managers in using established research techniques without special training in statistics or mathematics. Chapters cover marketing research, sales records use, how to use customer comment cards, analyzing trading area, evaluating customer perceptions, and how to conduct a competitive analysis.

62. National Restaurant Association. *Who's Who in the Foodservice Industry.* Washington, DC, 1984– . (Annual)

A directory of the National Restaurant Association members arranged alphabetically by state, city, and then by name of restaurant. An alphabetical index by the name of members' restaurants is found in the back. Association officers and a calendar of National Restaurant Association events are also included. This publication continues *Who's Who in the Restaurant Industry.*

63. National Restaurant Association and Laventhol & Horwath. *Restaurant Industry Operations Report for the United States.* Washington, DC. (Annual)

Based on over 700 questionnaires from restaurants, this report provides financial operating results of all types of restaurants from full service to fast food. Data is presented in charts based on type of restaurant, location, affiliation, years of operation, sales volume, and menu theme. The operating results are expressed as amounts per seat and ratios to total sales. Medium and upper and lower quartiles are reported. A worksheet is included so a restaurant can compare their operation with the industry. Continues *Restaurant Operations.*

64. National Restaurant Association, Research and Information Services Department. *Foodservice Numbers: A Statistical Digest for the Foodservice Industry.* Washington, DC, 1986. 107 p.

This is a digest of National Restaurant Association statistical information from 1970–84. The book is divided into six sections: "Industry Food and Beverage Sales and Purchases," "Consumer Research Highlights," "Characteristics of the Restaurant Occasion," "Restaurant Operations," "Industry Trends," and "Major Economic Indicators." The second section is of special interest, giving highlights of research on consumer preferences, expectations, and nutritional concerns as well as why, where, and how often various types of people eat out.

65. Ninemeier, Jack D. *Beverage Management: Business Systems for Restaurants, Hotels and Clubs.* New York: Chain Store Publishing Corp., 1982. 277 p.

This handbook presents in Standard Operating Procedure style (SOP), a practical sequence for planning and controlling beverage costs in restaurants, hotels, and clubs. For every topic, there is a SOP outline explaining procedures. Forms and instructions are included.

66. Ninemeier, Jack D. *Principles of Food and Beverage Operations.* East Lansing, MI: Educational Institute of the American Hotel & Motel Association, 1984. 451 p.

This is an introductory text on foodservice management. The author uses a marketing approach that focuses on the customer. The book is divided into (1) "Overview of the Food Service Industry," (2) "Customer Expectations," (3) "Satisfying Customer Expectations," and (4) "Planning Food and Beverage Operations."

67. Ninemeier, Jack D., and Kasavana, Michael L. *Planning and Control for Food and Beverage Operations.* 2d ed. East Lansing, MI: Educational Institute of the American Hotel & Motel Association, 1986. 395 p.

The objective of this book is to explain control in relation to food, beverages, labor, and sales income. It presents a framework of control systems developed by the Food and Beverage Committee of American Hotel & Motel Association. This second edition has a new chapter on menu planning and new information on computers, precosting, budgeting in multiunit operations, and other topics. Discussion questions have been added to the end of each chapter.

68. Oaksford, Margaret J. *Bibliography of Hotel and Restaurant Administration and Related Subjects.* Ithaca, NY: School of Hotel Administration, Cornell University. 1951–1987. (Annual)

This was the major index in the hotel and restaurant industry, published annually since the 1950s. It indexed books, pamphlets, and periodical articles. The index is arranged by subjects relevant to the field; a full bibliographic citation is given with each entry. The final publication indexed journals published during 1985. Starting in 1987, Cornell School of Hotel Administration, Purdue University, and University of Wisconsin-Stout are working together on the *Lodging and Restaurant Index* which will replace this publication.

69. Radice, Judi, and National Restaurant Association. *Menu Design 2: Marketing the Restaurant through Graphics.* New York: PBC International Inc., 1987. 256 p.

By the author of *Menu Design,* this second book is an all new collection of over 200 menus showing exceptional design qualities. Each menu is superbly photographed in color and carefully described. The restaurant's name and location are included along with the names of the designers and specifications of size, paper, and printer. Chapters cover techniques of design, theme menus, ethnic dining, catering and special feasts, hotel menus, institutional menus, specialty menus, and children's menus.

70. Rey, Anthony M.; Wieland, Ferdinand; and Ninemeier, Jack D. *Managing Service in Food and Beverage Operations.* East Lansing, MI: Educational Institute of the American Hotel & Motel Association, 1985. 395 p.

This is an up-to-date textbook on the procedures necessary to plan for and manage food and beverages in all types of restaurants from cafeterias to hotel roomservice. Chapters include personnel administration, menu planning, food production systems, suppliers and equipment, dining service methods, controlling service, labor costs, and sales income control systems. This book is used as part of the American Hotel and Motel Association Certification program.

71. Rombauer, Irma, and Becker, Marion Rombauer. *Joy of Cooking.* Illustrated by Ginnie Hofmann and Ikki Matsumoto. Indianapolis, IN: Bobbs-Merrill, 1975. 915 p.
This is perhaps the most well-known and extensively used cookbook available. In addition to including thousands of recipes, this is a good source for explanation about why certain techniques or procedures are used.

72. Seaberg, Albin G. *Menu Design, Merchandising and Marketing.* 3d ed. New York: Van Nostrand Reinhold Co., 1983. 319 p.
Seaberg says the menu is written and produced to sell. With this in mind, he discusses the menu from all angles. He deals with general considerations such as menu copy, color, and type selection; special menus such as children's and roomservice menus; and specific aspects such as appetizers and salads. Other chapters deal with subjects less often covered, such as merchandising low calorie items and "What Americans Can Learn from Foreign Menus." There are many example menus.

73. Sherry, John H. *The Laws of Innkeepers: For Hotels, Motels, Restaurants, and Clubs.* rev. ed. Ithaca, NY: Cornell University Press, 1981. 674 p.
Sherry has updated this basic text, increasing the section on government regulations and their impact on the lodging business. "The text covers the applicable basic common-law principles throughout the United States and representative statutes and court decisions based on these principles." The book covers responsibilities of innkeepers, liability for safety, government regulations, liability for guests' property, and rights and responsibilities of innkeepers.

74. Shugart, Grace; Molt, Mary; and Wilson, Maxine. *Food for Fifty.* 7th ed. New York: Wiley, 1985. 641 p.
This is the best and most well-known book on quantity cooking; the first six editions were done by Bessie Brooks West. It is intended as both a text and a reference tool and includes many tables of weights and measures for recipe adjustment as well as offers guidelines for preparation and serving. It also includes a large collection of standardized recipes by menu category, each for fifty portions or more, and sections on menu planning and special meal service such as receptions and brunches.

75. Spears, Marian C., and Vaden, Allene G. *Foodservice Organizations: A Managerial and Systems Approach.* New York: Wiley, 1985. 737 p.
This text is intended for upper division students in foodservice management and is designed to be used over an academic year in two or three courses. It deals with the designing of overall foodservice systems and discusses subsystems such as procurement, production, distribution, sales, and maintenance. The management section deals with organizational structure, decision making, personnel, budget, and the like. It includes many topics not found in most other texts such as forecasting models and productivity analysis. Both commercial and institutional operations are covered.

76. Torgeson, Kathryn W., and Weinstein, Sylvia J. *The Garland Recipe Index.* Garland Reference Library of the Humanities; vol. 414. New York: Garland Publishing, 1984. 314 p.
This is an index to recipes in nearly fifty well-known cookbooks. The cookbooks were chosen from Mimi Sheraton's list of basic cookbooks published in the *New York Times* (August 15,1981). Recipes are indexed by name, principle ingredient, and cooking style. If the recipe is of ethnic origin, that is noted also.

77. Trader Vic (Victor Bergeron). *Trader Vic's Bartender's Guide, Revised.* Illustrated by Helen A. deWerd. Edited by Shirley Sarvis. Garden City, NY: Doubleday, 1972. 442 p.
This is a revised and updated version of the book originally published thirty years ago and is the most well-known bartenders guide published. The recipes are grouped according to basic liquor where possible, with sections on more complex drinks such as punches and rickeys. Drinks can also be found by name in the index.

78. U.S. Travel Data Center, and Business Research Division, University of Colorado. *Tourism's Top Twenty: Fast Facts on Travel and Tourism.* Special Studies in Travel Economy and Marketing. Washington, DC, 1980. 86 p.

This compilation of facts, figures, and statistics on travel and tourism covers both the United States and the world. It provides a ranking of the "top twenty" in advertising, airlines, attractions, world travel, hotels and resorts, recreation, and visitors to cities and states. There are eighty-one tables; each cites the source of the statistics. Addresses for the sources are included in the back of the publication.

79. Vallen, Jerome J. *Check In—Check Out: Principles of Effective Front Office Management.* 3d ed. Dubuque, IA: W. C. Brown Co., 1985. 432 p.

This basic text for hotel administration classes covers all aspects of running the front desk. The structure of the front office is fully explained, as are reservations, registration, and room assignment. Attention is given to the financial side with chapters on charges, credit, billing, and night audits. A full discussion of the use of the American Plan is included. A bibliography and glossary are included.

80. VanEgmond-Pannell, Dorothy. *School Foodservice.* 3d ed. Westport, CT: AVI Publishing Co., 1985. 440 p.

This third edition of a basic text gives history and development of school foodservices and provides chapters on all basic aspects: menu planning, management, purchasing, preparation, sanitation, and equipment. Interesting and more complex aspects such as the advisability of using foodservice management companies and satellite food systems are also included. New in this edition are chapters on promoting school foodservices and computerization.

81. Wenzel, George Leonard. *Wenzel's Menu Maker.* 2d ed. Boston: CBI Publishing Co., 1979. 1167 p.

This is one of the most important reference books in the foodservice industry. It has both purchasing specifications and recipes. Over 2,000 recipes are included; each has the approximate cooking time, ingredients needed for twenty-four and 100 portions, cooking instructions, and helpful hints. Also included is a section on foodservice management and a glossary of terms.

82. West, Bessie Brooks, et al. *Food Service in Institutions.* 5th ed. New York: Wiley, 1977. 839 p.

A revised and updated fifth edition of this basic text for students in food systems management, it is still arranged in three major sections. The first includes planning, selection, production, delivery, and service of foods; the second includes personnel, cost control, sanitation, and safety; and the third includes floor planning, furnishings, and equipment for kitchens and dining areas. An appendix has examples of floor plans, organization charts, and personnel lists for typical small and large college residence hall foodservices.

83. Wilkinson, Jule. *The Complete Book of Cooking Equipment.* 2d ed. Boston: CBI Publishing Co., 1981. 259 p.

What started as a seventy-two page pamphlet in 1964 has become a large book in this revised, updated, and greatly expanded second edition of Wilkinson's guide to cooking equipment. The author gives guidance in selecting, buying, operating, and maintaining most types of commercial kitchen equipment including ranges, steam cooking equipment, ovens, griddles/grills, fryers, broilers, infrared food-warming equipment, specialty equipment, refrigeration, and waste-handling equipment. A final chapter is called "How to Clean Equipment: Programmed Lessons."

84. Woodman, Julie G. *IFMA Encyclopedia of the Foodservice Industry.* 5th ed. Chicago: International Foodservice Manufacturers Association, 1985. 275 p.

This is an extensive reference book which lists food, equipment and supply companies, brokers, chain restaurant executives, publishers, market researchers, association executives, consultants, government agencies, libraries, HRI faculty, and advertising agencies. Also included are articles and statistical charts on trends, size and segment of the foodservice market, food consumed away from home, and many other timely topics.

85. Woodman, Julie G. *IFMA Encyclopedia of World Foodservice Markets*. Chicago: International Foodservice Manufacturers Association, 1978. 130 p.
This directory of overseas foodservice markets is aimed at the U.S. manufacturer seeking overseas sales. It provides extensive information on each country including basic country information such as population, language, and industry data; U.S. and overseas contacts; major market consultants; chains; suppliers; trade shows; associations; and publications. Statistical charts are included for major countries. The book is arranged by regions of the world and includes introductory information on foodservice markets of the world, for each region and for some countries.

JOURNALS

86. *The Consultant*. Seattle, WA: The Foodservice Consultants Society International. (Quarterly)
This magazine is aimed specifically at the professional foodservice consultant; articles cover sanitation, equipment, new cooking techniques such as cook-freeze, industry trends, and design. Regular columns include association news, book reviews, and industry news.

87. *Cornell Hotel and Restaurant Administration Quarterly*. Ithaca, NY: Cornell University, School of Hotel Administration. (Quarterly)
This is the most important journal in the industry. Full-length feature articles are scholarly studies from researchers in the hospitality field. All articles are double-blind reviewed. In addition, each issue also includes news items related to the industry. "Educators' Forum" is a special issue published in August of each year.

88. *FIU Hospitality Review*. Miami, FL: Florida International University. (Biannual)
Each issue of this scholarly journal from the Florida International University School of Hospitality Management contains about ten articles written primarily by faculty members from hospitality schools from around the country. Emphasis is on hotel and restaurant management education, but there are also articles of interest to the whole industry.

89. *Food Management*. Cleveland, OH: Harcourt Brace Jovanovich Publications. (Monthly)
This monthly trade journal focuses on management in the nonprofit segment of the foodservice industry. It includes articles about foodservice in healthcare facilities, schools, colleges, and business and industry. Each issue has two or three long articles on timely topics, as well as regular columns focusing on the four areas of nonprofit foodservice: schools, hospitals, colleges, and businesses. Several quantity recipes are included in each issue. Each spring the journal has a "Presidents' Forum" which features the leaders of the five major foodservice associations.

90. *Foodservice Equipment & Supplies Specialist*. Newton, MA: Cahners Publishing Company. (Monthly)
This is the trade journal for equipment manufacturers and suppliers. Regular columns include "Industry News," "Industry Trends," "Products & Literature," and "Association News." In addition, each issue has full-length articles on equipment topics. Annual feature articles are "The 100 Giants of Distribution," "Consultant and Chain Giants," "The FE&S Industry Forecast," and the "Product Knowledge Handbook" which is a catalog of products by category. Every February a special issue is published called "The Buyers Guide"; it is a comprehensive industry sourcebook with manufacturer sources for more than 500 products.

91. *Hospitality Education and Research Journal.* University Park, PA: Council on Hotel Restaurant and Institutional Education. (Biannually)
> This is the main journal in hospitality education. Articles emphasis empirical investigation and theoretical analysis. All full-length articles are refereed by members of the editorial board and other experts. Each issue contains about five lengthy articles and a section called "Viewpoints and Commentary" which has rejoinders, commentaries, and rebuttals on earlier articles. Occasionally there is a section called "Research Notes" which has brief reports on current research projects.

92. *Hotel and Motel Management.* Cleveland, OH: Harcourt Brace Jovanovich. (17/year)
> Called the *Newspaper for the Lodging Industry,* this tabloid-size magazine is the best source for tracking company activity in the industry. Also included are articles on trends and issues before the industry such as tax reform, automation, and all-suite hotels. Indexed in *Business Periodicals Index* and *Business Index.*

93. *Hotel & Resort Industry.* New York: Coastal Communications Corporation. (Monthly)
> Subtitled The Magazine for Lodging Management—Hotels, Resorts, Motor Hotels, this is one of the best trade journals in the lodging industry. Articles are longer and more substantial than those in most trade journals. Emphasis is on management for the first-class or luxury hotel and resort. Special issues include an annual economic forecast issue in December and semiannual franchise issues.

94. *Hotels and Restaurants International.* Newton, MA: Cahners Publishing Company. (Monthly)
> This trade journal covers industry news and features of major hotels and restaurants from around the world. Each issue has from six to ten articles. One article in each issue focuses on a worldwide chain. Other articles cover interior design, foodservice, computer technology, stories on famous hoteliers or restaurateurs. The December issue is *The Worldwide Buyers Guide* which lists sources for buyers from all over the world. Indexed in *Business Index* and *Food Science & Technology Abstracts.*

95. *International Journal of Hospitality Management.* Elmsford, NY: Pergamon Journals Inc. (Quarterly)
> This journal is supported by the International Association of Hotel Management Schools, whose membership is derived from colleges in eight European countries. Each issue has four to eight articles which are refereed by experts in the field. In addition to the full-length research articles, there is a section called "Reviews and Features" that includes research notes and book reviews.

96. *Journal of Foodservice Systems.* Westport, CT: Food & Nutrition Press, Inc. (Quarterly)
> This is the official publication of The Society of Foodservice Systems Professionals. It is a refereed journal that publishes about six articles each issue emphasizing research, methodology, and case histories in foodservice systems analysis, design, implementation, and management.

97. *Journal of Travel Research.* Boulder, CO: Business Research Division. (Quarterly)
> This quarterly publication of the Travel and Tourism Research Association publishes articles on new techniques, creative views, generalizations about travel research thought and practice, and a synthesis of travel research material. Articles are blind reviewed by members of the editorial board. Each issue has from six to twelve research articles, an annotated list of new publications in a section call "Travel Research Bookshelf," and a few critical reviews of new books in the field.

98. *Lodging.* New York: American Hotel Association Directory Corporation. (11/year)
This is the official publication of the American Hotel & Motel Association. In addition to news of the association and information on association meetings, the journal includes in-depth articles on marketing, franchising, management, and design for hotels and motels. The April issue is a directory of products and services for the industry.

99. *Lodging Hospitality.* Cleveland, OH: Penton Publishing, Inc. (Monthly)
This is an excellent trade journal in the lodging segment. Articles are written primarily by the editorial staff. Each issue includes five lengthy articles on marketing, foodservice, amenities, computers, interior design, housekeeping, etc. Frequently articles focus on one of the big hotel chains and reviews its management and marketing techniques. In addition, there are numerous columns such as "Equipment at Work," "Economic Outlook," and "Marketwatch."

100. *Meeting News.* New York: Gralla Publications. (16/year)
This tabloid-size trade journal includes practical articles and news for meeting planners. One of the most useful sections includes site selection articles which review facilities, hotels, convention centers, and attractions in selected cities and states. The January issue is a directory of sites, suppliers, and services in the industry.

101. *Meetings & Conventions.* Cherry Hill, NJ: Business Publications Division of Murdoch Magazines. (Monthly)
This monthly trade journal includes longer articles on trends and issues in the meeting industry. Regular columns include "Planner's Portfolio," which includes helpful, practical ideas, and "Area Guides," which reviews facilities and activities available in convention cities. The annual "Gavel" issue in March is an international directory of hotels, resorts, conference centers, speakers, consultants, etc.

102. *Nation's Restaurant News.* New York: Lebhar-Friedman, Inc. (Weekly)
Regular scanning of this tabloid-size magazine is the best way to keep informed on the news and events in the restaurant industry. Mergers and acquisitions, new menu items and marketing techniques, and food trends are all closely tracked.

103. *Resort & Hotel Management.* Solana Beach, CA: Source Communications, Inc. (8/year)
This journal includes brief articles on equipment, management, and design for resort hotels and many short columns including a "Software Review" and book reviews. The spring issue is a "Buyer's Guide."

104. *Restaurant/Hotel Design International.* New York: Bill Communications, Inc. (10/year)
This trade journal focuses on the interior and exterior design of restaurants and hotels. Each issue carries about seven articles focusing on new or remodeled facilities. In addition, there is a regular column "Solutions," which discusses design problems. Other regular columns are "On-Site," "Facilities," and "Marketplace." Lavishly illustrated. Formerly entitled *Restaurant Design* and *Restaurant and Hotel Design.*

105. *Restaurant Business.* New York: Bill Communications, Inc. (18/year)
This is one of the best trade journals in the restaurant field. Issued every three weeks, each issue has a major cover story article and several other feature articles that cover trends in the industry or focus on specific chains. Regular columns include "Menu Ideas" (with recipes) and "Drafts, Carafes & Spirits." In addition, there is information on mergers and acquisitions, marketing ideas, trade quotes, and new equipment.

106. *Restaurant Hospitality* Cleveland, OH: Penton Publishing, Inc. (Monthly)
This is a excellent trade journal in the restaurant segment of the industry. It emphasizes management techniques for profitable, efficient, and comfortable restaurants. Most articles are written by the editorial staff of the journal; each issue includes about seven long articles and many columns such as "Food Trends," "Business Barometer," "Equipment

Report," "Interior Design," and "Tabletop Design." There are many special issues; the most important ones are "RH 500" in June, "Top 100 Chains" in August, and "Forecast" in December.

107. *Restaurant Management.* Cleveland, OH: Electrical Information Publications, Inc. (Monthly)

Formerly entitled *Independent Restaurants,* this journal emphasizes management and marketing information to assist independent restaurateurs. Each issue has a cover article and three to four other long articles one of which focuses on an independent restaurateur. Other articles cover menu planning ideas, bar business, and food trends. Short columns cover sanitation, marketing, personnel management, decor, computers, etc.

108. *Restaurants & Institutions.* Denver, CO: Cahners Publishing Company. (Bi-weekly)

This trade journal services all aspects of foodservice, both profit and nonprofit segments. Emphasis is on high volume units; all articles are written by the staff. Each issue has about thirty articles; columns cover chains, independents, institutions, equipment, food, and beverage service. Special issues include "Buyers' Guide" in March, "Trends" in May, "R&I 400" in July, and "Tastes of America" in December.

109. *Restaurants USA.* Washington, DC: National Restaurant Association. (11/year)

Published by the National Restaurant Association, this journal's major value is the extensive statistical reports it publishes in the "Foodservice Trends" and "Crest (Consumer Report on Eating Share Trends) Reports." In addition, each issue has articles on managing and marketing restaurants and reports on current trends such as drive-thru restaurants, franchising, etc.

110. *School Food Service Journal.* Englewood, CO: American School Food Service Association. (11/year)

This association journal is aimed at the practicing school foodservice manager, not researchers in the field. Association news is thoroughly covered; many articles focus on ideas from local schools. Over the last year, there has been a series of articles written by various food industry groups that review the history of foods. Quantity recipes appropriate for schools are also included.

111. *School Food Service Research Review.* Denver, CO: American School Food Service Association. (2/year)

This is the refereed journal from the American School Food Service Association. It is designed to disseminate research finding and other relevant information applicable to school foodservice in the areas of foodservice facilities, food quality and production, management, program evaluation, nutrition standards, and nutrition education. The journal also includes book reviews and abstracts of articles from other journals of interest to school foodservice professionals.

112. *Successful Meetings.* New York: Bill Communications, Inc. (Monthly)

This is a trade journal which is subtitled the Authority on Meetings and Incentive Travel Management. Special quarterly issues sections cover "Incentive Travel" and "Travel/Transportation." Each issue includes about three features and numerous columns such as "Trade Show Trends" and "What's New in Sites." Also in-depth site reports on states are included. The February issue is a "Facilities Directory" which lists hotels, convention centers, and meeting services.

Accounting, Cost Control, and Financial Management

113. American Hotel & Motel Association. *Uniform System of Accounts and Expense Dictionary for Small Hotels and Motels.* 4th ed. East Lansing, MI: Educational Institute of the American Hotel & Motel Association, 1987. 182 p.
This is a manual for small hotels and motels. Part one gives examples of a balance sheet, with explanatory comments, and an example of a statement of income for operations without restaurants and one for operations with restaurants. The final forty pages contain an expense dictionary giving item and proper heading for "restaurant" and "no restaurant" operations. Part two explains how to use financial information including bookkeeping, financial statement formats, ratio analysis, operations budgeting, and break even analysis.

114. Bell, Donald A. *Food and Beverage Cost Control.* Berkeley, CA: McCutchan Publishing Corp., 1984. 344 p.
This is a comprehensive textbook on cost control in restaurants and foodservice. Food costs and quality control are considered together in section two. Section three covers alcoholic beverage control and considers techniques, procedures, and methods used to control this area. Labor costs and other expenses and fixed costs are covered in the last sections. The author's premise is that the manager must take action to control costs. Data collection is an aid in assessing problems and forecasting but is only a step toward control.

115. Boardman, R. D. *Hotel and Catering Costing and Budgets.* 3d ed. London: Heinemann, 1978. 201 p.
Written for British students in hotel and catering management, this text covers methods for determining food, labor, and overhead costs for restaurants and hotels.

116. Bolhuis, John L.; Wolff, Roger K.; and Editors of the National Institute for the Foodservice Industry. *The Financial Ingredient in Foodservice Management.* Illustrated by Jack Stockman. A NIFI Textbook. Lexington, MA: Heath, in cooperation with the National Institute for the Foodservice Industry, 1976. 211 p.
An introductory text on foodservice accounting for managers. It covers budgeting, cost control, and interpretation of financial records for those with little or no accounting experience. The book covers history and purpose, how to use accounting data, and accounting for profit.

117. Club Managers Association of America. *Uniform System of Accounts for Clubs.* 2d ed. Washington, DC, 1967. 140 p.
This is not an accounting or bookkeeping text. Rather, it presents a system that will provide a uniform method of reporting financial results and provide the basis for a standard chart of accounts on which any club's bookkeeping methods can be established. The text is divided into sections on city and country clubs, covering the balance sheet,

statement of income and expense (in long and short forms), and summary of gross receipts. Schedule outlines and guidelines are given for all areas of club accounts.

118. Coltman, Michael M. *Cost Control for the Hospitality Industry.* Boston: CBI Publishing Co., 1980. 353 p.

Coltman applies accounting principles to food, beverage, and labor costs in the hospitality industry, beginning with a study of how a cost was created and how this differs from the anticipated cost. The book then presents an accounting-oriented system that helps managers set objectives, policies, and procedures to attain the organizations goals.

119. Coltman, Michael M. *Financial Management for the Hospitality Industry.* Boston: CBI Publishing Co., 1979. 245 p.

This text is intended for hospitality management programs and is aimed at the more advanced students with knowledge of basic accounting. It discusses how to set company goals, obtain funding, and use it effectively. Chapters cover financial ratio analysis, cash budgeting, current asset and capital asset management, financing, use of leverage, business valuation, feasibility studies, franchising, and management contracts.

120. Coltman, Michael M. *Food and Beverage Cost Control.* Prentice-Hall Series in Foodservice Management. Englewood Cliffs, NJ: Prentice-Hall, 1977. 228 p.

This is a basic cost-control text that covers sales control, food purchasing, receiving and the receiving report, food stores and inventory control, food production, the evaluation of food cost results, and beverage cost control. It describes, illustrates, and explains the control systems in most common use.

121. Coltman, Michael M. *Hospitality Management Accounting.* 3d ed. New York: Van Nostrand Reinhold, 1987. 449 p.

· A basic textbook on accounting systems appropriate for hotels, restaurants, resorts, clubs, and volume feeding operations. The second edition incorporates changes reflected in the *Uniform System of Accounts for Hotels* (1977). This new third edition includes new chapters on feasibility studies and financial goals and information systems. Also, additional information on pricing and budgeting have been added. Topics include financial statement analysis, ratio analysis, cost control, and cost management. Glossary appended.

122. Croft, J. H. *Going Metric in Catering.* Library of Industrial and Commercial Education and Training, Catering Division. Oxford: Pergamon Press, 1969. 62 p.

Designed to supplement British texts on catering for food production, the purpose of this booklet is to help students understand cost prices, selling prices and gross profits. The first seven chapters are recipes using both regular and metric measures. After students have prepared the recipes, they are to calculate the costs. Chapters seven to ten are sets of questions on cost calculations.

123. Dittmer, Paul. *Accounting Practices for Hotels, Motels, and Restaurants.* Hotel-Motel Management Series. Indianapolis, IN: Bobbs-Merrill, 1971. 192 p.

This is a basic text for the beginning student of accounting in the hospitality industry. It covers basic accounting principles, sales, cash receipts, purchases, wages, cash disbursements, and departmentalized worksheets. The accounting cycle, accounting for small operations, and reports to management are also included. Discussion questions are included at the end of each chapter.

124. Dittmer, Paul, and Griffin, Gerald G. *Principles of Food, Beverage, & Labor Cost Controls for Hotels and Restaurants.* 3d ed. New York: Van Nostrand Reinhold Co., 1984. 352 p.

This college text is designed as an introduction to the process of cost and sales control. Principles are applied to purchasing, receiving, storing, issuing, and preparing of food and beverages. Labor control is also covered. Learning objectives are clearly stated at the beginning of each chapter, and problems and exercises are provided at the end.

125. Dreis, Timothy E. *A Survivor's Guide to Effective Restaurant Pricing Strategy.* New York: Chain Store Publishing Corp., 1982. 151 p.
Dreis presents a new approach to cost control based on a per-patron formula theory. The book begins with volume analysis based on per-patron information and continues through various cost categories including meat, plate, and labor costs. The final section covers general applications of the theory of over-all operation and implementation.

126. Dun & Bradstreet Credit Services. *The Restaurant Industry: A Strategic and Financial Analysis of Full Service and Fast Food Restaurants.* 2d ed. Strategic Industry Study. New York, 1985. 436 p.
A detailed study of the present and future trends of the industry based on key business ratios and industry norms from Dun's Financial Profiles and demographic and marketing information from Donnelley Marketing Information Services. National and regional analyses are provided. Continuing and newly emerging trends are discussed in detail. Extensive statistical charts and graphs included.

127. Escoffier, Marcel Robert, and Dennis-Escoffier, Shirley. *Restaurant Operations and Controls: A Practical Guide.* Englewood Cliffs, NJ: Prentice-Hall, 1986. 246 p.
A comprehensive guide to management and control with emphasis on the use of computers in the restaurant systems and a review of computers. Chapters on menu, purchasing, inventory, kitchen and bar management, payroll, sales and cost controls, special events and banquets, financial accounting, and long-range financial planning are also included. The accounting controls set up here can be done by hand, bookkeeping machine, or computer.

128. Fay, Clifford T., Jr.; Rhodes, Richard C.; and Rosenblatt, Robert L. *Managerial Accounting for the Hospitality Service Industries.* 2d ed. Dubuque, IA: W. C. Brown Co., 1976. 596 p.
A text on the use of practical accounting techniques in the hospitality industry. The authors, who are members of the accounting firm of Harris, Kerr, Forster, and Company, emphasize the role of accounting in managerial decision making. Chapters cover most aspects of basic accounting as it relates to the industry, including such subjects as financial statements and uniform systems, cost-volume-profit analysis, cost accounting, responsibility accounting in the hospitality service industries, capital budgeting, and income tax planning and decisions.

129. Fay, Clifford T., Jr., et al. *Basic Financial Accounting for the Hospitality Industry.* East Lansing, MI: Educational Institute of the American Hotel & Motel Association, 1982. 237 p.
This is an introductory text designed to replace *Basic Bookkeeping for the Hospitality Industry.* More emphasis and detail are given here to major financial statements, and a chapter on equities has been added. Organization and format have been revised. All basic aspects of accounting as it applies to the hospitality field are covered including front office, sales, and payroll accounting as well as other aspects such as fixed assets and inventory.

130. Fisher, William P. *Profitable Financial Management for Foodservice Operators thru Profit Planning.* Chicago: National Restaurant Association, 1973. 25 p.
This brief pamphlet outlines how to plan for profit in a restaurant through use of basic financial analysis. It explains in easy-to-understand language, how to calculate occupational, primary, and fixed costs and then to determine breakeven point from gross profit percentage and variable cost percentage.

131. Glascoff, Donald G., Jr. *Financing and Development of Commercial and Resort Hotels 1982.* Real Estate Law and Practice Course Handbook Series; no. 205. New York: Practicing Law Institute, 1982. 440 p.

This is a course handbook to supplement a course in real estate law prepared by the Practicing Law Institute. Chapters written by various authors include "Economic Feasibility Study," "Equity Commitment," "Hotel Joint Venture Agreement," "Tax Considerations in the Financing and Development of Resort Hotels," "Tax Aspects of the Formation and Operation of the Hotel Enterprise," "Hotel Management Agreement from Owner's Perspective," "Hotel Operating and Management Agreements," and "U.S. Lodging Industry 1980."

132. Horwath, Ernest B., and Toth, Louis. *Hotel Accounting.* 4th ed. Revised by John D. Lesure. New York: Wiley, 1978. 424 p.

This explains the basic accounting procedures necessary in the lodging industry. General procedures are based on conditions found in hotels of 350 to 400 rooms, but modifications of procedures for establishments of other types and sizes are explained. Records and reporting methods, controls forecasting, budgeting, payroll, and many other aspects of accounting are covered. Appendix A contains illustrative statements that show how financial statements should be presented. Appendix B is a selection of financial and operational statistics from the U.S. lodging industry.

133. Hotel Association of New York City. *Uniform System of Accounts for Hotels.* 7th rev. ed. New York: 1977. 129 p.

This is an updating of the useful work originally published in 1925 and periodically revised. It is a manual for preparing standard financial statements and schedules of the operating and productive units of a hotel. Its greatest value has always lain in providing a simple formula for the classification of accounts and a standardized method for presenting financial results that makes comparisons between hotels easier. Changes in this edition include revisions of the balance sheet and income statement sections and a Statement of Changes in Financial Position.

134. Ilich, John. *Restaurant Finance: A Handbook for Successful Management and Operations.* New York: Chain Store Age Books, 1975. 142 p.

This is a basic book on the key financial aspects of the restaurant business. Chapters are short but detailed enough to provide essential financial information. Chapters cover using financial projections, borrowing money, financing the land and building, leases and subleases, equipment, insurance, purchasing, forms of ownership, and franchising.

135. Kahrl, William L. *Food Service Cost Control.* Managing for Profit Series. New York: Chain Store Publishing Corp., 1978. 87 p.

This is part of the Managing for Profit Series in which each manual deals with a specific problem area common to all segments of the industry. Here Kahrl discusses cost control, covering purchasing, receiving, inventory, and other aspects of control including a production guide.

136. Kahrl, William L. *Wage Cost Control.* Managing for Profit Series. New York: Chain Store Publishing Corp., 1980. 94 p.

Part of a series of manuals by Kahrl each dealing with specific problems. Here the problem is cutting wage costs without necessarily cutting payroll. Many alternatives are explored for analyzing and utilizing the work force effectively.

137. Kaud, Faisal A. *Financial Management of the Hospital Food Service Department.* Chicago: American Hospital Association, 1983. 77 p.

This book was prepared to assist foodservice managers in choosing appropriate methods to evaluate the financial management of their departments. Chapters cover financial data for management, budgetary control process, capital investment analysis, evaluation of cost allocation methods, and management of clinical dietetics staff.

138. Keiser, James, and Kallio, Elmer. *Controlling and Analyzing Costs in Food Service Operations.* New York: Wiley, 1974. 291 p.

This is a text for cost-control courses. It contains both theory and practical suggestions to cut costs and increase productivity. Emphasis is placed on labor cost control and the control function. Chapters discuss cost control in purchasing, receiving, storage, preparation, menu control, sales, security, and utilities. Other chapters cover food cost accounting, financial statements, budgetary control, breakeven analysis, and cost analysis of a foodservice operation.

139. Keister, Douglas C. *How to Increase Profits with Portion Control.* Chicago: National Restaurant Association, n.d. 51 p.

Procedures and methods are presented here for improving food cost control systems. Chapters cover analysis of operations, menu planning, precosting, purchase specifications, receiving, storeroom, production, and sales control as well as sales analysis.

140. Keister, Douglas C. *How to Use the Uniform System of Accounts for Hotels and Restaurants.* 2d rev. ed. Washington, DC: National Restaurant Association, 1983. 50 p.

Designed to supplement basic accounting texts, this book is written specifically about hotel and restaurant accounting. It is intended to amplify topics presented in *The Uniform System of Accounts for Restaurants* (National Restaurant Association, 5th rev. ed., 1983) and *The Uniform System of Accounts for Hotels* (American Hotel & Motel Association, 7th rev. ed., 1977). Chapters cover accounting terms, posting, journals, cash, accounting, inventories, accrued expenses, and nearly sixty other topics. Separate practice sets are included for hotels and restaurants.

141. Kotas, Richard. *Accounting in the Hotel and Catering Industry.* 3d ed. London: Intertext Books, 1972. 319 p.

This textbook was written specifically for students in Great Britain seeking degrees and diplomas in hotel keeping and catering. It follows the accounting and bookkeeping standards of that country and is divided into three main sections: "Book-keeping," "Accounting," and "Accounting as an Aid in Management." This edition omits the chapter on wages and salaries and has two new chapters: "Assessment of Capital Projects" and "Uniform Accounts." The first half of this book is an exact reproduction of chapters one through eight of *Book-keeping in the Hotel and Catering Industry* (Intertext, 3d ed, 1972). (The fourth edition, 1981, has been published but was not available for review.)

142. Kotas, Richard. *Book-Keeping in the Hotel and Catering Industry.* 3d ed. London: Intertext Books, 1972. 143 p.

Written for British students seeking diplomas and degrees or sitting examinations in hotel and catering areas, the information in this book follows British procedures. Topics covered include double entry; accounting for cash, purchases, sales, and other matters; mechanized accounting; organization of accounts; maintaining full set of books; simple final accounts; department accounts; and forms of ownership. With the exception of the last three topics, this book is contained in *Accounting in the Hotel and Catering Industry* (3d ed., 1972) which also contains additional chapters on accounting. (The fourth edition, 1982, has been published but was not available for review.)

143. Kotas, Richard. *Management Accounting for Hotels and Restaurants.* 2d ed. Glasgow, Scotland: Surrey University Press, 1986. 337 p.

Management accounting is designed to help management in decision making and problem solving. The author presents this type of accounting in terms of a revenue rather than cost-oriented accounting method because it is more appropriate to the industry. The approach is practical rather than theoretical and covers pricing, sales, breakeven analysis, budgetary control, variance analysis, cost control, operating ratios, income tax, and operations research. This new edition is thoroughly revised and includes two new chapters on profit sensitivity and financial statement analysis and an analysis of department profitability.

144. Kotschevar, Lendal Henry. *Cost Containment in Foodservice Operation.* West Lafayette, IN: Purdue Research Foundation, 1984. 15 p.

Kotschevar presents brief discussion of how foodservices in the health industry can work to contain costs while providing more value for the money spent. Menu planning and quality assurance programs are discussed.

145. Laventhol & Horwath. *Uniform System of Accounts for Restaurants: Adopted and Recommended by the National Restaurant Association.* 5th rev. ed. Washington, DC: National Restaurant Association, 1983. 159 p.

The purpose of the uniform system is to give restaurants a common language for their accounting statements. Part one outlines the classification of income and expense items. It covers profit and loss statements and balance sheet accounts. Part two contains examples of the system using various types of restaurants, i.e., large, small, drive-in, hotel, and club. Part three has forms for keeping detailed records. Part four contains forms and explanations for record keeping in a small restaurant.

146. Levings, Pat. *Profit from Foodservice: A Q and A Approach.* Chicago: Institutions/Volume Feeding Magazine, 1974. 158 p.

Aimed at the independent restaurateur, this book deals with the usual topics in a question-answer format. It is divided into three broad areas. The first looks at the facts of the business such as food, equipment, and payroll costs. The second part is on discovering problems and covers food production and administrative procedures, personnel, and overhead. The last section is on making a profit.

147. Levinson, Charles. *Food and Beverage Operation: Cost Control and Systems Management.* Prentice-Hall Series in Foodservice Management. Englewood Cliffs, NJ: Prentice-Hall, 1976. 256 p.

This is a text on cost control management written for the food and beverage industry. The author's intent is to present the range of solutions available rather than to give specific answers to specific problems. Chapters cover cost control, inventory control, beverage service, cash receipts, food purchasing, receiving and storage, menu planning and pricing, labor cost control, and labor cost analysis.

148. Maizel, Bruno. *Food and Beverage Cost Controls.* Hotel-Motel Management Series. New York: ITT Educational Services, 1971. 202 p.

This is a text that explains the basic principles of cost control through an analysis of all aspects of the operation. Basic accounting, storeroom management, inventory, purchasing, menu costing and pricing, production, and banquet procedures are discussed as they relate to cost control. Chapters on forecasting, budget, and breakeven analysis are included.

149. Moncarz, Elisa S., and Portocarrero, Nestor de J. *Financial Accounting for Hospitality Management.* Westport, CT: AVI Publishing Co., 1986. 448 p.

An introductory text designed to provide students with basic accounting applied to the specific needs of the hospitality industry. It is divided into four parts: "The Accounting Framework"; "The Accounting Cycle and Procedures"; "Financial Statements"; and "Selected Topics"; including inventories, corporation accounting, and responsibility accounting, among other topics.

150. National Restaurant Association. *Building Profits: Controlling Costs, Discovering Profit Centers and Targeting Markets: Selected Articles from NRA News.* NRA News Operations Series; 2d. Washington, DC, 1985. 94 p.

These articles originally appeared in *NRA News.* They are arranged into four sections: the first covers food and beverage costs; the second examines consumer trends; the third analyzes the various markets such as singles, teen-agers, and elderly; and the fourth reviews insurance, taxation, and renovation.

151. Ninemeier, Jack D., and Kasavana, Michael L. *Planning and Control for Food and Beverage Operations.* 2d ed. East Lansing, MI: Educational Institute of the American Hotel & Motel Association, 1986. 395 p.

The objective of this book is to explain control in relation to food, beverages, labor, and sales income. It presents a framework of control systems developed by the Food and Beverage Committee of the American Hotel & Motel Association. This second edition has a new chapter on menu planning and new information on computers, precosting, budgeting in multiunit operations, and other topics. Discussion questions have been added to the end of each chapter.

152. Ninemeier, Jack D., and Schmidgall, Raymond S. *Basic Accounting Standards.* The L.J. Minor Foodservice Standards Series; vol. 3. Westport, CT: AVI Publishing Co., 1984. 204 p.

Standards for accounting in the foodservice industry have already been developed by the Financial Accounting Standards Board, the SEC, and the IRS. This book reviews the precepts of accounting already established to help the manager better utilize accounting systems to collect data to make better business decisions.

153. Paige, Grace. *Catering Costs and Control.* London: Cassell, 1977. 222 p.

This British publication is intended as a text for students studying for various British examinations and certificates. It gives instruction in basic principles of food costing and control. It also discusses how all operational information can be used to promote cost consciousness and effective management.

154. Powers, Thomas F., and Powers, Jo Marie. *Food Service Operations: Planning and Control.* Wiley Service Management Series. New York: Wiley, 1984. 372 p.

The aim of this textbook is to help students understand how cost control systems are used by profitable foodservice operators today. It deals primarily with food, beverage, and payroll control. Each chapter begins with a general purpose statement and concludes with review questions. Chapters cover menu planning, monitoring, purchasing, receiving, storage, forecasting, production controls, precosting, payroll control, and food and beverage cost control. An inventory cost analysis in Fortran is included in the appendix.

155. Schmidgall, Raymond S. *Hospitality Industry Managerial Accounting.* East Lansing, MI: Educational Institute of the American Hotel & Motel Association, 1986. 605 p.

This text presents managerial accounting concepts and explains how they apply to specific operations within the hospitality industry. It presupposes some background in basic accounting. Chapters end with discussion questions and problems. Subjects covered include ratio analysis, balance sheet, income statement, internal control, basic cost concepts, cost-volume-profit analysis, operations budgeting, cash management, capital budgeting, lease accounting, and income taxes, among others.

156. Stokes, Judy Ford. *Cost Effective Quality Food Service: An Institutional Guide.* 2d ed. Rockville, MD: Aspen Systems Corp., 1985. 492 p.

This book is concerned specifically with practical ways to contain costs in health care educational and correctional foodservices while continuing service and quality. To this end, the author deals with budget, menu, inventory, labor, and energy costs as well as the selecting of energy-efficient equipment. This new edition has chapters on DRGs (diagnosis related groups) and their impact on foodservice and computer applications in foodservice. Appendix A gives a large selection of weekly menus.

157. Sutton, Donald F. *Financial Management in Hotel and Catering Operations.* 2d ed. London: Heinemann, 1983. 331 p.

This is an accounting text for British students in hotel and catering management. Sutton presents basic principles and helps students apply them. He uses a case study approach which simulates the growing complexity of accounting that would naturally develop as a small establishment expanded.

158. U.S. Department of Agriculture. Food and Nutrition Service. *School Food Service Financial Management Handbook for Uniform Accounting.* Washington, DC, 1973. (Irregular)

This book is intended to assist those responsible for recording and reporting the finances of a school foodservice. It provides an introduction to the principles of accounting, definitions of terms, and procedures for preparing reports. It also includes an overview of the school foodservice fund accounting system and charts and explanations of the different types of accounts used in the system.

159. Witzky, Herbert K. *Practical Hotel-Motel Cost Reduction Handbook.* New York: Ahrens Publishing Co., 1970. 208 p.

This book covers cost control and effective use of human resources. Topics covered include cutting administration costs, simplifying executive reports, long-range planning, detection and prevention of embezzlement, handling fraud, controlling advertising expenses, work simplification, preventive maintenance controls, improving operating efficiency, establishing an action management program, and a final chapter which is a comprehensive checklist for the whole range of management functions.

Beverages and Beverage Management

160. Adams, Leon David. *The Commonsense Book of Wine.* rev. ed. New York: McGraw-Hill, 1986. 166 p.
   A revised updated version of this twenty-six-year-old classic, it provides an introduction to the world of wine including a pronunciation guide to 408 wines. It covers wine shoppers secrets, the interpreting of labels and vintages as well as wine tasting, wine ritual, and the joys of cooking with wine and building a wine cellar. Intended for the consumer, it is still a valuable source book for the restaurateur. A glossary is included.

161. Adams, Leon David. *The Wines of America.* Boston: Houghton Mifflin, 1973. 465 p.
   A comprehensive guide to wines in the United States. The author includes history and development information as well as evaluations of quality for wines from all over the country. Maps of the principle vineyard districts of the United States are included as are a glossary of wine terms, a chronology of wine in the United States, and brief chapters on the wines of Mexico and Canada.

162. Argiry, George P. *Catch the Sticky Fingers: An Operational Guide to Bar Management.* Canton, OH: Beninda Enterprises, 1977. 143 p.
   This guide to bar management deals with the problems of owning and running a bar, with special emphasis on controlling theft of stock and cash. Inventory control is recommended as a major tool of theft prevention.

163. Asher, Gerald. *On Wine.* rev. ed. New York: Vintage Books, 1986. 220 p.
   Based on articles written for *Gourmet* magazine, this book deals with wines by regions such as Bordeaux, Tuscany, and Piedmont. Each section has several chatty informative essays about the best wines of the area, their history, and their appreciation. An index helps locate particular wines mentioned in the text. Not for the beginner.

164. Axler, Bruce H. *Practical Wine Knowledge.* His Focus on...the Hospitality Industry. Indianapolis, IN: ITT Educational Publishing, 1974. 134 p.
   Part of the Focus on...the Hospitality Industry series which presents various topics in practical terms. This book gives basic guidelines for evaluation, purchasing, and serving of wines. It also describes varieties of French, Italian, German, and American wines.

165. Bell, Donald A. *The Spirits of Hospitality: An Overview of the Origin, History and Service of Alcoholic Beverages.* East Lansing, MI: Educational Institute of the American Hotel & Motel Association, 1976. 161 p.
   This booklet is intended as a primer on distilled spirits, wines, beers, and alcoholic beverage management. The first section covers the history of alcoholic beverages and the processes of production. The second section deals with the technology of wine making and reviews the major wine producing areas of the world. The third section, on beverage management, discusses the cost control and profit management.

166. Berberoğlu, H. *Mr. B's Booze Book: Alcoholic Beverages Explained.* Dubuque, IA: Kendall/Hunt Publishing Co., 1981. 248 p.
The author intends to provide the beginning student with a complete overview of the wines of the world. He also has chapters on beer, distilled products, mineral water, and carbonated beverages as well as a history of cocktails. The final chapters discuss compiling a beverage menu and merchandising. The book is particularly good on the wines of Canada.

167. Beveridge, N. E. *Cups of Valor.* Illustrated by Peter F. Copeland. Harrisburg, PA: Stackpole Books, 1968. 106 p.
A brief, clever history of the use of alcohol in the U.S. Armed Services. Short chapters cover drinking customs in the Revolutionary War, Civil War, frontier days, World Wars I and II, and in the Navy. There is a recipe section. Some of these are merely of historical interest such as recipes for spruce beer, grog, and jungle juice; but there are twenty-five or thirty usable drink recipes, mostly for potent rum and brandy punches made in quantity.

168. Brandt, Jane. *Drinks without Liquor: For Bashes, Beaches, BBQs and Birthdays.* Illustrated by Jerry Joyner. New York: Workman Publishing, 1983. 143 p.
With the growing popularity of nonalcoholic drinks and mocktails, this is a handy book to have available. It was compiled by a business woman and mother as a collection of such recipes gathered from friends, relations, and business acquaintances.

169. Buller, Jon. *Buller's Professional Course in Bartending for Home Study.* Boston: Harvard Common Press, 1983. 152 p.
This is a good introduction to the art of bartending for beginners. Buller gives instructions in making the thirty basic cocktails and the techniques of pouring and preparing that make them professional. He also deals with cash register technique, customer relations, tips, cleaning, and other important subjects.

170. Finigan, Robert. *Robert Finigan's Essentials of Wine: A Guide to Discovering the World's Most Pleasing Wines.* New York: Alfred A. Knopf, 1987. 385 p.
This is a detailed, authoritative, and up-to-date wine book. It covers wines from France, Italy, Germany, Spain, Portugal, and America as well as other countries. Region by region, Finigan describes wines from various vineyards. He is not afraid to recommend his favorites or note which wines he feels do not live up to their reputations and price tags. A chapter on food and wine and an annotated bibliography of wine books are included.

171. Green, Eric F.; Drake, Galen G.; and Sweeney, F. Jerome. *Profitable Food and Beverage Management: Operations.* Ahrens Series. Hasbrouck Heights, NJ: Hayden Book Co., 1978. 429 p.
A companion volume to *Profitable Food and Beverage Management: Planning*, this volume deals with the day-to-day operations and is intended as an introductory text. As such, it covers menu planning, purchasing, merchandising, cost controls, table service, personnel, maintenance, sanitation, and security. An extensive bibliography is included.

172. Green, Eric F.; Drake, Galen G.; and Sweeney, F. Jerome. *Profitable Food and Beverage Management: Planning.* Ahrens Series. Hasbrouck Heights, NJ: Hayden Book Co., 1978. 342 p.
A companion volume to *Profitable Food and Beverage Management: Operations*, this volume concentrates on planning and managing for profit. Topics covered include marketing and financial strategy, feasibility study, design, financial statements and budgeting, advertising, legal issues, union negotiations, and insurance. This two-volume set was originally published as *Profitable Food and Beverage Operations*.

173. Grossman, Harold J. *Grossman's Guide to Wines, Beers, and Spirits.* 7th rev. ed. Revised by Harriet Lembeck. New York: Scribner, 1983. 638 p.
Grossman's is one of the major texts and reference books in the field. Updated periodically, it has excellent information on wines from all over the world as well as information on beers, distilled spirits, and liqueurs. Information is included on how various alcoholic beverages are made and how they should be served. There are also chapters on bar operation, merchandising, beverage control, and beverage laws.

174. Houston, Joseph, and Glenesk, Neil. *The Professional Service of Food and Beverage.* London: Batsford Academic and Educational, 1982. 143 p.
This is a British publication designed to help trainees meet requirements for certain examinations such as TEC and HCIMA tests. It is a manual of knowledge, skills, and techniques required for proper table service and covers the basics of organization, hygiene, and attitude as well as equipment, serving methods, foodservice, and beverages. Illustrations, diagrams, and study questions are included.

175. Johnson, Hugh. *The Atlas of German Wines and Traveller's Guide to the Vineyards.* New York: Simon and Schuster, 1986. 232 p.
This is a comprehensive guide to every registered vineyard in West Germany. Some 2,500 vineyards are mapped and listed here. The atlas is divided into northwest, central, eastern, and southern zones covering all principle wine growing areas. Maps are large, clear, and in color. Producers, villages, and travel information are also included, cross-referenced to an alphabetical vineyard register.

176. Joseph, Robert, ed., and Abbott, Louise, assistant ed. *The Wine Lists.* Enfield, Middlesex, England: Guinness Superlatives Ltd., 1985. 175 p.
This book lists alphabetically all the wine producing countries of the world and discusses the most important regions, grape varieties, and local words used on labels. The author gives his own opinions of many wines and often includes lists of merchants and growers he recommends. The book also includes some interesting and entertaining articles interspersed in the text such as "Sherlock Holmes Stories in Which Wine Features" and "The Greatest Wine Theft of All Time."

177. Kahrl, William L. *Advanced Modern Food and Beverage Service.* Prentice-Hall Series in Foodservice Management. Englewood Cliffs, NJ: Prentice-Hall, 1977. 279 p.
Designed to follow *Introduction to Modern Food and Beverage Service,* this book is for advanced students or those who have some experience in the field. Many of the same subjects are covered at a more advanced level, and more complex aspects of the industry are introduced. Chapters cover menus and selling, forecasting and control, operations, purchasing and receiving, security, food preparation, service, warehandling, facility planning, equipment, training, and sanitation.

178. Kahrl, William L. *Introduction to Modern Food and Beverage Service.* Prentice-Hall Series in Foodservice Management. Englewood Cliffs, NJ: Prentice-Hall, 1976. 302 p.
One of a two-textbook set on foodservice, the second book entitled *Advanced Modern Food and Beverage Service* is designed for those who have completed the introductory course or who have some experience in the field. This text covers all the major aspects of the industry at an introductory level. It includes an overview of the industry, along with chapters on merchandising, buying, preparation, service, personnel, and many other basics of the industry. Emphasis is on simple, practical presentation.

179. Katsigris, Costas, and Porter, Mary. *The Bar and Beverage Book: Basics of Profitable Management.* Wiley Service Management Series. New York: Wiley, 1983. 453 p.
Here is an overview of bar and beverage management. It covers facility planning, selection of equipment and staff, and how to operate and manage a bar. A section about how drinks are made, purchased, and mixed is also included.

180. Keister, Douglas C. *Food and Beverage Control.* Prentice-Hall Series in Foodservice Management. Englewood Cliffs, NJ: Prentice-Hall, 1977. 415 p.

A textbook of management techniques for food and beverage control which explains procedures for controlling costs. Chapters cover food cost formulas, breakeven analysis, menu pricing, cash control, and the like. Emphasis is on the necessity of keeping accurate records. Objectives are listed at the beginning of each chapter. A glossary is included.

181. Lichine, Alexis, et al. *Alexis Lichine's New Encyclopedia of Wines & Spirits.* 5th rev. ed. New York: Alfred A. Knopf, 1987. 771 p.

This is a comprehensive encyclopedia covering wines and spirits, regions, vineyards, and wine terminology. Entries vary from single sentences to several pages. Brief chapters are included in the front of the book on the history of wine, serving wine, starting a cellar, and related topics.

182. Maizel, Bruno. *Food and Beverage Purchasing.* Hotel-Motel Management Series. Indianapolis, IN: Bobbs-Merrill, 1971. 243 p.

Short basic chapters cover the purchasing of all types of food for the hospitality industry. Chapter one covers principles including methods, standards, regulations, and techniques for day-to-day buying. The following chapters contain descriptions of meats, vegetables, beverages, dairy products, convenience foods, specialty items and general groceries for buyers. The last chapters cover subjects such as storage, receiving procedures, and issuing.

183. Moore, Philip. *Total Bar and Beverage Management.* New York: Chain Store Publishing Corp., 1981. 264 p.

The emphasis of this textbook is on controlling costs through management efforts. Areas covered are purchasing, inventory and sales control, merchandising, and training of bartenders and servers. The appendix includes training tests for bartenders, food servers, and cocktail servers.

184. Ninemeier, Jack D. *Beverage Management: Business Systems for Restaurants, Hotels and Clubs.* New York: Chain Store Publishing Corp., 1982. 277 p.

This handbook presents in standard operating procedure (SOP) style, a practical sequence for planning and controlling beverage costs in restaurants, hotels, and clubs. For every topic there is a SOP outline explaining procedures. Forms and instructions are included.

185. Ninemeier, Jack D. *Food and Beverage Security: A Manual for Restaurants, Hotels, and Clubs.* Boston: CBI Publishing Co., 1982–. (Loose-leaf)

This manual is designed to help the practicing food and beverage manager improve security. Each topic presents practical procedures to overcome specific problems. Main topics include security program and employee selection, procedures for sales income control, methods of employee theft, methods of customer theft, preventing food and beverage theft, building security control, lock control, and protection of guests.

186. Ninemeier, Jack D. *Principles of Food and Beverage Operations.* East Lansing, MI: Educational Institute of the American Hotel & Motel Association, 1984. 451 p.

This is an introductory text on foodservice management. The author uses marketing approach which focuses on the customer. The book is divided into "Overview of the Food Service Industry," "Customer Expectations," "Satisfying Customer Expectations," and "Planning Food and Beverage Operations."

187. Osterland, Edmund A. *Wine and the Bottom Line.* Washington, DC: National Restaurant Association, 1980. 79 p.

Written for restaurant managers, this book helps the restaurateurs take full advantage of wine service. It covers employee training and basics of wine selection including wine regions, labels, tasting, vintages, and service. It also includes effective merchandising and sales techniques.

188. Parker, Robert M., Jr. *Parker's Wine Buyer's Guide.* New York: Simon & Schuster, 1987. 731 p.
This comprehensive guide covers France, Italy, Germany, Portugal, Spain, and North America. It also includes a brief chapter on wines from other areas such as Australia and the Middle East. Each section includes the name of the viticultural regions, an introduction to the area, a summary of the qualities of recent vintages, a chart of the area's best producers, a two-year buying strategy, and specifics such as tasting commentary, numerical rating, and retail shop prices.

189. Rey, Anthony M.; Wieland, Ferdinand; and Ninemeier, Jack D. *Managing Service in Food and Beverage Operations.* East Lansing, MI: Educational Institute of the American Hotel & Motel Association, 1985. 395 p.
This is an up-to-date textbook on the procedures necessary to plan for and manage food and beverages in all types of restaurants from cafeterias to hotel room service. Chapters include personnel administration, menu planning, food production systems, suppliers and equipment, dining service methods, controlling service, labor costs, and sales income control systems. This book is used as part of the American Hotel & Motel Association certification program.

190. Simmons, Marie, and Lagowski, Barbara J. *Good Spirits: Alcohol-Free Drinks for All Occasions.* New York: New American Library, 1986. 160 p.
Over 100 recipes for unspiked drinks are included in this cookbook. The recipes are arranged by occasion, i.e., New Year's, Valentine's Day, and tailgate parties. It also includes a chapter on stocking the alcohol-free bar and shopping for ingredients. Eight full-color plates illustrate many of the drinks.

191. Sutcliffe, Serena. *The Wine Handbook.* rev. ed. New York: Simon and Schuster, 1987. 224 p.
Sutcliffe gives all the basics for appreciating wine. In "The Range of Wine," she discusses types of wines and when to serve them. In "The Wine Producers," she tells where various wines are found and recommends trusted names in various regions. "Enjoying Wines" covers many subjects such as decanting, serving temperatures, wine lists, and wine cellars. The book also includes vintage notes, glossary, and pronunciation guide.

192. Thorner, Marvin Edward, and Herzberg, Ronald J. *Non-Alcoholic Food Service Beverage Handbook.* 2d ed. Westport, CT: AVI Publishing Co., 1978. 343 p.
First published in 1970 as *Food Beverage Service Handbook,* this 1978 edition has been updated and partly reorganized. It covers the production, handling and service of nonalcoholic beverages. All common restaurant beverages are included: coffee, tea, cocoa, juices, dairy products, and soft drinks. Sanitation and water treatment are also discussed as they relate to beverages.

193. Tourism Education Corporation. *Wine Service Procedures.* Boston: Cahners Books International, 1976. 132 p.
This book presents standard task procedures for training employees in every aspect of the proper serving of wine. The process is broken into twenty-three separate tasks. Each is described in detail and accompanied by illustrations. A glossary, selected bibliography, and brief information on wine types and labels are included.

194. Trader Vic (Victor Bergeron). *Trader Vic's Bartender's Guide, Revised.* Illustrated by Helen A. deWerd. Edited by Shirley Sarvis. Garden City, NY: Doubleday, 1972. 442 p.
This is a revised and updated version of the book originally published thirty years ago, and is the most well-known bartenders guide published. The recipes are grouped according to basic liquor where possible, with sections on more complex drinks such as punches and rickeys. Drinks can also be found by name through the index.

195. Van Kleek, Peter E. *Beverage Management and Bartending.* Boston: CBI Publishing Co., 1981. 164 p.

This is an introduction to beverage management and bartending. Separate chapters on beer, wine, whiskey, gin, vodka and tequila, brandy, and liqueurs and cordials discuss varieties of various liquors and how they are made. The chapter on "Bar Setup" looks at the four major types of bars and essential equipment and implements for bar operation. Bartending as a profession, as well as the important aspects of beverage management such as purchasing, receiving, storage, and issuing, are covered. There is a short section on beverage law and a basic drink recipe section.

196. Vedel, André, ed. *The Hachette Guide to French Wines.* New York: Alfred A. Knopf, 1986. 741 p.

This is the definitive guide to over 5,000 French wines. Each short entry has a wealth of information, including average production, price, and best vintage years, as well as addresses and symbols indicating whether the wine is vinified in stainless steel, aged in wood, available directly from the producers, and so forth. Labels on pages indicate particularly good choices. There are also essays on buying, serving, and storing wines. Forty-eight new maps of French wine regions are provided. Wines are arranged by region with indexes giving access by wine type and appellations.

Career Planning

197. Baker, Marilyn Carruth. *Exploring Occupations in Food Service and Home Economics.* Edited by Charles S. Winn. Careers in Focus. New York: Gregg Division, McGraw-Hill, 1976. 152 p.
> Written and designed to help young people choose a career, this booklet and related filmstrip contains information on home economics careers including restaurant management, cooking, and baking. Each unit begins with a fictional story detailing duties, problems, and working conditions and concludes with a hands-on activity. Worksheets, a filmstrip, and three interview cassettes are available for this book.

198. Bernbach, Linda. *Food Service Supervisor: School Lunch Manager.* 2d ed. New York: Arco, 1979. 256 p.
> This book contains practice exams and review text for the Civil Service Foodservice Supervisor test. The review material covers nutrition and menu planning, management and supervision, sanitation and safety as well as test-taking techniques.

199. Breithaupt, Herman A., and Herring, Betty L. *Chef Herman's Story: How We Started Students on Successful Foodservice Careers.* Edited by Jule Wilkinson. Boston: Institutions/Volume Feeding Magazine, 1972. 241 p.
> Breithaupt established one of the first high school programs preparing students as cooks. This book presents an anecdotal history of the Commercial Foods Program at Chadsey High School in Detroit. It also follows the lives of several graduates. It is intended for those considering a career in foodservices and those organizing education programs in the field.

200. Caprione, Carol Ann. *Opportunities in Food Services.* VGM Career Horizons Series. Lincolnwood, IL: VGM Career Horizons, 1984. 150 p.
> This is a guide to jobs in foodservices. Short, simple chapters cover career opportunities; job qualifications; education requirements; and entry level, middle, and management positions, with earning potential. Appendices list one-, two-, and four-year programs in Hotel, Restaurant, and Institutional Management.

201. Cavallaro, Ann. *Careers in Food Services.* New York: Elsevier/Nelson Books, 1981. 147 p.
> Cavallaro is a professional career counselor. The wide range of opportunities in foodservices is examined, and guidance is given on how to choose and train for a career in foodservices. Interviews with professionals in the field are included. Emphasis is on the tremendous variety of jobs available in this area.

202. Cornelius, Ethelwyn G. *Food Service Careers.* rev. ed. Edited by Marion L. Cronan. A Bennett Career Book. Peoria, IL: C. A. Bennett, 1979. 336 p.
> A text for beginning students of foodservice, it includes lab and on-the-job practice exercises as well as basic information. The book covers training requirements and descriptions of many types of jobs. Chapters cover general subjects like the operation of

foodservice units and specific aspects such as catering, waiting on customers, and preparation of food. Jobs are discussed in food preparation, service, and management areas.

203. Creasy, Donna Newberry. *Food Careers.* Consulting editor, Xenia F. Fane. Englewood Cliffs, NJ: Prentice-Hall, 1977. 122 p.
This is an introductory career manual aimed at high school and beginning students giving guidance to types of jobs available in the food industry. Qualifications, job descriptions, conditions, prospects, and pay are discussed for positions in volume feeding, food production and processing, merchandising, nutrition and dietetics, communication, and education. The presentation is very brief and basic. Sources for further information are included at the end of each chapter.

204. Hayter, Roy. *A Career in Catering: Choosing a Course.* International Series in Hospitality Management. Oxford: Pergamon Press, 1980. 226 p.
This British publication is a guide to preparation for careers in catering. It gives detailed information on eighty-five different courses of study available in the United Kingdom, from skills training to professional degrees. Syllabus, entry requirements, and other specific information is provided.

205. Henkin, Shepard. *Opportunities in Hotel and Motel Management.* VGM Career Horizon Series. Lincolnwood, IL: VGM Career Horizons, 1985. 148 p.
Aimed at students considering a career in the lodging industry, this is a thorough but easy-to-read overview of the field. It includes information on the industry and the employment outlook and a discussion of positions in the front of the house and in the back of the house. A list of two- and four-year college programs is appended.

206. Humphers, Sandra. *Exploring Careers in the Hotel and Motel Industry.* New York: Rosen Publishing Group, 1983. 121 p.
This is a basic introduction to the hospitality industry. Humphers discusses both the food and lodging aspects of the industry and helps the student decide whether it is for them. Examples of course descriptions from various schools are included.

207. Lattin, Gerald W., and Ninemeier, Jack D.*The Lodging and Food Service Industry.* East Lansing, MI: Educational Institute of the American Hotel & Motel Association, 1985. 299 p.
This is an introduction to the lodging and foodservice industry put out by the American Hotel & Motel Association. Emphasis is on career opportunities. Sections cover an overview of both the lodging industry and the foodservice industry and opportunities in the industries.

208. Morton, Alexander Clark. *The Official Guide to Food Service and Hospitality Management Careers.* Miami Springs, FL: International Publishing Co. of America, 1982. 119 p.
This is a compilation of information that includes an overview of the industry and job classifications. Job descriptions list qualifications, duties, and salary ranges and other pertinent information. The book includes career ladders in hotels, restaurants, institutions, schools and universities, business, transportation, and catering. There are lists of schools and universities with foodservice programs and of associations and trade journals.

209. National Institute for the Foodservice Industry and National Restaurant Association, comps. *Junior/Community College and Culinary School Programs in Hotel, Restaurant, and Institutional Management in the United States.* Chicago, 1984. 40 p.
A pamphlet by the National Restaurant Association and the National Institute for the Foodservice Industry giving addresses and phone numbers of schools throughout the country with Hotel, Restaurant, and Institutional Management programs. The entries are for nonbaccalaureate, postsecondary programs in hospitality management and commercial cooking.

210. National Institute for the Foodservice Industry and National Restaurant Association, comps. *Senior College Programs in Hotel, Restaurant, and Institutional Management in the United States.* Chicago, 1984. 16 p.

A pamphlet by the National Restaurant Association and the National Institute for the Foodservice Industry giving addresses and phone numbers of schools throughout the country with Hotel, Restaurant, and Institutional Management programs. Entries for schools that emphasize dietetics rather than commercial foodservice are flagged with a "D." An "M" indicates postgraduate degrees are offered.

211. National Restaurant Association. *Career Ladders in the Foodservice Industry.* Washington, DC, 1971. 26 p.

This report is a summary of the major findings and recommendations of the report, *A Study of Career Ladders and Manpower Development for Non-Management Personnel in the Foodservice Industry.* It offers a model for a large foodservice operation and emphasizes the importance of career ladders—"not just a job"—in the industry. The full report is available from the Clearinghouse for Federal Scientific and Technical Information, Springfield, VA.

212. Smith, William O. *Food Services.* Edited by Richard L. Lynch. Career Competencies in Marketing Series. New York: McGraw-Hill, 1979. 186 p.

This is part of the Career Competencies in Marketing series, appropriate for beginning students or as a training manual for people entering the foodservice industry. As all books in the series, it is divided into four parts: "Introduction to and Overview of the Industry," "Basic and Social Skills," "Product and Service Technology," and "Marketing Skills." Information is clearly if briefly presented. Exercises in each section are good, calling for thought and requiring written answers.

213. Sonnabend, Roger P. *Your Future in Hotel Management.* rev. ed. Careers in Depth; 113. New York: Rosen Press, 1975. 150 p.

This is an introduction to the lodging profession for prospective students of hotel management. There are chapters on the general attraction of innkeeping, as well as an emphasis on the role of management in the system. Chapters cover front and back of the house, food and beverage management, budget and control, personnel, motivation, marketing, creating the image, and tourism.

214. Spradley, James P., and Mann, Brenda J. *The Cocktail Waitress: Woman's Work in a Man's World.* New York: Wiley, 1975. 154 p.

Subtitled Woman's Work in a Man's World, this book is an ethnographic study of the role of the cocktail waitress in our culture. The data was collected between July 1971–July 1972 in a college bar in the Midwest. The social structure and social network territoriality and other aspects are presented in a descriptive format that is both informative and interesting.

215. Vorndran, Barbara Sethney. *Exploring Occupations in Personal Services, Hospitality, and Recreation.* Edited by Charles S. Winn. Careers in Focus. New York: Gregg Division, McGraw-Hill, 1976. 152 p.

Designed as a textbook for high school level students choosing a career, this volume in the series covers hotel and motel occupations along with several other service and recreation careers. Each unit begins with a fictional account of a worker that presents a realistic description of the problems and working conditions of the career. An accompanying filmstrip and three cassettes can be used to help bring the occupations to life for students.

216. Westbrook, James H. *Aim for a Job in Restaurants and Food Service.* Arco Career Guidance Series. New York: Arco, 1971 (1980 printing). 191 p.

Part of the Arco vocational series, this book is intended to introduce young people to the opportunities in the foodservice field. It gives a description of the wide variety and great size of the industry as well as discussing typical jobs, giving descriptions and conditions, earnings, and prospects. Training and qualifications are also presented. There are chapters listing other sources of information including schools and professional organizations.

Some of the information and figures are getting dated, but the introduction to various jobs in the field is still essentially accurate.

217. Witzky, Herbert K. *Your Career in Hotels and Motels.* New York: Dodd, Mead, 1971. 202 p.
> This is a general introduction to hotel management. Chapters discuss the history and development of the lodging industry and the role of management. There are also chapters on getting started in hotel management, getting a first job, moving ahead, and the future of the field.

218. Witzman, Joseph, and Block, Jack. *Food Service Careers: A Handy Guidebook for Those Seeking a Career in the Hospitality Industry.* Illustrated by Robin Olimb. Hospitality Heritage Career Series. San Diego, CA: Educators' Publications, 1985. 243 p.
> Part one of this guidebook describes jobs, requirements, training, preparation, and career planning. Part two, "Work Experience Supplement," includes extra chapters on related subjects such as service and marketing challenge. These help give an overall introduction and feeling for the industry. The National Restaurant Association and the National Institute of Foodservice Industry *Directory of Food Service Educational Programs* is included.

Computers and Automation

219. American Hotel & Motel Association. *The State of Technology in the Lodging Industry 1983: An Update of a Multi-billion Dollar Market.* New York, 1983. 128 p.

Summary report of results from a 1983 survey conducted by the American Hotel & Motel Association which updates previous surveys in 1970, 1976, and 1980. The survey is focused on six aspects of hotel technology: information processing, telecommunications, energy control, security systems, life (fire) safety systems, and audio and visual systems. Includes survey highlights and summary reports.

220. Chaban, Joel. *Practical Foodservice Spreadsheets with Lotus 1-2-3.* New York: Van Nostrand Reinhold Co., 1987. 179 p.

This is the most complete book available on using spreadsheets in foodservice management. It does not assume that the reader has any computer expertise and starts with a clear explanation of DOS commands. Then it gives examples of how to set up spreadsheets for purchase register, inventory, labor reports, and cash/sales reports. Later chapters cover tip reporting spreadsheets and recipe costing and menu pricing reports. The spreadsheets described and illustrated in the book are available for purchase on floppy disks from the author.

221. Club Managers Association of America, Information & Publications Department. *Focus on Clubs & the Computer.* Bethesda, MD, 198?. 176 p.

This collection of articles, most of which have been published in trade journals before, is compiled to help the club manager select or upgrade a computer system. "The 1985 Guide to Computers" is a chart of the various systems available and their capabilities.

222. Eudy, Charles L. *Automating Hotel/Motel Sales Functions: A How-to Manual on Computerizing the Sales Department.* East Lansing, MI: Educational Institute of the American Hotel & Motel Association, 1986. 68 p.

Written specifically for small and medium-sized hotels, this brief manual describes how to automate the marketing and sales department. It includes a list of software available and examples of screens and reports.

223. Godwin, Nadine. *Complete Guide to Travel Agency Automation.* Wheaton, IL: Merton House Publishing Co., 1982. 148 p.

Godwin, who is senior editor of *Travel Weekly,* discusses the application of computers and automated systems to travel work. She covers teleticketing and automated reservation systems. She also presents the features, economics, and problems of a back office system for computerized accounting.

224. Kasavana, Michael L. *Computer Systems for Foodservice Operations.* New York: Van Nostrand Reinhold Co., 1984. 259 p.

A book intended to help incorporate the computer into foodservice management, it explains computer terminology, point-of-sale systems, control systems, and accounting-based systems for the foodservice area. Electronic cash register configurations, automated precheck systems, precost systems, menu engineering, and beverage control through computerization are among the topics included. Diagrams, summaries, and lists of key concepts in each chapter facilitate understanding for the nonexpert.

225. Kasavana, Michael L. *Hotel Information Systems: A Contemporary Approach to Front Office Procedures.* Boston: CBI Publishing Co., 1978. 269 p.
This book on the use of computers in hotel management focuses specifically on the monitoring and controlling of the guest cycle through effective management information systems. Part one discusses hotel operations, in general. Part two is about basic computer operations. Part three presents specific hotel information systems (HIS). The concepts and specifications of HIS systems are described and particular modules presented, such as HIS Reservations, HIS Guest Accounting, and HIS Rooms Management.

226. Kasavana, Michael L., and Kolodin, Dennis L. *Before You Decide to Computerize.* East Lansing, MI: Educational Institute of the American Hotel & Motel Association, 1979. 46 p.
Designed as a guide for hotels and motels considering computerization, this guide explains how to accumulate and evaluate information on computer systems and discusses indirect cost analysis. Charts are provided for cost justifications. The guide covers systems techniques, maintenance options, and purchase agreements. It includes a glossary of computer terms.

227. Kasavana, Michael L., and Kolodin, Dennis L. *A Practical Guide to Hotel/Motel Automation.* New York: Hospitality Information Systems, 1978. 35 p.
This manual provides a ten-step methodology for evaluating computer systems and their application to the needs and problems of hotels and motels. Each step is carefully outlined to help the innkeeper examine all important aspects before making a decision on computer equipment.

228. Levine, Jack B., and Van Wijk, Alfons. *Counting on Computers: The New Tool for Restaurant Management.* New York: Chain Store Publishing Corp., 1980. 289 p.
This book is intended to help restaurants make use of the computer. Part one, "Introduction to the Computer," explains how the computer became a useful tool for restaurants and what restaurants need to know about computers. Part two is on computer application in the restaurant industry. Part three covers choosing the right type of hard- and software as well as looking at the perspectives on the future.

229. Moore, Aimee N., ed., and Tuthill, Byrdine H., ed. *Computer-Assisted Food Management Systems.* Columbia, MO: Technical Education Services, 1971. 102 p.
A collection of fourteen articles presented at the conference of the same name held at the University of Missouri-Columbia in July 1969. Representative titles include "Concepts of Food Systems Management," "Systems Design and Evaluation," "Development of a Standardized Recipe Data File for Computer Systems," "Application of Linear Programming to Menu Planning by Computer," "Acquiring Computer-Assisted Methods in the Dietetics Department."

230. Pellegrino, Thomas W. *Selecting a Computer-Assisted System for Volume Food Service.* Chicago: American Hospital Publishing, Inc., 1986. 124 p.
This book is divided into eight sections which cover the entire process of selecting a computer system. The author discusses defining the needs, problems, and solutions of the present system; conducting feasibility studies; evaluating vendor proposals; selecting, implementing, and evaluating the new system. Checklists and a case study are included.

231. Pine, Ray. *Management of Technological Change in the Catering Industry.* Brookfield, VT: Avebury, 1987. 114 p.

This book provides both an introduction to the theories and concepts of technology and practical recommendations for their implementation in the catering industry. Part one presents an overview of technology and its relationship to man power and management. Part two deals with technology in the catering industry. Part three presents actual recommendations to managers for the management of technological change.

232. Smaller Properties Advisory Council; Committee on Operations, Education, and Technical Assistance of the American Hotel & Motel Association, and MDR Associates. *Property Management and Point of Sale Systems: Guide to Selection.* Washington, DC: s.n., 1985. 43 p.

This guide has been prepared to help hotel and motel operators systematically evaluate and select a computer system to automate their property management and point of sales systems. Chapters cover assessing the need for computers, vendor qualifications, site visits, proposal requests and evaluations, and final selection.

Energy Management

233. Arnold and O'Sheridan, Inc. *Energy Conservation Manual, Wisconsin Hotels, Motels & Resorts.* Madison, WI: University of Wisconsin—Extension, Recreation Resources Center, 1978?. 101 p.

> Wisconsin was one of ten states selected to serve as pilots for energy programs, and it was the only state to target the hospitality industries for the program. This manual was designed to help restaurant and hotel managers set up an energy conservation program to reduce consumption by 15 percent. It includes many checklists and charts which can form the basis of an individual properties program.

234. Aulbach, Robert E., and Conrade, George R. *Energy Management.* East Lansing, MI: Educational Institute of the American Hotel & Motel Association, 1984. 243 p.

> This is a practical guide to the development and implementation of an energy management program for the hospitality industry. Part one is an overview of the energy problem. Part two, an action plan for energy management, deals with the development and organization of a program. Part three covers procedures for implementing an energy program such as analyzing utility bills, using surveys and audits, and utilizing energy management for food and beverage departments. Part four focuses on the future, especially in new designs and renovations.

235. Fulweiler, John H. *Profitable Energy Management for Retailers and Shopping Centers.* New York: Chain Store Age Books, 1975. 211 p.

> This is intended as a practical guide to getting the most from the energy dollar. Many of the recommendations are based on articles from periodicals such as *Chain Store Age* and *Nation's Restaurant News*. Chapter five (p p. 101–126) is on "Restaurants and the Energy/Cost." Other chapters cover other types of retail stores and energy management, in general.

236. Hospitality, Lodging & Travel Research Foundation. *Energy Conservation Manual: A Tool for Energy Management.* rev. ed. New York: HL&T Research Foundation, 1977. 362 p.

> Practical energy conservation techniques for hotels and motels are covered here. The book centers mainly on inexpensive opportunities that can cut energy use up to 30 percent. Each department is analyzed separately: front office, food and beverage, meetings and conventions, engineering, maintenance, laundry, and security. There is also a section on more costly methods for energy recovery and increased energy efficiency. Instructions are given for organizing a conservation program. The Appendix includes engineering data and other useful technical information.

237. National Restaurant Association. *Foodservice and the Energy Outlook for 1985 and Beyond.* National Restaurant Association Current Issues Report. Washington, DC, 1984. 20 p.

> This analysis of current and potential energy sources looks at the supply, demand, and prices of oil, natural gas, propane, coal, and electricity. Solar energy and synthetic fuels

are also considered as alternate energy sources. The pamphlet concludes with a section on emergency energy preparedness.

238. Unklesbay, Nan, and Unklesbay, Kenneth. *Energy Management in Foodservice.* Westport, CT: AVI Publishing Co., 1982. 437 p.
This text presents an approach to energy management based on five overall policies. Part one is an overview of energy consumption, in general. Part two includes a primer on basic energy principles and also presents the five policies. The rest of the book applies these policies to direct and indirect energy consumption in foodservices and presents techniques for energy accounting systems and implementing conservation programs.

239. U.S. Federal Energy Administration, Office of Energy Conservation and Environment. *Guide to Energy Conservation for Food Service.* Washington, DC: Government Printing Office, 1975. 74 p.
This is a government guide to energy conservation built on research done by the National Restaurant Association and FEA/NBA publication known as *EPIC (Energy Conservation Program Guide for Industry and Commerce).* This guide differs from the *EPIC* mainly in offering specific how-to conservation procedures that foodservice operators can perform themselves along with the more technical recommendations. Chapters cover food preparation and storage, light, heating and air conditioning, ventilation, and sanitation. Each chapter is divided into sections on operations, maintenance, and planning.

Equipment

240. Avery, Arthur C. *A Modern Guide to Foodservice Equipment.* rev. ed. New York: CBI Publishing Co., 1985. 358 p.

This is the basic textbook on foodservice equipment. It is a digest of research done by the U. S. Navy Food Science and Engineering Division, which Avery directed for years. Each type of equipment, such as microwave ovens and griddles, is covered in a separate chapter. In addition to being an excellent textbook, it also serves as the source of specification details and capacity information on equipment for quantity cooking.

241. Glew, G., ed. *Catering Equipment and Systems Design.* London: Applied Science Publishers, 1977. 481 p.

A collection of papers from a symposium organized by Leeds University discussing the future of the catering industry in terms of equipment. Caterers, architects, scientists, and engineers all contributed. The thirty-five papers are presented in seven sections: "Catering Policy and Planning"; "Parameters for Equipment Design"; "Modern Concepts of Cooking and Food Handling"; "Designs for Total Catering Systems"; "Catering Systems, Food Distribution, Nutrition and Hygiene"; "Catering Equipment—New Ideas and Their Evaluation and the Teaching of Catering Equipment Design"; and "The Use of Computers in Equipment and Facilities Design."

242. Greaves, Roland E. *The Commercial Food Equipment Repair and Maintenance Manual.* New York: Van Nostrand Reinhold Co., 1987. 189 p.

This practical manual provides information on making minor repairs, adjustments and preventive maintenance on foodservice equipment. The author includes information on food preparation, cooking, sanitation, serving, and beverage equipment. Some black-and-white diagrams of equipment are included.

243. Greaves, Roland E. *Food Equipment Repair and Maintenance.* Rochester, NY: F.E.R.M. [Food, Equipment Repair Maintenance], 1984. 293 p.

General information on maintenance given here enables the reader to perform some minor repairs and avoid unnecessary service calls. Over forty pieces of equipment are covered including preparation and cooking equipment, serving equipment, dishwashers and disposals, ice makers, toasters and related items, and beverage equipment. The final chapter on miscellaneous equipment is about repairing conveyers and ventilating units. Each section covers maintenance, preventive maintenance schedules, trouble shooting, parts, and common problems. Presentation is step by step.

244. Groen. *Problem Solving Foodservice Equipment.* Educational Series/Application Stories. Elk Grove Village, IL: Groen Division, Dover Corp., 1978?. (Loose-leaf)

This is a collection of single sheets that give tips on how to make most effective use of Groen kettles and related equipment. Each sheet features some restaurant where the particular type of equipment is in use.

245. *Hotel and Catering.* Equipment Planning Guide for Vocational and Technical Training and Education Programmes; vol. 16. Geneva, Switzerland: International Labour Office, 1983. 222 p.

> This is one of a series of equipment planning guides designed to help government departments and national institutes in developing countries understand the technical specifications for equipment. This volume covers hotels and foodservice industries. The bulk of the work is an equipment guide list. Also included is information on planning equipment requirements and layouts of kitchens and laundries.

246. Jernigan, Anna Katherine, and Ross, Lynne Nannen. *Food Service Equipment.* 2d ed. Ames, IA: Iowa State University Press, 1980. 132 p.

> Designed for use by foodservice managers in hospitals, schools, and restaurants. This book covers selection, placement and use of foodservice equipment. It also covers how to maintain efficient operation of the equipment and standards that regulate the equipment. All types of equipment are covered: receiving and storing, food preparation, serving, and sanitizing (dishwashing) equipment.

247. Kahrl, William L. *Food Service Equipment.* Managing for Profit Series. New York: Chain Store Publishing Corp., 1978. 87 p.

> Part of the Managing for Profit Series, this manual covers both selection and use of equipment. It sets out guidelines that will assist in equipment selection and tells how to get maximum efficient use out of both new and existing equipment.

248. Kotschevar, Lendal Henry, and Terrell, Margaret E. *Foodservice Planning: Layout and Equipment.* 3d ed. New York: Macmillan, 1986. 543 p.

> A textbook dealing with the overall arrangement and layout of foodservices and equipment. Section one on planning discusses the design of the facilities, layout characteristics, and space allocation. Section two is on functional areas of food facilities such as receiving and storage. Section three is on supporting factors such as lighting and energy. Section four is on equipment selection.

249. Ley, Sandra J. *Foodservice Refrigeration.* Boston: CBI Publishing Co., 1980. 354 p.

> This is a concise overview of refrigeration in the foodservice industry. Basic refrigeration principles are covered and scientific aspects such as enzymes and microbial contamination as they relate to storage temperatures. The book also provides a guide for selecting dependable refrigeration systems whether uprights or walk-ins, and a chapter on preventive maintenance. Sanitation and energy conservation are included as are new concepts in food production that affect refrigeration. Appendices list refrigerator manufacturers and various suppliers of refrigeration necessities.

250. Milson, A., and Kirk, D. *Principles of Design and Operation of Catering Equipment.* Ellis Horwood Series in Food Science and Technology. Chichester, England: Horwood; Westport, CT: AVI Publishing Co., 1980. 440 p.

> This is a book on process engineering as applied to the study of catering equipment. The authors wish to explain the basic concepts on which the processes of food preparation are based and show how they apply in the design and operation of catering equipment. Chapters cover mass and heat balances, fluid flow, conduction, convection, radiation, microwaves, freezing and thawing, multimode heat transfer, mass transfer, energy sources, foodhandling equipment, and dishwashers.

251. Myers, James R. *Commercial Kitchens.* 6th ed. Edited by James R. Modlin and Harry C. Anderson. Arlington, VA: American Gas Association, 1979. 349 p.

> Published by the American Gas Association, this book discusses the effective use of commercial kitchens. Emphasis is naturally on the advantages of gas appliances though others are discussed. There are good chapters on foodservice layouts and kitchen design as well as comparisons of gas to other fuels in terms of cost and efficiency. The main part of the book provides detailed descriptions of most types of gas appliances for commercial kitchens.

252. National Sanitation Foundation. *Manual on Sanitation Aspects of Installation of Food Service Equipment.* Ann Arbor, MI, 1968. 43 p.

This manual gives guidelines for the installation of foodservice equipment to meet minimum acceptable public health criteria. Chapters cover warewashing facilities, hot water generating equipment, and walk-in refrigerators and storage freezers.

253. Scriven, Carl, and Stevens, James. *Food Equipment Facts: A Handbook for the Food Service Industry.* New York: Wiley, 1982. 429 p.

This is a handbook of facts and statistics on a wide variety of foodservice equipment. It includes production capacity charts, lists of options, portion control charts, helpful hints, and dimensional and power specifications. Items described were selected as typical and cover every type of equipment from storage and receiving through cooking and serving to maintenance and warehandling equipment.

254. Thorner, Marvin Edward. *Convenience and Fast Food Handbook.* Westport, CT: AVI Publishing Co., 1973. 358 p.

This is a handbook on the use of equipment and its effects on food, handling, and preservation. It is divided into two main sections. The first covers preparation systems, storage, production areas, microwave cooking, and deep frying. The second section is on control, evaluation, and handling of efficiency foods. The first chapter is a review of the history of convenience and fast food.

255. Wilkinson, Jule. *The Complete Book of Cooking Equipment.* 2d ed. Boston: CBI Publishing Co., 1981. 259 p.

What started as a seventy-two page pamphlet in 1964 has become a large book in this revised, updated, and greatly expanded second edition of Wilkinson's guide to cooking equipment. The author gives guidance in selecting, buying, operating, and maintaining most types of commercial kitchen equipment including ranges, steam cooking equipment, ovens, griddles/grills, fryers, broilers, infrared food-warming equipment, specialty equipment, refrigeration, and waste-handling equipment. A final chapter is called "How to Clean Equipment: Programmed Lessons."

256. Williams, Chuck. *The Williams-Sonoma Cookbook and Guide to Kitchenware.* New York: Random House, 1986. 304 p.

Written by the chairman of the Williams-Sonoma Company kitchen equipment catalog and stores, the first half of the book covers all types of cooking equipment. There are line drawings of each item next to a short explanation of its uses. The second half has over 150 recipes in all menu categories. These mostly come from the catalog where they have appeared as recipes for specific pieces of equipment, but there are some new ones as well. Emphasis is on simple recipes using fresh ingredients.

Facility Design and Interior Decoration

257. Aloi, Giampiero. *Ristoranti: Testo e Didascalie in Italiano ed Inglese, 37 Tavole a Calori, 297 Illustrazioni in Nero, 343 Disegni.* Milano, Italy: Ulrico Hoepli Editore Spa, 1972. 319 p.

> Written in both Italian and English, this book presents photographs, descriptions and floor plans for more than fifty restaurants. Restaurants from all over the world are included, but emphasis is on Italian restaurants with unique architectural design and style.

258. Angelo, Rocco M. *Understanding Feasibility Studies: A Practical Guide.* East Lansing, MI: Educational Institute of the American Hotel & Motel Association, 1985. 51 p.

> This is a guide to feasibility studies for the hospitality industry. It explains how to read and analyze a study and what can be expected when commissioning one. It clears up some misconceptions and discusses how feasibility studies can be used to greatest advantage. Chapters include the proposal letter, feasibility report opening sections, market area characteristics, project site and area evaluation, competition analysis, demand analysis, recommended facilities and services, and estimating operating results.

259. Buchanan, Robert D., et al. *The Anatomy of Foodservice Design 1.* Edited by Jule Wilkinson. Boston: Cahners Books, 1975. 218 p.

> This book is intended to meet the design needs of many types of foodservices. Each chapter is written by specialists in the planning of facilities in a particular segment of the industry. Chapters cover planning objectives, sites, equipment, special relationships, and other aspects. Many illustrations and floor plans are provided. Included in this volume are college and university foodservice, coffee shops, fast foods, industrial foodservice, school foodservice, and employee foodservice.

260. Cohen, Edie Lee, and Emery, Sherman R. *Dining by Design: Interior Design's Handbook of Dining and Restaurant Facilities.* New York: Cahners Publishing Co., 1984. 223 p.

> This is an interior design handbook about restaurants. The book includes floor plans, pictures, and descriptions of more than fifty well-designed restaurant interiors under such categories as theme restaurants, fast food facilities, hotel dining areas, ballrooms, clubs and discoteques, historic restorations, and corporate dining facilities. Interviews and special features discuss trends and problems in current restaurant design. Lavishly illustrated with color photographs.

261. Colgan, Susan. *Restaurant Design: Ninety-Five Spaces That Work.* New York: Whitney Library of Design, 1987. 255 p.

> Fully illustrated with color photographs, this book presents ninety-five successful restaurant designs. Each restaurant covered includes the design need and the way that need was addressed by the designer and contractor. The chapters are arranged by type of restaurant:

destination restaurants, fast food, ethnic restaurants, cafeterias, and nightspots. Each restaurant is photographed; many floor plans are also included.

262. Garvey, Audrey, ed., and Wilkinson, Jule, ed. *Institutions Award: Food Service, Interiors.* Chicago: Medalist Publications, Inc., 1967. vol. 1. 206 p.

This book gives pictures, descriptions, and floor plans of restaurants winning the Total Design Award given by *Institutions Magazine.* Chapters called "Design International" and "Idea Inventory" give ideas and information for efficient and aesthetically pleasing foodservice interiors, illustrated with many examples of effective restaurants. "Design Data" contains tabular information on subjects such as operating ratios and installation costs by region. Includes lists of past winners and an index.

263. Hess, Alan. *Googie: Fifties Coffee Shop Architecture.* San Francisco, CA: Chronicle Books, 1986. 144 p.

Hess traces the development of coffee shops and drive-in design in the fifties emphasizing California. Though not dated, "modern" shapes of glass and metal were once called the Googie School after a particularly outlandish example of the style in Los Angeles. Hess examines this passing phase of architecture and relates it to the car culture and social outlook of the fifties. Illustrations are included with photographs of McDonald's and a guided tour of Googie.

264. Kahrl, William L. *Modern Food Service Planning.* CSPC Managing for Profit Series. New York: Chain Store Publishing Corp., 1975. 91 p.

This is one of the Managing for Profit Series manuals. Each manual deals with a specific problem common to all segments of the industry and offers suggested solutions. This volume is a guide to analyzing and planning for remodeling and for new operations. Part one, on remodeling, includes guidance in gathering information, evaluating needs and priorities, preliminary planning, evaluation, engaging an architect or general contractor, completed plans, and examples of actual remodeling jobs. Part two discusses the major differences between remodeling and starting a new operation.

265. Kahrl, William L. *Planning and Operating a Successful Food Service Operation.* rev. ed. New York: Chain Store Publishing Corp., 1979. 256 p.

This is a comprehensive book of restaurant planning. Part one deals with location, basic planning, and layout. The other sections cover equipment planning, planning for efficient operation and for growth and change, and maximizing the benefits of good planning. Kahrl brings forty years of experience to this book. He gives excellent advice and suggestions for effective operation. Every complex operation is broken into simple parts for easier understanding.

266. Kazarian, Edward A. *Foodservice Facilities Planning.* 2d ed. Westport, CT: AVI Publishing Co., 1983. 308 p.

This textbook covers facility design for all types of foodservices from fast food restaurants to hospitals. The major emphasis is on the planning process including the feasibility study, planning for functional use and for atmosphere. Space requirements for workers and equipment and layouts are also included.

267. Kazarian, Edward A. *Work Analysis and Design for Hotels, Restaurants, and Institutions.* 2d ed. Westport, CT: AVI Publishing Co., 1979. 390 p.

Drawing upon the field of industrial engineering, this textbook presents the techniques needed to analyze and design efficient work systems and thereby increase employee productivity in the hospitality industries. Topics covered include design for safety, functional and activity analysis, motion analysis, and time study. This new edition has a complete new unit on task sequencing.

268. Langdon, Philip. *Orange Roofs, Golden Arches: The Architecture of American Chain Restaurants.* New York: Alfred A. Knopf, 1986. 223 p.

Langdon provides a look at the history and development of chain restaurant architecture in the United States. He traces the decor and design from the origins of chain restaurants to the present. The author's thesis is that these restaurants embody the spirit of their times. Chapters include origins of the chain restaurant industry, standardizing the image, drive-ins, Googie-style coffee shops, and design since 1975.

269. Lawson, Fred R. *Restaurant Planning and Design*. London: Van Nostrand Reinhold Co., 1973. 180 p.
Major internal and external design factors are discussed here with more emphasis on practical technical details than is usual with books of this type. Business and functional requirements are taken into consideration along with service, atmosphere, engineering, interior construction, tableware, and menu design. A "Briefing Guide" gives a detailed outline of design procedure.

270. National Golf Foundation. *Planning the Golf Clubhouse*. 3d ed. rev. North Palm Beach, FL, 1986. 268 p.
This book presents a cross-section of ideas and trends in the golf clubhouse design and operation so clubhouse builders have criteria to compare their own concepts and ideas and avoid some mistakes. It is a collection of articles, each by a different author, on the various elements of planning and developing the design of a golf clubhouse. Diagrams, floor plans, site plans, and cost information are included; but color photographs are omitted from this edition.

271. Rutes, Walter A., and Penner, Richard H. *Hotel Planning and Design*. New York: Whitney Library of Design, 1985. 256 p.
This book surveys emerging trends in hotel design and provides practical information for planning and designing new facilities. Part one covers twelve different hotel types including downtown and suburban, resort, convention, and residential hotels. Part two, "Design Guide," deals with the effective design of guest rooms, public space offices, and other aspects of design as well as construction. Part three discusses feasibility studies, hotel operations, and professional practices including consultants, contracts, and fees. There are many illustrations and floor plans.

272. Schirmbeck, Egon. *Restaurants, Architecture and Ambience*. New York: Architectural Books Publishing Co., 1983. 143 p.
Written in German and English side by side, this book begins with a brief discussion of the various aspects of modern restaurant design including lighting, material, and decoration. The main body of the book consists of descriptions, floor plans, and pictures of nearly forty restaurants in the United States and Europe (all opened since 1970) where contemporary designs have been successfully used.

273. Seltz, David D. *The Entrepreneur's Guide to Restaurant Expansion*. New York: Chain Store Publishing Corp., 1982. 238 p.
This book is intended to help the restaurant owner know when to expand operations and how to avoid the pitfalls of expansion. The chapters cover organizing and planning expansion, obtaining investment capital, and many other aspects of the subject including chapters on bottom line figures and breakeven analysis.

274. Smith, Douglas. *Hotel and Restaurant Design*. London: Design Council Publications, 1978. 137 p.
This book is intended for the owners and operators of small and medium-sized hotels and restaurants. Examples and illustrations are British. Chapters cover landscape, interior design, equipment, and British legislation and regulations.

275. Wood, Charles, et al. *The Anatomy of Foodservice Design 2*. Edited by Jule Wilkinson. Boston: CBI Publishing Co., 1978. 214 p.
This volume gives management's relationship to design in the lodging industry as well as covering other foodservice industry design needs not discussed in volume one. As with the first book, each chapter is written by a design specialist in the particular field and includes many illustrations and floor plans. Chapters include hospitals, day care centers, cafeterias, and hotels and motels. An appendix gives important tips for facility planning design.

Fast Food

276. Bertram, Peter. *Fast Food Operations*. London: Barrie & Jenkins Ltd., 1975. 223 p.

A careful examination of the spread of the demand for fast food in Great Britain. The author discusses the revolution he sees in the British restaurant industry and the planning and equipment necessary to begin a successful fast food operation there.

277. Business Trend Analysts, Inc. *The Fast Food and Multi-Unit Restaurant Business: A Strategic Marketing Analysis and Biennial Review*. Commack, NY, 1984. 388 p.

This is a report providing market analysis and commentary. It is intended as an aid to evaluation and planning for fast food chains and related businesses. Statistics with brief analysis and summary are presented for the multiunit restaurant market as a whole and by section including the hamburger, pizza, chicken, Mexican, seafood, and sandwich segments, among others. Statistics are given on sales, advertising, location, and other pertinent subjects. Additional sections appear on demographic trends, financial profiles, company developments, and international activities. A directory of major companies is included.

278. Charner, Ivan, and Fraser, Bryna Shore. *Fast Food Jobs: National Study of Fast Food Employment*. Washington, DC: National Institute for Work & Learning, 1984. 144 p.

This study looks at fast food employees: what they do, how they are trained and supervised, and the benefit and effect of their work. The research here is based upon a survey of hourly employees called "The National Study of Fast Food Employment." It offers insights to the largest employment area for young people.

279. Emerson, Robert L. *Fast Food: The Endless Shakeout*. rev. ed. New York: Chain Store Publishing Corp., 1982. 345 p.

Emerson is a securities analyst, so his book offers an outsider's view of the chain restaurant industry. He looks at why some chains have succeeded where others have failed, the keys to consumer acceptance of fast food, and how to manage and control rapid growth of a chain. Interviews with chain executives from McDonald's, Wendy's, Pizza Hut, Kentucky Fried Chicken, and Burger King discuss strategic decisions and past mistakes, and future prospects are included.

280. Jacobson, Michael, and Fritschner, Sarah. *The Fast-Food Guide: What's Good, What's Bad, and How to Tell the Difference*. New York: Workman Publishing, 1986. 225 p.

This book provides nutritional information on all major fast food chains. Lists show which foods are highest in fat, sodium, calcium and calories, etc. Ingredients are listed. In the section on the fast food meal, chains are listed alphabetically with ingredients and nutritional values given for various menu items. The most healthful choices are indicated.

Food Preparation

281. Axler, Bruce H. *Breakfast Cookery.* His Focus on...the Hospitality Industry. Indianapolis, IN: ITT Educational Publishing, 1974. 134 p.

This brief booklet is another in Axler's series on the hospitality industry. This one covers breakfast cooking and service. Topics include purchasing equipment, cooking techniques, beverages, and menu planning. No recipes are included.

282. Belsinger, Susan, and Dille, Carolyn. *Cooking with Herbs.* New York: Van Nostrand Reinhold Co., 1984. 261 p.

Recipes are collected here for using the twenty best known herbs. Chapters on each herb include herblore, culinary suggestions and growing tips as well as a dozen or so recipes. A final chapter lists complementary herb combinations and the use of dried herbs. An appendix lists herb sources in many states. Herbs covered include basil, bay, chervil, chives, coriander, cress, dill, garlic, lemon balm, marjoram and oregano, the mints, parsley, rosemary, sage, sorrel, summer and winter savory, tarragon, and thyme.

283. Boykin-Stith, Lorraine, and Williams, Barbara Kern. *A Comprehensive Review of Food Preparation and Storage Application.* Old Westbury, NY: Westville Publishing Co., 1982. 124 p.

This is a study guide of multiple-choice questions designed to help students review the material covered in college textbooks on food preparation and storage. Answers are given at the end of each section.

284. Boyle, Peter T. *Sugar Work: Blown- and Pulled-Sugar Techniques.* New York: Van Nostrand Reinhold Co., 1988. 130 p.

Blown- and pulled-sugar techniques are explained and illustrated in this how-to manual. The technique calls for cooked sugar which can be stored for over one month and then warmed under heat lamps and blown or pulled, similar to glass blowing. Step-by-step instructions are given for a variety of projects such as a fruit bowl, flowers, a swan, and Christmas ornaments. This fascinating art form has been used by European chefs, and this book now makes the techniques available for American chefs.

285. Cooke, Phillip S., ed. *The Second Symposium of American Cuisine.* New York: Van Nostrand Reinhold Co., 1984. 240 p.

This is the edited transcripts of speeches presented at the Second Symposium on American Cuisine. Nearly twenty speeches are included, and they cover topics such as influence of nouvelle cuisine, creole cooking, merchandising, California influence, Cajun cooking, and American wines. Biographies and favorite recipes of the speakers are included.

286. Culinary Institute of America, Learning Resources Center. *The Professional Chef's Knife.* The Professional Chef's Photo-text Series; no. 1. New York: Van Nostrand Reinhold Co., 1978. 63 p.

This is a comprehensive photo-text on the chef's knife. It covers nomenclature, care, balance, and other basics about the knives themselves as well as sharpening stones and steels. General techniques for using the knife and specific cutting techniques for various meats, vegetables, and fruits are included. Most photographs are taken from the chef's point of view facilitating the learning of proper hand and knife positions.

287. Durocher, Joseph F., and Goodman, Raymond J., Jr. *The Essentials of Tableside Cookery*. Ithaca, NY: School of Hotel Administration, Cornell University, 1978?. 72 p.
This is an instruction book on the basics of tableside preparation. It includes sections on techniques, equipment, staffing requirements, and pricing. There are recipes for a variety of tableside dishes including appetizers, salads, various entrees, desserts, and beverages.

288. Emery, William. *Culinary Design and Decoration*. Illustrated by Joyce Tuhill. Boston: CBI Publishing Co., 1980. 135 p.
The basic principles of good design are applied to food presentation. The suggestions in this book emphasize the simple use of color and shape to achieve attractive dishes. These principles are applied to appetizers, salads, soups, sandwiches, meat, and desserts. Color plates enhance the appeal of the book.

289. Escoffier, A. *The Escoffier Cook Book: A Guide to the Fine Art of Cookery*. New York: Crown Publishers, 1941. 923 p.
This cookbook is a translation and adaptation for U.S. cooks of *Le Guide Culinaire* by A. Escoffier. It is divided into two main sections: "Cooking Techniques," which includes techniques for making sauces, garnishing, and basic cooking methods; and "Recipes." Wherever French terms are used, they are italicized and defined in the glossary.

290. Field, Michael. *Michael Field's Cooking School; A Selection of Great Recipes Demonstrating the Pleasures and Principles of Fine Cooking*. Drawings by Roderick Wells. New York: M. Barrows, 1965. 369 p.
A collection of about 100 recipes in all common menu categories with special chapters on casseroles and rice, pasta, and kasha. Emphasis is on recipes that demonstrate basic culinary principles. Chapters begin with a summary of things to be learned, and text carefully explains preparation to students. A chapter at the end includes menus with appropriate wine suggestions.

291. Fuller, John. *Guéridon and Lamp Cookery*. London: Hutchinson, 1980. 162 p.
Guéridon means tableside cookery; this book covers both guéridon and flamed cooking. It includes recipes and procedures for dishes that are completely prepared in front of the customer. Chapters cover the purpose of lamp cooking, equipment needed, liquors used in flambé, directions for guéridon preparations, flamed savory dishes, flamed fruits and desserts, tableside carving, salads, and coffee and liquor service at the table. A glossary is included also.

292. Fussell, Betty Harper. *I Hear America Cooking*. New York: Viking, 1986. 516 p.
A collection of recipes that reflect the diversity of American food. Recipes appear by regions: "Mexamerican Desert," "The Delta South," "Southeast Dixie," "The New England Coast," and "The Great Lakes of the Midwest." Some recipes are primarily of historic interest, but most are usable by any cook. Text gives history and background on American cuisine. Quite a few Native American recipes are included.

293. Gould, Wilbur A. *Food Quality Assurance*. rev. ed. Westport, CT: AVI Publishing Co., 1983. 314 p.
This is a quality control manual. Each chapter deals with major quality attributes of various foods such as odor, texture, consistency, and acidity and methods for their evaluation. The technologist is provided with quality valuation and assurance procedures for a wide variety of food products.

294. Gregg, Joseph G. *Cooking for Food Managers: A Laboratory Text.* Brown Restaurant and Hotel Management Series. Dubuque, IA: W. C. Brown Co. 1967. 148 p.

> This is a laboratory text for foodservice management majors. It is intended for teaching principles and basic concepts of good food production rather than to train professional cooks. It covers menu planning and basic cooking knowledge, safety, and sanitation but also provides instructions and recipes for preparing basic hors d'oeuvres, sandwiches, egg, bread, meat, poultry, seafood, fruit, and vegetable dishes. Lesson plans and objective tests are available through the author.

295. Haines, Robert G. *Food Preparation for Hotels, Restaurants, and Cafeterias.* 2d ed. Chicago: American Technical Society, 1973. 678 p.

> An introductory cooking text containing over 770 recipes for common preparations used in most restaurants and cafeterias. Early chapters give basic information on equipment and procedures. Many recipes start with learning objectives and are presented step by step. Suggestions for garnishing and serving are included. Final chapter deals with selecting and writing menus. This edition includes information on new equipment, use of convenience foods, an expanded glossary, and two new chapters on breakfast and specialty desserts.

296. Iowa Dietetic Association. *Simplified Diet Manual with Meal Patterns.* 5th ed. Ames, IA: Iowa State University Press, 1984. 108 p.

> Written to provide guidance for doctors prescribing diets and for hospital and nursing home staff in following those prescriptions, this brief manual has been widely used and accepted. Diets are explained and sample menus are given for special diets (such as high calorie); soft, liquid, and diabetic diets; and calorie-, fat-, and sodium-restricted diets. This new edition includes protein- and purine-restricted diets.

297. Janericco, Terence. *The Book of Great Breakfasts and Brunches.* Boston: CBI Publishing Co., 1983. 217 p.

> Over 250 recipes for breakfast, brunch, and lunch are compiled here by Janericco, the owner and operator of La Cuisine Cooking Classes in Boston. The recipes in this volume serve six to eight people and are intended for the homemaker but are usable by restaurateurs.

298. Kahrl, William L. *Food Preparation.* Managing for Profit Series. New York: Chain Store Publishing Corp., 1978. 78 p.

> Part of the Managing for Profit Series, this book discusses the use of convenience foods in restaurants. Kahrl presents the varieties and sources of convenience foods in the first part of his book. In the second part, "Convenience Foods vs. from Scratch Preparation," he shows that they compare favorably in terms of costs, contamination, safety, need for skilled personnel, and speed of service. He also shows that acceptance of such foods is growing. Reconstituting equipment is also discussed.

299. Knight, John Barton, and Salter, Charles A. *Foodservice Standards in Resorts.* The L. J. Minor Foodservice Standards Series, vol. 7. New York: Van Nostrand Reinhold Co., 1987. 242 p.

> This volume in the L. J. Minor Foodservice Standard Series covers foodservice in resorts. It is divided into two main parts. Part one is an overview that covers resort management, food purchasing, food preparation, service, merchandising, and guest satisfaction. Part two is a series of case studies.

300. Lappé, Frances Moore. *Diet for a Small Planet.* 10th rev ed. Illustrated by Marika Hahn. New York: Ballantine Books, 1982. 496 p.

> This is one of the most famous and most influential books on diet, nutrition and health. The author advocates a change in eating habits away from processed foods to meals rich in vegetable protein. Hundreds of recipes are included which combine nonmeat items into complete proteins. The book is aimed at the home cook but would be of interest to restaurateurs seeking to capitalize on the natural food trend.

301. Lawson, Harry W. *Standards for Fats & Oils.* The L.J. Minor Foodservice Standards Series, vol. 5. Westport, CT: AVI Publishing Co., 1985. 235 p.
Written to help foodservice employees understand how and why certain types of fats and oils work in cooking. Standards for using fats and oils for frying, baking, and salad dressings are included as are quantity recipes. The book also covers the chemistry and technology of fats, nutrition and dietary considerations, and sanitary and quality control of fats.

302. Lundberg, Donald E., and Kotschevar, Lendal Henry. *Understanding Cooking.* rev. ed. Holyoke, MA: Marcus Printing Co., 1985. 463 p.
This is a programmed textbook where students uncover the answers as they work through the questions. It covers the principles of cooking meat, eggs, vegetables, sauces, baked products, and salads.

303. Medved, Eva. *Food: Preparation and Theory.* Englewood Cliffs, NJ: Prentice-Hall, 1986. 409 p.
This book is a text for college classes in food study, covering basic principles and techniques of food preparation. It is aimed at giving the student a grasp of how foods respond to preparation. Chapters cover food preparation; components; assessment; individual types of food such as cereals, eggs, etc.; and how they respond to preparation. Food safety and microwave cooking are also included.

304. Mizer, David A.; Porter, Mary; and Sonnier, Beth. *Food Preparation for the Professional.* 2d ed. Wiley Service Management Series. New York: Wiley, 1987. 526 p.
This is a text for beginning students covering the principles and the techniques of food preparation. The text is centered on the actual preparation of food. It also provides basic vocabulary and terminology of cooking and menu items as well as giving an introduction to foods, equipment, and quality standards. The first six chapters give basics such as sanitation, prepreparation, cooking techniques, and measurement. The remaining chapters center on preparation of specific food.

305. Moosberg, Frank O. *Simplified Manual for Cooks.* rev. ed.? Des Moines, IA: s.n. 1973. 233 p.
This manual on cooking techniques was written to be used in vocational education courses or on-the-job training. It emphasizes efficient movement in the kitchen. Topics covered include organization, tools and equipment, and food preparation techniques. Many recipes are included. Each unit begins with an objective and ends with a set of questions. Black-and-white photographs are used to illustrate techniques and equipment throughout the book.

306. Mosimann, Anton. *Cuisine Naturelle.* Photographs by John Lee. Illustrated by Jane Human. New York: Atheneum, 1986. 263 p.
The author explains cuisine naturelle as a technique for producing fine food that is also healthy food. Mosimann starts with fresh, natural ingredients and stresses the use of steaming, poaching, broiling and dry sautéing. He eliminates butter, oil, and alcohol while cutting the use of salt and sugar to a minimum. Recipes appear for stocks and sauce bases, appetizers, soups, fish, shellfish, meat, poultry, game and game birds, vegetables, desserts, and breads.

307. Mueller, T. G. *The Professional Chef's Book of Charcuterie: Pates, Terrines, Timbales, Galantines, Sausages, and Other Culinary Delights.* New York: Van Nostrand Reinhold: 1987. 276 p.
"Charcuterie" literally means cooked meat and was used during the Middle Ages to describe products from the pork butcher's shop. No longer limited to just cooked pork, the word now describes a method of cooking and serving food. Savory pies and filled pastries, sausages, meats, fish, and vegetables made into galantines or ballotines can be prepared in this method. Over 300 recipes specifically collected for restaurateurs and caterers are included.

308. Nickerson, John T. R., and Ronsivalli, Louis J. *Elementary Food Science.* 2d ed. Westport, CT: AVI Publishing Co., 1980. 441 p.
This textbook is aimed at the junior college level student or lower undergraduate student who plans a career in food handling in restaurants, hotels, or airlines or in food processing plants. It covers microbial, enzyme, and chemical food changes; food processing methods such as heating, drying, and freezing; and food handling techniques of meat, dairy products, fish, grains, bakery items, sugars, fruits, vegetables, fats, and oils.

309. Pauli, Eugen. *Classical Cooking the Modern Way.* Edited by M. Arkwright. Translated by P. March and M. Levine. Boston: CBI Publishing Co., 1979. 625 p.
A translation of a European text, this book is a manual for students in foodservices. It covers basic principles of kitchen management and organization. It also presents fundamental principles of cooking based on classical French cookery as well as the latest developments in the industry. The cookery section includes many excellent recipes in all menu categories intended for students.

310. Pellaprat, Henri Paul. *The Great Book of French Cuisine.* Edited by René Kramer and David White. Adapted by Avanelle Day. New York: Vendome Press, 1982. 1,171 p.
This is an American edition of Pellaprat's *L'Art Culinaire Moderne* published in 1935, the classical work on French cooking. It was first translated into English under the title *Modern French Culinary Art* (1966). Pellaprat was a famous chef and teacher at the Cordon Bleu Cooking School in Paris. The book begins with a chapter on entertaining and one on wines. Following that, the book is divided into the standard menu categories. Most recipes make four servings.

311. Polak, Jeanne. *Food Service for Fitness: A Guide to Healthful Eating.* Plycon Press Home Economics Series. Minneapolis, MN: Plycon Press, 1981. 84 p.
This booklet contains recipes for school lunch programs which meet the national dietary goals as developed by the Senate Select Committee on Nutrition and Human needs. All recipes are low in saturated fats, low in cholesterol, high in nutrients, and low in calories. All are in fifty portion servings. Also included in the book is the "Report of the Select Committee, U.S. Dietary Guidelines, National School Lunch Program Requirements of 1980" and the basic requirements for breakfast and lunch patterns.

312. Robins, G. V. *Food Science in Catering.* London: Heinemann, 1980. 234 p.
This British publication provides a nonspecialist introduction to food science. The book concentrates on the composition, structure, and behavior of food during phases of preparation without overwhelming the student in scientific theory. The first three chapters cover food and heat, the constitution of food, and basics of food-related organic chemistry. Chapters four through seven deal with the various food groups such as lipids and proteins and also cover the aesthetic value of food. Final chapters deal with such related subjects as additives and preservation.

313. Rombauer, Irma, and Becker, Marion Rombauer. *Joy of Cooking.* Illustrated by Ginnie Hofmann and Ikki Matsumoto. Indianapolis, IN: Bobbs-Merrill, 1975. 915 p.
This is perhaps the most well-known and extensively used cookbook available. In addition to including thousands of recipes, this is a good source for explanation of why certain techniques or procedures are used.

314. Rosenberg, Barbara S. *How to Succeed with Chicken without Even Frying.* Edited by Frances Rosenberg Hendrick. Illustrated by Alice H. Balterman. Cincinnati, OH: MarLance, 1984. 204 p.
As consumer tastes are demanding less fattening, low cholesterol meats, the popularity of chicken is on the rise. This cookbook contains hundreds of recipes for the nutrition-minded chef. Included are tips on how to prepare and freeze staples that you can use later

and what steps in each recipe can be done ahead of time. Recipes serve four to eight people.

315. Simms, A. E., ed., and Quin, Mabel, assistant. ed. *Fish and Shell-fish.* London: Virtue, 1973. 504 p.

This cookbook is the most comprehensive one available on the preparation of fish and shellfish. It starts with an illustrated dictionary of fish and goes on to cover purchasing and cooking preparations and methods. Black-and-white photographs are used to illustrate techniques and service procedures. Recipes for international dishes constitute about two-thirds of the volume; many are illustrated in full color.

316. Southey, Paul. *The Vegetarian Gourmet Cookbook.* New York: Van Nostrand Reinhold Co., 1980. 224 p.

As food preferences are changing to less emphasis on meat, restaurateurs will find this cookbook an inspiration for menu planning. Southey has compiled over 400 recipes using vegetables in an elegant and epicurean way. Each recipe starts with a list of calories, protein content, and preparation time, making it possible to plan a completely adequate diet using these recipes. Emphasis is on fresh fruits and vegetables, eggs, and dairy products. The book starts with a beautifully illustrated glossary of ingredients and concludes with a chapter on nutrition. Color photographs and line drawings add to the visual appeal.

317. Sutherland, Elizabeth, et al. *Food Preparation Principles and Procedures.* 6th ed. Dubuque, IA: W. C. Brown Co., 1973. 292 p.

This manual is designed to present the scientific principles of food preparation. It is divided into chapters on types of food and cooking techniques. The laboratory exercises start with a stated problem which relates to a scientific technique.

318. Terrell, Margaret E. *Professional Food Preparation.* 2d ed. New York: Wiley, 1979. 741 p.

This text covers the important basic principles of food preparation in large kitchens. Section one includes basic organization and procedures in quantity cooking. Section two covers fruits, vegetables, sauces, and soups. Section three is about pantry items such as salads, beverages, and sandwiches. Section four discusses the cooking of meat and dairy products. Section five is about baking. In each section, representative items of equipment are explained. This edition takes into account changes resulting from new developments in commodities, equipment, and handling methods.

319. Vastano, Joseph F. *Elements of Food Production and Baking.* 2d ed. Indianapolis, IN: Bobbs-Merrill Educational Publishing, 1978. 452 p.

This is a text for beginning students in foodservices and food preparation. It covers sanitation and safety, tools and equipment, and basic cooking methods as well as providing chapters with both recipes and general instructions on various types of foods. Meats, seafoods, vegetables, salads, hors d'oeuvres, pies, pastry, cakes, cookies, and other desserts as well as convenience foods and microwave cooking are covered.

320. Zaccarelli, Herman E. *The Cookbook That Tells You How: The Retirement Food and Nutrition Manual.* Boston: Cahners Books, 1975. 355 p.

Intended as a manual for retired people, this book provides over 1,095 menus that are nutritious and interesting while fitting certain dietary needs and limited budgets. In addition to regular diets, there are recipes for sodium-restricted, low fat, high carbohydrate, high protein, liquid, diabetic, and special allergy diets. Checklists help make the most of food purchases and preparations on limited income.

APPETIZERS AND GARNISHES

321. *Beginning Again: More Hors D'Oeuvres.* Cincinnati, OH: Rockdale Ridge Press, 1981. 224 p.
> This collection of hors d'oeuvres recipes supplements an earlier collection called *In the Beginning.* Recipes are from restaurants, newspapers, and cookbook editors. Included are soups, canapés, quiches, dips, spreads, vegetables, drinks, and breads. The last chapter includes recipes from outstanding restaurants and food writers.

322. Casas, Penelope. *Tapas, the Little Dishes of Spain.* Photographs by Tom Hopkins. New York: Alfred A. Knopf, 1985. 219 p.
> Tapas are little appetizer-type dishes popular in Spain. This is a collection of many recipes for tapas in the following categories: sauces, marinades, patés, salads, tapas with bread or pastry, and tapas with some last-minute preparation. A short glossary, tapas menus, and recommended tapas bars in Spain are included.

323. Forster, August Ernst. *American Culinary Art.* 2d ed. New York: Ahrens Publishing Co., 1958. 253 p.
> This is a guide to the techniques of garnishing, food carving, and platter decorations and other aspects of food artistry. Twenty-five sections are presented including how to carve meats and fish, fruit carving, decorating with sugar, and many others as well as nonfood decorations such as wax work and clay designs. Illustrated by line drawings.

324. Haydock, Yukiko, and Haydock, Bob. *Japanese Garnishes: The Ancient Art of Mukimono.* New York: Holt, Rinehart and Winston, 1980. 103 p.
> The authors explain, for Westerners, some of the exquisite fruit and vegetable garnishes of Japan. The book is organized by fruit or vegetable, and is illustrated with line drawings and some color plates.

325. Haydock, Yukiko, and Haydock, Bob. *More Japanese Garnishes.* New York: Holt, Rinehart and Winston, 1983. 118 p.
> Similar to its companion, *Japanese Garnishes: The Ancient Art of Mukimono,* this book includes descriptions and illustrations of garnishes in Japanese style.

326. Haydock, Yukiko, and Haydock, Bob. *Oriental Appetizers.* New York: Holt, Rinehart and Winston, 1984. 145 p.
> The authors present fifty-four recipes from China, Japan, India, Burma, Thailand, Indonesia, and the Philippines for appetizers in the following categories: "Deep Fried"; "Pan Fried"; "Steamed"; "Oven Cooked"; "Barbecued"; "Others"; and "Sauces, Dips, and Dough." Each recipe gives careful, numbered steps accompanied by illustrations. Unusual ingredients are defined in the front of the book. Recipes vary in size from eight to forty portions.

327. Hoffman, Mable, and Hoffman, Gar. *Appetizers.* Tucson, AZ: H.P. Books, 1980?. 160 p.
> This illustrated cookbook contains hundreds of recipes for appetizers divided into the following chapters: "Meat"; "Cheese and Egg"; "Fish and Seafood"; "Poultry"; "Vegetables"; "Pastries and Puffs"; "Pates, Molds, and Spreads"; "Dips, Nibblers, and Dippers"; and "Party Sandwiches."

328. Huang, Shu-hui. *Chinese Appetizers and Garnishes.* Translated by Chen Chang-Yen. Monterey Park, CA: Wei Chuan's Cooking, 1982. 151 p.
> This is a lavishly illustrated guide to Chinese garnishes and appetizers which are presented according to difficulty, ingredients, and occasions when served. Both simple and complex arrangements are included. All items are keyed to a section where instructions for making them are given accompanied by step-by-step photographs. Text is in Chinese as well as English.

329. *In the Beginning: A Collection of Hors D'Oeuvres.* rev. Cincinnati, OH: Rockdale Ridge Press, 1983. 201 p.

This is an updated and enhanced printing of the original. It includes hundreds of recipes for elegant, but easy to prepare hors d'oeuvres. All kinds of appetizers, canapés, and soups are gathered together. In addition, it includes a chapter on party drinks, both alcoholic and nonalcoholic. Additional recipes are available in the companion volume *Beginning Again.*

330. Janericco, Terence. *The Book of Great Hors d'Oeuvre.* Boston: CBI Publishing Co., 1982. 513 p.

Over 800 recipes for all types of hors d'oeuvres are collected here for the home and professional chef. Chapters cover nuts and olives, sauces, dips, spreads, patés, canapés, croquettes, skewered foods, cheese/meat/fish balls, pickled foods, stuffed vegetables/meats, pastry, crackers and pastries, and Dim Sum—the Chinese equivalent of hors d'oeuvres.

331. Kokko, Margo. *The Final Touch: Decorative Garnishes.* 2d ed. Illustrated by Buzz Gorder. Photography by Bruce Beauchamp. Boston: CBI Publishing Co., 1982. 160 p.

Unlike many garnishing books that illustrate how to make specific garnishes, this one starts with a discussion of the selection and care of knives and goes on to describe the various cuts of vegetables from the Japanese art of garnishing. Illustrated with line drawings and many full color plates, this book is an inspiration for any cook or chef.

332. Larousse, David Paul. *Edible Art: Forty-Eight Garnishes for the Professional.* New York: Van Nostrand Reinhold Co., 1987. 94 p.

This book presents forty-eight unusual garnishes in Larousse's "California Mukimono" style based on Japanese artistic concepts. Emphasis is on flower shapes. Each step is illustrated by line drawings, and beautiful color photographs of completed garnishes and arrangements are included.

333. Nicolas, Jean F. *Elegant and Easy: Decorative Ideas for Food Presentation.* Boston: CBI Publishing Co., 1983. 118 p.

This book presents very easy to do garnish designs illustrated with pen drawings. Designs are arranged into six broad categories: fruits, vegetables, sheets of color (stiff gelatin), meringues and decorations using butter, bread, and eggs. Four color plates are included.

334. Rosen, Harvey. *How to Garnish: Illustrated Step-by-Step Instructions.* Edited by Robert J. Rosen. Elberon, NJ: International Culinary Consultants, 1983. 96 p.

This book includes easy-to-follow instructions, diagrams, and color photographs to create garnishes from readily available vegetables and fruits. The tools needed for preparation are included with the book.

335. Siple, Molly, and Sax, Irene. *Foodstyle: The Art of Presenting Food Beautifully.* Drawings by Ralph Moseley. New York: Crown Publishers, 1982. 311 p.

This book is primarily an alphabetical guide to various food items showing how to garnish, arrange, and present them beautifully. The book also covers the basic principles of food arrangement and garnishing. Additional short sections give table styling techniques for all occasions, holidays, and international dinners.

336. Weinberg, Julia. *The Big Beautiful Book of Hors d'Oeuvres.* Piscataway, NJ: New Century, 1980. 176 p.

This is a recipe and instruction book for making a wide variety of hors d'oeuvres, both simple and complex. The author emphasizes beauty as much as taste. This book is designed to incorporate splendid recipes with the artistry of food. Short chapters on garnishes and gourmet gadgets for making hors d'oeuvres are included.

BAKING

337. Amendola, Joseph. *The Bakers' Manual for Quantity Baking and Pastry Making.* 3d rev. ed. New York: Ahrens Publishing Co., 1972. 191 p.
Amendola, an instructor of the Culinary Institute, explains the fundamentals of quantity baking of cakes, cookies, pies, puddings, yeast products, and pastries. All recipes are easy to follow and have been tested at the institute. Illustrated with line drawings and photographs.

338. Amendola, Joseph. *The Professional Chef's Baking Recipes.* Edited by Jule Wilkinson. Boston: CBI Publishing Co., 1974. 80 p.
This collection of over 200 recipes was selected from the baking columns in *Institutions/Volume Feeding* magazine. Breads, buns, cakes, pastries, and pies are included along with muffins, rolls, cookies, icings, puddings, and pizza. Three or more recipes appear on each page usually with information on yield along with ingredient lists and short basic instructions. Many are for quantity baking.

339. Amendola, Joseph, and Lundberg, Donald E.*Understanding Baking.* Chicago: Institutions Magazine, 1970. 216 p.
Short basic chapters on all aspects of baking, from selecting the right flour to layouts for bake shops. Chapters are arranged in short paragraphs with keywords and concepts printed in the margin to facilitate study. Quick review questions are provided at the end of each paragraph and at the end of chapters. Covers breads, pies, cakes, cookies, eclairs, and cream puffs. There are also sections on frostings, fillings, puddings, sugar, and syrups.

340. Burbidge, Cile Bellefleur. *The Fine Art of Cake Decorating.* New York: Van Nostrand Reinhold Co., 1984. 225 p.
The author, a professional cake decorator, provides step-by-step instructions for the novice. Black-and-white line drawings help illustrate instructions for roses, stars, leaves, scrolls, lattices, and borders. It also covers frosting making, colors, designing the cake, and making sugar molds. Over thirty specialty cakes are described and illustrated in full color.

341. Cotton, Nathan S. *Breads, Pastries, Pies, and Cookies: Quantity Baking Recipes.* Boston: CBI Publishing Co., 1983. 292 p.
Cotton, a retired baker, has collected nearly 300 of his own recipes into this book. The ingredients, quantities, and formulas are exactly those he used in his bakery shops. The volume is spiral bound for easy use in the kitchen. A companion volume is *Cakes, Icings, and Cheese Cakes.*

342. Cotton, Nathan S. *Cakes, Icings, and Cheese Cakes: Quantity Baking Recipes.* Boston: CBI Publishing Co., 1983. 303 p.
This is a companion volume to *Breads, Pastries, Pies, and Cookies.* Both books have recipes developed and used by Cotton in his bakery. This volume has over 270 recipes for batter cakes, angel food, chiffon cakes, and cheesecakes. Formulas and ingredients are exactly those used by Cotton. All recipes call for weighing ingredients instead of measuring them. A glossary is included.

343. Crane, Warren E. *Delectable Desserts.* New York: Ahrens Book Co., 1964. 122 p.
The author collected these recipes from restaurants and hotels in the U.S. and Mexico. Recipes include cakes, cookies, custards, gelatin desserts, summer desserts, pear desserts, pies, puddings, and tortes. All yield twenty-five servings. Also included are special Hawaiian and Mexican desserts and holiday desserts.

344. Dodge, Jim, and Ratner, Elaine. *The American Baker: Exquisite Desserts from the Pastry Chef of the Stanford Court.* Illustrated by Susan Mattmann. Photographs by Michael Lamotte. New York: Simon and Schuster, 1987. 350 p.
Jim Dodge is pastry chef at Stanford Court in San Francisco. His delicious desserts have gained him wide fame. The recipes included in this volume are adapted for home use and

include sponge cakes, creams, tarts, pies and cobblers, cakes, puddings, pastries, cookies, ice cream and sherbets, and fruit desserts. Black-and-white line drawings illustrate techniques, and sixteen color photographs enhance the volume.

345. Fance, Wilfred J., ed. *The New International Confectioner: Confectionery, Cakes, Pastries, Desserts and Ices, Savouries.* 5th ed. Revised by Michael Small. London: Virtue, 1981. 890 p.

Designed for the professional patisserie as taught in Europe, this is a very extensive and beautiful book. It covers the history of baking, bakery technology, raw materials, decorating of cakes and pastries, and hundreds of recipes on preparing all types of confections. Recipes are given in British measurements, and many are illustrated with color photographs.

346. Fiske, Rosalie Cheney, and Potee, Joanne Koch. *The Bread Baker's Manual: The How's and Why's of Creative Bread Making.* Illustrated by Barbara Sleigh Ellis. The Creative Cooking Series. Englewood Cliffs, NJ: Prentice-Hall, 1978. 171 p.

Written for the novice breadmaker, this book gives detailed explanations of the ingredients and techniques used in bread baking. Over seventy-five recipes are included for breads using various whole grains, spices, herbs, and vegetables. Breads for special occasions are also included. Most recipes yield two loaves.

347. Friberg, Bo. *The Professional Pastry Chef.* New York: Van Nostrand Reinhold Co., 1985. 273 p.

Friberg was trained in Sweden and now is a chef teaching culinary arts at the California Culinary Academy. He has compiled hundreds of recipes that he has developed and tested. The book starts with a detailed chapter on ingredients and equipment. This is followed by precisely described recipes on pastries, tarts, breads, cakes, meringues, cookies, custards, frozen desserts, and decorations.

348. Gilman, Marion Blatsos, and Gilman, Richard. *Desserts and Pastries: A Professional Primer.* New York: Van Nostrand Reinhold Co., 1984. 225 p.

The authors present fine pastry techniques emphasizing ingredients and flavors popular with American consumers such as chocolate, lemon, and strawberry. The first part of the book covers ingredients, techniques and preparation. The second and largest part includes recipes for tarts and pies, puff pastries, cakes and tortes, meringues, mousses and soufflés, individual pastries, and petits fours.

349. Gisslen, Wayne. *Professional Baking.* New York: Wiley, 1985. 346 p.

Originally designed as a text for students, this book is also aimed at amateurs who wish to learn professional techniques. Basic theory and principles as well as proper procedures for professional baking are explained. The approximately 400 recipes have been selected to reinforce the techniques explained in each chapter. All basic baking categories are covered including breads, doughnuts, pies, pastries, cakes, cookies, and other desserts as well as icings, sauces, and decorating techniques.

350. Sultan, William J. *Modern Pastry Chef: Volume 1.* Westport, CT: AVI Publishing Co., 1977. 360 p.

Aimed at the professional baker, this book covers ingredients, procedures, and baking of specialty quick breads and rolls, yeast-raised products, doughnuts, pies, puff paste and choux paste products, and Gateaux. Recipes serve approximately 100 diners.

351. Sultan, William J. *Modern Pastry Chef: Volume 2.* Westport, CT: AVI Publishing Co., 1977. 348 p.

This, and its companion volume one, is written for the professional baker. It covers pancakes, crepés, and fritters; custards, puddings, mousses, and soufflés; French pastries, petits fours, and cookies; tarts, fruitcakes, and strudel; cheesecakes; frozen desserts; and cake decorating. All recipes are for 100 servings.

352. Sultan, William J. *The Pastry Chef.* Westport, CT: AVI Publishing Co., 1983. 674 p.

A reference book for the baker and pastry chef, this book evolved from the two-volume *Modern Pastry Chef.* It is updated and deals with modern products and equipment, dough conditioners, and prepared mixes as well as presents recipes, methods, and formulas for most desserts and other baked items included on most menus. Recipes are constructed to serve about 100.

353. Sultan, William J. *Practical Baking.* 4th ed. Westport, CT: AVI Publishing Co., 1986. 712 p.

This thorough manual on baking is both a textbook for students and a reference manual for bakery chefs. Each chapter begins with a discussion of the chemistry and technology. This is followed by recipes with step-by-step instructions and numerous line drawings illustrating the procedures. Sections cover bread, rolls, sweet yeast products, biscuits, muffins, doughnuts, pies, cakes, cookies, and specialty baking.

354. Szathmáry, Louis. *The Bakery Restaurant Cookbook.* Boston: CBI Publishing Co., 1981. 325 p.

The Bakery Restaurant is located in Chicago, and Chef Louis is a well-recognized leader in the field of cooking. This collection of his recipes is arranged in standard menu categories and includes hundreds of recipes in serving proportions appropriate for small dinner parties.

355. Zenker, John J. *Artistic Cake Decorating from A to Z.* rev. ed. Palos Verdes, CA: Continental Publications, 1976. 288 p.

Zenker worked as pastry chef at several prestigious Chicago restaurants and won prizes for his huge and elaborate cakes. Here he presents for the beginner and the experienced chef the techniques of fancy cake decorating. He starts with borders and scroll work, then goes on to flowers, gum paste plaques, baskets, and fancy cakes. He also covers jelly designs and inlaid sugar designs. Fancy cake designs such as sugar vases, architectural design, and special uses of sugar are also included. The book concludes with a short chapter on ice carving.

CATERING SERVICES

356. Blanchard, Marjorie P. *Cater from Your Kitchen: Income from Your Own Home Business.* Indianapolis, IN: Bobbs-Merrill, 1981. 244 p.

The knowledge and experience of the author, a successful caterer, cookbook compiler, and cooking school teacher, are relayed here for the entrepreneur who wants to start a catering service using a home kitchen. Over half the book is devoted to recipes specifically for caterers. The other half of the book covers information on equipping and organizing the kitchen, menu planning, purchasing, advertising, and legal and tax matters.

357. Finance, Charles. *Buffet Catering.* Rochelle Park, NJ: Ahrens Publishing Co., 1958. 256 p.

Finance is a former professor of Culinary Arts at the Swiss Hotel School in Lucern who has also been executive chef in Western and Hilton hotels. His book is designed to help the chef produce a creative cold buffet. The basic set up, organization, decorating, and raw materials are discussed. Recipes from many cold dishes of all buffet types are clearly presented along with instructions on artistic arrangement. There is a short chapter on ice sculpture. Black-and-white pictures and diagrams facilitate proper preparation.

358. Glew, G., ed. Advances in Catering Technology: Proceedings of the Second International Symposium on Catering Systems Design. London: Applied Science Publishers Ltd., 1980. 492 p.

This is the proceedings of the Second International Symposium on Catering Services. The theme was looking ahead to 1990 and beyond to predict the future of the industry. The first section of the book deals with trends and forecasts. The second deals with the "value for money" because consumers are expected to be more interested in quality and nutrition. The third section deals with catering technology.

359. Glew, G., ed. *Advances in Catering Technology-3: Proceedings of the Third International Symposium on Catering Systems Design.* London: Applied Science Publishers, 1985. 293 p.

This is a collection of the papers from the third International Symposium on Catering Systems Design, 1984. Papers from the first two are published in *Catering Equipment and Systems Design* (1977) and *Advances in Catering Technology* (1980). New themes in this collection include management, waste, and sanitation. The twenty-five symposium papers appear under five headings: "The Catering Industry and Some Approaches to Planning," "Improvement of Cooking and Meal Production Techniques," "Waste Control," "Cleaning and Sanitation," and "Management and Technology."

360. Glew, G., ed. *Cook-Freeze Catering: An Introduction to Its Technology.* London: Faber and Faber, 1973. 168 p.

This book discusses the use of precooked frozen food in the catering industry. Emphasis is on technical and scientific aspects such as physical and chemical changes caused by food processing, microbial growth, and factors affecting heat transfer in freezing and reheating. There is also a chapter on packaging.

361. *The ICI Catering Manual.* 3d ed. London: Barrie & Rockliff, 1967. 130 p.

The third edition of the original 1954 publication is intended as a text in catering operations. Basic principles and recipes remain largely unchanged, the costing supplement has been eliminated. Part one covers principles and techniques for budgetary control, special catering, service, butchery, and carving, as well as storage, safety hygiene, and a glossary of kitchen terms. Part two is a catering recipe book containing 579 recipes in all menu categories including a good selection of savouries and hors d'oeuvres.

362. Ketterer, Manfred. *How to Manage a Successful Catering Business.* Rochelle Park, NJ: Hayden Book Co., 1982. 294 p.

This book reviews the factors involved in organizing catered events and operating a catering business. Both on-premises and off-premises events are covered. It covers financial and legal considerations; sales; menus, with an emphasis on weddings and bar mitzvahs as the most profitable functions; organizing and supervising; serving; kitchen operations; serviceware; purchasing and cleanup; and expanding the business.

363. Mengelatte, Pierre; Bickel, Walter; and Abelanet, Albin. *Buffets and Receptions.* 4th ed. Edited by Michael Small and Mabel Quin. London: Virtue, 1983. 1,221 p.

This is the most complete and elaborate book on buffets available. Originally published in French, it is intended to accompany *Modern French Culinary Art* by Pellaprat. Part one, "Functions," gives guidelines on various forms of parties. Part two, "Customs and Traditions," covers eating habits from other countries. These sections are followed by the main part of the book which is a collection of recipes from chefs around the world. Illustrated with full color plates. The fourth edition varies only slightly from earlier editions; it actually is more a reprint than a new edition.

364. Miller, Donna. *A Guide to Catering: Catering Your Own Events or Hiring Professionals.* Portland, OR: DJ's Guides, 1986. 104 leaves.

This book is designed to help a beginning caterer organize, determine costs and prepare food for a major catered event. The first chapter is an outline to be filled out for the event. It prompts all the necessary questions from number of guests to entertainment. Many quantity recipes are included; portions vary from eight to fifty portions. This edition is an expansion and revision of *DJ's Guide to Catering* (1984).

365. *More Thoughts for Buffets.* Boston: Houghton Mifflin, 1984. 440 p.

This cookbook supplements *Thoughts for Buffets* (1958). It is aimed at the home cook but includes recipes useful to professional caterers as well. Recipes are arranged according to type of buffet, e.g., brunch, ethnic, party, holiday, summer, or microwave. Most recipes serve six people, some ten to twelve people.

366. Smith, Henry. *Successful Food Costing and Portion Control: A Modern Guide to Profitable Catering Management.* 3d ed. Successful Catering Series, no. 1. London: Barrie & Rockliff, 1964. 100 p.

This is a costing and control manual for caterers. Part one, "The Science of Food Costing," includes food cost charts and steps to ensure food costing and profit, as well as related subjects of cost control. Part two, "Portion Control," covers subjects such as how large portions should be and how much they should cost. It also includes portion control charts and information on equipment.

367. Splaver, Bernard R. *Successful Catering.* 2d ed. Boston: CBI Publishing Co., 1982. 294 p.

Written for the entrepreneur who wants to start an off-premise catering business, this practical book covers sanitation, foodservice equipment, transportation equipment, contracting, accommodator service, arrangements, and bar service. Also included are menus, recipes, an inventory control sheet, and a list of fifty food additives.

368. Weiss, Edith, and Weiss, Hal. *Catering Handbook.* New York: Ahrens Publishing Co., 1971. 290 p.

Written by a pair of caterers with many years of experience, this book is designed to cover all aspects of catering and point out problems likely to trouble the beginner. The book covers banquet hall, off-premises, and mobile unit catering, and compares the three. There are sections on equipment, kitchen, staff, how to start, selling the service, and even basic business practices. The specifics on the actual catering services cover arranging the affair, bar service, special cakes for special occasions, centerpieces, and food decoration. The book ends with sample menus and recipes and a list of catering schools.

369. Wilkinson, Jule, ed. *The Professional Chef's Catering Recipes.* Chicago: Institutions Magazine/Volume Feeding Management, 1971. 88 p.

Here is a collection of over 120 recipes from catering companies and other sources for dishes especially suited for catering. Recipes for appetizers, entrees, vegetables, salads, and desserts appear. Most serve between twenty and fifty people.

ICE CARVING

370. Amendola, Joseph. *Ice Carving Made Easy.* rev. ed. New Haven, CT, 1969. 127 p.

Amendola, instructor at the Culinary Institute of America in New Haven, discusses the technique of ice carving. He teaches proper method and discusses the tools and equipment needed. Over forty-five designs for ice carvings are provided including photographs, block line diagrams, and step-by-step instructions. A short section on styrofoam carving is also included.

371. Durocher, Joseph F., *Practical Ice Carving.* Boston: CBI Publishing Co., 1981. 87 p.

The basic procedures of ice carving are presented in a how-to style. The author's goal is to simplify ice carving. Chapters include tools, techniques, and carving some basic and advanced forms. He also includes a chapter on alternatives to carving. The book ends with a series of templates.

372. Hasegawa, Hideo. *Ice Carving.* Edited by Jackie Athey. Translated by Norman Braslow. Palos Verdes, CA: Continental Publications, 1978. 326 p.

The author presents seventy-five designs for ice sculptures illustrated with photographs and design drawings. Chapter one covers how to select ice, plan the carving, compose the outline, and other basics including tools. The carving designs are divided into basic pieces (eight designs), beginning pieces (ten designs), intermediate pieces (seventeen designs), advanced pieces (twenty-six designs), and combined pieces (seven designs).

QUANTITY COOKING

373. Albert, Helen M. *Serving Successful Salads: A Merchandising Cookbook.* Edited by Jule Wilkinson. Illustrated by Louisa M. Boshardy. Boston: Cahners Books, 1975. 183 p.

This collection of recipes for salads includes a novel addition: each recipe has a merchandising idea designed to increase demand for the salad. The author suggests tableside salad preparation or salad displays as the most effective marketing techniques. If this is not possible, she encourages detailed description in the menu. Chapters cover appetizer salads, fruit salads, molded salads, entree salads, salad dressings, and dessert salads. Quantity portions for 170 recipes are included. All have been tested.

374. Amendola, Joseph, and Berrini, James M. *Practical Cooking and Baking for Schools and Institutions.* New York: Ahrens Publishing Co., 1971. 198 p.

This is an extensive collection of recipes intended for use in schools, hospitals, nursing homes, and other institutions. It includes some guidance in cooking methods and procedures. All recipes were tested in the International Food Research and Education Center Test Kitchen, and many are designed to make use of government food commodities. A chapter is included on bakeshop equipment and maintenance.

375. American Dietetic Association. *Dietitians' Food Favorites: Recipes from Members of the American Dietetic Association.* Des Plaines, IL: Cahners Publishing Co., 1985. 360 p.

Recipes that are both healthy and palatable have been collected from hundreds of dietitians. Each recipe includes a nutrient analysis and is accompanied by symbols indicating its suitability for low fat, low cholesterol, high fiber, or low salt diets. In addition, each recipe is given for family-size quantity (four to eight portions) and for institution quantity (twenty to twenty-four portions). All menu categories from appetizers to desserts are included.

376. American Spice Trade Association. Food Service Department. *Food Service Seasoning Guide: A Guide for Chefs on the Use of Spices, Seeds, Herbs, Seasoning Blends and Dehydrated Vegetable Seasonings in Food Service Cookery.* New York, 1969. 93 p.

This manual discusses the use of spices and seasonings in quantity cooking. Many spices and herbs are listed with brief notes telling origin and description, usages and availability. Spice charts show what quantity to use in large recipes. A chart for converting fresh to dehydrated vegetables is included. The last half of the book is a recipe collection suitable for foodservice cooking.

377. Asmussen, Patricia D. *Simplified Recipes for Day Care Centers.* Edited by Jule Wilkinson. Boston: Cahners Books, 1973. 218 p.

This spiral book contains recipes designed to please the appetites of children from two to six years of age. Because most day care centers are small, recipes are set up for twenty-five portions. Nearly 200 recipes are included. Also included is a food buying chart which lists, by food, how much to purchase by weight and package size.

378. Blair, Eulalia C., comp. *Breakfast & Brunch Dishes for Foodservice Menu Planning.* Edited by Jule Wilkinson. Foodservice Menu Planning Series. Boston: Cahners Books, 1975?. 256 p.

Blair has compiled over 240 breakfast and brunch recipes for quantity cooking. Portions for recipes vary, but most are for twenty-four or fifty servings. Included are recipes for fruit and juices, french toast, eggs, pancakes, waffles, cereals, meat, fish and chicken dishes, potatoes, and breads.

379. Blair, Eulalia C. *Casseroles and Vegetables for Foodservice Menu Planning.* Edited by Jule Wilkinson. Foodservice Menu Planning Series. Boston: Cahners Books International, 1976. 278 p.

Another title in the Foodservice Menu Planning Series for professional menu planners, this one covers two related topics. The vegetable section has 125 recipes and tips on handling, seasoning, stuffing, and combining vegetables. Part two includes 142 recipes for casseroles made with cheese, eggs, poultry, meat, and vegetables. Portions for each recipe vary from twenty-four to 100 servings.

380. Blair, Eulalia C., comp. *Dishes for Special Occasions: For Foodservice Menu Planning.* Edited by Jule Wilkinson. Foodservice Menu Planning Series. Boston: Cahners Books, 1975. 312 p.

As with other volumes in the series, this book has recipes selected from the recipe file of *Volume Feeding Management.* It includes appetizers, tea breads, sandwiches, cakes, cookies, and punch bowls. Salads are omitted from this volume because they are in *Salads for Foodservice Menu Planning* (Van Nostrand Reinhold Co., 1988) Many of the recipes are for dishes especially for buffets.

381. Blair, Eulalia C., comp. *Fish & Seafood Dishes for Foodservice Menu Planning.* Edited by Jule Wilkinson. Foodservice Menu Planning Series. Boston: Cahners Books, 1975. 234 p.

Blair has compiled more than 200 quantity recipes which have appeared in *Volume Feeding Management, Institutions Magazine* and *Institutions/Volume Feeding.* Portions vary for each recipe, although most serve twenty-four portions. The book starts with an introduction covering definitions, handling, storage, and fish cookery methods. The recipes are divided into the standard menu categories: appetizers, soups, salads, etc.

382. Blair, Eulalia C. *Garnishes, Relishes, and Sauces for Foodservice Menu Planning.* Edited by Jule Wilkinson. Boston: CBI Publishing Co., 1977. 181 p.

This book includes recipes for fruit, vegetable, and molded relishes. The garnish chapter is short with lists of suggested garnishes for various dishes and beverages followed by directions for cutting attractive citrus garnishes. The section on sauces is the most complete. There are recipes for cocktail, white, and tomato sauces as well as various meat sauces, flavored butters, and gravies. A large separate chapter deals with dessert sauces.

383. Blair, Eulalia C., comp. *Luncheon and Supper Dishes.* Edited by Jule Wilkinson. Boston: Institutions/Volume Feeding Magazine, 1973. 213 p.

This collection of recipes is from the issues of *Institutions/Volume Feeding* magazine. They are arranged into standard categories: soup, sandwiches, salads, vegetables, rice and pasta, eggs, cheese, fish, poultry, and meats. Portions for each recipe vary from sixteen to ninety-six servings. All recipes are for lighter meals appropriate for supper or luncheon.

384. Blair, Eulalia C. *Meat & Poultry Entrees for Foodservice Menu Planning.* Cahners Foodservice Menu Planning Series. Boston: CBI Publishing Co., 1978. 247 p.

A collection of 260 recipes for entrees made with beef, pork, veal, lamb, chicken, and turkey. Most recipes are for twenty-five, fifty, or 100 portions. Illustrated with black-and-white photographs.

385. Blair, Eulalia C. *Mini-Meals for Foodservice Menu Planning.* Edited by Jule Wilkinson. Foodservice Menu Planning Series. Boston: Cahners Books International, 1976. 230 p.

The author presents quantity recipes for small meals and between-meal snacks aimed at the current trend toward smaller, less regular, and more frequent meals. Some 250 recipes and suggestions are given for soups, breads, cheese dishes, and desserts as well as minimeal entrees of meat, poultry, and seafood and quick service minimeals. Most recipes are for twelve, twenty-four, or forty-eight servings.

386. Blair, Eulalia C., ed. *Professional's Recipe Master.* New York: Ahrens Publishing Co., 1967. 403 p.

Blair has selected over 400 quantity recipes from the past issues of *Volume Feeding* magazine (now entitled *Restaurants and Institutions*). Recipes are printed in large type, and the book is bound in a spiral binding so that it can be propped on a table for easy reference. Portions for each recipe vary from twenty to 200 servings.

387. Blair, Eulalia C. *Quick-to-Fix Desserts for Foodservice Menu Planning.* Boston: CBI Publishing Co., 1980. 309 p.

Over 250 recipes which utilize fruit, ice cream, purchased baked goods (pie shells and cakes), and prepared-in-advance items to make quick desserts. Included are recipes for chiffon, open-faced pies, puddings, gelatins, no-bake cheesecake, and cakes. There is also a section on toppings, fillings, and sauces and a section on dessert cheeses. Most recipes are for twenty-four or forty-eight servings.

388. Blair, Eulalia C. *Salads for Foodservice Menu Planning.* New York: Van Nostrand Reinhold Co., 1988. 201 p.

Blair passes along her treasury of salad-making tips in this cookbook of quantity recipes. Nearly 220 recipes of green salads, gelatins, main dishes, vegetable salads, fruit salads, pasta salads, and salad dressings are included. There also is a chapter on salad bars and one on garnishes. This book revises and updates the author's *Salads and Salad Dressing for Foodservice Menu Planning* and includes over 174 new, fully tested recipes.

389. Boltman, Brigid. *Cook-Freeze Catering Systems.* London: Applied Science Publishers, 1978. 247 p.

South Africa has been an acknowledged leader in cook-freeze technology since the early 1970s. The National Building Research Institute in South Africa pioneered research studies and pilot projects in newly constructed hospitals in Pretoria. This book is based on the major research reports and several papers presented at a symposium held in 1975. The three parts of the book include "Assessment of Conventional and Cook-Freeze Catering Systems," "Chemical, Physical, Microbiological and Hygiene Aspects of Food Relevant to Cook-Freeze Systems," and "Introduction of a Cook-Freeze Production Process."

390. Box, Doris. *The Church Kitchen.* Nashville, TN: Broadman Press, 1976. 238 p.

The author divides her book into "Management," "Menus," and "Recipes." In the management section, she gives basic guidelines for staffing, equipment, sanitation, planning, serving, and budget in the church kitchen. The menus section gives suggestions for the use of leftovers as well as menus for such functions as family nights, ladies luncheons, and special occasions. The final three-quarters of the book is a collection of recipes that the author has prepared in her own church kitchen. These include salads, breads, meats, sauces, vegetables, and desserts.

391. Boyd, Grace M.; McKinley, Marjorie M.; and Dana, Janice T. *Standardized Quantity Recipe File for Quality & Cost Control.* Ames, IA: Iowa State University Press, 1971.

This card file of recipes for 100 portions is a successor to Lenore Sullivan's *Quantity Recipe File*. Each recipe has been tested in the Institute Management Laboratory of Iowa State University. They are appropriate for use in any quantity cooking setting: restaurants, hotels, schools, colleges, hospitals, or nursing homes. The file is divided into the standard menu categories. A guide card for each category lists all recipes in it. Within each division, the cards are numbered for easy refiling.

392. Bristow, Linda Kay. *Bread & Breakfast: The Best Recipes from North America's Bed & Breakfast Inns.* Illustrated by Roy Killeen & Others. San Francisco, CA: 101 Productions, 1985. 134 p.
Over 150 recipes gathered from bed and breakfast inns across the country are included in this cookbook. Recipes are arranged by the area of the country where the B&B is located. Descriptions of the inn, a line drawing of it, and a menu are included with each entry. A recipe index and inn directory are included at the end.

393. Cavaiani, Mabel, and Urbashich, Muriel. *Simplified Quantity Recipes: Nursing/Convalescent Homes and Hospitals.* rev. ed. Washington, DC: National Restaurant Association, 1986. 316 p.
This quantity cookbook provides simplified recipes for nursing homes and hospitals. Economical cooking that can be done by staff with limited training is emphasized. Dietary information is included with each recipe. This edition emphasizes recipes with lower calories, sugar, and saturated fat but higher in fiber content. All recipes yield fifty portions.

394. Cavaiani, Mabel; Urbashich, Muriel; and Nielsen, Frances. *Simplified Quantity Ethnic Recipes.* Ahrens Series. Rochelle Park, NJ: Hayden Book Co., 1980. 266 p.
Over 200 recipes for ethnic foods have been selected for this cookbook. All are for fifty portions and can be made using basic equipment and easily obtainable ingredients. Instructions are easy to follow and do not presume any foodservice training or education. Dietary information is included with each recipe to assist those working in hospitals and nursing homes.

395. Cavaiani, Mabel; Urbashich, Muriel; and Nielsen, Frances. *Simplified Quantity Regional Recipes.* Ahrens Series. Rochelle Park, NJ: Hayden Book Co., 1979. 214 p.
The approximately 180 recipes here use basic equipment, nationally available ingredients, and require a minimum of cooking expertise. The region of origin is included with each recipe. They are intended to be interesting while retaining broad appeal. Each recipe serves about fifty. Dietary information is included with each recipe. Instructions are clear and brief. All menu categories are represented.

396. Church, Charles F. *Wisconsin Quantity Cuisine: The Foods that Make Wisconsin Famous.* Boston: Cahners Books International, 1976. 238 p.
This was the first of an intended series of merchandising cookbooks planned by Cahner Books. Each was to feature a state, city, or region. This one, arranged by regions, centers on Wisconsin. Selected restaurants and foodservice operations in each region are described, and featured recipes are included. Servings per recipe vary; many serve over twenty-five people. Merchandising techniques such as menus and table tents are reproduced.

397. Cornell University, School of Hotel Administration. *Quantity Recipes.* Revised by Myrtle H. Ericson. Ithaca, NY, 197?. (Loose-leaf)
Arranged in standard menu categories, this loose-leaf notebook contains hundreds of recipes for quantity cooking. Servings vary from recipe to recipe, but most serve between twenty-five and 100 portions. All recipes were compiled by the Department of Institutional Management at Cornell.

398. Criswell, Cleta, comp. *Group Feeding: Quality Recipes and Diet Modification.* Edited by Alene Griffin. Drawings by Betty Mills. Philadelphia, PA: George F. Stickley, 1983. 268 p.
This is a collection of recipes intended for health care centers and other institutions catering to special dietary needs of the elderly. In all menu categories, fat and sodium

have been reduced, and yield is adapted to smaller portions in keeping with reduced calorie needs. Special diet adaptations are included with each recipe for diabetic, fat-restricted and sodium-restricted diets.

399. Culinary Institute of America, and Editors of Institutions Magazine. *The Professional Chef.* 4th ed. Edited by LeRoi Al Folsom. Boston: CBI Publishing Co., 1974. 470 p.

First published in 1962, this is the most comprehensive study of professional cooking available. It includes information on equipment, formulas, techniques, and recipes from many nations. Most recipes are for fifty portions. The introductory chapters cover chefs, foodservice occupations, sanitation, safety, cost, and converting recipes. The bulk of the book presents quantity recipes.

400. Deacon, Gene E. *Kid Tested Menus with Kitchen and Lunchroom Techniques for Day Care Centers.* North Wilkesboro, NC: Gold Crest Publishing, 1981. 93 p.

This menu planning and recipe book for day care centers emphasizes easy-to-prepare food which is nutritious, appealing to children, and low cost. Part one is an essay on making the lunchroom a learning experience. Part two is a short section on menu planning and purchasing. Part three is the set of recipes; all serve forty to fifty children.

401. Deuel, William K. *Kitchen Management for Institutions: Economies in Purchasing, Portioning, and Preparation.* Ahrens Series. Rochelle Park, NJ: Hayden Book Co., 1975. 178 p.

This is a handbook for the professional kitchen manager. Part one deals with management subjects like portion control, buying, pricing, equipment, personnel and the like. Part two is on the actual preparation of food. It covers methods and recipes for quantity cooking in most menu categories. The final chapter provides "Volume Preparation Methods for Twenty-five Low-Cost Entrees."

402. Evans, Michele. *Fearless Cooking for Crowds: Beautiful Food for Groups of Eight Through Fifty.* New York: Times Books, 1986. 328 p.

A collection of over 300 recipes for groups. All menu categories including hors d'oeuvres are included. Dishes specifically for eight, twelve, sixteen, thirty-six, and fifty are presented in each category. Tips are given for planning, organizing and preparing a large meal. This book is aimed at the private host but would be of use to any establishment catering large meals and parties.

403. *Food Services Handbook.* NAVSHIPSTO Publication, no. 13. Brooklyn, NY: U.S. Navy Ship's Store Office, 1950?. 205 p.

A loose-leaf binder for Navy foodservices divided into sixteen sections. Very detailed instruction is given for soda fountain operation including sections on soda fountain maintenance, syrups, toppings and ice cream dispensing, milk and milk drinks, ice cream sodas, ice cream sundaes, and toppings. Contains much information on quantity food preparation and food specifications. Sections on salads, sandwiches, and hot food are also included.

404. Fuller, John, and Renold, Edward. *The Chef's Compendium of Professional Recipes.* 2d rev ed. Westport, CT: AVI Publishing Co., 1972 (1985 printing). 340 p.

Fuller presents conventional French-style cooking simplified and adapted for the professional chef for use in hotels, restaurants, and other catering establishments. Most recipes are sufficiently simple for use by trainees and amateurs as well. A glossary of kitchen French is included. All recipes designed to serve eight.

405. General Mills. *Institutional Cook Book and Menu Planner.* rev. ed. Minneapolis, MN: General Mills, 1963. (Loose-leaf)

A loose-leaf collection of basic quantity recipes. The soups, salads, vegetables, main courses, desserts, and baked specialties sections often (but not always) use GM products. These are followed by a large section on baking with General Mills' mixes. It includes cakes and icings, cookies, muffins and hot breads, soft rolls and sweet rolls, pies and pie fillings, pancakes and waffles, doughnuts, and specialty varieties such as brownies. Charts and guides are included for high temperature baking, meat cuts, and cooking temperatures.

406. Gisslen, Wayne. *Professional Cooking.* New York: Wiley, 1983. 680 p.

This is one of the best textbooks teaching basic cooking skills for any type of foodservice operation. It has a dual goal of understanding and performing, and it includes over 800 recipes applying procedures and techniques presented. Illustrated with drawings, photographs, and color plates.

407. Harder, Eulalia L. *Blast Freezing Quantity Recipes.* Boston: CBI Publishing Co., 1979. 315 p.

A companion volume of recipes to accompany *Blast Freezing Systems for Quantity Foods.*

408. Harder, Eulalia L. *Blast Freezing System for Quantity Foods.* Boston: CBI Publishing Co., 1979. 384 p.

This is a guide to on-premise preparation, packaging, and blast freezing of foods. The author presents the case for blast freezing in terms of cost savings, quality, and nutrient retention. The book covers the technology for processing various types of food as well as methods for holding, storing, tempering, and reheating frozen foods. Quality control and system testing is included. The book is designed to work with a collection of recipes developed for the system published separately as *Blast Freezing Quantity Recipes.*

409. Hardwick, Geraline B., and Kennedy, Robert L. *Fundamentals of Quantity Food Preparation: Appetizers, Salad Dressings, and Salads.* Fundamentals of Quantity Food Preparation. Boston: CBI Publishing Co., 1982. 360 p.

This is the third volume in a series of books on quantity food preparation. The quantity formula approach continues to be used for most recipes though modifications in format appear in the section on appetizers which are not often prepared in substantial quantities. Each recipe includes ingredient guides for various numbers of portions, from twenty-four to several hundred servings.

410. Hardwick, Geraline B., and Kennedy, Robert L. *Fundamentals of Quantity Food Preparation: Desserts & Beverages.* Edited by Jule Wilkinson. Fundamentals of Quantity Food Preparation. Boston: Cahners Books, 1975?. 338 p.

The authors provide general instructions and formulas for quantity preparation of pies, cakes and cookies, puddings, gelatin desserts, and beverages. Explanation is given of how food formulas differ from regular recipes.

411. Janericco, Terence. *Breakfast & Brunch Dishes for the Professional Chef.* Boston: CBI Publishing Co., 1983. 106 p.

This cookbook shows foodservice managers how to prepare elaborate brunches using lower cost food. Chapters include poached, hard cooked, shirred, and baked eggs; quiches; soufflés; crepes; fish; meat and poultry dishes; and sauces. Full color photographs are included.

412. Janericco, Terence. *The Complete Book of Sandwiches for the Professional Chef.* Boston: CBI Publishing Co., 1984. 134 p.

This collection of recipes is written specifically for chefs and foodservice managers to add variety and easy, low-cost items to restaurant menus. Hot and cold, simple and fancy, tea sandwiches and ethnic specialties are included. Twelve pages of color plates illustrate how to present many of the sandwiches.

413. Johnston, Harriet, comp. *Quality, Quantity Cuisine I.* Edited by Jule Wilkinson. Boston: Cahners Books, 1976. 312 p.
> Harriet Johnston, registered dietitian, has selected quantity recipes that are easy and economical to prepare while being appealing and nutritious. Most recipes are for 100 portions. Tables to convert the recipes to different serving portions are included. Color and black-and-white photographs add to the appeal of this book.

414. Jones, Lila M., and Fischer, Barbara R. *Simplified Recipes for Adult Care Centers.* Boston: CBI Publishing Co., 1981. 298 p.
> All the recipes in this book can be prepared using only basic equipment and standard measures and pan sizes, and all serve fifty people. They are arranged into standard menu categories and were selected especially for retirement residences, nursing homes, and meals on wheels. Also included is general information on food purchasing for fifty servings, how to adjust recipes to various quantities and substitutions. The spiral binding makes it easy to use in the kitchen. No illustrations or photographs are included.

415. Mario, Thomas. *Quantity Cooking.* Westport, CT: AVI Publishing Co., 1978. 450 p.
> Mario presents the basic kitchen skills in their traditional stations. This is not because cooks remain rigidly classified but because these are important job prototypes. Once these skills are mastered, the cook can go on to greater versatility. Many basic quantity recipes are included. Chapters include using the French knife, stocks and soup cook, fry cook, broiler cook, roast cook, sauce cook, cold meat preparer, vegetable cook, breakfast cook, sandwich maker, pantry worker, salad maker, coffee maker, and dessert cook.

416. McNatt, Martha. *Feeding the Flock.* Minneapolis, MN: Bethany House Publishing, 1987. 176 p.
> Written specifically for churches and clubs, this book covers equipment, menu planning, food purchasing, and preparation techniques for feeding groups. The recipe sections include recipes for 100 servings, women's luncheon recipes for fifty servings, and recipes for children and youth groups.

417. Meyer, Barbara Friedlander. *Cooking for a Crowd Naturally.* Fort Lee, NJ: Stamlyn Publishing Co., 1984. 181 p.
> This is a collection of over 200 quantity recipes for vegetarian meals. Part one covers equipment, ordering and storing. Part two discusses menu planning and methods for cooking vegetables and grains and other topics. Part three, "Recipes," is the main body of the book and includes over 200 recipes with directions given for ten, twenty-five, fifty, and 100 servings. Recipes appear in the following categories: grain dishes, bean dishes, tofu, main and side dish vegetables, desserts, and breakfasts.

418. Millross, Janice, et al. *The Utilisation of the Cook-Freeze Catering System for School Meals: A Report of an Experiment Conducted in the City of Leeds.* Leeds, England: Procter Department of Food and Leather Science, University of Leeds, 1973. 216 p.
> This is a report of research conducted at the University of Leeds on the application of cook-freeze technology. Food is prepared, cooked, portioned and frozen and stored at −20°C. It is then reheated in convection ovens. The report constitutes the first fifty pages of the book. This is followed by appendices that cover equipment, organization, food production and recipes, end-kitchen design, general assessment, and costs.

419. Morgan, William J., Jr. *Food Production Principles.* East Lansing, MI: Educational Institute of the American Hotel & Motel Association, 1981. 231 p.
> This is an introduction to all aspects of quantity food production. It is designed to train the new foodservice manager to administer food production using the new techniques of processing and control necessitated by larger more centralized methods. Within this context, it covers the history, composition, and function of food, pantry items, salads, meat, poultry, fish, soups and sauces, vegetables and fruits, dairy products, cereals, bakery products, spices, condiments, and fats. There is also a chapter on service and merchandising.

420. Perry, Rick. *Hurricane Kitchen: How to Cook Healthy Foods for Large Groups and Institutions.* Illustrated by Douglas Alvord. Augusta, ME: L. Tapley, 1988. 172 p.

> The author has been cooking at the Hurricane Island Outward Bound School in Maine for over ten years. He advocates using natural foods to make less expensive, healthier food. His book begins with a discussion of menu planning and an analysis of the most important natural foods: whole grains, oils, sweeteners, red meat, seaweed, yogurt and spices. The major portion of the book is the recipe section. Ingredients for portions of fifteen to 120 people are included. This book was first published as *The Integration of Natural Foods in an Institutional Setting* in 1985.

421. Pomeroy, Elizabeth. *Cooking by the Dozen.* London: Hamlyn, 1984. 192 p.

> This book is for the family cook who needs to prepare food for a large group or is interested in catering services. The introduction covers the theories of adapting and equipping the kitchen, cooking techniques and adapting recipes for large quantities. The main portion of the book is a collection of recipes for six, twelve, twenty-four, and forty-eight portions arranged in the standard categories: hors d'oeuvres, soups, fish, meat, etc. Full color plates enhance the visual appeal of the book.

422. Sanders, Edward E. *Meals for Many: A Complete Guide to Banquets and Buffets for Groups of All Sizes.* Bountiful, UT: Horizon Publishers, 1979. 155 p.

> This is a clearly written book for an amateur needing to prepare food for a large group. It includes checklists and advice for planning and organizing the event, purchasing, preparing and serving the food, and cleaning up afterward. Also included are twelve menus and recipes with charts on how much to purchase and how to prepare the food for groups of twelve to 500 people. American favorites such as meatloaf, swiss steak, and spaghetti are emphasized. An excellent book for church groups.

423. Shugart, Grace; Molt, Mary; and Wilson, Maxine. *Food for Fifty.* 7th ed. New York: Wiley, 1985. 641 p.

> This is the best and most well-known book on quantity cooking; the first through the sixth editions were done by Bessie Brooks West. It is intended as both a text and reference tool and includes many tables of weights and measures for recipe adjustment as well as guidelines for preparation and serving. It also includes a large collection of standardized recipes by menu category, each for fifty portions or more, and sections on menu planning and special meal service such as receptions and brunches.

424. Shurtleff, William, and Aoyagi, Akiko. *Using Tofu, Tempeh & Other Soyfoods in Restaurants, Delis & Cafeterias.* Lafayette, CA: Soyfoods Center, 1982. Various pagings.

> The most useful part of this book is a collection of over 250 recipes using tofu, tempeh and soyfoods; many of these recipes serve twenty-five to fifty people. In addition, the book lists distributors of soyfoods and names and addresses of soyfood restaurants. Nearly twenty articles about soyfood restaurants are reproduced.

425. Sonnenschmidt, Frederic H., and Nicolas, Jean F. *The Professional Chef's Art of Garde Manger.* 3d ed. New York: Van Nostrand Reinhold Co., 1982. 248 p.

> A text on the preparation of artistic cold buffet food, this third edition reflects the current trend toward simpler, more natural looking dishes while maintaining a high degree of display quality. Chapters deal with buffet planning and presentation as well as offer specific recipes and instructions for gelée, aspic, hors d'oeuvres, patés, galantines, mousse, marinades, salads, and other cold buffet items. There is a chapter on nonedible displays and one on low calorie buffets.

426. St. Laurent, Georges C., and Holden, Chet. *Buffets: A Guide for Professionals.* New York: Wiley, 1986. 368 p.
This book gives over 300 buffet recipes with suggestions for proper service and possible variations. Ingredients are given for test quantities of eight and service for fifty. Recipes appear in the following categories: appetizers, salads, soups, meats, seafood, poultry, side dishes, desserts, and brunch.

427. Sublette, Louise, and Shepherd, Ruth. *Lunch at School: The 'How-to' Book for the Planning and Preparation of Low Cost, Nutritionally Adequate Meals for Children Who Eat at School.* Jackson, TN: McCowat-Mercer Press, 1963. 132 p.
This is a loose-leaf book of menus, recipes, and mixes to assist managers and supervisors of school lunch programs in preparing nutritious and low-cost meals. Menus for the entire school year and special holiday menus are included.

428. Treat, Nola, and Richards, Lenore. *Quantity Cookery: Menu Planning and Cooking for Large Numbers.* 4th rev. ed. Boston: Little, Brown, 1966. 660 p.
This book includes detailed instructions on quantity cooking and recipes used in the Richards Treat Cafeterias. Intended for use in the field as well as a text, it stresses the use of scales, accurate recipes, proper buying and standardized serving sizes to maintain quality in quantity cooking. Part one is a close look at menu planning. Part two gives suggestion lists, tips for using leftovers, and tables of weights and measures. Part three is a collection of recipes in standard menu categories. Part four presents a look at the future of quantity foodservice.

429. U.S. Army, et al. *Armed Forces Recipe Service.* rev. ed. Washington, DC: Government Printing Office, 1985. (Cards)
This card file of quantity recipes is a joint effort of the various military agencies to provide military foodservice personnel with the most advanced concepts and techniques in food preparation and foodservice.

430. U.S. Department of Agriculture. *Recipes for Quantity Service.* rev. ed. Home Economics Research Report, no. 5. Washington, DC: Government Printing Office, 1972. (Cards)
This card file contains standardized recipes for quantity cooking divided into eight menu categories. Each recipe yields 100 portions and includes quantities to purchase and the preparation directions.

431. U.S. Department of Health, Education, and Welfare, Manpower Development and Training Program. *Quantity Food Preparation, A Suggested Guide.* Washington, DC: Government Printing Office, 1967. 39 p.
This is guide for the development of training programs in quantity food preparation at secondary and postsecondary school levels. Information is arranged by areas of study and includes food preparation, science, mathematics, and safety instruction. Each area outlines the essential skills and knowledge to be acquired, the scope of instruction, and technical and related information.

432. U.S. Food and Nutrition Service, Nutrition and Technical Services Staff; U.S. Department of Agriculture, Agricultural Research Service, Consumer and Food Economics Research Division; and U.S. Department of Commerce, National Oceanic and Atmospheric Administration, National Marine Fisheries Service. *Quantity Recipes for Type A School Lunches.* rev. ed. Washington, DC: Government Printing Office, 1971. 203 cards.
This card file provides quantity recipes to prepare "Type A" lunches in schools participating in the National School Lunch Program. Cards are divided into menu categories. All recipes were planned to appeal to children, make good use of U.S. Department of Agriculture donated foods, and yield 100 servings.

433. Waldner, George K., and Mitterhauser, Klaus. *The Professional Chef's Book of Buffets.* Edited by Jule Wilkinson. Chicago: Institutions Magazine, 1968. 232 p.

This is a complete but concise book on buffets. It includes instructions on preparing most types of buffet foods, recipes, decorating ideas, themes for buffets, and steps and diagrams for setting up.

434. Wallace, Jane Young, ed. *American Quantity Cookbook: Tracing Our Food Traditions.* Boston: Cahners Books International, 1976. 239 p.

This book is a collection of recipes that represent American cookery—old, well-known, and typical. The core of materials came from the series of bicentennial articles prepared by the editorial staff of *Institutions/Volume Feeding* magazine under the guidance of Jane Young Wallace, editor. Many of the recipes here could not be included in the magazine series because of space limitations. Organized by regions, the book is lavishly illustrated and includes articles on the history of American cooking and foodservice.

435. Wenzel, George Leonard. *Wenzel's Menu Maker.* 2d ed. Boston: CBI Publishing Co., 1979. 1,167 p.

This is one of the most important reference books in the foodservice industry. It has both purchasing specifications and recipes. Over 2,000 recipes are included; each has the approximate cooking time, ingredients needed for twenty-four and one hundred portions, cooking instructions and helpful hints. Also included is a section on foodservice management and a glossary of terms.

436. Wilkinson, Jule, comp. *Making the Most of Fruit on Foodservice Menus.* Boston: CBI Publishing Co., 1977. 245 p.

Because fruit is increasing in popularity, this compilation of recipes is a welcome one to foodservice managers. It includes hundreds of recipes using fruit in beverages, compotes, salads, main dishes, pancakes, pies, cakes, puddings, frozen desserts, and sauces. Most recipes serve forty-eight portions. Black-and-white photographs of many of them enhance the book.

437. Wilkinson, Jule, ed. *Seasonings Cookbook for Quantity Cuisine.* Boston: CBI Publishing Co., 1980. 273 p.

Designed to provide alternatives to bland quantity cooking, this is a collection of over 150 recipes in all menu categories for quantity cooking with seasonings. Each recipe includes a "featured seasoning" list telling which seasonings provide the distinctive flavor of the dish. It also includes a good glossary of seasonings and seasoning charts.

438. Wood, Marion Aurelia, and Harris, Katharine W. *Quantity Recipes.* Revised by Dorothy M. Proud. Ithaca, NY: New York State College of Home Economics at Cornell University, 1966. 233 p.

This is a revision of *Meals for Many* (Cornell Extension Bulletin 477). It includes recipes for fifty portions and guidelines for quantity food preparation, such as temperatures for cooking; ingredients; instructions for cooking milk, cheese, eggs, macaroni, and rice; and deep-fat frying.

RECIPES FROM FAMOUS RESTAURANTS OR CHEFS

439. Bergeron, Victor J. (Trader Vic). *Trader Vic's Book of Mexican Cooking.* Drawings by Cheryl Olsen. Garden City, NY: Doubleday, 1973. 271 p.

Trader Vic developed the Señor Pico restaurant in Ghirardelli Square in San Francisco. Prior to opening the restaurant, he traveled all over Mexico, eating and collecting recipes to adapt to American tastes. Here he reproduces many of them for the home cook. Illustrations include color photographs and black-and-white drawings.

440. Bery, Odette J. *Another Season Cookbook: Recipes for Every Season from the Chef/Owner of Boston's Another Season Restaurant.* Illustrated by Ippy Patterson. Chester, CT: Globe Pequot Press, 1986. 568 p.
Odette Bery, chef of the Boston Another Season Restaurant, has compiled 370 of her recipes emphasizing fresh, seasonal ingredients. Ms. Bery was trained in London and Paris; she and has traveled and worked in Africa, Europe, and the Americas. Her recipes reflect her international knowledge.

441. *The Best of Gourmet.* New York: Conde Nast/Random House, 1986–. (Annual)
Gourmet's first yearly collection of menus and recipes from the 1985 issues of the magazine. Part one is a menu collection which has twenty complete menus for occasions throughout the year. Part two is a compendium of over 500 recipes. There is a special guide to find recipes in the menu collection. There is also a general index, an index by recipe titles, and an index to forty-five minute recipes. Lavishly illustrated.

442. Blake, Anthony, and Crewe, Quentin. *Great Chefs of France: The Masters of Haute Cuisine and Their Secrets.* New York: Harry N. Abrams, 1978. 239 p.
The authors tell the history of French haute cuisine as well as presenting the culinary biographies of twelve outstanding chefs. The final part of the book includes menus, recipes, and advice from the great kitchens of France.

443. Brody, Jerome. *The Grand Central Oyster Bar & Restaurant Seafood Cookbook.* New York: Crown Publishers, 1977. 192 p.
The recipes from the Famous Grand Central Oyster Bar and Restaurant in New York City are collected here for the home chef.

444. Burns, Jim, and Brown, Betty Ann. *Women Chefs: A Collection of Portraits and Recipes from California's Culinary Pioneers.* Berkeley, CA: Aris Books, 1987. 218 p.
Forty women chefs of California are included in this cookbook. Several famous chefs are featured with a profile telling her story and philosophy and including several signature recipes and a photograph. The chefs include Amaryll Schwertner, Cindy Black, Susan Feniger, Mary Sue Milliken, Margaret Fox, Elka Gilmore, Joyce Goldstein, Mimi Hébert, Maggie Blyth Klein, Wendy and Ann Little, Cindy Pawlcyn, and Annie Somerville. Twenty-five other chefs are included in a section called "Snapshots." Each of these entries includes a short statement by or about the chef, one recipe, and a photograph.

445. Cozzi, Ciro, and Cozzi, Alethea. *Ciro & Sal's Cookbook: Recipes, Tips and Lore from the Acclaimed Chef of Provincetown's Famous Italian Restaurant, Ciro & Sal's.* New York: Donald I. Fine, 1987. 244 p.
Over 200 recipes from Ciro Cozzi's files are included in this cookbook by the chef of the famous Italian restaurant Ciro & Sal's in Provincetown, MA. Also included is a history of the restaurant from its opening as an informal sandwich shop in the 1950s to today. Recipes are arranged in standard categories, and most are in four portions.

446. Czarnecki, Jack. *Joe's Book of Mushroom Cookery.* New York: Atheneum, 1986. 340 p.
Over 300 recipes using many varieties of mushrooms written by the proprietor of one of the only gourmet mushroom restaurants in the world. Czarnecki is undoubtedly the authority on this subject. He includes a good deal of information on selecting, preserving, and preparing mushrooms. Included are recipes for sauces, extracts, soups, and complete mushroom dishes as well as recipes that combine mushrooms with almost every item on the menu. A list of Mycological Clubs in the United States is included.

447. D'Ermo, Dominique. *Dominique's.* New York: Dutton, 1987, 252 p.
Recipes from Dominique's prize-winning restaurants in Washington, DC, and Miami Beach, FL, are adapted for home use in this cookbook. They include appetizers, pastas, soups, vegetables, salads, and desserts as well as famous entrees using meat, fish, chicken, and game.

448. Foley, Joan, and Foley, Joe. *The Steakhouse Cookbook: A Collection of the Best Recipes from the Great Steakhouses of the U.S.* New York: Freundlich Books, 1985. 152 p.
Foley presents a collection of recipes from better-known steakhouses nationwide. Recipes appear under the following categories: appetizers and soups, beef, potatoes, vegetables, salad, bread, and desserts. A unique aspect of this book is the arrangement of a menu where all recipe items are presented. The reader can select a complete meal as in a restaurant, then turn to the recipes section to find out how to prepare it.

449. Glassman, Helen, and Postal, Susan. *The Greyston Bakery Cookbook.* Photographs by Lou Manna. Illustrations by Lyn Wohlers. Boston: Shambhala, 1986. 148 p.
A collection of eighty recipes from the Greyston Bakery operated by the Zen Community of New York. All recipes use only natural ingredients. Recipes, adapted for home use, are divided into seven categories: breakfast and brunch specialties, breads, pastries, cookies, tarts and pies, cakes, and chiffon layer cakes.

450. Hettich, Arthur, and Seranne, Ann. *The Four Star Kitchen: Classic Recipes from New York's Great Restaurants.* New York: Times Books, 1986. 318 p.
This is a collection of over 250 recipes from eighty-five of New York City's best restaurants. The restaurants are presented in alphabetical order with an address and short description of each followed by three or four recipes. The recipes include careful instructions given in numbered steps. An index assists in finding recipes by name and type of dish.

451. Hyatt International Hotels. *Deliciously Hyatt.* Chicago, 1985. 33 p.
Hyatt Hotel restaurants specialize in serving dishes using locally available ingredients and emphasizing the regional cuisine. Now, for the first time, some of these ethnic recipes have been collected in a small pamphlet so hotel patrons can reproduce them at home. Arrangement of the booklet is by country or region, including America, Egypt, Europe, India, Indonesia and South Pacific, Korea, Mexico, Pacific, and Thailand.

452. Klapthor, Margaret Brown. *The First Ladies Cook Book: Favorite Recipes of All the Presidents of the United States.* Consulting editor, Helen Duprey Bullock. New York: Parents Magazine Enterprises, 1982. 238 p.
Klapthor has collected about 150 recipes said to be the favorite recipes of all the U.S. Presidents. There is a separate section on each President which includes a great deal of historical information and anecdote, as well as some beautiful pictures. The recipes are at the end of each section and include main courses, desserts, and some side dishes.

453. Kramer, Rene. *Meat Dishes in the International Cuisine.* Edited by John Fuller. London: Virtue, 1984. 1058 p.
This huge and beautifully illustrated cookbook is a collection of recipes from over 100 chefs representing thirty countries. Part one covers food preparation topics such as buying meat, cooking methods, carving, and wine choices. The chapter on techniques includes over 250 black-and-white photographs. Part two, the recipe section, is divided into garnishes, sauces, hors d'oeuvres, savories, soups, buffet dishes and main dishes (subdivided by meat), hot-pots, cold main dishes, and accompaniments. There is an index by nationality as well as a general index.

454. Lawrence, Barbara. *Fisherman's Wharf Cookbook.* Illustrated by Mike Nelson. Concord, CA: Nitty Gritty Productions, 1971. 173 p.
This is a small collection of gourmet fish recipes from fifteen restaurants on Fisherman's Wharf. It is arranged alphabetically by name of the restaurants. The illustrations are delightful paintings of the restaurants and the "happenings" on the wharf.

455. LeHuédé, Henri. *Dining on the France.* New York: Vendome Press, 1981. 255 p.
This is a collection of over 400 recipes compiled by Henri Le Huede, former chef of the SS *France.* The ship's first class dining room was considered one of the great restaurants of the world. Appearing in all menu categories, these recipes have been adapted for home use. French names and English translations are given for each dish with indexing under both. There are thirty-seven suggested menus included.

456. Lesberg, Sandy. *The Master Chefs Cookbook: Recipes from the Finest Restaurants Compiled with the Cooperation of Carte Blanche.* New York: McGraw-Hill, 1980. 180 p.
This cookbook is a collection of over 350 signature recipes in all menu categories. Each includes the name of the restaurant of origin and usually the name of the senior chef as well. There are both classic and innovative recipes represented in this book. Some are rather challenging and require careful attention to instructions. There is an index by restaurant, location, and chef as well as a standard alphabetical index.

457. Lesberg, Sandy. *Specialty of the House.* Englewood Cliffs, NJ: Prentice-Hall, 1970. 213 p.
This is a collection of specialty dishes from the chefs of over 300 fine restaurants in the U.S. and elsewhere. Because the chefs decided which recipes to send, the collection has a preponderance of entrees. Section one includes appetizers and soups. Section two is divided into fish entrees, poultry entrees, oriental entrees, meat entrees, vegetables, salads, dressings, eggs, and sauces. Section three covers crepes, soufflés, and desserts. Recipes are headed by the name of the restaurant and usually the chef. A wine suggestion is included with each. Most recipes have never been printed before.

458. Levy, Faye. *LaVarenne Tour Book.* Edited by Judith Hill. Drawings by Sarah Kensington. Seattle, WA: Peanut Butter Publishing, 1979. 171 p.
This cookbook is a collection of recipes chosen by five chefs at La Varenne in Paris: Fernand Chambrette, Claude Vauguet, Gregory Usher, Albert Jorant, and Anne Willan. Each recipe serves four people, and ingredient quantities have been adjusted to U.S. measures.

459. Madison, Deborah, and Brown, Edward Espe. *The Greens Cookbook.* Toronto, ON: Bantam Books, 1987. 396 p.
This is a collection of more than 260 vegetarian recipes from the Greens Restaurant in San Francisco. Included are many excellent salad recipes. Recipes appear for soups, sandwiches, breads, pizzas, pasta, gratins, stews and casseroles, crepes, roulades, tarts, timbales, and desserts among others. Along with good directions, special tips are given at the head of each recipe.

460. Margittai, Tom, and Kovi, Paul. *The Four Seasons.* Edited by Barbara Kafka. Recipes created by Chef Joset Renggli. New York: Simon and Schuster, 1980. 573 p.
The Four Seasons restaurant in New York City has been the epitome of fine dining since 1959. In 1973, Tom Margittai and Paul Kovi became the new owners. With Chef Seppi Renggli, the tradition of fine seasonal food has continued. This cookbook is a collection of Chef Renggli's recipes. It includes cold and hot appetizers, soups, sorbets, main courses, special dinners, vegetables, and desserts. Recipes serve from six to ten people. Color photographs of the restaurant are included.

461. McLaughlin, Michael. *The Manhattan Chili Co. Southwest-American Cookbook: A Spicy Pot of Chilies, Fixins', and Other Regional Favorites.* New York: Crown Publishers, 1986. 120 p.

McLaughlin is chef and coowner of the Manhattan Chili Co. restaurant in New York City. He presents over sixty recipes for southwestern cooking with the emphasis on chili dishes. Appetizers, desserts, side dishes which complement chili and recipes for a few other items are included, but the central theme is chili, McLaughlin's specialty. A list of mail-order sources for less common southwestern ingredients is provided.

462. Méras, Phyllis, and Conway, Linda Glick. *The New Carry-Out Cuisine.* Boston: Houghton Mifflin, 1986. 374 p.

A sequel to the authors' *Carry-Out Cuisine* published in 1982, this book includes 330 recipes from the chefs and cooks of over 100 gourmet take-out shops. Regional recipes, home cooking, and recipes using popular new fruits and vegetables are emphasized. Although no photographs are included, the book is very attractively printed and sturdily bound.

463. Metz, Ferdinand E., and U.S. ACF Culinary Olympic Team. *Culinary Olympics Cookbook: U.S. Team Recipes from the 15th International Culinary Competition.* Edited by Chet Holden. Des Plaines, IL: Cahners Publishing Co., 1983. 144 p.

Primarily a collection of recipes presented by the American Culinary Olympics team members, this book includes among some 300 recipes, "Black Sea Bass St. Augustine" and "Turkey Breast Oklahoma," the two dishes that won America its first place gold medals at the 1980 competition. Recipes include ingredients and instructions for six portions and for twenty to twenty-four portions. Also included is information on the Olympics and team members.

464. Metz, Ferdinand E., and U.S. Culinary Team. *The Culinary Olympics Cookbook: US Team Recipes from the Culinary Olympics.* Edited by Steve M. Weiss. Boston: CBI Publishing Co., 1979. 291 p.

U.S. Team recipes from the International Culinary Olympics of 1976 in Frankfurt are included in this book. It also includes information on the Olympics including names of team members, precompetition activities, and competition menus and dishes. The main body of the book is favorite recipes of the team members in all major menu categories.

465. Miles, Darrell, and Bigley, William. *Quantity Cooking: Tested Recipes for Twenty or More.* New York: Dover Publications, 1976. 56 p.

This is a collection of about eighty recipes originally prepared for use on the USS *Semmes*, an award winning Navy mess. All menu categories are represented. Recipes are basic, easy-to-prepare items with broad appeal. Most will yield twenty-four measured portions. This is a corrected republication of *Dare to Excel in Cooking* published by the Government Printing Office, 1966.

466. Mosimann, Anton. *Cuisine a la Carte.* Boston: CBI Publishing Co., 1981. 304 p.

Anton Mosimann is one of the finest modern chefs. Here he has collected over 200 recipes, each serving four people. The book is arranged in standard recipe categories and is illustrated with over twenty full-color photographs. A long introduction by Quentin Crewe includes black-and-white photographs of Chef Mosimann.

467. O'Brien, Dawn, and Scheck, Rebecca. *Maryland's Historic Restaurants and Their Recipes.* Drawings by Bob Anderson. Winston-Salem, NC: J. F. Blair, 1985. 204 p.

The authors provide a description of the history and interiors of some fifty Maryland restaurants with three or four recipes given from each one. There are over 140 recipes in all, including a number of house and local specialties. Accompanied by line drawings of the restaurants.

468. O'Brien, Dawn, and Walter, Claire. *Pennsylvania's Historic Restaurants and Their Recipes.* Illustrated by Patsy Faires. Winston-Salem, NC: J. F. Blair, 1986. 204 p.

A brief description and history of some fifty Pennsylvania restaurants are presented here along with several specialty recipes from each. The 150 recipes include dishes from every menu category as well as some cocktails and salad dressings. Included are such recipes as Stokesay Castle's Veal Picante and The George Washington Tavern's Strawberries Flambé.

469. Peddersen, Raymond B. *Prize Winners: Recipes and Menu Ideas from Award-Winning Foodservice Personalities.* Boston: CBI Publishing Co., 1983. 316 p.

This book starts with brief chapters on foodservice, inventory control, sanitation, recipe standardization, and purchasing. Following these chapters are the favorite recipes of some of the most famous people in foodservice. Each recipe is preceded by a biographical sketch of the contributor and a list of awards won. In most cases, recipes are in six portions.

470. Prudhomme, Paul. *Chef Paul Prudhomme's Louisiana Kitchen.* Photographs by Tom Jimison. New York: W. Morrow, 1984. 351 p.

This basic Cajun/Creole cookbook is by the well-known Louisiana cook. Recipes are simple enough to be done in a normal home kitchen, yet are authentic. In "Notes from Our Test Kitchen," the author explains Cajun cooking terms and gives information on ingredients and procedures that are special to Louisiana cooking. Besides normal menu categories, special chapters are included on gumbos and jambalayas. Recipes are arranged by beginning each chapter with the easiest. Recipes are usually designed for six servings but vary in size from two to twenty.

471. Puck, Wolfgang. *The Wolfgang Puck Cookbook: Recipes from Spago, Chinois, and Points East and West.* New York: Random House, 1986. 304 p.

This cookbook contains over 200 recipes by Puck whose Spago and Chinois on Main restaurants are famous in Los Angeles. Puck's recipes are part of the emerging new American cuisine. They are inventive and are based on his interest in blending different types of food in original ways. Examples include Ravioli with Foie Gras and Truffles and Lobster with Sweet Ginger. All menu categories are included with a special section on pizza.

472. Renggli, Josef, and Grodnick, Susan. *The Four Seasons Spa Cuisine.* New York: Simon and Schuster, 1986. 348 p.

The famous Four Seasons Restaurant in New York is the source of this collection of healthful recipes. Renggli, well-known as a innovative chef, presents over 100 recipes arranged in forty-six menus. All are excellent cuisine while remaining low in fat and salt. Calories, salt, cholesterol, fiber, and other nutritional contents are given for every dish and each menu as a whole.

473. Salmon, Alice Wooledge, and Dunn-Meynell, Hugo. *The Wine & Food Society Menu Book: Recipes for Celebration.* Illustrated by Soun Vannithone. New York: Van Nostrand Reinhold Co., 1983. 234 p.

This collection of recipes arranged by menus includes six luncheons, nine dinners, a breakfast, and a picnic. Recipes are from members of the International Wine & Food Society and restaurateurs from all over the world. The appropriate wine or beverage for each meal is suggested.

474. Sedlar, John, and Kolpas, Norman. *Modern Southwest Cuisine.* Photographs by Richard Clark. New York: Simon and Schuster, 1986. 222 p.

This is a collection of recipes by John Sedlar of the Saint Estèphe restaurant in California. Dishes combine Mexican and American food with the techniques of French preparation. Many dishes are artistically presented and will be of interest to caterers (i.e., Zebra of Red and Green Chiles Rellenos with Lobster Sauce). Recipes appear in all menu categories, and a southwest pantry of basic preparations such as tortilla chips and sopapillas is included.

475. Stanforth, Deirdre. *The New Orleans Restaurant Cookbook.* rev. ed. Garden City, NY: Doubleday, 1976. 256 p.
> This book is both a restaurant guide and a cookbook. The first half includes a thorough description of the famous restaurants in New Orleans covering their history. Black-and-white photographs of the exterior and interior are included for most entries. The second half of the book is a collection of recipes arranged into standard menu categories. The restaurant contributing each recipe is cited.

476. Stern, Jane, and Stern, Michael. *Real American Food: From Yankee Red Flannel Hash and the Ultimate Navajo Taco to Beautiful Swimmer Crab Cakes and General Store Fudge Pie.* Illustrated by Jane Stern. New York: Alfred A. Knopf, 1986. 335 p.
> A book of over 300 recipes collected from the restaurants recommended by the Sterns in their books *Roadfood* and *Goodfood*. Recipes appear from East, South, West, and Midwest. There is no fancy cuisine; emphasis is on popular local specialties such as Memphis-style Barbecue Pizza and Mama Lo's Broccoli Casserole. Entries include some background on recipe sources.

477. Szathmáry, Louis. *The Chef's Secret Cook Book.* Illustrated by Carolyn Amundson. New York: Quadrangle/New York Times Books Co., 1971. 288 p.
> Louis Szathmáry, chef of The Bakery restaurant in Chicago, presents a collection of recipes largely from his personal files for dishes in all major menu categories. Though French, Italian, Hungarian, Mexican, and Far Eastern dishes are included, Szathmáry simplifies both techniques and ingredients to make his recipes usable by the less experienced cook. Drawings help explain some more difficult steps. There is a "Chef's Secret" section after each recipe giving special techniques, small tricks, and explanations.

478. Tower, Jeremiah. *Jeremiah Tower's New American Classics.* Photographs by Ed Carey. New York: Harper & Row, 1986. 233 p.
> This is a collection of best recipes by Tower, a well-known West Coast chef; nearly 250 recipes are included that combine classic and innovative aspects and making use of many locally available items (for example, Lobster Gazpacho and Braised Rabbit with Leeks and Prunes).

479. Troisgros, Jean, and Troisgros, Pierre. *The Nouvelle Cuisine of Jean & Pierre Troisgros.* Translated by Roberta Wolfe Smoler. New York: Morrow, 1978. 254 p.
> The nouvelle cuisine—the new French cooking—is a departure from the classical technique to a more creative, innovative, and lighter style. The Troisgros brothers are masters of the new cooking and owners of the Troisgros restaurant in the Hotel des Platanes. This book is a collection of their recipes carefully translated into English and tested in the translator's American homè. Substitutions for unobtainable French ingredients are noted in italic type.

480. Vergé, Roger. *Roger Vergé's Entertaining in the French Style.* Photographed by Pierre Hussenot. New York: Stewart, Tabori & Chang, 1986. 318 p.
> Roger Vergé is a famous chef and owner of Moulin de Mougins. He has chosen 120 recipes arranged into twenty seasonal menus for special dinners. All recipes serve six people. Each lists preparation time required, difficulty, and cost (i.e., expensive, inexpensive). The book is illustrated with many full-color plates printed on glossy paper.

481. Vergnes, Jean. *A Seasoned Chef: Recipes and Remembrances from the Chef and Former Co-Owner of New York's Famous Le Cirque.* New York: D. I. Fine, 1987. 250 p.
> Trained in France in the classic French tradition, Jean Vergnes has been a chef at the Waldorf-Astoria, the Colony Restaurant, and Le Cirque in New York City. In this

autobiography, he recounts his years in training and successful years as a chef. Each chapter includes recipes he developed or adapted. Over 150 recipes are given including Spaghetti Primavera, Supreme de Volaille Gismonda, and Clams Blini. All recipes are adapted for home use.

482. Vyhnanek, John J. *The Ritz-Carlton Cookbook.* San Diego, CA: Harcourt Brace Jovanovich, 1986. 216 p.

This is a collection of recipes from the Ritz-Carlton in Boston and a selection of local specialties from Ritz-Carltons in other locations. Recipes appear for appetizers, soups and stocks, pasta and rice, seafood, poultry, meat, sauces, vegetables, salads, savories, and desserts. Traditional and innovative dishes are included. Most recipes serve between two and six portions.

483. Wakefield, Ruth Graves. *Toll House Cook Book.* rev. ed. Drawings by Barbara Corrigan. Boston: Little, Brown, 1953. 381 p.

This cookbook is written by the original owner and cook of the famous Toll House restaurant located in a historic Cape Cod house which served as the toll house between Boston and New Bedford. Most of the recipes serve four to six people and emphasize the use of real butter; cream; whole milk; and fresh eggs, fruit, and vegetables. One chapter gives recipes for 100 servings. The famous Toll House Chocolate Crunch Cookies recipe (chocolate chip cookies) is on page 208.

484. Waters, Alice, and Guenzel, Linda P. *The Chez Panisse Menu Cookbook.* Recipes edited by Carolyn Dille. Illustrated by David L. Goines. New York: Random House, 1982. 312 p.

Chez Panisse is an internationally famous restaurant in San Francisco. The cuisine is American with a French flavor. Since the restaurant opened in 1971, it has served five-course dinners seldom repeating a meal. In this cookbook, Alice Waters, owner and chef, has compiled 120 classic French dishes from the meals served at Chez Panisse for the home chef. Recipes serve six to eight people.

485. Wilkinson, Jule. *Selected Recipes from IVY Award Winners.* Boston: Cahners Books, 1976. 224 p.

The Ivy Award has been given annually since 1971 by *Institutions/Volume Feeding* magazine (now *Restaurants and Institutions*) to the restaurateurs and foodservice operators who are elected for the award by their peers. It is a prestigious award that is given for life. This book is a collection of recipes from the forty-five winners from 1971 to 1975. Recipes are organized into standard menu categories. A biographic sketch is included also for each winner.

486. Wise, Victoria; Potenziani, James; and Jenanyan, Arayah. *American Charcuterie: Recipes from Pig-by-the-Tail.* New York: Viking, 1986. 300 p.

This is a collection of recipes from Pig-by-the-Tail, the original American charcuterie in Berkeley, California. In France, charcuterie began as the profession of preparing pork and other meats. Such shops now specialize in take-out food of many sorts. The recipes here combine French and American elements in unique ways. Recipes appear in the following categories: terrines, patés and galantines; preserved meats, fish and fowl; main dishes; cold compositions; savories; and sweets.

Food Purchasing

487. Association of School Business Officials, and American School Food Service Association. *School Food Purchasing Guide.* Chicago: Research Corp. of the Association of School Business Officials in the U.S. and Canada; Denver, CO: American School Food Service Association, 1968. 144 p.

This is a guide to school food purchasing. Chapters cover market regulations and the purchasing factors of various products. Sample bid requests are included in the chapter on purchasing. There is also a chapter on the purchasing process which includes methods of purchasing and sample contract, requisition, and purchase order forms. Although somewhat dated, this book still includes useful information. A glossary and bibliography are provided.

488. Axler, Bruce H. *Buying and Using Convenience Foods.* His Focus on...the Hospitality Industry. Indianapolis, IN: ITT Educational Publishing, 1974. 116 p.

Part of the Focus on... series, this book discusses the uses of convenience foods and their impact on quantity cooking, and foodservice. Buying principles and buyers' guides are given for convenience meats, fruits, vegetables, entrees, baked goods, desserts, beverages, and convenience components.

489. Beau, Frank N. *Quantity Food Purchasing Guide.* Chicago: Institutions Magazine, 1970. 84 p.

Beau provides a carefully worked out "multiplier" for easy guidance in quantity food purchasing. The guide is divided into dry stores, dairy and related products, fish, meat, poultry, fresh produce, and frozen produce. Each entry gives the normal unit of measure, the multiplier, suggested temperature range for storage, and approximate shelf life.

490. Berberoğlu, H. *Restaurateurs' and Hoteliers' Purchasing Book.* Dubuque, IA: Kendall/Hunt Publishing Co., 1981. 234 p.

The author provides a guide to purchasing of food, beverage and equipment. Part one discusses the purchasing function, receiving, and storage. Part two is a guide to many types of merchandise including descriptions of quality, type, and yield, where applicable. In addition to food items such as produce, meat, and seafood, there are chapters on tableware, kitchen equipment, housekeeping items, and other nonfood operational necessities.

491. Blue Goose Growers. *The Buying Guide for Fresh Fruits, Vegetables, Herbs, and Nuts.* 8th ed. s.l., 1986. 136 p.

This is the eighth revised edition of the *Blue Goose Buying Guide* first published in 1946. It remains the most complete and authoritative compilation of such information available. It is a consumer guide to fresh fruits, vegetables, nuts, and herbs arranged in short articles on each item of produce. These are written in a popular style and cover selection, storage, supply, and nutritional information and sometimes a bit of history about their origin and development. There are color illustrations of most items included. The book also contains brief information on the grading and waxing of produce.

492. Davis, Bernard. *Food Commodities.* London: Heinemann, 1978. 346 p.
This is a comprehensive textbook covering all foods—cereals, sugar, fats and oils, dairy products, fruits and vegetables, herbs and spices, beverages, meat, poultry, and fish. Each chapter contains an introduction, classification, methods of production, grading, uses in foodservice, storage requirements, and nutritional aspects. Although it is intended as a textbook for British students, it has a wealth of information useful to all food purchasers.

493. Dore, Ian. *Frozen Seafood, the Buyer's Handbook: A Guide to Profitable Buying for Commercial Users.* Osprey Seafood Handbooks. Huntington, NY: Osprey Books, 1982. 310 p.
This is a buyers' guide in dictionary format. It gives both seafoods and seafood terms. Items are classified by basic substance name with cross-references and index. Short additional chapters cover related subjects such as grading, packaging, processing, and substitutions as they relate to the frozen seafood market. A chapter on resources gives names and addresses of organizations that help seafood users. Good short bibliography.

494. Fabbricante, Thomas, and Sultan, William J. *Practical Meat Cutting and Merchandising: Volume 1: Beef.* 3d ed. New York: Van Nostrand Reinhold Co., 1987. 324 p.
This is an illustrated manual on the purchasing, processing, merchandising, distribution, and preparation of beef cuts. It is arranged by the various cuts such as flank, rounds, loins, brisket, rib, chuck, etc. Questions are included with each chapter. New developments in beef processing, and changes in identification of beef cuts, processing, and uses are included in this thorough revision.

495. Fabbricante, Thomas, and Sultan, William J. *Practical Meat Cutting and Merchandising: Volume 2: Pork, Lamb, Veal.* Westport, CT: AVI Publishing Co., 1975. 206 p.
Similar in format and goals to volume one on beef, each unit gives the steps of making particular cuts accompanied by line drawings. Merchandising aspects include methods for displaying and cooking the particular cut and suggested dishes to accompany it. A glossary of trade terms is included. Index and reading list appended.

496. *Food Buying Guide for Child Nutrition Programs.* Washington, DC: United States Department of Agriculture, 1984. 149 p.
The guide gives average yield information on over 600 food items. This information is necessary in calculating quantities for food purchase. Using the guide will help ensure that nutrition program requirements will be met by school lunches and breakfasts. Information is presented in chart form that includes purchase unit information and a column on serving size or portion and contribution to the meal requirement. Headings include meat and meat alternates, vegetables and fruits, bread and bread alternates, milk, and other foods. There is an index by individual food names also.

497. Kelly, Hugh J. *Food Service Purchasing: Principles and Practices.* New York: Chain Store Publishing Corp., 1976. 239 p.
Written as a practical guide and textbook, this book covers purchasing of alcoholic beverages, tabletop items, equipment, and capital items. It also covers buying strategies, portion control, quality control, training purchasing personnel, and vendor relationships.

498. Kotschevar, Lendal Henry. *Quantity Food Purchasing.* 2d ed. New York: Wiley, 1975. 684 p.
This is the most well-known textbook and reference handbook in food purchasing. Emphasizing the product information needed to purchase food, it is divided into chapters based on food categories, i.e., fruits and vegetables, dairy products. Each food is then described; various kinds are compared; and sizes, qualities, and seasons are listed. Alcoholic beverages and some nonfood supplies such as linen and tableware are also included.

499. Levie, Albert. *Meat Handbook.* 4th ed. Westport, CT: AVI Publishing Co., 1979. 338 p.
> Levie covers the entire product cycle of meat, from livestock to meat cuts. There are chapters on the history and purpose of grading and many aspects of meat handling such as distribution, purchasing, specifications and merchandising. Detailed chapters on meat cuts for beef, veal, lamb, and pork as well as processed, smoked, and variety meats are included. There is a short chapter on the cooking of meat.

500. Magoon, Charles. *Buying, Handling & Using Fresh Fruits.* 2d ed. Alexandria, VA: United Fresh Fruit and Vegetable Association, 1983. 19 p.
> This buying guide lists the availability, varieties, uses, quality, grades, and handling for thirty-five fruits. Each fruit is also illustrated with a black-and-white photograph of a dish using the fruit such as a pie or cake.

501. Magoon, Charles. *Buying, Handling & Using Fresh Vegetables.* 2d ed. Alexandria, VA: United Fresh Fruit and Vegetable Association, 1984. 20 p.
> Thirty-four vegetables are listed in this guide for buyers. For each one the availability, types, uses, quality, grades, and handling is given.

502. Mutkoski, Stephen A., and Schurer, Marcia L. *Meat and Fish Management.* North Scituate, MA: Breton Publishers, 1981. 296 p.
> The authors state that their reason for writing this text was to integrate the meat science approach and the management approach in one book for foodservice-oriented meat courses. To this end, chapters appear on the composition and structure of meat, and detailed information on government inspection and grading are included. But there are also chapters for meat buyers on all important meat types including fish and even soy and processed meat products. In addition, there are operational chapters on purchasing, receiving, storage, cooking, costing, and menu pricing.

503. National Association of Meat Purveyors. *The Meat Buyers Guide.* McLean, VA, 1976. 118 p.
> This is an updated compilation of two previous guides: *The Standardized Meat Buyer's Guide* and *The Portion Control Meat Cuts Guide.* It provides basic reference standards for the procurement of meat and meat products. Ordering data, primal cuts, and portion cuts are covered for beef, lamb, veal, and pork. (No organ meats are covered.) Color photographs of the various cuts are included.

504. National Live Stock and Meat Board, Foodservice Department. *Meat in the Foodservice Industry.* 2d ed. Chicago, 1977. 80 p.
> This is a primer for the beginning foodservice worker that contains information on meat cuts, where they come from, and how to judge their quality. It covers the purchasing, receiving, storing and inventorying of meat cuts. It also describes basic types of equipment and the principles of quantity meat cookery.

505. National Restaurant Association. *Profitable Purchasing: Proceedings from NRA's Second Annual National Conference on Purchasing.* Washington, DC, 1982. 76 p.
> This is an edited version of the transcripts of the Second National Conference on Purchasing. Purchasers, purveyors, and industry specialists looked at the trends in food purchasing and at innovations that will effect the industry in the future.

506. Ninemeier, Jack D. *Purchasing, Receiving, and Storage: A Systems Manual for Restaurants, Hotels, and Clubs.* Boston: CBI Publishing Co., 1983– . (Loose-leaf)
> This is a systems manual in a three-ring binder. It is written in standard operating procedure (SOP) format, intended for use in the field with topics being read as needed. The first nineteen chapters are primarily about purchasing and include such subjects as calculation of quantity purchasing, supplier selection, and the legal aspects of purchasing. The final two chapters cover receiving, inventory, and storage. Twenty-four sample forms

are included for such documents as "Purchase Specifications" and "Quotation Call Sheets." A detailed table of contents makes finding specific topics easier.

507. Padberg, Daniel I. *Today's Food Broker: Vital Link in the Distribution Cycle.* New York: Chain Store Age Books, 1971. 200 p.
Padberg covers the role of the food broker, the history of this type of work, and its importance to the food industry. The two major types of food processors—the National Brand Processor and the Private Label Processor—are examined in detail, and the way in which the broker services each of them is discussed. There are also chapters about the brokers' relationship with retailers, foodservices, and industrial markets. The growth and future of the profession are examined, and appendices present policy guidelines and practices.

508. Peddersen, Raymond B. *Foodservice and Hotel Purchasing.* Boston: CBI Publishing Co., 1981. 708 p.
Primarily designed as a textbook on purchasing, this book covers purchasing of most food items, alcoholic beverages, major equipment, tableware, and smallware. Chapters are also included on energy and chemicals. The author uses a management-of-materials approach and gives attention to guiding the development of standards, procedures, and controls along with the specifics of effective purchasing.

509. Peddersen, Raymond B. *SPECS: The Comprehensive Foodservice Purchasing and Specification Manual.* Edited by Jule Wilkinson. Boston: Cahners Books International, 1977. 1,185 p.
The U.S. government departments have developed detailed specifications for every raw food product on the market. This author has brought together the most important of these specifications for the food purchaser. Arrangement is by food categories: meat, poultry, eggs, dairy products, fish and shellfish, convenience food, kosher products, and produce.

510. Quality Assurance Department, National Institutional Food Distributor Associates, Inc., comp. *Canned Goods Specifications Manual.* Atlanta, GA: NIFDA, Inc., 1983. 254 p.
Intended as a reference manual, this book provides information on canned fruits and vegetable products. It includes USDA Quality Factors, as well as Acceptable Quality Levels (AQL) and the Cumulative Sum Sample (CUSUM) USDA Grading System. Descriptions, specifications, and short histories of each canned item are given.

511. Ross, Lynne Nannen. *Purchasing for Food Service: Self-Instruction.* Ames, IA: Iowa State University Press, 1985. 157 p.
A self-paced introduction to purchasing, it covers accounting procedures and product specifications for most areas of food buying as well as receiving and storage procedures. Students are to read a paragraph, answer a comprehension question, and proceed to the next paragraph.

512. Schneider, Elizabeth. *Uncommon Fruits & Vegetables: A Commonsense Guide.* Illustrated by Soun Vannithorne. New York: Harper & Row, 1986. 546 p.
This alphabetical guide to unusual produce gives instructions for selecting, storing, and preparing such items as ugli fruit, tamarillo, and spaghetti squash. Several recipes appear with most entries. There is also a recipe guide by menu category.

513. Stefanelli, John M. *Purchasing: Selection and Procurement for the Hospitality Industry.* 2d ed. Wiley Service Management Series. New York: Wiley, 1985. 541 p.
A textbook aimed at the hospitality student covering buying techniques and product information. It also addresses issues and problems related to purchasing that must be understood at the managerial level. Part one gives an overview of purchasing. Part two discusses the principles of selection and procurement such as ordering procedures, purchasing specifications, and storage management. Part three covers selection and procure-

ment of specific items. Each chapter begins with a stated learning objective and ends with questions and problems. This edition has a new chapter on furniture and equipment.

514. U.S. Food and Nutrition Service. *Food Buying Guide for Type A School Lunches.* Washington, DC: Government Printing Office, 1972. 92 p.

A "Type A" lunch must contain meat or meat alternate, vegetables and fruits, bread, butter or fortified margarine, and whole milk. This book provides purchase tables in all the above categories which list purchase unit, servings per purchase unit, serving size or portion, purchase units for 100 servings, and additional yield information. There is an additional section on other foods that covers items like catsup, cereals, and potato chips. Though the purchase unit pricing is out of date, the tables of amounts needed for quantity cooking are still excellent guides.

515. Virts, William B., and Ninemeier, Jack D.*Purchasing for Hospitality Operations.* East Lansing, MI: Educational Institute of the American Hotel & Motel Association, 1987. 282 p.

This textbook is a good balance of theoretical and practical information on purchasing. Part one introduces management concepts, and part two applies these concepts to commodities. The authors purpose is to change the attitude of the purchaser from just maintaining supplies to a cost-saving branch of the business. The most up-to-date techniques including cost-plus and forward contracting are covered.

516. Warfel, Marshall C., and Cremer, Marion L. *Purchasing for Food Service Managers.* Berkeley, CA: McCutchan Publishing Corp., 1985. 446 p.

This book seeks to explain the process of purchasing to foodservice managers who will have buyers under them. It demonstrates how purchasing fits into the management system of the industry. Standards, principles, and procedures for quantity food purchasing are discussed. The various commodities such as meat, dairy products, poultry, seafoods, and groceries are each covered in specific chapters that include information on specifications and governmental regulations. Cost control and supplies such as china, linen, and flatware are also covered. A bibliography is included.

517. Warfel, Marshall C., and Waskey, Frank H.*The Professional Food Buyer: Standards, Principles, and Procedures.* Illustrated by Terry Down. Berkeley, CA: McCutchan Publishing Corp., 1979. 363 p.

Warfel explains the job of food purchasing, gives a history, and discusses the future of the profession as well as principles such as specifications, procedures, and the basic mechanics of food buying. Receiving, controls, common market practices, and ethical considerations are included. The appendix provides tables of purchase guides.

518. Zaccarelli, Herman E., and Maggiore, Josephine. *Nursing Home Menu Planning—Food Purchasing, Management.* Edited by Jule Wilkinson. Chicago: Institutions/Volume Feeding Magazine, 1972. 359 p.

Almost 1,100 menus (not recipes) for fifty-two weeks of the year are included in this book, which is designed to help the food director of a nursing home plan meals. In addition, there are menus for holidays and special diets. Recipes for each dish listed are available in *The Professional Chef* or *The Professional Chef's Baking Recipes,* (Chicago: Institutions/Volume Feeding Magazine). Also included are chapters on nutrition and feeding of aged persons, how to organize a dietary department, and how to purchase food in quantities.

Food Sanitation and Safety

519. Axler, Bruce H. *Kitchen Sanitation and Food Hygiene.* His Focus on...the Hospitality Industry. Indianapolis, IN: ITT Educational Publishing, 1974. 169 p.

This is part of the Focus on...the Hospitality Industry series by Axler, which deals with various topics in practical terms using short, basic presentations of information and techniques. This book gives the basics on sanitation and hygiene. Chapters include information on management of kitchens, food hygiene, public health, food spoilage, training personnel, food handling, dishwashing, housekeeping, equipment sanitation, environmental sanitation, and pest control.

520. Border, Barbara A. *Food Safety and Sanitation.* Edited by Elizabeth Simpson. Careers in Home Economics New York: McGraw-Hill, 1979. 159 p.

This is a basic text for foodservice personnel and trainees explaining the need for safety and sanitation. It gives general instructions and procedures. Chapters cover standards, problems, and safety procedures as well as food storage, microorganisms, and the cleaning of premises and equipment. Cartoons, dialogue, and chapter summaries help students retain important facts and ideas.

521. Cichy, Ronald F. *Sanitation Management: Strategies for Success.* East Lansing, MI: Educational Institute of the American Hotel & Motel Association, 1984. 481 p.

This book approaches foodservice sanitation in terms of subsystems or control points integrating these with what the author calls the four resources (personnel, inventory, equipment, and facilities). Part one discusses general aspects of spoilage and preservation as well as regulations and management. Part two deals with each of ten control points such as purchasing, receiving, service, and maintenance. The first chapter of part three is specifically related to the lodging industry. The final chapter integrates the book's ideas into a workable system.

522. Cohen, Gerald, and Cohen, Nancy E. *Food Service Sanitation Handbook.* Rochelle Park, NJ: Hayden Book Co., 1982. 161 p.

Written to help students and foodservice operators comply with government regulations, this book is a guide to maintaining clean and hygienic conditions wherever food is handled. It discusses microorganisms, how they relate to foodborne illnesses, and how they can be controlled through proper cleaning procedures. Rodent and insect control are also covered.

523. Guthrie, Rufus K. *Food Sanitation.* Westport, CT: AVI Publishing Co., 1972. 247 p.

This book is intended for foodservice workers and students. It provides an introduction to microbiology and pollution as they relate to sanitation. Along with basics on microorganisms, wastes, and chemicals, specific chapters appear on sanitation in dairy plants, canning plants, food preparation, service, storage, and equipment.

524. Hobbs, Betty C., and Gilbert, Richard J. *Food Poisoning and Food Hygiene.* 4th ed. London: Edward Arnold, 1978. 366 p.

This British publication covers causes and prevention of food poisoning. Part one, "Food Poisoning and Food-borne Infection," discusses elementary bacteriology and microbiology, reservoirs and vehicles of infection, and the ecology of microorganisms in food. Part two, "Food Hygiene in the Prevention of Food Poisoning," covers personal hygiene, storage, and preparation procedures, cleaning and disinfecting methods, legislation, and education.

525. Kahrl, William L. *Food Service Sanitation/Safety.* Managing for Profit Series. New York: Chain Store Publishing Corp., 1978. 85 p.

A part of the Managing for Profit Series, this manual is a guide to safety and sanitation. Kahrl discusses regulations and laws as well as instructions and guidelines for safe and clean facilities. He emphasizes that money spent on safety and sanitation is not wasted but adds to efficiency and increases profits.

526. Kahrl, William L. *Food Service Warehandling.* Managing for Profit Series. New York: Chain Store Publishing Corp., 1978. 61 p.

This Managing for Profit Series manual covers warehandling which includes dishwashing and related operations. Kahrl points out that this neglected operation is the single largest function in all of foodservice in terms of expense and effort. In this manual, he presents the entire warehandling operation in detail and outlines effective programs for efficient warehandling systems.

527. Longreé, Karla, and Armbruster, Gertrude. *Quantity Food Sanitation.* 4th ed. New York: Wiley, 1987. 452 p.

This is a detailed guide to the prevention of foodborne illness with proper sanitation. Early chapters give basics on spoilage and microorganisms and other agents of foodborne illness. Several chapters deal with reservoirs of microorganisms causing gastroenteritic outbreaks. Others deal with procurement and proper storage, sources of contamination within the foodservice establishment, and multiplication of bacterial contaminants in ingredients. There are also chapters on control of contaminants and the education of personnel. This edition has a special section on microwaves and discusses their effect on microbial life.

528. Longreé, Karla, and Blaker, Gertrude G. *Sanitary Techniques in Foodservice.* 2d ed. New York: Wiley, 1982. 271 p.

The theory and application of good sanitation is covered in this text. Sanitary techniques for preparing, holding, and serving food are covered along with sanitary care of equipment and facilities. Basic scientific background information is included. The book covers food sanitation and microbiology, food spoilage and foodborne illnesses, sanitary practice, and training in sanitation of foodservice personnel.

529. Minor, Lewis J. *Sanitation, Safety & Environmental Standards.* The L.J. Minor Foodservice Standards Series, vol. 2. Westport, CT: AVI Publishing Co., 1983. 245 p.

This, the second volume in the series, provides guidelines for foodservice managers in controlling microbial and other food hazards, employee safety, dishwashing and other environmental standards and food waste standards. Also included is a chapter on food definitions, grades, and labeling.

530. National Institute for the Foodservice Industry. *Applied Foodservice Sanitation.* 3rd ed. A NIFI Textbook. Dubuque, IA: W. C. Brown Co., 1985. 299 p.

This updated edition of the National Institute for the Foodservice Industry's sanitation management text includes changes in Federal Drug Administration standards and new equipment. Chapters cover sanitation and health, purchasing, storage, and preparation, as well as cleaning, facilities and equipment, pest control, employee training, and sanitation management. A chapter is included on sanitation and safety regulations and standards.

531. National Restaurant Association. *Non-Uniformity of Regulations and the Foodservice Industry.* National Restaurant Association Current Issues Report. Washington, DC, 1986. 8 p.

Sanitation and food safety laws vary widely from state to state and even within states because municipal laws govern in some areas. The laws also vary from kind of restaurant because snack bars and convenience stores come under different regulations than do full service restaurants. To document these problems, the National Restaurant Association surveyed all the health departments in the U.S. This report summarizes these findings. It also includes recommendations from the National Conference on Food Protection, 1984.

532. National Restaurant Association, Public Health and Safety Department. *Sanitation Operations Manual.* Chicago, 1979. (Loose-leaf)

This loose-leaf manual provides a specific guide to meeting public health requirements and regulations. The wording of the Food and Drug Administration's 1976 Foodservice Model Ordinance is included, and the first four sections "Food Care," "Personnel," "Equipment," and "Facilities," deal with its requirements. There are additional sections on local ordinances, program development, microbiology, and foodborne diseases as well as public health and National Restaurant Association information and assistance available.

533. National Sanitation Foundation. *Reference Guide: Sanitation Aspects of Food Service Facility Plan Preparation and Review.* Ann Arbor, MI, 1978. 102 p.

This guide is intended to be a primary reference source providing general information and guidance to foodservice sanitation. It also presents the fundamentals of food plan preparation. The appendix includes sample forms, checklist, glossary, and a six-chapter "Manual on Sanitation Aspects of Installation of Food Service Equipment."

534. Richardson, Treva M., and Nicodemus, Wade R. *Sanitation for Foodservice Workers.* 3d ed. Boston: CBI Publishing Co., 1981. 275 p.

A textbook for foodservice students, this book covers the origins and consequences of foodborne illnesses and how they can be prevented. It also includes information on regulations and procedures necessary to maintain a sanitary establishment. The six main sections include organisms that cause foodborne illnesses, histories and major characteristics of food poisoning in the U.S., pest control, dishwashing, personnel training, and legal issues.

535. U.S. Division of Retail Food Protection. *Food Service Sanitation Manual: Including a Model Food Service Sanitation Ordinance: 1976 Recommendations of the Food and Drug Administration.* DHEW Publication, no. (FDA) 78-2081. Washington, DC: Government Printing Office, 1978. 96 p.

The major portion of this government document is the text of a recommended uniform food sanitation ordinance for adoption by state and municipal governments. It has sections on food care, personnel, equipment, sanitation, physical maintenance of facilities, temporary foodservice places, and compliance procedures.

Franchising

536. Friedlander, Mark P., Jr., and Gurney, Gene. *Handbook of Successful Franchising.* 2d ed. New York: Van Nostrand Reinhold Co., 1985. 453 p.
Intended to be a reference book for the prospective franchisee, this book consolidates material from the *Franchise Opportunities Handbook* and *Franchising in the Economy.* It is arranged by businesses and includes a description of the operation, number of franchisees, date business started, equity capital needed, and training and managerial assistance provided. The appendices list government and nongovernment assistance programs available and an excellent bibliography.

537. Hammond, Alexander. *Franchisee Rights: A Self-Defense Manual for Dealers, Distributors, Wholesalers, and Other Franchisees.* Greenvale, NY: Panel Publishers, 1979. 360 p.
This book explains the legal rights of the franchisee, dealer, distributor, wholesaler, licensee, or sales representative. Though not aimed at lawyers, it deals with issues in terms of laws and legal procedures and covers protecting yourself from termination, contract rights, litigation, Federal Antitrust Laws, price-fixing, tying, territorial restrictions, and price discrimination.

538. Kostecka, Andrew, comp. *Franchise Opportunities Handbook.* Washington, DC: Government Printing Office. (Annual)
This is the twentieth edition of the handbook. The main body of the book lists hundreds of franchise companies alphabetically by category. Each entry includes address, description of operation, number of franchisees, length of time in business, equity capital needed, financial assistance available, training provided, managerial assistance available, and the date when the information was submitted.

539. Luxenberg, Stan. *Roadside Empires: How the Chains Franchised America.* New York: Viking, 1985. 313 p.
The author looks at the proliferation of all kinds of chains and franchises and discusses their effect on America. He points out the chains' less appealing aspects while documenting their rapid spread. Much is revealed about how major chains operate, locate, and hire, as well as many other aspects of some major chain enterprises.

540. Naisbitt Group. *The Future of Franchising: Looking 25 Years Ahead to the Year 2010.* Washington, DC: International Franchise Association, 1986. 27 p.
This study was commissioned by the International Franchise Association to determine trends in franchising. Over 100 franchisors and franchisees were interviewed. The researchers also utilized secondary data sources and thematic content analysis. The top ten franchise businesses are identified; each is reviewed for its growth potential to 1990. The top three industries are restaurants, retailing, and hotels/motels/campgrounds.

541. National Restaurant Association, Research Department. *Franchise Restaurants: A Statistical Appendix to Foodservice Trends.* Washington, DC, 1987. 78 p.
This book provides statistics on the franchise restaurant industry through 1985 based on data from the annual *Franchising in the Economy* survey published by the U.S. Department of Commerce. Sections include "Sales and Establishment Data on the Franchise Restaurant Industry," "Sales and Establishment Data on Types of Franchise Restaurants," "Sales and Establishment Data on Donut and Ice Cream/Yogurt Franchise Restaurants," "Financial, Ownership and Employment Statistics," "Franchise Restaurant Establishments by State and Region," "International Restaurant Franchising."

542. U.S. Department of Commerce. *Franchising in the Economy.* Washington, DC: Government Printing Office, 1971?–. (Annual)
This is a statistical handbook on all types of franchises in the U.S. It is based on questionnaires mailed to all known business formats. Automobile dealers, gasoline service stations, and soft drink bottlers dominate the franchise field, but restaurants are a growing portion. Statistics from 1969 to 1987 are included in the 1985-1987 edition.

543. Vaughn, Charles L. *Franchising, Its Nature, Scope, Advantages, and Development.* 2d rev. ed. Lexington, MA: Lexington Books, 1979. 281 p.
This is a thorough introduction to franchising for both the franchisor and franchisee. Chapters cover history of franchising, marketing, the advantages and disadvantages of franchising, starting a franchise, recruiting and training franchisees, financing the operation, real estate program, and international franchising. Sample franchise contracts and agreements are provided in the appendix.

544. Webster, Bryce. *The Insider's Guide to Franchising.* New York: AMACOM, 1986. 309 p.
Webster covers all the practical aspects of running a franchise. In part one, he covers fundamentals such as location and starting costs. In part two, he covers setting up and running a successful operation, relations with the franchisor, and the use of marketing techniques. There is a special chapter on women and franchising. Part three, "The Best Franchises in the United States," teaches how to rate a franchise before buying and lists over 100 of what Webster judges to be the best franchises in the country.

History

545. Alberts, Robert C. *Mount Washington Tavern: The Story of a Famous Inn, a Great Road, and the People Who Used Them.* Illustrated by A. Snyder. Washington, DC: Eastern National Park & Monument Association, 1976. 32 p.
  The history of the National Road (or Cumberland Road) built from Maryland to Illinois in the early 1800s and this famous tavern on the road near Uniontown, PA, is told in this short book. The tavern is now a museum administered by the National Park Service who published this booklet.

546. Anoff, I. S. *Food Service Equipment Industry.* Sponsoring editor, Russ Carpenter. Chicago: Institutions/Volume Feeding Magazine, 1972. 255 p.
  This is the first history ever written of the foodservice equipment industry. The author presents its pioneers, merchandise, trade associations, dealers, and manufacturers. He also discusses its future. Chapters are filled with names and dates more than with analysis. As such, it might be a useful reference tool for researching the history of companies.

547. Bernstein, Charles. *Great Restaurant Innovators: Profiles in Success.* New York: Chain Store Publishing Corp., 1981. 221 p.
  The author presents success stories of various entrepreneurs whose creativity have effected the current restaurant world. The book is divided into sections on fast-food pioneers, conglomerate foodservice leaders, entrepreneurs, independents, and creative consultants. Included are the stories of such people as Don Smith of Pizza Hut and Taco Bell, Stuart Anderson of Black Angus, and Dave Thomas of Wendy's.

548. Bryant, Carol A., et al. *The Cultural Feast: An Introduction to Food and Society.* St. Paul, MN: West Publishing Co., 1985. 481 p.
  A scholarly work on nutrition and culture, the first three chapters look at human evolution and history and their impact on food practices. Chapters four through six discuss how culture, society's knowledge, traditions, beliefs, and values effect food practices. Chapters seven and eight cover world hunger both in terms of politics and production. The final two chapters focus on changes in dietary practices and ways to improve them in our own and other societies.

549. Cross, Wilbur, and Steinman, Jerry. *Service Imperative; The Past, Present, and Future of the Linen Supply Industry.* Miami Beach, FL: Linen Supply Association of America, 1970. 240 p.
  The linen supply business provides towels, uniforms, aprons, and the like on a rental basis. This is a history of the linen supply industry from its beginning in the nineteenth century to the present. The appendix includes many tables and statistics including sales trends 1953–68 and a very complete glossary of linen items carefully defined and illustrated.

550. Décsy, Gyula. *Hamburger for America and the World: A Handbook of the Transworld Hamburger Culture.* Transworld Identity Series. Bloomington, IN: EURORA, European Research Association, 1984. 133 p.
    Briefly tells the history and legends of the development of the American hamburger. The main body of the book is a compilation of over 800 burger names for commercial hamburgers with sources noted.

551. Feifer, Maxine. *Tourism in History: From Imperial Rome to the Present.* New York: Stein and Day, 1986. 288 p.
    Feifer traces the experience of tourism from Roman times to the present. Chapters look at medieval pilgrims, Elizabethan, Romantic, and Victorian tourists and at the recent explosion in tourism. The author creates a prototypical tourist for each epoch. But all the elements, the socio-geographic details, opinions, and reactions, have been drawn from factual research not from invention. The list of sources is a good basic bibliography of historical accounts of tours and travels.

552. Ford, Willard Stanley. *Some Administrative Problems of the High School Cafeteria.* New York: AMS Press, 1972. 147 p.
    First published in 1926 as part of the Teachers College, Columbia University's Contribution to Education, no. 238, this work is now available in reprint format. It traces the history of the development of the high school cafeteria in the U.S. from 1909–1926 and goes on to deal with the problems facing administrators in the 1920s. Topics covered include predicting number of students who will buy a school lunch, building provisions, equipment need, management of the cafeteria, accounting systems, educational opportunities offered by the cafeteria, and a summary. It is a fascinating historical study.

553. Gomes, Albert J. *Hospitality in Transition: A Retrospective and Prospective Look at the U.S. Lodging Industry.* Houston, TX: Pannell, Kerr, Forster, Houston Administrative Office, 1985. 166 p.
    A clear and scholarly review of the hotel and motel industry's history, composition, and impact on the economy in general. Many statistical charts are included.

554. Helberg, Kristin. *The Belvedere and the Man Who Saved It.* Baltimore, MD: Pumpkin Publications, 1986. 111 p.
    Told mostly in photographs discovered in the Maryland Historical Society Archives, this book tells the history of the Belvedere Hotel from construction in 1902 until today. It also tells the story of Victor Frenkil, the author's father, who worked to renovate and save the grand hotel of Baltimore.

555. Hilton, Conrad N. *Be My Guest.* Englewood Cliffs, NJ: Prentice-Hall, 1957. 288 p.
    This autobiography of Conrad Hilton covers his childhood and early struggles as well as the growth of his hotel empire. It is full of personal recollections and philosophy that give insight into Hilton's climb to success.

556. Josephson, Matthew. *Union House, Union Bar; The History of the Hotel and Restaurant Employees and Bartenders International Union, AFL-CIO.* New York: Random House, 1956. 369 p.
    This is the history of the Hotel and Restaurant Employees and Bartenders International Union told from its beginnings in the 1890s to the early fifties. The author, a professional historian, was commissioned to write this book for the 1953 convention of the union.

557. Kroc, Ray, and Anderson, Robert. *Grinding It Out: The Making of McDonald's.* New York: Berkley Books, 1978. 218 p.
    The history of McDonald's is one of America's biggest success stories. Here, Ray Kroc, founder of the world's largest hamburger franchise, tells his own story of building the multibillion dollar business from scratch in a popular, entertaining style that reveals his business philosophy and operating strategies. Becoming somewhat dated now because it was written in 1976.

558. Love, John F. *McDonald's: Behind the Arches.* New York: Bantam Books, 1986. 470 p.
> Written by an independent journalist, this book traces the history of the McDonald's Corporation. Emphasis is on the innovative strategies and creative approach that have made McDonald's the most successful franchise system in the world.

559. Morgan, Howard E. *The Motel Industry in the United States: Small Business in Transition.* Small Business Management Research Reports. Tucson, AZ: Bureau of Business and Public Research, University of Arizona, 1964. 218 p.
> A descriptive and analytical study done during the 1960s which gives a comprehensive profile of the motel industry at that time. It also analyzed various environmental and managerial factors that affected sales, profitability, and survival of motels. The findings are based on samplings from 2,000 motels and guests in 100 locations. Bibliography included.

560. Moss, Peter. *Meals Through the Ages.* London: G. Harrap, 1958. 176 p.
> Meals in eight eras of British history are described here in entertaining story format. A feel for the customs and attitudes of the period as well as the foodserving and utensils of the time is given. Time periods covered are Roman Britain, Anglo-Saxon England, the Middle Ages, Tudor England, Seventeenth-Century England, the Late Eighteenth Century, Victorian England, and Twentieth-Century England.

561. National Restaurant Association. *A Financial Analysis of the Restaurant Industry; Corporations, Partnerships, and Individually Owned Operations.* Washington, DC, 1963. 94 p.
> A look at financial structure and operating histories of restaurants in the U.S. from 1954 to 1961. Emphasis is on sales, costs, assets, net worth, and profits. There are several chapters on financial ratios including how to prepare a financial ratio analysis for your foodservice operation.

562. O'Brien, Robert. *Marriott: The J. Willard Marriott Story.* Salt Lake City, UT: Deseret Book Co., 1978. 336 p.
> A biography of Marriott written by a long-time friend. It traces his Mormon heritage and youthful years in Utah as well as the story of his success with the chain of Hot Shoppe restaurants and Marriott hotels. This biography provides insights into the man and his business methods.

563. Palmer, Arnold. *Movable Feasts.* London: Oxford University Press, 1952. 153 p.
> Relying largely on novels, Palmer discusses the changing meal times and customs in England through a period of 170 years beginning with 1780. He traces the origins of breakfast, lunch, and afternoon tea and their changing quirks and customs.

564. Patrick, Ted, and Spitzer, Silas. *Great Restaurants of America.* Illustrated by Ronald Searle. Philadelphia, PA: Lippincott, 1960. 383 p.
> This guide lists 100 fine restaurants all over the U.S.A. Each entry includes address and the name of the proprietor, maitre d'hotel, and chef where available, followed by a page or two of personal comment and description by the authors. Somewhat out of date now, because it was published in the 1960s, it is still an interesting look at some famous restaurants and includes about seventy-five recipes in the back of the book.

565. Staples, Loring M. *The West Hotel Story, 1884–1940: Memories of Past Splendor.* Minneapolis, MN: Carlson Print Co., 1979. 136 p.
> This book tells the history of a famous Minneapolis hotel. The book covers the building of the hotel and some of its past glories and disasters, as well as its final demolition.

566. Stuart, Sandra Lee. *The Pink Palace: Behind Closed Doors at the Beverly Hills Hotel.* Secaucus, NJ: L. Stuart, 1978. 231 p.

Stuart tells the story of the Beverly Hills Hotel, the old fashioned, elegant and still highly successful hotel where Hollywood celebrities spend their recreation time. She tells of its history and relates some of the many stories that have grown around it.

567. Volant, F., and Warren, J. R., comps. and eds. *Memoirs of Alexis Soyer.* Rottingdean, Sussex, England: Cooks Books, 1985. 303 p.

This is a facsimile reprint of the original 1859 edition of the biography of Alexis Soyer. Soyer was a very famous nineteenth-century chef of the Reform Club in England. He also wrote three very influential cookbooks *The Gastronomic Regenerator, The Modern Housewife* and *A Shilling Cookery for the People.*

568. Watts, Stephen. *The Ritz of Paris.* New York: Norton, 1964. 214 p.

This is the story of the Hotel Ritz, which is the only hotel whose name has become a common English word. The story of Cesar Ritz, who started the hotel, and of the hotel through 1963 is told in chapters that give a real feel for the elegance and tradition of the Ritz. Chapters on the Ritz bars and food and wine contain some interesting ideas that could be adapted for use elsewhere, but no actual recipes are included.

Opening a Small Restaurant or Inn

569. Breen, James J., and Sanderson, William D. *How to Start a Successful Restaurant: An Entrepreneur's Guide.* New York: Chain Store Publishing Corp., 1981. 117 p.

In this book, the authors outline how to use marketing techniques to write a proposal for a new restaurant. A written proposal will help the developers gain financing, interest others in the restaurant, and illustrate good organization to employees. The book starts with a discussion of each section of the proposal including restaurant concept, customer profile, locating competition, marketing plan, organization, operating growth strategy, and financial plan. A sample proposal is included. The last chapter covers related topics such as accounting systems, advertising, leases, licenses, permits, and taxes.

570. Brown, Douglas Robert. *The Restaurant Manager's Handbook: How to Set Up, Operate, and Manage a Financially Successful Restaurant.* Silver Springs, FL: Atlantic Publishing Co., 1982. 312 p.

The author has written a manual especially for those with minimal experience who are just opening or thinking of opening a new restaurant. Particularly good is the first chapter on pre-opening activities covering all pertinent laws, licenses, and regulations as well as promotion and the various types of services that must be engaged. Other chapters cover menu planning, bar and kitchen management, supplies, service procedures, employee relations, bookkeeping and monthly audit, and cost projecting. Many useful forms are included that may be freely reproduced.

571. Buchanan, Robert D., and Espeseth, Robert D. *Developing a Bed and Breakfast Business Plan.* North Central Regional Extension Publication, no. 273. s.l. s.n., 1987. 59 p.

This brief pamphlet outlines a series of steps to help one analyze the market and develop a business plan for a bed and breakfast home or small inn.

572. Chiffriller, Thomas F., Jr. *Successful Restaurant Operation.* Boston: CBI Publishing Co., 1982. 278 p.

Writing from his own experience as an independent restaurateur, the author outlines for the inexperienced person how to get started in a small restaurant operation. He covers financing, legal requirements, personnel, kitchen equipment and sanitation, cost management, menu, beverage management, advertising, energy, and utilities.

573. Coltman, Michael M. *Start and Run a Profitable Restaurant: A Step-by-Step Business Plan.* North Vancouver, BC: International Self-Counsel Press Ltd., 1983. 141 p.

This is a guide to starting in the restaurant business. Basic information and suggestions are given for every stage from concept, menu, site, construction, equipment, and financing through personnel, purchasing, advertising, and insurance. Throughout the book, illustrative samples are given of such documents as balance sheets, market analysis question-naires, financing proposals, and requisition forms.

574. Davies, Mary E., et al. *So...You Want to Be an Innkeeper.* Illustrated by Jen-Ann Kirchmeier and Sharyl Duskin. San Francisco, CA: 101 Productions, 1985. 218 p.

This practical guide to starting and operating a bed and breakfast inn was written for novices and dreamers by four successful innkeepers. It covers site selection, choosing a legal structure, financial planning, renovating and decorating, meal planning, marketing and advertising, reservation procedures, insurance, and staffing.

575. Dukas, Peter. *How to Plan and Operate a Restaurant.* rev. 2d ed. Ahrens Series. Rochelle Park, NJ: Hayden Book Co., 1973. 268 p.

This book is aimed at management problems and decisions in the restaurant business. In section one, "How to Organize a Profitable Restaurant," Dukas discusses concepts of business organization, where to obtain capital, location, menu, equipment, layout, and insurance. In section two, "How to Operate a Profitable Restaurant," he discusses employees, promotion, cost controls, accounting, record keeping, and planning.

576. Dyer, Dewey A. *So You Want to Start a Restaurant?* rev. ed. Boston: CBI Publishing Co., 1981. 168 p.

Dyer points out that a restaurant is a combination of a manufacturing business and a retail outlet. He covers planning, design, staffing, training, management, and other major concerns for the prospective restaurant owner. This updated edition gives more space to energy considerations as well as reflects changes in cost and marketing emphasis since 1971.

577. Etsell, Karen L., and Brennan, Elaine C. *How to Open (and Successfully Operate) a Country Inn.* Illustrated by Leo Garel. Stockbridge, MA: Berkshire Traveller Press, 1983. 191 p.

The authors of this practical guide operate the Bramble Inn in Brewster, Cape Cod. Drawing upon their own experience, they outline how to turn a dream into a reality for the entrepreneur who dreams of owning a country inn. Topics covered include developing a preliminary study; locating an inn to purchase; defining your market and clientele; getting the inn ready to open; hiring, redecorating, and purchasing food and equipment; and the basic operating procedures of running an inn.

578. Fairbrook, Paul. *Starting and Managing a Small Restaurant.* Starting and Managing Series, no. 9. Washington, DC: Small Business Administration, 1964. 116 p.

One of the Starting and Managing Series published by the Small Business Administration, it is divided into three parts. Part one helps the beginner decide whether he or she has the capital and abilities necessary for success. It also discusses the process of running a restaurant as well as franchises and other options. Part two covers the basics of getting started including location, organization, and opening day. Part three covers proper management and accounting and how to plan for the future. This is a good basic book written in a clear and simple style.

579. Herbert, Jack. *Creating a Successful Restaurant.* New York: St. Martin's Press, 1985. 210 p.

An expert's fact-filled handbook for anyone going into (or even thinking about going into) the restaurant business. This is a step-by-step guide for the new restaurant owner. The author deals with location and type of restaurant, financing, menu planning, design, food purchasing, regulations, staffing, advertising, and most other aspects of getting started. Chapters are short and basic.

580. Johnson, R. H. *Running Your Own Restaurant.* 2d ed. London: Hutchinson, 1982. 185 p.

Written in Britain, this book covers all aspects of restaurant ownership. Chapters focus on locality, layout, equipment, staffing, operation and routine, control, records, accounts, costing, purchasing, stores, menu, advertising, and other important areas for the beginning entrepreneur.

581. Kleeman, Elayne J., and Voltz, Jeanne A. *How to Turn a Passion for Food into Profit.* New York: Berkley Books, 1983. 215 p.

Aimed at the general layperson, this book outlines how to start a restaurant or gourmet shop, operate a cooking school, start a mail-order food business, or begin a catering service. In addition, it covers pricing, taxes, advertising and promotion, and other financial questions.

582. Lundberg, Donald E. *The Restaurant: From Concept to Operation.* New York: Wiley, 1985. 308 p.

This book is aimed at those who want to have their own restaurant. It provides guidance for every step from concept and location through menu development, cost projection, financing, organizing, staffing and equipment purchasing to marketing, managing, food purchasing, and customer relations. There are chapters on laws and regulations, employee training, and bar operations as well.

583. Miller, Daniel. *Starting a Small Restaurant: A Guide to Excellence in Purveying of Public Victuals.* rev. ed. Harvard, MA: Harvard Common Press, 1983. 206 p.

This book is aimed at those without professional restaurant experience who wish to open a small restaurant. After frankly pointing out the difficulties in the first chapter, Miller covers all the aspects of a restaurant including kitchen design, dining room practice, decor, supplies, personnel, advertising, pricing, and profits. An informative book written in a popular style, this revised edition has a new chapter on automation.

584. Mooney, Sean, and Green, George. *Sean Mooney's Practical Guide to Running a Pub.* Chicago: Nelson-Hall, 1979. 241 p.

This is a guide to all the procedures and pitfalls in bar ownership. Mooney talks about buying the property, getting fixtures and equipment, security, and employees as well as basic drinks, pricing, problems, and inventory control. He also gives highlights of relevant federal and state laws. Intermixed are many interesting and entertaining stories from his own experiences.

585. National Restaurant Association. *Conducting a Feasibility Study for a New Restaurant: A Do-It-Yourself Handbook.* Washington, DC, 1983. 130 p.

This is a step-by-step guide to using marketing techniques in determining the success of a proposed restaurant. The guide divides the process into five major steps: "Researching Your Market Area," "Surveying Potential Competitors," "Analyzing the Selected Site," "Developing a Restaurant Concept," and "Constructing a Pro Forma Financial Statement."

586. Notarius, Barbara, and Brewer, Gail Sforza. *Open Your Own Bed & Breakfast.* New York: Wiley, 1987. 223 p.

Notarius is the well-known expert who started Bed & Breakfast USA, Ltd., a reservation service for B&Bs. In this volume, she outlines the responsibilities of the innkeeper; how to promote and advertize; what to charge; and how to keep records and deal with insurance, legal, and tax issues. A nice addition to the volume is a set of breakfast recipes and an appendix which lists reservation services.

587. Petteruto, Ray. *How to Open and Operate a Restaurant: A Step-by-Step Guide to Financial Success.* New York: Van Nostrand Reinhold Co., 1979. 269 p.

This is a step-by-step guide for those entering the restaurant field. It covers basics such as financing, menu, location, and equipment as well as management techniques, merchandising, and decor. A checklist of things to be done in setting up a new business is provided. There is a bibliography of government publications and one of foodservice magazines and newspapers.

588. Robbins, Charles. *So You Want to Open a Restaurant: Making Your Favorite Fantasy Real.* San Francisco, CA: Harbor Publishing, 1982. 217 p.

This is a practical guide to the various aspects of starting and running a restaurant for those new to the business. Chapters cover menu, location, leasing, capital costs, financing, kitchen design, construction, hiring, supervision, daily operations, and liquor operations. A foodservice equipment directory is provided.

589. Shown, Janet. *Freelance Foodcrafting: How to Become Profitably Self-Employed in Your Own Creative Cooking Business.* Boulder, CO: Live Oak Publications, 1983. 172 p.

The author believes there is a ready market for specialty and gourmet foods that can be produced in your own kitchen or in a small business. Her book is an inspiration to would-be freelancers and covers product development, market analysis, and legal concerns. Besides specialty foods, she covers catering, mail-order foods, cooking classes, take-out shops, and gourmet food stores. The last chapter is on financing your business.

590. Siegel, William L. *How to Run a Successful Restaurant.* Edited by David M. Brownstone. Wiley Small Business Series. New York: Wiley, 1977. 115.

This concise overview of the restaurant business reviews the basic information needed by an inexperienced restaurant owner. Chapters cover planning, menu design, advertising, purchasing, sanitation, hiring and training, and personnel management, laws and taxes, financing, and grand opening.

591. Stankus, Jan. *How to Open and Operate a Bed & Breakfast Home.* Chester, CT: Globe Pequot Press, 1986. 290 p.

Based on information gathered from many B&B hosts and other authorities, this book covers what it takes to run a successful B&B home. It includes how to get started, publicity, pricing, insurance, zoning, and other useful topics. Appendices list reservation services and tourist offices as well as a "Helping Hand Network" which includes names and addresses of B&B hosts willing to answer beginners' questions. Worksheets, checklists, and quizes are interspersed throughout.

592. Stevenson, W. C. *Making and Managing a Pub.* North Pomfret, VT: David & Charles, 1979. 144 p.

The author, a successful public house owner, has written a helpful little book for those who want to own and manage a pub in Britain. Material on license laws, regulations, and tenancy is not applicable in the U.S. However, chapters on hiring, training, and dealing with problem patrons will be useful to U.S. readers.

593. Tracey, Patrick A., Jr. *How to Open a Small, Sophisticated Restaurant and What Everyone Should Know about Dining Out.* Smithtown, NY: Exposition Press, 1984. 128 p.

This is a specific guide to opening a linen-covered, jacket-required restaurant seating forty people. Tracey discusses menu, location, financing, insurance, taxes, employees, and equipment in brief, clear paragraphs that cover most elements necessary to a successful small operation of this type.

594. Vellacott, Audrey, and Christmas, Liz. *Doing Bed & Breakfast.* Newton Abbot, England; North Pomfret, VT: David & Charles, 1982. 96 p.

Bed and Breakfast accommodations have been a popular alternative to hotels in England for years. In this book, two British women cover the basic information needed to set up and run a B&B in England. Topics covered include financing, retaining your own privacy, insurance, advertising, health and hygiene, planning and preparing breakfast, and many recipes and menus. Much of the legal and regulation information is very British oriented, but the recipes and philosophy of innkeeping would be valuable to U.S. entrepreneurs interested in B&B business.

595. Ware, Richard, and Rudnick, James. *The Restaurant Book: The Definitive Guide to Starting Your Own Restaurant.* New York: Facts on File, 1984. 198 p.

This is a step-by-step guide to opening a restaurant. In a conversational style, the authors cover everything from business aspects, starting costs, location, layout, and personnel to the type of experts new restaurant owners will need to consult. They also deal with advertising, suppliers, systems and controls, and the pros and cons of franchises. The appendix lists associations and trade shows where further information can be obtained.

596. Zander, Mary. *How to Start Your Own Bed & Breakfast: A Guide to Hosting Paying Guests in Your House or Apartment.* Spencertown, NY: Golden Hill Press, 1985. 201 p.

Zander provides clear step-by-step instructions on how to turn your home into a Bed and Breakfast. She covers zoning, licensing regulations, health and sanitary considerations, advertising, and marketing. Reservation service organizations (RSOs) are explained and listed. Also included are guidebooks in which to list your B&B and a list of state historic preservation offices and state tourism offices.

Law and Legal Issues

597. Anderson, Ronald Aberdeen. *The Hotelman's Basic Law.* Ocean City, NJ: Insurance Press, 1965. 493 p.

A guide to legal principles which concern the hospitality industry. Part one covers definitions, accommodations and discrimination, liability-imposing conduct, the hotel's supervisory liability, the hotel's vicarious liability, causal relationship, intentional torts and death claims, negligence, and contributory negligence and assumption of risk. Part two is on particular situations and includes chapters on specific aspects of liability such as liability for condition of premises as well as such other subjects as checks and credit cards, liens and eviction, labor law, crime, and the anatomy of a lawsuit.

598. Branch and Swann. *The Wage and Hour Law Handbook for the Lodging and Foodservice Industry.* Atlanta, GA: The Publishers, Inc., 1980–. (Loose-leaf)

Written by members of the Branch and Swann law firm, this loose-leaf handbook is a practical guide to the Fair Labor Standards Act wage and hour laws. Chapters give basic clear explanations of the law's various provisions and record-keeping requirements. Among other things, chapters cover tip credit, exemptions, compliance audits, equal pay, federal wage garnishment law, and age discrimination in employment. A summary of various state laws is also provided.

599. Cournoyer, Norman G., and Marshall, Anthony G. *Hotel, Restaurant & Travel Law.* 2d ed. North Scituate, MA: Breton Publishers, 1983. 675 p.

This book's purpose is to educate hoteliers and restaurateurs on legal problems and how they can be avoided. It covers the laws and regulations in labor relations, safety rules, and product liability as well as local, state, and federal regulations specifically related to the industry. The case method approach is used with the intent of training future managers to consider the legal aspects of their decisions.

600. Dickerson, Thomas A. *Travel Law.* New York: Law Journal Seminars-Press, 1981–. (Loose-leaf)

This is a legal loose-leaf service which is updated regularly to keep up with the changes in the law. It is aimed at the practicing lawyer and those with some legal knowledge. Each section begins with a brief discussion which is followed by extensive footnotes citing court cases, regulations, articles, and state laws. Areas covered include airlines, travel agents and tour operators, and travel consumer class actions. The appendices include the "Warsaw Convention," the "Montreal Convention," and several association readings.

601. *Employment Law in the 50 States: A Reference for Employers.* rev. ed. Washington, DC: CUE/NAM, 1987. 101 p.

Subtitled *A Reference for Employers,* this is a state-by-state presentation of the pertinent laws effecting employers in lay language. Legislation and court cases are presented in brief paragraphs. Fines and penalties are included. The overall headings for each state are General Employment-at-will Rule, Whistleblowers, Plant Closure, Employee Access to Personnel and Other Records, Polygraph Examinations and Alcohol and Drug Testing, Legislation Requiring Disclosure of Toxic Substances, and Other Significant State Laws.

Not all of these are of use to the foodservice industry, but enough are to make this a handy book.

602. Goodwin, John R. *Hotel Law: Principles and Cases.* Columbus, OH: Publishing Horizons, 1987. 693 p.

A college-level textbook, this examines the laws and regulations in the travel and hotel industries and emphasizes management principles that are necessary to comply with the laws. It is arranged by business topics in the industry. Topics covered include sales contracts, agents and contractors, employee relations, credit cards, business organization, ownership and management of property, duties and rights of innkeepers and guests, legal liability, reservations and check-in, guest's property and injuries, restaurant and bar law, travel agent law, and carrier law.

603. Goodwin, John R., and Rovelstad, James M. *Travel and Lodging Law: Principles, Statutes, and Cases.* Grid Series in Law. Columbus, OH: Grid Publishing, 1980. 456 p.

This college-level textbook combines the law on travel and hotels into one volume. Its purpose is to examine the historical evolution of laws in the hospitality industries and to show how principles of law are applied in the lodging and travel field. Chapters cover contracts, employee relations, commercial paper, types of organization, property, ownership, control and management of property, construction and mortgage financing, rights and duties of innkeepers, guest reservations and check-in, property and injury liability, travel agents, and restaurants.

604. Griffith, Clyde L. *The Legal Problem Solver for Foodservice Operators.* 3d rev. ed. Washington, DC: National Restaurant Association, 1983. (Loose-leaf)

A National Restaurant Association publication which covers basic legal information in nonlegal language on such topics as minimum wage, working hours, tips, overtime, hiring, record keeping, tax problems, and using the polygraph, among others. Supplements tabulate wage, hour, and child labor laws by state.

605. Hotel Law Publishing Service. *Hotel & Motel Laws.* Canoga Park, CA, 1977–. (Loose-leaf)

This is a legal loose-leaf service which covers federal and state statutes related to the operation of hotels and motels in the U.S. Administrative regulations and judicial opinions are cited but not reproduced in the set. Replacement and supplemental pages are regularly mailed to subscribers to keep the set current.

606. Jefferies, Jack P. *Understanding Hotel/Motel Law.* East Lansing, MI: Educational Institute of the American Hotel & Motel Association, 1983. 310 p.

This book deals in lay terms with basic legal principles that affect the lodging industry. Special emphasis is given to federal regulations including OSHA regulations and the National Labor Relations Act. The book covers the hotel guest and employees, laws relating to general operations, taxes, antitrust laws, franchises, convention, and group contracts. Appendices include a glossary of legal terms and illustrative cases.

607. Kalt, Nathan. *Legal Aspects of Hotel, Motel, and Restaurant Operation.* Hotel-Motel Management Series. New York: ITT Educational Services, 1971. 434 p.

This textbook is designed to introduce the legal issues and problems in the industry to students. It begins by defining terms and then covers hotel-guest relationship, duties of innkeepers to protect guests and their property, contracts, crimes against innkeepers, and forms of business organization.

608. *Legal and Business Problems of Hotels and Restaurants.* Seattle, WA: Washington State Bar Association, 1981. 350 p.

The material and forms in this book were prepared for a one-day seminar in Washington state on the practical application of law in Washington to the hotel and restaurant industries. The book is aimed at owners and operators and at the practicing attorney as well. It covers the rights of patrons, the rights of employees (including the right to organize), and regulatory activities of government bodies. It excludes information on acquiring or selling property and the negotiation and termination of franchises.

609. Miller, Jeffrey R. *Legal Aspects of Travel Agency Operation.* Wheaton, IL: Merton House Publishing Co., 1982. 192 p.
Designed as a general guide to the legal questions of the travel industry, this book covers the rights and obligations of the travel agent under the law. Chapters, which include case studies and keyword reviews, cover subjects such as insurance, contracts, advertising, employees, buying, selling, and closing a travel agency.

610. National Restaurant Association. *Familiarize Yourself with Basic Requirements of the Federal Minimum Wage Law.* rev. ed. Washington, DC, 1987. 4 p.
This four-page pamphlet summarizes the major requirements of the Minimum Wage Law for restaurateurs. It covers minimum wage, tips, exemption for management, student employment, uniforms, and required record keeping.

611. National Restaurant Association. *Food Product Information: An Historical Perspective for Foodservice.* National Restaurant Association Current Issues Report. Washington, DC, 1986. 15 p.
This booklet reviews the interest of consumers in food ingredients and nutrition information over the past twenty years. It looks at how aware consumers are and how they use labels. The study concludes that restaurateurs can anticipate increased concern from consumers about ingredients. The National Restaurant Association opposes mandatory ingredient labeling on restaurant food and advocates voluntary labeling. No solutions are outlined; the purpose of this report is to supply a historical perspective on the problem.

612. Service, J. Gregory. *Hotel-Motel Law: A Primer on Innkeeper Liability.* Springfield, IL: C. C. Thomas, 1983. 114 p.
In this brief book, the author considers the laws in which hotel and motel owners most frequently find themselves involved in lawsuits. It outlines the duties of innkeepers and potential liabilities so that hoteliers can eliminate or reduce the likelihood of occurrence. The text is written for nonlawyers and covers loss of guest property, foodservice liability, acts of employees, acts of third parties, security, and injuries.

613. Sherry, John E. H. *The Laws of Innkeepers: For Hotels, Motels, Restaurants, and Clubs.* rev. ed. Ithaca, NY: Cornell University Press, 1981. 674 p.
Sherry has updated this basic text, increasing the section on government regulations and their impact on the lodging business. "The text covers the applicable basic common-law principles throughout the United States and representative statutes and court decisions based on these principles." The book discusses responsibilities of innkeeper, liability for safety, government regulations, liability for guests' property, and rights and responsibilities of innkeepers.

614. Sherry, John E. H. *Legal Aspects of Foodservice Management.* A NIFI Textbook. Dubuque, IA: W. C. Brown Co., 1984. 334 p.
A law textbook for managers and students designed to explain legal subjects relevant to foodservice. Employee relations, food and beverage liability, government regulations, patron civil rights, contracts, and property rights are covered as are bankruptcy, court and out-of-court settlement, and choosing an attorney. Each chapter is clearly outlined.

615. Women's Legal Defense Fund, and Coalition of Labor Union Women, DC Chapter...,et al. *The Waitresses Handbook: A Guide to the Legal Rights of Waitresses and Other Restaurant Workers.* Washington, DC, 1986. 99 p.
This is a guide to legal rights of restaurant workers with special emphasis on women's rights. Chapters cover discrimination of all types, wages, tips and other money matters, health and safety, workers compensation, unemployment insurance, unionizing, filing a complaint, finding a lawyer, and where to get help.

616. Zwarensteyn, Hendrik. *Legal Aspects of Hotel Administration: Cases and Materials.* rev. ed. Revised by Milton B. Dickerson. East Lansing, MI: Department of Business Law, Insurance & Office Administration, College of Business, Michigan State University, 1975. 317 p.

This is a sourcebook of legal cases and materials intended for courses in hotel administration. Over 150 actual cases are presented in the nineteen chapters. They illustrate such legal issues as the innkeeper-guest relationship, the right to refuse and eject, the responsibility of the innkeeper for the safety of guests, liability for loss of property, and more. This 1975 edition has added cases decided since 1961 and includes a chapter on travel agents and their role in the hospitality industry.

Maintenance and Housekeeping Services

617. Axler, Bruce H. *Building Care for Hospitality Operations.* His Focus on...the Hospitality Industry. Indianapolis, IN: ITT Educational Publishing, 1974. 129 p.

This is another practical booklet in Axler's series. It covers cleaning equipment and procedures; floor care; wall and ceiling cleaning; special projects such as lamp shades and screens; sanitation; plumbing and electrical systems; and care of building exteriors.

618. Axler, Bruce H. *Room Care for Hotels and Motels.* His Focus on...the Hospitality Industry. Indianapolis, IN: ITT Educational Publishing, 1974. 122 p.

As other books in this series, this is a brief and practical overview to housekeeping services. Besides covering the techniques of cleaning a room—floor care, bathroom cleaning, and bedmaking—it also covers planning and organizing the work and stresses the importance of the maid, or roomkeeper, to effectively represent the hotel management to the guests.

619. Borsenik, Frank D. *Maintenance and Engineering for Lodging and Foodservice Facilities.* rev. ed. East Lansing, MI: Educational Institute of the American Hotel & Motel Association, 1977. 264 p.

The purpose of this book is to provide hotel and restaurant management personnel with the knowledge needed to work with engineers. Topics include blueprint reading, electrical systems and appliances, plumbing, swimming pools, heating systems, refrigeration, and ventilation systems, air conditioners, elevators and escalators, sound control, pollution, safety systems, and energy conservation.

620. Borsenik, Frank D. *The Management of Maintenance and Engineering Systems in Hospitality Industries.* 2d. ed. Wiley Service Management Series. New York: Wiley, 1987. 553 p.

A textbook for energy, maintenance, and engineering management, the book begins with management principles as they apply to this area of the industry. Basic terms and concepts as well as management techniques are covered for heating, refrigeration, ventilation, air conditioning, electricity, water, laundry, sound systems, and building transportation systems. Emphasis is on conservation, and the appendix gives a detailed outline for an energy reduction program. All sectors of the industry are covered: clubs, institutions, restaurants, and hotels. Only minimal mathematics skills are needed to understand the text. This second edition includes new chapters on life safety systems, foodservice equipment maintenance, and energy management.

621. Borsenik, Frank D. *Property Management.* East Lansing, MI: Educational Institute of the American Hotel & Motel Association, 1974. 208 p.
Property management is the term in the lodging industry that covers housekeeping, engineering, service, and food and beverage. This book is a text for training property managers. It includes chapters on planning, staffing, personnel assignments, and equipment replacement as well as basics on the role of the property manager, expenses, and long-term trends.

622. Branson, Joan Cameron, and Lennox, Margaret. *Hotel, Hostel and Hospital Housekeeping.* 4th ed. London: Edward Arnold, 1982. 310 p.
Written primarily for British students seeking TEC certificates and diplomas, this book covers the management of the executive housekeeping department in hotels and hospitals. It starts with the organization of the department and then covers the cleaning and servicing of fabrics, soft furnishings, floors, carpets, walls, bedding, and furniture. It also covers interior design, planning trends, and security.

623. Brigham, Grace H. *Housekeeping for Hotels, Motels, Hospitals, Clubs, Schools.* rev. ed. New York: Ahrens Publishing Co., 1962. 158 p.
This book covers the skills and responsibilities required of the housekeeping manager. The book covers the housekeeper's duties, employees, organization and management, purchasing and care of furnishings, and the principles of decoration.

624. Chase, Mildred L. *Administrative Housekeeping for Institutions.* rev. ed. Gallipolis, OH: National Executive Housekeepers Association, 1968. 122 p.
A guide for the training of directors of housekeeping. Short chapters arranged in outline form cover general basics such as business psychology and communications as they apply to housekeeping as well as more specific subjects such as training, procedure manuals, maintenance, and controls and sanitation. Examples of various job order specification forms, rating sheets, and equipment and maintenance records forms are included.

625. Chase, Mildred L. *The Theory of Institutional Housekeeping Management.* Kettering, OH: Kettering Medical Center Press, 1972. 115 p.
An overview of the relationship of housekeeping to the institutional setting. Covers the functions and responsibilities of housekeeping departments in hospital organizations. Management objectives and procedures are discussed. Includes a technical bibliography.

626. Fales, John T. *Functional Housekeeping in Hotels and Motels.* Hotel-Motel Management Series. Indianapolis, IN: Bobbs-Merrill Educational Publishing, 1971. 183 p.
This is a basic text on housekeeping for the lodging industry. Chapters cover the general theory of housekeeping, the selection of personnel, training, organizing, controlling, and scheduling as well as general operating procedures. There are chapters on equipment, floor and carpet care, linen service, and safety hazards.

627. Feldman, Edwin B. *Housekeeping Handbook for Institutions, Business & Industry.* rev. ed. New York: Frederick Fell Publishing, Inc., 1978. 502 p.
Feldman is a member of Service Engineering Associates, Inc., a firm of engineers specializing in custodial consulting. His book is designed to help analyze and organize all aspects of a housekeeping department. Part one, on management, discusses in detail the process of setting up a program to meet the needs of the particular institution. Part two is about implementing a program at the supervisory level. Part three covers specifics of operations such as equipment, chemicals, floor care, and graffiti control. Based on extensive consulting experience with many firms through the U.S. and Canada.

628. Hurst, Rosemary. *Housekeeping Management for Hotels and Residential Establishments.* rev. ed. London: Heinemann, 1980. 165 p.
With its companion volume *Services and Maintenance for Hotels and Residential Establishments,* this book is intended to meet certain British examination requirements of the Hotel Catering and Institutional Management Association. It does, however, stand on its

own as a good basic housekeeping guide to furniture, tableware and linen purchasing, and general cleaning.

629. Hurst, Rosemary. *Services and Maintenance for Hotels and Residential Establishments.* London: Heinemann, 1982. 144 p.

Along with its companion volume *Housekeeping Management for Hotels and Residential Establishments,* this book is intended for British students and meets examination requirements of the Hotel Catering and Institutional Management Association in that country. It does, however, provide good general grounding in various types of maintenance including lighting, plumbing, heating, ventilation, and insulation.

630. Kotschevar, Lendal Henry. *How to Select and Care for Serviceware, Textiles, Cleaning Compounds.* Chicago: Institutions Magazine, 1969. 201 p.

A book for the buyer who must have quick basic information on these types of purchases. Questions at the end of each paragraph help reinforce what is learned. The section on serviceware includes glassware, china, plastic, disposables, silver, and stainless. The section on textiles includes information on fabrics, sheets, towels, blankets, curtains, upholstery, carpets, and apparel. Cleaning compounds covers dishwashing, water, laundry, and floor cleaners. The secion on laundry and dry cleaning discusses the planning and operation of these facilities.

631. Martin, Robert J. *Professional Management of Housekeeping Operations.* New York: Wiley, 1986. 514 p.

This book is the textbook for the National Executive Housekeeper's Association's certification program. It includes background information and practical applications for opening, operating, and being accountable for housekeeping operations.

632. Nuerge, William. *Training Yourself to Efficiently Clean and Sanitize a Restroom.* Training Yourself Series, no. 2. Minneapolis, MN: Restaurant Hotel Aids, 1967. 64 p.

This is a simple step-by-step procedure for cleaning restrooms. Each step is illustrated, and key points are summarized periodically. The manual includes a list of the ten most often missed steps, a checklist of proper cleaning steps and a quiz.

633. Pfeiffer, William B., and Voegele, Walter O. *The Correct Maid for Hotels and Motels.* Illustrated by Paula Hoffman. Rochelle Park, NJ: Hayden Book Co., 1965. 64 p.

Designed as an instruction booklet to help maids understand their duties, this practical manual also emphasizes the importance of housekeeping services to the success of a hotel or motel. Chapters include responsibilities, room reports, and step-by-step procedures on cleaning a room.

634. Tucker, Georgina, and Schneider, Madelin Severson. *The Professional Housekeeper.* 2d ed. Boston: CBI Publishing Co., 1982. 451 p.

Intended as a resource and textbook for the professional housekeeper, this book covers all aspects of setting up and managing a housekeeping staff for hotels, motels, and institutions such as clubs and dormitories. Basic information about equipment and cleaning procedures are included as well as managerial subjects such as hiring, record keeping, purchasing, and control. Includes a glossary and an index.

635. Tucker, Gina. *The Science of Housekeeping.* 2d ed. Chicago: Institutions/Volume Feeding Magazine, 1973. 118 p.

Written by the director of housekeeping at Century Plaza Hotel, Los Angeles, this book provides recommendations for planning and staffing as well as a step-by-step guide to various housekeeping operations. Chapters cover planning a housekeeping department, staffing, cleaning of public areas, the linen room, and care of furnishings. There are also chapters on hiring, OSHA legislation, record keeping, uniforms, new products and services, and other subjects. Chapters include specifics on bedmaking, bathroom cleaning, and other standard housekeeping operations with illustrations.

Management

636. Albrecht, Karl, and Zemke, Ron. *Service America!: Doing Business in the New Economy.* Homewood, IL: Dow Jones-Irwin, 1985. 203 p.

Based on the premise that service is becoming ever more important in the American economy, the authors discuss key factors that govern service quality. Customer service is seen as a strategic business tool. Management personnel are told to think of their jobs as service positions too. Presents a new model for service management based on the authors' theories.

637. Axler, Bruce H. *Management of Hospitality Operations.* Hotel-Motel Management Series. Indianapolis, IN: Bobbs-Merrill, 1976. 351 p.

This is a management text for the operational manager. This type of manager is defined as having primary responsibility but not complete authority. In contrast to administrators and executive managers who formulate policy, the operational managers are concerned with implementation of policy directly and on a daily basis. Chapters include operational management, techniques and concepts of management, management of work and material, controls and profits, management of business activity, and guest relations.

638. Brymer, Robert A., ed. *Introduction to Hotel and Restaurant Management: A Book of Readings.* 4th ed. Dubuque, IA: Kendall/Hunt Publishing Co., 1984. 305 p.

A book of readings containing articles by various experts. In this edition, the majority of articles are written by hospitality educators rather than by executives out in the industry. The articles are grouped under the following headings: "Hospitality Industry," "Hospitality Corporations," "Hospitality Operations" (which includes management, marketing, cost control, property management, and service), and "Allied Fields" (which looks at tourism, clubs, theme parks, hospitals, and casinos). Taken as a whole, these forty-four articles cover most subjects found in the hospitality curricula.

639. Bullaro, John J., and Edginton, Christopher R. *Commercial Leisure Services: Managing for Profit, Service, and Personal Satisfaction.* New York: Macmillan, 1986. 364 p.

This is a text on the basic skills and knowledge necessary for the successful management of a commercial leisure service organization. It deals with marketing and managing as well as with theoretical and practical aspects. Chapters appear on starting a leisure service, financial management, accounting, organizing, marketing, commercial leisure service and the law, and the application of the computer.

640. Cassee, Ewout, ed., and Reuland, Rudolf, ed. *The Management of Hospitality.* International Series in Hospitality Management. Oxford: Pergamon Press, 1983. 219 p.

This is a collection of ten papers presented at the International Jubilee Conference on Management of Hospitality in October 1979, at the Hague, Netherlands. Titles include "External Influences on the Hospitality Industry," "Marketing in the Hospitality Industry," "Hotel Management Education," "Industrial Catering," "Management of Fast-Food Chains" and others.

641. Crawford, H. W., and McDowell, M. C. *Math Workbook—Food Service/Lodging.* 2d ed. Edited by Jule Wilkinson. Chicago: CBI Publishing Co. 1981. 247 p.
   This is a workbook to be used by students in hospitality career courses. It first reviews arithmetic including addition, subtraction, multiplication and division, fractions and ratios. Section two applies mathematical principles to problems in the foodservice industry for practical application. Sample applications include converting standard recipes and figuring inflation and menu pricing.

642. Friedman, Bill. *Casino Management.* rev. ed. Secaucus, NJ: L. Stuart, 1982. 542 p.
   This is an updated edition of the most thorough and widely used book on the gaming industry. It includes all financial aspects of the Nevada gaming industry plus a new section specifically on Atlantic City. One other new chapter covers sports books. The text covers casino organization, credit (including cage and rim credit, authorization, and collection), hotel marketing (including hosting, comps, junkets, entertainment, and value of various groups), accounting procedures (covering the operation of each game, responsibility of the personnel, and theft prevention systems), and government regulations.

643. Gullen, Harold V., and Rhodes, Geoffrey E. *Management in the Hotel and Catering Industry.* London: Batsford Academic and Educational, 1983. 146 p.
   This is an introductory text on management which will be especially useful for British students taking TEC qualification exams. Chapters cover management, objective setting, management by objective, planning, organization, coordination and communication, control, purchasing and materials management, work study, and decision making.

644. Heskett, James L. *Managing in the Service Economy.* Boston: Harvard Business School Press, 1986. 211 p.
   Presents Heskett's "Strategic Service Vision," a four-part guide for service managers. His steps involve targeting a market segment, conceptualizing customer reaction, developing an operating strategy, and designing efficient service delivery. Heskett also traces the development of the multinational service industries and discusses the future of the service economy.

645. Keiser, James. *Principles and Practice of Management in the Hospitality Industry.* Boston: CBI Publishing Co., 1979. 430 p.
   The author wrote this textbook specifically to meet the hospitality students' needs for a book with strong management theory and that dealt with the problems of law, labor relations, finance, and marketing in restaurants and hotels.

646. Keister, Douglas C., ed., and Wilson, Ralph D., ed. *Selected Readings for an Introduction to Hotel and Restaurant Management.* Berkeley, CA: McCutchan Publishing Corp., 1971. 446 p.
   A collection of forty-seven published articles representing an overview and cross-section of the field, this book is intended as a supplement to lecture courses on hotel and restaurant management and can be used as the basis of discussion. For this reason, various points of view are presented. Articles come from many of the important publications in the field as well as from some lesser known ones. Included are articles from *Forbes, Hotel and Motel Management, Hospitality, Volume Feeding Management, Cornell H.R.A. Quarterly,* and *Franchise Journal,* among others.

647. Khan, Mahmood A. *Foodservice Operations.* Westport, CT: AVI Publishing Co., 1987. 382 p.
   This is an introductory textbook to the systems for both commercial and institutional foodservice, appropriate for restaurant management, institutional management, and dietitian students. It is arranged using the system approach. Topics covered include menu

planning, facility design, equipment selection, purchasing and storage of food, sanitation, food preparation, and management of the system and personnel. Included are example forms and checklists for good service.

648. Kreck, Lothar A. *Operational Problem Solving for the Hotel and Restaurant Industry: The Pullman Method.* Boston: CBI Publishing Co., 1978. 167 p.
This book describes the Pullman method of management. Part one draws a sharp line between problem analysis and searching for solutions. Part two presents the ten actions of the Pullman Method: define outcome, describe the symptoms, verify the symptoms, are there any trends?, which critical areas?, critical principles, comparisons, solutions, testing, comparing. Part three presents an actual situation where the method is used and discusses problem prevention.

649. Kreck, Lothar A., ed., and McCracken, John W., ed. *Dimensions of Hospitality Management: An Industry Performance in Seven Acts, Volume 1.* Boston: Cahners Books, 1975. 351 p.
The first of a two-volume set on management in the hospitality industry. The table of contents is set up like a play bill: Act I is "Corporate Administration"; Act II is "Management," and Act III is "The Employees." In each act articles appear by various experts on new developments in the field. The intent is to be thought provoking and entertaining.

650. Kreck, Lothar A., ed., and McCracken, John W., ed. *Dimensions of Hospitality Management: An Industry Performance in Seven Acts, Volume 2.* Boston: Cahners Books, 1975. 460 p.
Whimsically arranged in seven acts like a play, these two volumes include articles by various experts on different aspects of hospitality management. This volume includes Act IV, "Operations," which covers finance, accounting, and data processing; marketing and public relations; and safety and security. Act V, "The Physical Setting," is divided into design and maintenance. Act VI, "Guests," covers consumerism and law. Act VII, "Environs," deals with research and development, convenience foods, franchises, and tourism.

651. Lane, Harold E., and Van Hartesvelt, Mark. *Essentials of Hospitality Administration.* Reston, VA: Reston Publishing Co., 1983. 386 p.
This book is intended as a core text in hospitality administration. Chapters cover markets, economics, and growth potential of the industry; basic concepts and theory of management; labor relations; architecture; important elements of pre-opening management; feasibility studies; energy conservation; pricing and analyzing profitability; trends and feasibility analysis; and strategic planning.

652. Lasher, Willard K. *The Banquet Chairman's Manual; Planning that Brings Applause and Merits Praise.* Chicago: American Technical Society, 1962. 68 p.
This is a simple, basic manual for the novice banquet chairman. It has chapters on planning the banquet, where to hold it, the agenda, table arrangements, selling the local affair, and national and district sales meetings. The author is often entertaining and points out clearly the various pitfalls the nonexpert may encounter.

653. Lewis, Robert, et al., eds. *The Practice of Hospitality Management II: Profitability in a Changing Environment.* Westport, CT: AVI Publishing Co., 1984. 554 p.
A collection of fifty essays from the World Hospitality Congress II. "Profitability in a Changing Environment" was the theme of the congress. Essays include the following topics: search for quality, growth and development of the industry, operations management, applications of emerging technologies, developing human resources, food and beverage management, marketing management, analyzing market opportunities, segmentation marketing, profiling, and analyzing the consumer.

654. Lundberg, Donald E. *The Hotel and Restaurant Business.* 4th ed. New York: Van Nostrand Reinhold Co., 1984. 352 p.
Lundberg gives a history of the industry and a look at the scope and variety of technology, skill, and temperament that can be put to use in hotel and restaurant management. Included are chapters on the early inn, the developing hotels and motels, finances and building operations, food and beverage operations in hotels and restaurants, kitchen, fast food, franchising, and private clubs. Biographical sketches of industry leaders are contained in each chapter. Topics added to this edition include computerization, video conference, and timesharing.

655. Pizam, A.; Lewis, R. C.; and Manning, P., eds. *The Practice of Hospitality Management.* Westport, CT: AVI Publishing Co., 1982. 530 p.
This is a collection of articles presented at The World Hospitality Congress—Hospitality Management held March 9–12, 1981 in Boston. Fifty-one articles appear in seven categories: "The Economic Contribution of the Hospitality Industry," "Strategic Planning," "Financial Aspects," "Operations Management," "Human Resources," "Marketing," and "The Hospitality Tomorrow."

656. Powers, Thomas F. *Introduction to Management in the Hospitality Industry.* 3d ed. Wiley Service Management Series. New York: Wiley, 1988. 591 p.
This introductory text for hospitality management programs offers an overview and detailed look at some of the major segments of the hospitality industry. Chapters cover restaurants, institutional and school foodservices, hotels and motels, and some of the new emerging operations such as campgrounds and play environments including theme parks. Other chapters give basic management concepts for the industry. Planning, organizing, staffing, controlling, and leading or directing are each given a chapter. The final chapter looks at the future of the industry. This edition is a thorough revision and includes new chapters on lodging, tourism, and franchising.

657. Sapienza, Dunnovan L.; Abbey, James R.; and Vallen, Jerome J., eds. *Readings on Managing Hotels/Restaurants/Institutions.* Ahrens Series. Rochelle Park, NJ: Hayden Book Co., 1977. 394 p.
Drawing upon the writings from the business, accounting, psychology, and sociology fields, this book pulls together current and historical material that reflects the rudiments and concerns of foodservice and lodging management.

658. Schmidt, Arno. *The Banquet Business.* Boston: CBI Publishing Co., 1981. 282 p.
Written for hotels, clubs, and other foodservice operations that serve banquets, this book offers advice on how to sell banquets. The premise of the author is that fun, informal elegance and value in food are necessary to a successful banquet instead of formal dinners and speakers. Topics covered include planning the meal, writing menus, working with the chef, kitchen layout, and beverage sale. Sample form letters are included.

659. Vallen, Jerome J.; Abbey, James R.; and Sapienza, Dunnovan L. *The Art and Science of Managing Hotels/Restaurants/Institutions.* Ahrens Series. Rochelle Park, NJ: Hayden Book Co., 1978. 275 p.
This textbook presents an overview of management principles applied to hotels, restaurants, and institutions. Chapters cover communications, accounting, human relations, personnel administration, marketing and sales promotions, and future of the industry. A companion volume entitled *Readings on Managing Hotels/Restaurants/Institutions* (Sapienza, Abbey, Vallen) provides additional background readings and is designed to accompany this book. Formerly entitled *The Art and Science of Modern Innkeeping.*

660. Voss, Christopher, et al. *Operations Management in Service Industries and the Public Sector: Text and Cases.* Chichester, England: Wiley, 1985. 318 p.
This is primarily a casebook on the use of operations management and production principles in service fields. Written in Great Britain, it is intended for graduate classes in management. There are some substantial differences between English and American

service fields, especially in the public sector. Chapters cover design of service operations, human resource management, capacity management, operations control, quality management, field service management, queueing systems design, material management, site location, and operation strategy.

661. Wyckoff, D. Daryl, and Sasser, W. Earl. *U.S. Lodging Industry.* Lexington Casebook Series in Industry Analysis. Lexington, MA: Lexington Books, 1981. 255 p.

Part of a series in which each book focuses on a selected industry, this book presents case studies of real situations and decisions of various firms such as Hyatt Regency Cambridge and Universal Inns, Inc. The authors refer to their approach as situational analysis because the situation is given but not the outcome. Originally intended as texts for teaching industrial analysis, these cases are designed to make the readers think about these actual industry situations and reach their own conclusions.

CLUBS

662. Barbour, Henry Ogden. *Private Club Administration.* Washington, DC: Club Managers Association of America, 1968. 630 p.

This book joins modern management techniques with private club principles and philosophies. Early chapters cover club charters, bylaws and boards of directors. Later chapters discuss club financing and the effective administrative use of committees. Appendices give examples of charters, bylaws, rules for various facilities, and membership forms as well as profiles, job descriptions, and contract examples for club managers and major staff positions.

663. Club Managers Association of America. *Club Management Operations.* Dubuque, IA: Kendall/Hunt Publishing Co., 1980. 292 p.

This text is designed to improve the efficiency of club management. Chapters are written by experienced club managers and other experts. Aimed primarily at beginners in the field, it covers cost controls, housekeeping (both interior and exterior) financing, communications and public relations, recreation and sports program management, insurance, security, taxes, and regulations, as well as gives an overview of how and why private clubs operate.

664. White, Ted E. *Club Operations and Management.* Boston: CBI Publishing Co., 1979. 253 p.

This text is intended to introduce the student or new club manager to the details of club management. The author presents a look at the major aspects of the field and gives insights into problem areas. Topics covered include history, physical organization of the club, personnel management, operating club departments, accounting and cost control, advertising, and entertainment.

HOTELS

665. American Hotel & Motel Association. *The Hubbart Formula for Evaluating Rate Structures of Hotel Rooms.* New York, 1952. 11 p.

The "Hubbart Formula" was developed in the late 1940s as a standard for computing hotel rates. As outlined in this pamphlet, it can be used for transient, residential, or resort hotels.

666. Arnold, David E., et al. *Hotel/Motel Development.* Washington, DC: Urban Land Institute, 1984. 212 p.

A discussion of current aspects and development in the hospitality industry, this book begins with an overview from World War II onward and continues with a wealth of statistics and financial data as it discusses all major aspects of development. Chapters cover history, markets, the development process, financing, and trends in hotel development. Case studies are included in the end.

667. Beavis, J. R. S.; Medlik, S.; and Pullen, R. A. *A Manual of Hotel Reception.* 3d ed. London: Heinemann, 1981. 257 p.

The authors view the hotel reception office as the main sales outlet of the hotel and a central communication link to all other departments. The text is intended primarily for students seeking degrees and diplomas in Great Britain. Topics covered include records, advance bookings, visitor accounts, cash and banking, computerized and mechanized billings, communication, and statistics.

668. Dix, Colin. *Accommodation Operations: Front Office.* 2d ed. The M&E Hotel, Catering, and Tourism Series, 0265–3109. Estover, Plymouth, England: Macdonald and Evans, 1984. 166 p.

This British publication is part of the M & E Hotel, Catering, and Tourism Series. It is aimed at meeting the needs of students studying for BTEC and HCIMA examinations, but it can also serve as a reference source. Chapters cover all aspects of front office work, from reservations, registration and billing to methods of payment, tours, booking methods, and statistics and report preparation. There are also chapters on selling and computers in the front office.

669. Dukas, Peter. *Hotel Front Office Management and Operation.* 3d ed. Dubuque, IA: W. C. Brown Co., 1970. 174 p.

This is a text of front office procedures which includes an introduction to the lodging industry. Accounting and quantitative analysis are also included. Topics covered include procedures used to serve guests, salesmanship, registration procedures, procedures for unusual events, credit, records of food, accounting records for charges, the transcript, financial statements, and quantitative analysis.

670. Educational Institute of the American Hotel & Motel Association. *Relieving Reservation Headaches.* East Lansing, MI, 1979. 30 p.

A practical guide to efficient reservation procedures. Chapters cover community research (about knowing your local profile, guest history, and markets), reservation process, procedures for handling guaranteed reservations, understays and overstays, needs of special groups, forecasting, handling walk-in guests, and a conclusion including the American Hotel & Motel Association's "Guest Reservation Pledge." There is also a glossary of reservation terms.

671. Eyster, James J. *The Negotiation and Administration of Hotel Management Contracts.* 2d ed. Ithaca, NY: School of Hotel Administration, Cornell University, 1980. 209 p.

The author discusses owner/operator management contracts used by most hotel chains. Approaching from the point of view of business objectives rather than primarily from legal considerations, Eyster concentrates on the concerns and problem areas of these contracts. Sections cover concerns both during negotiations and during the term of the contract and preparing for successful negotiations. Appendices include "Description of Management-Contract Provisions," "Factors Influencing the Adoption of Management Contracts," and "Reference Tables."

672. Gray, William S., and Liguori, Salvatore C. *Hotel and Motel Management and Operations.* Englewood Cliffs, NJ: Prentice-Hall, 1980. 360 p.

This is a basic introductory overview text of the lodging industry. Sections cover history and development of the field, types of hotels, operations structures, staff organization, basic operations and departments, accounting and controls, and the future trends of the industry for the beginning students.

673. Gunnar, Peter M., and Burkhart, Judith A. *The Management of Hotel and Motel Condominiums.* Ithaca, NY: School of Hotel Administration, Cornell University, 1978. 275 p.

A condominium hotel is one that is owned by condominium owners but intended to operate as a hotel or motel. This arrangement makes management even more difficult. Assuming the reader has training or experience in conventional hotel management, the authors address taxation, insurance, the role of the condominium owners' association, regulations, management contracts, operations, marketing, and accounting.

674. Haszonics, Joseph J. *Front Office Operation.* Hotel-Motel Management Series. Indianapolis, IN: Bobbs-Merrill Educational Publishing, 1971. 182 p.

This is a text about the basics and principles of front office procedure. Much of what is given on equipment such as the NCR 42 and 52 is less useful in the computer age, but the chapters on guest relations, rooming procedures, and other basics are still effective.

675. Hotton, Georgia. *Introduction to Resort Management.* Illustrated by M. Oliver. Chicago: Nelson-Hall, 1982. 201 p.

This is a good basic introduction to resort management. Part one covers the nature of the resort business. Part two discusses accounting, public relations, and marketing as the three basic skills necessary for success. Part three is called "Quality Service and Quality Leadership." Part four is about planning for operations and growth. Part five deals with legal and ethical obligations, operating details, and the overall appeal and challenge of resort management.

676. Jones, Christine, and Paul, Val. *Accommodation Management: A Systems Approach.* London: Batsford Academic and Educational, 1985. 270 p.

This practical British textbook applies the system approach to housekeeping, maintenance, and reception (front office) management. All types of accommodations are covered: hotels, hospitals, public buildings, schools, industries. It covers the building, housekeeping services, personnel control, purchasing and supplies, and the front office.

677. Kalt, Nathan. *Introduction to the Hospitality Industry.* Hotel-Motel Management Series. Indianapolis, IN: Bobbs-Merrill Educational Publishing, 1971. 158 p.

This introductory textbook covers the operations of the various departments and their relationships to each other in a hotel or motel. Chapters cover the history and future of hospitality, an overview of the motel industry and hotel management, and information on each department, front of the house, accounting, food and beverage, sales and promotion, engineering, and personnel.

678. Kasavana, Michael L. *Effective Front Office Operations.* New York: Van Nostrand Reinhold Co., 1981. 308 p.

Covering principles, operations, and procedures of the hotel front office, this textbook begins with an overview of the industry and an introduction to the guest cycle. This is followed by chapters on each department and its function: reservations, registration, room status, guest accounting, and checkout. Equipment and information systems are also covered. Each chapter begins with objectives and ends with a list of key concepts and discussion questions. A glossary is also included.

679. Lattin, Gerald W.; Warfel, Marshall C.; and Lattin, Thomas W. *Modern Hotel and Motel Management.* 3d ed. San Francisco, CA: W. H. Freeman, 1977. 289 p.

An introductory text that covers the history and future trends of the hospitality industry as well as the basics of hotel operations including: food, beverage, personnel, and sales. An appendix lists colleges with hotel administration majors and junior and technical colleges with hotel industry training courses.

680. Medlik, S. *The Business of Hotels.* London: Heinemann, 1980. 176 p.
Published in England, this is a comprehensive book on hotels written by an experienced manager, teacher, and consultant. Part one includes an introduction to hotels, products, markets, policies, and strategies. Part two has chapters on accommodations, food and drink, and services such as telephones and concessions. Part three discusses hotel organization, staffing, and productivity. Part four covers marketing, ownership, and management. Part five includes information on the small hotel, hotel groups, and international hotel operations.

681. Paananen, Donna. *Selling Out: A How-to Manual on Reservations Management.* East Lansing, MI: Educational Institute of the American Hotel & Motel Association, 1985. 43 p.
This is a manual on hotel and motel reservations management. Part one gives the basic details of the reservation process, including guaranteed reservation information, changes and cancellations, front desk relations, and various types of reservation difficulties. Part two gives facts, figures, and suggestions on the effective use of forecasting and reservations to avoid over-booking while still managing to maximize sales, even to the point of "selling out" whenever possible.

682. Paige, Grace, and Paige, Jane. *The Hotel Receptionist.* 2d ed. London: Holt, Rinehart and Winston, 1984. 210 p.
This British publication is intended for students studying for City and Guild Hotel Reception Examinations and other British certificates. As a textbook, it covers all aspects of front office training. It includes social skills, reception tasks, selling, bookkeeping, business practice, and other elements of hotel work related to the receptionist job.

683. Podd, George O., and Lesure, John D. *Planning and Operating Motels and Motor Hotels.* New York: Ahrens Book Co., 1964. 343 p.
This is an introduction to the motel business. It discusses the development of the field and the process of getting started. It includes chapters on such subjects as site selection, facilities, personnel, advertising, and accounting.

684. Renner, Peter Franz. *Basic Hotel Front Office Procedures.* Boston: CBI Publishing Co., 1981. 256 p.
This is a book on the specific tasks of the front office clerk. Chapters cover all aspects and technical skills step by step including organization of a hotel and the front office, front office equipment, communication skills, reservation and rooming procedures, accounting, credit, and computer systems.

685. Rosenzweig, Stan. *Hotel/Motel Telephone Systems: Opportunities Through Deregulation.* East Lansing, MI: Educational Institute of the American Hotel & Motel Association, 1982. 138 p.
This is a manual designed to facilitate setting up an effective telecommunications system. It also analyzes various call rating systems and alternative telephone systems. Chapters discuss all subjects relevant to motel/hotel phone systems including consultants, how to buy phones, your own phone system, and satellite communications. It is aimed mostly at the large chains.

686. Schmidt, Arno. *Food and Beverage Management in Hotels.* New York: Van Nostrand Reinhold Co., 1987. 230 p.
This book emphasizes what is different about food and beverage service and management in hotels as opposed to restaurants and other foodservice businesses. Chapters cover such areas as room service and catering as well as dining room service and various aspects of personnel and management.

687. Scholz, William. *Profitable Hotel/Motel Management.* Englewood Cliffs, NJ: Prentice-Hall, 1975. 206 p.
> Written by the previous director of marketing and public relations for the American Hotel & Motel Association, this book emphasizes practical techniques for maximizing profits. The chapters give experience-proven advice on most aspects of the hotel industry. Many of the ideas in the book are presented in checklist or outline form.

688. Steadmon, Charles E. *Managing Front Office Operations.* East Lansing, MI: Educational Institute of the American Hotel & Motel Association, 1985. 267 p.
> This book gives guidelines, procedures, and methods of front office operations. It includes a discussion of the organization and mission of hotels as well as specific front office tasks such a reservations, guest accounting, night audit, front office management, registration, complaints, and security.

689. Taylor, Derek. *Sales Management for Hotels.* New York: Van Nostrand Reinhold Co., 1987. 164 p.
> This is a text for executives and students explaining the role of the sales manager and the importance of sales management. Chapters cover sales management, selection and recruiting, sales training, supervision and building a sales team, relations with superiors, internal and external public relations, and advertising.

690. Taylor, Derek, and Thomason, Richard. *Profitable Hotel Reception.* International Series in Hospitality Management. New York: Pergamon Press, 1982. 225 p.
> This is a British publication that sees the reception department, or the front office, as the most important department of a hotel. The author discusses how to increase profits by turning this department into a sales department. Chapters include booking the hotel, sales promotion, management, accounts, and computerization.

691. Vallen, Jerome J. *Check In—Check Out: Principles of Effective Front Office Management.* 3d ed. Dubuque, IA: W. C. Brown Co., 1985. 432 p.
> This basic text for hotel administration classes covers all aspects of running the front desk. The structure of the front office is fully explained, as are reservations, registration, and room assignment. Attention is given to the financial side with chapters on charges, credit, billing, and night audits. A full discussion of the use of the American Plan is included. A bibliography and glossary are included.

692. Venison, Peter. *Managing Hotels.* London: Heinemann, 1983. 140 p.
> Venison, a successful British hotelier, feels that hotel managers need to come out of their offices and work out front, meeting their guests and working directly with employees. Only then can they understand the needs of their guests. He also encourages hoteliers to frequent competitive hotels as guests to better be able to manage their hotels with a guest-centered philosophy.

693. White, Paul B., and Beckley, Helen. *Hotel Reception.* 4th ed. London: Edward Arnold, 1982. 195 p.
> This is a British publication intended as a textbook on hotel reception. It covers the basics including tasks and techniques as well as security, bookkeeping, and other related aspects of the lodging industry.

694. Witzky, Herbert K. *Modern Hotel-Motel Management Methods.* rev. 2d ed. Ahrens Series. Rochelle Park, NJ: Hayden Book Co., 1976. 275 p.
> Unlike many other hotel management texts, this one starts with a section on communication, both written and oral. This is followed by a section on industrial relations, which covers managerial and cost controls, and information on executive methods and controls, executive compensation, business promotion, and executive development.

MEETINGS AND CONVENTIONS

695. Astroff, Milton T., and Abbey, James R. *Convention Sales and Services.* Dubuque, IA: W. C. Brown Co., 1978. 448 p.
> This book is intended as a guide and primer covering all parts of the convention business. Part one, on convention sales, helps the reader analyze and define the convention market for a particular facility. It also gives advice on selling to various markets and negotiating contracts. Part two, on convention services, covers the requirements for making a convention successful and for gaining repeat business. Chapters on guest rooms, food, exhibits, and meeting rooms are among those included. There is also a chapter on convention billing and post-convention review.

696. Berkman, Frank W.; Dorf, David C.; and Oakes, Leonard R. *Convention Management & Service.* East Lansing, MI: Educational Institute of the American Hotel & Motel Association, 1978. 230 p.
> This book is designed to present related areas of convention servicing and management together for use by those in the field. It includes information on convention management, corporate meetings, exhibitions and trade shows, geographic considerations, purchasing from both the buyer's and the seller's viewpoint, customer service, rebooking or referral, and convention servicing.

697. Hanlon, Al. *Trade Shows in the Marketing Mix: Where They Fit and How to Make Them Pay Off.* rev. ed. Shrewsbury, MA: Wordsworth Publishers, 1982. 248 p.
> This book is intended to show how proper use of the trade show exhibit can be a valuable marketing technique. The author, who is an experienced salesman, exhibitor, and company president, presents the thesis that trade shows are for developing new business and advance sales and actually reducing the cost of selling. The following subjects are included among others in the twenty chapters selecting the right show, exhibit concept and design, booking sales at the show, and evaluating trade show investment.

698. Kreul, Lee M.; Lohr, Judi; and Ellis, Raymond C., Jr. *Meeting Planners Facilities and Services: Results of a Survey by the Research Committee, American Hotel and Motel Association.* New York: American Hotel & Motel Association, 1985. 51 p.
> Details the results of a survey based on questionnaires sent to members of the National Association of Exposition Managers (NAEM) in January 1984. Preferences for various services and facilities are tabulated. Copy of the questionnaire is included.

699. McGee, Regina M., and the Convention Liaison Council Editorial Committee. *The Convention Liaison Council Manual: A Working Guide for Successful Conventions.* 4th ed. Alexandria, VA: Convention Liaison Council, 1985. 107 p.
> The manual is a working guide to the managing of a successful convention. Though it is aimed primarily at association meeting planners, it would be useful for anyone connected with the convention business. Chapters cover every aspect of planning and managing a convention from site selection and transportation to food and beverage, gratuities, and postmeeting evaluations.

NONCOMMERCIAL FOODSERVICE INSTITUTIONS

700. American Society for Hospital Food Service Administrators. *Hospital Food Service Management Review.* Chicago, 1980. 72 p.
> A checklist of operational statements designed as a comprehensive review of administrative practices. "NO" answers will identify deficiencies in various areas of management. "ASSIGNED TO" and "TARGET DATE" columns facilitate its use as a management tool for setting short and long-term goals for improvement. Chapters cover planning, budgeting

and financial analysis, departmental administration, total systems management, safety and sanitation control, personnel management, and clinical dietetics administration.

701. Buchanan, Polly W. *Quantity Food Preparation: Standardizing Recipes and Controlling Ingredients.* Chicago: American Dietetic Association, 1983. 33 p.
Written as a basic reference on recipe standardization for students studying production control techniques, this book is also useful to professionals who are now implementing controls. Specific information on starting an ingredients room and computer-assisted food production is included in this edition, which is a revision of *Standardizing Recipes for Institutional Use* (Pearl J. Aldrich and Grace A. Miller, 1967).

702. Carlin, Joseph M. *A Food Service Guide to Nutrition Programs for the Elderly.* s.l.: s.n., 1975. 64 p.
This is a manual for foodservice workers with the National Nutrition Programs for the Elderly (Title VII). Sections cover standards, procedures, recipes, menu cycles, portion control, sanitation, safety, and related subjects.

703. Casola, Matteo. *Successful Mass Catering and Volume Feeding.* s.l.: Continental Publications, 1980. 382 p.
This basic text for professional foodservices is a revised edition of *Successful Mass Cookery and Volume Feeding* (1969). Part one covers basic functions such as kitchen management, menu planning, food buying, and merchandising. It also includes a detailed chapter of job descriptions for various members of the kitchen staff. Part two gives basic cooking principles and recipes for all menu categories. Glossary, charts, and conversion tables are provided.

704. Caton, Jay, and Nix, Mary. *I Can Manage: A Practical Approach to School Foodservice Management.* New York: Van Nostrand Reinhold Co., 1986. 131 p.
Management skills for those who operate local school foodservice programs are interspersed with biographical chapters about "Miss Jessie," a pioneer school foodservice manager in Tennessee. Management image, time management, job analysis, staffing, and menu planning are discussed at a very basic level.

705. Cloyd, Frances, ed. *Guide to Foodservice Management.* Chicago: Institutions/Volume Feeding Magazine, 1972. 184 p.
A collection of twenty-four articles and essays by members of the NACUFS (National Association of College and University Food Services) intended as a resource book for foodservice administrators of universities. Essays discuss various aspects including management training and effectiveness, the use of computers, efficiency, sanitation, and public relations. The "Monotony Breakers for Foodservice" provides a menu rotation plan and special suggestions from eleven different regions. Ideas for party and holiday dinners are also included. A bibliography is also included.

706. Cronan, Marion Louise. *The School Lunch.* Peoria, IL: C. A. Bennett, 1962. 512 p.
Cronan's textbook covers all phases of the school lunchroom operation: policies, personnel, nutrition, menu planning, purchasing, food production, records, equipment, sanitation, and safety. The roles of administration, director, manager, teacher, and cook are defined. Nearly half the book is recipes appropriate for schools; most are in serving portions for fifty.

707. Crusius, Vera Claussen. *Quantity Food Management: Principles and Applications.* Minneapolis, MN: Burgess Publishing Co., 1981. 186 p.
This is an overview in concise form, usable as a supplement for classes or as a review. Designed as a lab manual for food management and based on the second edition of *Handbook on Quantity Food Management* (E. E. Smith and V. C. Crusius), it includes a plan for organizing and managing a laboratory in quantity food preparation. The fourteen chapters give basics on such subjects as sanitation, equipment, menu planning, preparation, task organization, merchandising, purchasing, personnel, and cost control.

708. Dow, Clista. *Lunchroom Waste: A Study of "How Much and How Come."* The Triad Prototype Series. Mansfield Center, CT: Creative Learning Press, 1978. 39 p.
This brief booklet describes a curricular unit used with gifted and talented students in the fifth grade over several months. The students investigated why students at their intermediate school wasted food. Their conclusion was that the current laws governing school lunch programs are the problems because students would prefer to select the foods they would eat rather than being given a balanced meal.

709. Eckel, Peter J., Jr. *College & University Foodservice Management Standards.* The L. J. Minor Foodservice Standards Series, vol. 6. Westport, CT: AVI Publishing Co., 1985. 175 p.
This book is about managing foodservices in colleges and universities through the use of standards. Topics covered are public relations (to attract and keep students in residence halls), menu planning, purchasing, accounting, budgeting, theft, sanitation, and vending machine operation.

710. Fairbrook, Paul, and Milano, John. *College & University Food Service Manual.* Stockton, CA: Colman Publishers, 1979. 438 p.
This manual is intended as a guide and reference tool for managers and supervisors of college and university foodservices. Chapters include guidance in planning and organizing, purchasing, budgets, internal controls, personnel, residence halls, and cash operations as well as vending, catering, special events, and public relations. There are also helpful chapters on relations with students and faculty as well as building your image on campus. Appendices include a wealth of information and suggestions including menu and newsletter examples.

711. Fredrick, Len. *Fast Food Gets an "A" in School Lunch.* Boston: Cahners Books International, 1977. 245 p.
Following the philosophy "If you can't lick 'em, join 'em," this book shows how school foodservice managers can serve a Type A school lunch that appeals to students by serving milk shakes, hamburgers, ham and cheese sandwiches, etc. This book is a step-by-step guide and the story of how student participation was greatly increased by using this approach.

712. Gardner, Jerry G. *Contract Foodservice/Vending.* Edited by Jule Wilkinson. Chicago: Institutions/Volume Feeding Magazine, 1973. 157 p.
This book considers the problems and difficulties of company-operated cafeterias and examines the alternatives of hiring an outside contractor or installing vending machines. Chapters also cover planning the cafeteria menu, appropriate selling prices of food, understanding a contractor's profit and loss statement, type of contractor arrangements, kinds of vending services available, and the history of independent contractors and the trend of vending in plants.

713. Holmberg, Rita. *Meal Management Today.* Belmont, CA: Wadsworth Publishing Co., 1983. 394 p.
This text gives the basics of meal management. It emphasizes cost and energy control and also includes general purchasing guidelines for major food groups. It is intended for use in home economics courses as well as foodservice courses.

714. Jernigan, Anna Katherine; Dennler, Louise; and McHenry, Roberta. *Food Service Management: Study Course.* Ames, IA: Iowa State University Press, 1977. 109 p.
This is a self-study textbook designed to be used with guidance from a dietary consultant. It covers the organization, procedures, and planning of menus for foodservice in a hospital or nursing home. Topics include ordering, receiving and storing food, keeping records, and employee supervision and training.

715. Kahrl, William L. *Foodservice on a Budget for Schools, Senior Citizens, Colleges, Nursing Homes, Hospitals, Industrial, Correctional Institutions.* Edited by Jule Wilkinson. Boston: Institutions/Volume Feeding Magazine, 1974. 198 p.
Kahrl discusses the problems of running noncommercial foodservices economically and efficiently. Part one covers problems common to all facilities such as control, design, productivity, and operating systems. Part two deals with seven segments of the field individually including schools, elderly and poor, colleges, hospitals, nursing homes, industrial, and correctional institutions.

716. Kaud, Faisal A.; Miller, R. Paul; and Underwood, Robert F. *Cafeteria Management for Hospitals.* Chicago: American Hospital Association, 1982. 152 p.
This book deals with hospital foodservice for the nonpatient. It outlines how to operate a cafeteria to provide customer satisfaction and employee productivity and yet meet the institutions' financial objectives. The book is divided into two broad categories: "Management Functions," which covers menu planning and pricing, food cost, scheduling labor, productivity, cash controls, vending machines, and merchandising; and "Audit and Marketing Techniques," which covers market surveys, cash register sales analysis, food cost analysis, product movement study, transaction analysis, and other accounting-management strategies.

717. Kotschevar, Lendal Henry. *Foodservice for the Extended Care Facility.* Edited by Jule Wilkinson. Chicago: Institutions/Volume Feeding Magazine, 1973. 509 p.
This book is intended as a basic text in foodservice with emphasis on the special needs of health care facilities and nursing homes. Chapters include health care and the extended care facility, personnel management, foodservice controls, nutrition and menu planning, food production, purchasing, sanitation and safety, layout and equipment.

718. Mahaffey, Mary J.; Mennes, Mary E.; and Miller, Bonnie B. *Food Service Manual for Health Care Institutions.* Chicago: American Hospital Association, 1981. 381 p.
This is a revision of the *Hospital Food Service Manual* first published in 1954. It is designed especially for smaller hospitals. This edition has been completely rewritten and includes current information on state and federal agency requirements. The chapters cover organization and management, personnel management, food production and service systems, food protection, financial management, menu planning, food procurement and selection, quality assurance, food production processes, and equipment design.

719. Miller, Edmund, ed. *Profitable Cafeteria Operation.* New York: Ahrens Book Co., 1966. 340 p.
This is a collection of twenty articles by various authorities on all facets of cafeteria operation. Articles appear on managing, training, menu planning, purchasing, and equipment. There are also articles on school lunchrooms, hospitals, and in-plant cafeterias. Promotion, safety, control, and some aspects of facility design are included. The book is edited by partners of Harris, Kerr, Forster, and Co. who also edited *Profitable Food and Beverage Operation.*

720. Powers, Jo Marie. *Basics of Quantity Food Production.* Wiley Service Management Series. New York: Wiley, 1979. 514 p.
This is an introductory text on quantity foodservice. Section one covers both production planning and raw food costing. Section two deals with preparation including meat cookery and various kitchen stations such as sandwich, breakfast, vegetable, and salad stations. There are also chapters on preparation problems and service. Section three includes sanitation as well as the preparation of manufactured and convenience foods and special dietary needs.

721. Rose, James C., ed. *Handbook for Health Care Food Service Management.* Rockville, MD: Aspen Systems Corp., 1984. 369 p.

Containing chapters by thirty-nine different specialists in health care foodservice management, this is a comprehensive work which examines issues of the industry. Part one covers overall issues such as organization, facility design, budgeting, and selection and training. Part two deals with specifics such as menu planning, scheduling, equipment, and production controls. Part three addresses subjects such as diet order transmittal systems, outpatient and community nutrition services, and the like. The book assumes basic knowledge of foodservice management.

722. Smith, E. Evelyn, and Crusius, Vera Claussen. *A Handbook on Quantity Food Management.* 2d ed. Illustrated by John A. Cole. Minneapolis, MN: Burgess Publishing Co., 1970. 191 p.

A lab manual for quantity cooking classes, chapters cover organization and planning, standardization of recipes and portions, waste and cost control, modern food units, work simplification, personnel, sanitation, accident prevention, merchandising, and service of food. An appendix gives suggestions for the organization of a quantity cookery laboratory course, suggested studies, bibliographies and short lists of journal articles and visual aids.

723. Stokes, John Wesley. *Food Service in Industry and Institutions.* 2d ed. Dubuque, IA: W. C. Brown Co., 1973. 260 p.

This is a text covering foodservice in hospitals, schools, colleges, and industrial plants. It includes a basic overview, objectives and policies, management, organization, and supervision as well as the specifics of purchasing, menu planning, preparation, sanitation, cost control, and merchandising. There are chapters on statements, reports, and budgets as well as on laws and regulations. Photographs of equipment and floor plans of kitchens and service areas are included.

724. Sullivan, Catherine F. *Management of Medical Foodservice.* Westport, CT: AVI Publishing Co., 1985. 410 p.

A text and reference for students and administrators in health care facilities that promotes the idea that the menu is the hub of the foodservice system and that all subsystems revolve around it. Chapter one is an overview of the systems approach. Chapters two through ten cover basic systems management. Chapters eleven through seventeen discuss subsystems one by one. Subjects such as safety, sanitation, and energy conservation are dealt with collectively as they relate to each subsystem.

725. University of Massachusetts, Cooperative Extension Service. *Food Management Manual, no. 1–5.* Amherst, MA, 1964?

This is a five-manual series resulting from a contract program at the University of Massachusetts Extension Service. The program tested methods, procedures, and materials for conducting educational work in the foodservice industry.

726. VanEgmond-Pannell, Dorothy. *School Foodservice.* 3d ed. Westport, CT: AVI Publishing Co., 1985. 440 p.

This third edition of a basic text, gives history and development of school foodservices and provides chapters on all basic aspects: menu planning, management, purchasing, preparation, sanitation, and equipment. Interesting and more complex aspects such as the advisability of using foodservice management companies and satellite food systems are also included. New in this edition are chapters on promoting school foodservices and computerization.

727. Warner, Mickey. *Industrial Foodservice and Cafeteria Management.* Edited by Jule Wilkinson. Chicago: Institutions/Volume Feeding Magazine, 1973. 181 p.

This text covers the basics of management in industrial and institution foodservices. Chapters cover management principles, operating goals, budget, accounting, menu, personnel cycle, cost control, operating reports, coffee cart services, sanitation and maintenance, vending, insurance, and the future of the industry. The book looks at foodservice in plants and factories, office buildings, schools and colleges, hospitals, and institutions.

728. Watson, Olive B. *School and Institutional Lunchroom Management.* West Nyack, NY: Parker Publishing Co., 1968. 310 p.

This is a basic technical handbook on lunchroom management. It covers management of the lunchroom and the physical plant, food management. All major areas are covered from basic planning and setup of the physical plant to personnel, equipment, safety, and sanitation. Basic nutrition, menu planning, and display are also presented. It also includes worksheet examples and teaching suggestions for vocational teachers using the book as a text.

729. West, Bessie Brooks, et al. *Food Service in Institutions.* 5th ed. New York: Wiley, 1977. 839 p.

A revised and updated fifth edition of this basic text for students in food systems management, it is still arranged in three major sections. The first includes planning, selection, production, delivery, and service of foods; the second includes personnel, cost control, sanitation, and safety; and the third includes floor planning, furnishings, and equipment for kitchens and dining areas. An appendix has examples of floor plans, organization charts, and personnel lists for typical small and large college residence hall foodservices.

RESTAURANTS

730. Anderson, Henry William. *The Modern Food Service Industry: An Introductory Guide.* Dubuque, IA: W. C. Brown Co., 1976. 340 p.

This is an introductory text for those beginning a career in foodservice. Part one traces foodservice in history. Part two looks at current operations in various types of restaurants and institutions. Part three is about restaurant ownership. Part four describes over sixty jobs and gives career planning guidance. Part five includes directories and a glossary, as well as a list of over 100 periodicals.

731. Atkinson, David. *Hotel and Catering French: A New Approach for Advanced Students and Practitioners.* Oxford: Pergamon Press, 1980. 210 p.

This textbook is designed for students with some proficiency in French. It is divided into five lessons each comprising about thirty hours of work. Each lesson has six readings including a passage on a gastronomic topic, a regional recipe, a principle of cooking, and a biography of a famous chef. The book also includes extensive French-English and English-French glossaries.

732. Axler, Bruce H. *Foodservice: A Managerial Approach.* s.l.: D.C. Heath and Company, 1979. 498 p.

Taking the systems approach, this book analyzes the various parts of foodservice and how they relate and interact. Marketing research, promotion, and menu planning are stressed. Includes a bibliography and index. Published in cooperation with the National Institute of the Foodservice Industry.

733. Axler, Bruce H. *Showmanship in the Dining Room.* His Focus on...the Hospitality Industry. Indianapolis, IN: ITT Educational Publishing, 1974. 116 p.

Part of the *Focus on...* series, this book discusses the principles of profitable showmanship in restaurants and covers most aspects of the techniques. Display courses, customer cooking, carving techniques, flambéing, and other tableside preparations are described as are rolling cart service and special dining room personnel.

734. Axler, Bruce H. *Tableservice Techniques.* His Focus on... the Hospitality Industry. Indianapolis, IN: ITT Educational Publishing, 1974. 136 p.

Intended as a training tool and management aid, this book covers all aspects of tableservice with step-by-step instructions in many basic operations, as well as guidance for special situations. Chapters include modern tableservice, sidework, preparation of garnishes, preparing for the guests' arrival, beverage service, special tableservice situations, solving people problems, and the business of tableservice. A glossary defines tableservice terms and phrases.

735. Berberoğlu, H. *The World of the Restaurateur.* Dubuque, IA: Kendall/Hunt Publishing Co., 1981. 249 p.

This textbook covers all aspects of restaurant management in a very concise style. It is intended by the author to introduce students to the restaurant business. The chapters on foods and cuisines of the countries of the world are particularly valuable. The book also covers food presentation, table side cooking and carving, dining room service, menu planning, sanitation, marketing, design and layout of kitchens and dining rooms, purchasing, personnel management, and cost control.

736. Beznoska, Dennis; Gaehler, Heinz V.; and Kraus, Emil. *The HDE Most Complete Manual of Fine Restaurant Service.* Pompano Beach, FL: Exposition Press of Florida, Inc., 1985. 103 p.

The authors of this manual for waiters were trained in European schools and since immigration to the U.S. have worked as managers and maitre d's in fine hotels in the U.S. The book covers table settings; silver and china; job descriptions of waiter staff from maitre d' hotel to busboys; directions for food prepared at the table; definitions of culinary terms; descriptions of famous dishes; and information on wines, champagnes, spirits, and liqueurs.

737. Birchfield, John C. *Foodservice Operations Manual: A Guide for Hotels, Restaurants, and Institutions.* Boston: CBI Publishing Co., 1979. 500 p.

This loose-leaf manual contains 115 operations procedures that are standard to all food operations. It is intended to serve as a basis for developing your own procedures manual. It includes the following topics: menu planning, purchasing, food production, sanitation, cost controls, and personnel.

738. Boykin-Stith, Lorraine, and Williams, Barbara Kern. *A Basic Primer of Food Service Administration.* Old Westbury, NY: Westville Publishing Co., 1982. 260 p.

This is an entry level text for foodservice management students. All chapters include multiple-choice review questions with answers. Chapters cover communications, sanitation and safety, labor policy, menu planning, food preparation, additives, storing, cost control equipment layout, and food specifications.

739. Boykin-Stith, Lorraine; Williams, Barbara Kern; and D'Angelo, Rosemary. *A Comprehensive Review of Food Service Administration.* Old Westbury, NY: Westville Publishing Co., 1981. 138 p.

This is designed as a study guide to supplement texts in foodservice. Using a multiple-choice format, with answers provided, the review covers administrative skills and support systems as well as laws and unions, food cost determination, terminology, meal planning and food purchasing, inventory, storage, delivery, and record keeping. There are chapters on pre-readiness and food preparation and kitchen environment, food safety, and dishwashing.

740. Brodner, Joseph; Carlson, Howard M.; and Maschal, Henry T., eds. *Profitable Food and Beverage Operation.* 4th rev. ed. New York: Ahrens Publishing Co., 1962. 458 p.

This book focuses on the business management side of foodservice in restaurants and hotels. It covers the broad field of management methods, practices and policies applying them to the hospitality industry. Topics covered include menu planning and merchandising, food purchasing, storage and preparation, employee training, advertising, sanitation, wine cellar operation, kitchen planning, food and liquor controls, payroll analysis, and control. New to this edition is a chapter on vending machines.

741. Buchanan, Robert D. *Selected Articles on Food Service Management.* Madison, WI: Food Service Marketing, 1977. 80 p.

This is the first volume of a series of selected articles reprinted from *Food Service Marketing.* Each of the fifteen articles reprinted here is aimed at improving foodservice management skills. Among the topics are employee training programs, selecting sources of supply, and purchasing trends.

742. Coffman, James P. *Introduction to Professional Food Service.* rev. ed. New York: Van Nostrand Reinhold Co., 1974. 311 p.

A text for entry level personnel with the objective of giving the trainee a foundation in related foodservice subjects that will be a basis for the study of actual food preparation. Basic information is given on organization, sanitation, food poisoning, nutrition, purchasing, storage, menu planning, food processing, principles of food production, table service, and record keeping.

743. Dietz, Susan M. *The Correct Waitress.* New York: Ahrens Publishing Co., 1965. 58 p.

This is a very brief practical manual written for use by waitresses. Topics covered include types of restaurant service; table setting; serving beer, wine, and mixed drinks; sanitation; and merchandising.

744. Dukas, Peter. *Planning Profits in the Food and Lodging Industry.* Edited by Jule Wilkinson. Boston: Cahners Books, 1976. 180 p.

In four major sections, Dukas provides guidance in the use of profit planning which is especially aimed at foodservice operations with an annual sales volume under $400,000. Part one teaches the effective use of information provided by a general profit planning and expense control system. Part two deals with food sales profit control. Part three provides methods for increased profit through labor cost control. Part four gives the details of a general system for liquor sales and cost control.

745. Elliott, Travis. *Profitable Foodservice Management.* 2d ed. Revised by Scott Barns. Washington, DC: National Restaurant Association, 1983. 9 pamphlets.

A series of nine pamphlets issued by the National Restaurant Association intended to promote good management techniques. Each pamphlet is short, with clear basic information on various aspects of management. Where appropriate (as in the hiring process) step-by-step instruction is given. They are variously titled: (1) *Job Analysis Descriptions and Specifications,* (2) *Employee and Management Meetings,* (3) *Good Supervision,* (4) *Reduction of Employee Turnover,* (5) *Job Evaluation,* (6) *Worker Motivation,* (7) *Performance Appraisals,* (8) *Counselling and Intercommunications,* and (9) *Recruitment Selection of Employees.*

746. Eshbach, Charles E., ed. *Food Service Trends: Selected Articles from Publications of the Society for the Advancement of Food Service Research.* Boston: Cahners Books, 1974. 326 p.

This book provides a look at trends in the foodservice industry. Each chapter is made up of papers presented by different experts for the Society of the Advancement of Food Service Research. Over-all chapter headings include "Making Changes in the Food Service Industry," "Motivation and Productivity: Employee Training Education," "Changes in Systems, Products and Services," "Engineered Foods—Products of Great Promise," "School and Institutional Feeding," and "Standards, Quality and Consumers."

747. Eshbach, Charles E. *Foodservice Management.* 3d ed. Boston: CBI Publishing Co., 1979. 324 p.

Aimed at identifying and solving or preventing the kind of problems characteristic of foodservice management. Covers subjects such as receiving, storage, menu, frozen foods, food poisoning, kitchen layout, food costs, financial statements, operating budgets, break-even analysis, employee training, purchasing, and communication. There is also a chapter on foodservice and the computer. This edition is updated and has questions added at the end of each chapter.

748. Fisher, William P. *Fisher's Laws: The Thinker's Guide to Management Action.* Chicago: National Restaurant Association, 1978. 124 p.
Fisher's Laws originally appeared monthly from 1972–1977 in the *NRA News.* Fisher presents the wisdom culled from years in the field in brief page-and-a-half essays that deal with all aspects of management. Each essay is summarized in one of fifty pithy "laws" for the role of management in restaurants. Included are such gems as Law 17—"A poor plan well executed is always superior to a good plan poorly executed"—and Law 50—"If you don't have anything more to say, don't say anything more."

749. Foodservice Editors of CBI. *The Professional Host.* Boston: CBI Publishing Co., 1981. 175 p.
The focus of this book is the techniques of tableservice in America. Every aspect is covered from folding linens and setting the table to handling the payment for the dinner. Also covered are staff personnel and dining room organization, food sanitation, beverage service, cooking at the table, reservations, and serving a banquet. A glossary of food and tableservice terms is included in the appendix.

750. Fuller, John. *Professional Kitchen Management.* London: Batsford Academic and Educational, 1981. 410 p.
This is a revision of the 1962 title first published as *Chef's Manual of Kitchen Management.* It covers supervision, layout and equipment, and foods and menus. Coverage is thorough, and a glossary of kitchen terms is included. Topics such as training and employment have been reduced in this edition, and some topics such as kitchen planning, equipment, food buying, records and controls, safety, and supervision have been expanded. The whole edition has been substantially rewritten.

751. Fuller, John; Knight, John Barton; and Salter, Charles A. *The Professional Chef's Guide to Kitchen Management.* New York: Van Nostrand Reinhold Co., 1985. 238 p.
A practical textbook for chefs and managers. Part one, on the professional chef, covers the history of foodservice, a description of the vocation and responsibilities of chefs, and a review of the tools and utensils and safety considerations. Part two, on kitchen management, presents organization, layout, staffing, equipment, menu planning, purchasing, and controls. This volume was "inspired" by *Professional Kitchen Management* by John Fuller.

752. Ginders, James R. *A Guide to Napkin Folding.* 2d ed. Illustrated by E. R. Capps. Boston: CBI Publishing Co., 1980. 88 p.
Clearly illustrated with line drawings and colored plates, this guide includes over forty different folding patterns. Each pattern is rated as to how difficult it is.

753. Goodman, Raymond J., Jr. *The Management of Service for the Restaurant Manager.* Edited by Jerry Vallen. Dubuque, IA: W. C. Brown Co., 1979. 302 p.
This textbook is divided into sections on "Management" and "Technical Procedures." It is designed to give specific managerial and procedural guidelines fitting most service systems. Chapters cover psychology of service, human relations, personnel, equipment, sanitation, tableside service and beverage service.

754. Gordon, Robert T. *Restaurant Management Guide.* Englewood Cliffs, NJ: Institute for Business Planning, 1985. (Loose-leaf)
Written by a restaurateur and consultant, this is a practical guide to restaurant management. He considers the menu to be the keystone of success. Other topics covered include purchasing, personnel management, accounting, advertising and promotions, remodeling, and tax planning.

755. Gottlieb, Leon. *The Best of Gottlieb's Bottom Line: A Practical Profit Guide for Today's Foodservice Operator.* New York: Chain Store Publishing Corp., 1980. 169
This is a collection of articles first published in the author's monthly newsletter, *Gottlieb's Bottom Line.* The collection gives very practical advice in a problem-solution format,

emphasizing the three Ps—patrons, personnel, and profits. Articles cover the following topics: hiring, training, security, cost saving techniques, sales promotion, advertising and public relations, and management policies.

756. Hitchcock, Mary J. *Foodservice Systems Administration.* New York: Macmillan, 1980. 216 p.

This is an introductory text on foodservice administration with emphasis on control of management resources. Foodservice is seen as a system with interrelated parts. Chapters cover each management resource and its control through management functions. Different types of delivery systems and legal responsibilities of a foodservice administrator are also included.

757. Ireland, Richard C. *The Professional Waitress.* 2d ed. Wheaton, IL: Hospitality Institute, 1974. 5 vols.

A series of five short instructional manuals for perspective serving personnel. Each manual has a programed self-instruction section. *About Food Service* is an overview of the foodservice industry. *Your Duties and Responsibilities* gives basic tasks and procedures including tableservice, menu, serving food, and liquor. *The Important Personal Skills* discusses human relations, communication, appearance, and attitude. *All about Your Customer* discusses why people eat out and the ways to know and please the customer. *Selling in the Restaurant* covers basic in-house selling philosophy and techniques.

758. Jacobs, Jay. *Winning the Restaurant Game.* Drawings by Ronald Searle. New York: McGraw-Hill, 1980. 198 p.

Jacobs, restaurant reviewer for *Gourmet* magazine, presents a humorous but informative guide to restaurant one-up-manship. As well as being a clever guide to what many customers are up to when eating out, it includes real information on menu and wine terminology in the second half of the book.

759. Kahrl, William L. *Improving Food Service.* Managing for Profit Series. New York: Chain Store Publishing Corp., 1978. 83 p.

In this booklet, Kahrl emphasizes the importance of good service to the success of a restaurant. He examines the problems and offers practical tips to solve them.

760. Kahrl, William L. *Increasing Productivity and Sales.* Managing for Profit Series New York: Chain Store Publishing Corp., 1980. 96 p.

This is part of the Managing for Profit Series written by Kahrl. Each manual focuses on a specific aspect of the restaurant industry. Part one of the volume discusses what productivity is and the steps for increasing it. Parts two and three cover such subjects as measuring sales, sales analysis, and increasing sales.

761. Kahrl, William L. *Meeting Challenges in Food Service: A Guide for Solving Present and Future Problems.* New York: Chain Store Age Books, 1974. 182 p.

Aimed at all areas of the foodservice industry, Kahrl's book is designed to help solve current and future difficulties by greater efficiency and better equipment and methods. Chapters discuss inefficient existing facilities; labor, training, productivity, and utilization; supply of food and materials; energy; sanitation and safety; profit or loss; operating guidelines; management problems; capital expenditures; and research and development. The final chapter gives conclusions and ideas for the future.

762. King, Carol A. *Professional Dining Room Management.* 2d ed. New York: Van Nostrand Reinhold Co., 1988. 214 p.

This book is for those who supervise the serving functions in a restaurant. It covers types of dining room service, dining room service standards, organization, operation, and sales procedures. It also deals with the basics of supervision, motivation, cost control, revenue control, training, and unions. Some of the material in this book was first developed for *Profitable Food and Beverage Management: Operations* by Eric Green, Galen Drake, and Jerome Sweeney (1978).

763. Kinton, Ronald, and Ceserani, Victor. *The Theory of Catering.* 5th ed. London: Edward Arnold, 1984. 438 p.

This basic text from Great Britain is designed to help students pass examinations in catering operations. The information is mostly given in outline form to use as review material. Chapters cover safety, hygiene, gas, electricity, water, kitchen equipment, elementary nutrition, commodities, preservation of foods, storekeeping, kitchen organization and supervision, kitchen French, menu planning or menu compilation, food buying and costing, computers, service, types of catering, and a guide to study.

764. Kotschevar, Lendal Henry. *Standards, Principles, and Techniques in Quantity Food Production.* 3d ed. Boston: Cahners Books, 1974. 661 p.

A text written for managers as well as students and trainees that contains detailed information on the procedures for quantity production for most menu categories and information on planning and administration. The three major sections cover management in quantity food production, kitchen production, and bakeshop production. Though exercises for students are included at the end of each chapter, this book is also intended as a working manual and reference source for supervisors and administrators of quantity food production.

765. Kramer, Amihud, and Twigg, Bernard A. *Quality Control for the Food Industry. Volume I: Fundamentals.* 3d ed. Westport, CT: AVI Publishing Co., 1970.

The first of a two-volume set on quality control. Volume one deals with general principles and fundamentals. Application is reserved for volume two. The first half of this book deals with tests and measurements for qualities such as color and gloss, size and shape. The last half is on the utilization of measurements in setting grades and standards. Production control and operations research are also covered. Appendix one is an outline of statistical methods. Appendix two is a large glossary of symbols and terms. This is a revision of *Fundamentals of Quality Control for the Food Industry.*

766. Lehrman, Lewis E. *Dining Room Service.* Hotel-Motel Management Series. Indianapolis, IN: Bobbs-Merrill Educational Publishing, 1971 (1980 printing). 204 p.

Part of the *Hotel-Motel Management Series,* this text deals with all aspects of dining room management and service. Early chapters are aimed at the manager and cover the manager's role, planning, day-to-day management, equipment, supplies, and personnel. Later chapters cover specifics such as types of service, preparing the dining room, seating guests, and the essentials of food and beverage service. There are also chapters on showmanship in dining room service and on special service situations. Appendices list wines, cocktails, and menu terms.

767. Livingston, G. E., and Chang, Charlotte M., eds. *Food Service Systems: Analysis, Design, and Implementation.* New York: Academic Press, 1979. 483 p.

This is the revised and updated proceedings from the 1976 Food Service Association seminar conducted in Framingham, Massachusetts. Emphasis is on analysis, design, and implementation. Twenty-seven articles appear under the following subtitles: "Systems and Their Study," "Food Selection and Menu Planning," "Utilizing Labor Effectively," "Equipment and Facility Planning," "Insuring Food Quality and Wholesomeness," "Case Histories of Successful Food Service Systems Implementation."

768. Martin, William B. *Quality Service: The Restaurant Manager's Bible.* Ithaca, NY: Cornell University, School of Hotel Administration, 1986. 175 p.

This is not a training manual for employees; it is a guide for managers. It provides an explanation of the nature of service and analyzes the components that make up good service. It also gives practical guidance for producing quality service through service improvement strategies and the use of feedback, recognition, and related methods.

769. Minno, Maurice P. *How to Prepare a Restaurant Operations Manual: A Do-It-Yourself Handbook for Preparing an Operations Manual.* Washington, DC: National Restaurant Association, 1982. 133 p.

This handbook is designed to help the restaurateur develop an operations or procedures manual. A step-by-step guide to writing a manual along with worksheets and forms for duplication are included. Pointers on keeping the manual up to date are also included.

770. Minor, Lewis J. *Nutritional Standards.* The L. J. Minor Foodservice Standards Series, vol. 1. Westport, CT: AVI Publishing Co., 1983. 281 p.

This is the first volume of a series on foodservice standards. Its aim is to explain the factors that influence the wholesomeness, nutritive value, flavor, color, texture, appearance, and preservation of food products. It also provides guidelines for quality standards for foodservice. Chapters cover product standards, food additive standards, monosodium glutamate, flavor standards, nutrition standards, new food product development standards, and a laboratory guide to food evaluation theory and practice.

771. Minor, Lewis J., and Cichy, Ronald F. *Foodservice Systems Management.* Westport, CT: AVI Publishing Co., 1984. 285 p.

This book gives a detailed discussion of foodservice systems management, its problems, and resources. Chapters cover foodservice systems, menu management, purchasing, service management, sanitation, human resources management, equipment, and quality assurance/quality control management.

772. Monaghan, Thomas S., and Anderson, Robert. *Pizza Tiger.* New York: Random House, 1986. 346 p.

This is the autobiography of Tom Monaghan who developed the Domino's Pizza business. His book tells in an entertaining style how he turned his original $500 investment into a multimillion dollar empire which includes ownership of the Detroit Tigers.

773. Morgan, William J., Jr. *Food and Beverage Management and Service.* East Lansing, MI: Educational Institute of the American Hotel & Motel Association, 1981. 245 p.

Food preparation and related subjects such as sanitation, cost controls, purchasing, and merchandising are covered in this text for foodservice management students. Morgan also discusses the history and future of foodservice, management structures and functions, some of the newer forms of food preparation, techniques, terminology, equipment, menu planning, recipes, and beverage management.

774. Morgan, William J., Jr. *Supervision and Management of Quantity Food Preparation: Principles and Procedures.* 2d ed. Berkeley, CA: McCutchan Publishing Corp., 1981. 449 p.

A text designed for the systems approach to hospitality management covering all aspects of food preparation. The book is divided into two parts. Part one deals with the manager's side of preparation including purchasing, storage, sanitation, and safety. Part two covers the actual process of preparing and serving items in major menu categories, as well as merchandising. This second edition has added chapters on newer forms of food preparation, personnel management, and beverage management. Current concerns such as smoking, truth in menus, and energy efficiency are discussed.

775. National Restaurant Association. *Help Prevent Drunk Driving: A Restaurateur's Guide.* Washington, DC, 1984. 12 p.

This pamphlet gives useful suggestions to prevent drunk driving accidents such as introducing food at your bar and providing alternative transportation programs. There are also some interesting suggestions for promotion without encouraging overindulgence. Instead of a happy hour for instance, they suggest guest bartender nights, theme nights, and specials on bar food and nonalcoholic drinks.

776. National Restaurant Association. *National Symposium: The Crisis in Product and Service Liability: Washington, DC, January 29, 1986.* Washington, DC, 1986. 66 p.
This is an edited transcript from the symposium sponsored by Pennsylvania State University and National Restaurant Association on January 29, 1986 in Washington DC. Papers and panel discussions presented cover tort law reform, liability insurance, professional liability, service liability, government liability, congressional view, and Dram Shop law. Summation is by William P. Fisher, Executive Vice President of the National Restaurant Association.

777. National Restaurant Association. *A Restaurateur's Guide, Operation Prom/Graduation.* Washington, DC, 1986. 15 p.
This brief brochure is designed to help restaurant owners serve their community by participating in a campaign to reduce alcohol-related deaths during graduation and prom season. A variety of activities are described which can be implemented, and table tents samples and camera-ready art work for newspaper ads are included.

778. National Restaurant Association. *A Restaurateur's Guide to the Insurance Crisis.* National Restaurant Association Current Issues Report. Washington, DC, 1986. 10 p.
This report is divided into two parts. The first deals with how restaurateurs can cope with the rising liability insurance costs. It encourages restaurant operators to become their own risk managers. Part two is background information on the current state of the insurance industry, describing the causes and affects of the crisis in the industry.

779. National Restaurant Association, Technical Services Department. *Facilities Operations Manual.* Washington, DC, 1986. 150 p.
This is one of the National Restaurant Association's self-help manuals. This one provides an awareness of the interacting technical systems in foodservice operations. It covers building structures, building systems, foodservice equipment, energy management, and maintenance. Sources of additional technical information are also listed.

780. Palan, Earl R., and Stadler, Judith A. *Preparing for the Foodservice Industry: An Introductory Approach.* Westport, CT: AVI Publishing Co., 1986. 372 p.
Designed as a text for secondary and postsecondary foodservices, this is a very clear and basic introduction to skills and concepts needed by the beginning student. The first seven chapters discuss entry level skills and include the basics of human relations, sanitation, and nutrition as well as a general introduction to the industry. The remaining chapters give basic preparation principles and methods for various food types.

781. Peddersen, Raymond B., et al. *Increasing Productivity in Foodservice.* Edited by Jule Wilkinson. Chicago: Institutions/Volume Feeding Magazine, 1973. 206 p.
Wilkinson has gathered productivity know-how of five industry leaders. Raymond Peddersen writes on motivation and worker productivity. Arthur Avery covers equipment arrangements for worker productivity. Ruth Richard discusses task planning, motion studies, and equipment placement. Using slack time is covered by James Osenton in a chapter on "Stored Labor Concept." Studies by Lendal Kotschevar on work simplification are reproduced. Convenience food, disposable, and automation are covered by Raymond Peddersen. The book concludes with Harry Pope's summary chapter on utilization.

782. Poledor, Andrew P. *Determining the Feasibility of a Total Convenience Food System.* Boston: CBI Publishing Co., 1977. 132 p.
Because the foodservice industry faces two chronic problems—shortage of personnel and decreasing productivity—the author suggests extensive use of convenience foods. This book is designed to help a foodservice operator decide the feasibility of converting to total use of convenience foods or designing a new operation using convenience foods. It provides guidance for collecting statistics to make this decision. Several case studies are included.

783. School of Hotel Administration, Cornell University. *The Essentials of Good Table Service.* rev. ed. Ithaca, NY: Cornell Hotel & Restaurant Administration Quarterly, 1975. 68 p.
> This is an illustrated guide to correct serving. Chapters cover the headwaiter, American service, French service, Russian service, buffet service, banquet service, bar service, and glassware. The appendix includes such additional subjects as French menu terms, table service arrangements, napkin folding, how to carve meat and poultry, and decorative ice carving.

784. Solomon, Edward S. *Service Is an Honorable Profession.* rev. ed. Vermilion, OH, Solomon, 1979. 83 p.
> This is a basic training guide for waitresses. Brief chapters followed by review questions cover all aspects of tableservice from setup and service sequence to presenting the guest check. Chapters appear on wine and beverage service, selling, tips, and restaurant jargon. Emphasis is on being cheerful and customer oriented.

785. Solomon, Kenneth Ira, and Katz, Norman. *Profitable Restaurant Management.* 2d ed. Englewood Cliffs, NJ: Prentice-Hall, 1981. 298 p.
> A theoretical and practical guide to restaurant management, each chapter includes examples from the real experience of the authors, who are partners in a successful hospitality accounting consulting firm. The chapters cover restaurant organization, personnel management, food and beverage control, streamlining food handling procedures, maximizing operating procedures, equipment management, long-range financial planning, streamlining accounting, financial ratios and analysis, tax and tax planning implications, industry trends, site selection, feasibility, and location planning.

786. Spears, Marian C., and Vaden, Allene G. *Foodservice Organizations: A Managerial and Systems Approach.* New York: Wiley, 1985. 737 p.
> This text is intended for upper division students in foodservice management and is designed to be used over an academic year in two or three courses. It deals with the designing of overall foodservice systems and discusses subsystems such as procurement, production, distribution, sales, and maintenance. The management section deals with organizational structure, decision making, personnel, budget, and the like. It includes many topics not found in most other texts such as forecasting models and productivity analysis. Both commercial and institutional operations are covered.

787. Stokes, John Wesley. *How to Manage a Restaurant or Institutional Food Service.* 4th ed. Dubuque, IA: W. C. Brown Co., 1982. 393 p.
> This is a comprehensive text that covers the general principles of effective management and foodservice organization as well as having specific chapters on planning the menu, styles of foodservice, principles of design, kitchen equipment and layout, engineering facilities, purchasing, receiving and storage, and food preparation and cooking. There are also chapters on controlling food and labor cost, management control through accounting, merchandising and public relations, sanitation, safety, and security. The final chapter discusses relevant laws and regulations affecting foodservice.

788. Stretch, J. Audrey, and Southgate, H. A.*The Science of Catering.* London: Edward Arnold, 1986. 266 p.
> Intended for British catering students, this book is primarily concerned with buying, storing, cooking, and serving at the practical level. Most chapters, however, have a section for practical skills information and a section dealing with the scientific information related to the same subjects. Chapters appear on plant and animal foods, storage, cooking, nutrition, preservation, fermentation, hygiene, and cleaning operations.

789. Thayse, Harris. *Professional Food Service Management.* Englewood Cliffs, NJ: Prentice-Hall, 1983. 228 p.
> The author presents systems and procedures for operational success in the hospitality industry. The various food systems are covered separately and then integrated into one overall system of management procedures. Thayse breaks the system into thirty chapters

including food purchasing controls, item cost analysis, menu breakdown analysis, and many other specifics.

790. Thorner, Marvin Edward, and Manning, Peter Burnam. *Quality Control in Foodservice.* rev. ed. Westport, CT: AVI Publishing Co., 1983. 366 p.

This revised edition continues to emphasize the need for effective, comprehensive quality control programs in foodservices. Every phase of a foodservice facility is explored, and simplified control procedures are offered. The author's stated purpose is the development of simplified inspection skills, usable without technical training, which would serve as effective guides for checking quality parameters at all stages of an operation. A newly revised chapter on energy management appears in this edition, and a new final chapter on preventive and corrective maintenance.

791. Tolve, Arthur P. *Standardizing Foodservice for Quality and Efficiency.* Westport, CT: AVI Publishing Co., 1984. 221 p.

Written primarily as an introductory text, this book presents the benefits of standardization to the foodservices student. Chapters cover the use of a checklist as a means to standardization, training for standardization, standardizing the operation, the menu and recipes, the costing process, and pricing the menu.

792. Van Duyn, J. A. *Successful Kitchen Operation and Staff Management Handbook.* Englewood Cliffs, NJ: Prentice-Hall, 1979. 234 p.

This guide to kitchen management is aimed at making the profit-oriented kitchen more efficient and successful. It covers all aspects of food and staff management and includes interviews with successful operators which provide insight into actual procedures in a number of efficient kitchens.

793. Villano, Caesar. *Restaurant Management and Control: The Profitable Approach.* 2d ed. New York: Chain Store Publishing Corp., 1985. 172 p.

This book is intended as a guide for managers, investors, and potential owners of restaurants. It is intended to teach methods for structuring a profitable operation, and emphasis is on financial controls. The book has four major sections: "Putting a Restaurant Package Together," "Structuring for Profit," "Restaurant Management," and "Presenting the Restaurant Image to the Public."

794. Villella, Joseph A. *The Hospitality Industry: The World of Food Service.* 2d ed. New York: McGraw-Hill, 1975. 342 p.

This is an introductory survey text for beginning courses in foodservice. Chapters cover history of the industry, front of the house and back of the house—job titles, departments, stations, and equipment—facility design, sanitation, foods, and employees.

Marketing, Advertising, and Promotions

795. Axler, Bruce H. *Increasing Lodging Revenues and Restaurant Checks.* His Focus on...the Hospitality Industry. Indianapolis, IN: ITT Educational Publishing, 1974. 104 p.

This brief booklet outlines how restaurant and hotel employees can increase profits by suggestive selling. It covers food and beverage sales, developing regular clientele, selling guest rooms, and other retail sales. The booklet has a very practical approach as do others in the series.

796. Blomstrom, Robert L. *The Commercial Lodging Market.* East Lansing, MI: Michigan State University, 1967. 233 p.

The results of phase two of a five-phase research project conducted at Michigan State University in the late 1960s. The objective was to find out as much as possible about commercial lodging customers so that managers or owners of commercial lodging establishments might more effectively define existing markets or develop new markets. Chapters with information in tabular and graph form include "About the Study," "The Lodging Customer" (demographic statistics), "Travel Patterns," "Purpose of Travel," "Hotel and Motel Customers," "The Pricing Structure," "Expense Accounts and Credit Card Use," "Customer Eating Pattern," and "Markets and Marketing."

797. Blomstrom, Robert L., ed. *Strategic Marketing Planning in the Hospitality Industry.* East Lansing, MI: Educational Institute of the American Hotel & Motel Association, 1983. 322 p.

This is a collection of about fifty articles intended to supplement the teaching of marketing in the hospitality industry. It is not intended as a primary text. Articles appear under the following headings: "Strategic Marketing Planning—The Concept," "Strategic Marketing Planning—The Process," "Research for Strategic Marketing Planning," "Market Segmentation and Target Marketing," "Positioning Strategy," "Advertising," and "The 'How to' Cases."

798. Coffman, C. DeWitt. *Hospitality for Sale: Techniques of Promoting Business for Hospitality Establishments.* East Lansing, MI: Educational Institute of the American Hotel & Motel Association, 1980. 339 p.

This is a textbook on marketing techniques for the hotel and motel industry. The goal is very specific—to plan and carry out sales programs in the restaurant and lodging industries. It is divided into five parts: "Pre-sale" (planning), "Selling Instruments" (advertising, publicity, and public relations), "Sales Agents" (use of outside organizations), "Act of Selling," and "Post-Sale" (evaluation.)

799. Coffman, C. DeWitt. *Marketing for a Full House: A Complete Guide to Profitable Hotel/Motel Operational Planning.* Edited by Helen J. Recknagel. Ithaca, NY: School of Hotel Administration, Cornell University, 1975 (1984 printing). 384 p.
> This is a simplified explanation of marketing that is aimed at helping hotel operators develop a marketing plan coordinating all departments for maximum business flow. The author presents the major concepts of marketing under five headings: "People," "Product," "Package," "Promote," and "Performance." Although the statistics and operating data are out of date, the book is still valuable for the marketing information and philosophy it contains. The 1984 printing is an unmodified reprint of the 1975 edition.

800. Crissy, William J. E.; Boewadt, Robert J.; and Laudadio, Dante M. *Marketing of Hospitality Services: Food, Travel, Lodging.* East Lansing, MI: Educational Institute of the American Hotel & Motel Association, 1975. 269 p.
> Emphasis in this text on hospitality marketing is on a guest-oriented approach for the entire staff. There are chapters on advertising, sales promotion, merchandising, pricing, inside and outside selling, and public relations. Sources of marketing information and the financial aspects of marketing are also covered. It is a thorough introduction to this aspect of the hospitality field intended for the advanced student.

801. Darrah, Lawrence B. *Food Marketing.* rev. ed. New York: Ronald Press, 1971. 387 p.
> An introductory text for marketing classes. This book presents general marketing principles and practices, marketing services and concepts as well as food purchasing patterns, marketing agencies, marketing costs, and pricing.

802. Eison, Irving I. *Strategic Marketing in Food Service: Planning for Change.* New York: Lebhar-Friedman Books, 1980. 142 p.
> This book is about strategic planning to meet the changing market. Eison shows how preparing to meet change creatively can provide long-range feasibility for foodservice operations. Chapters include "Adopt the Marketing Perspective," "Analysis: Who You Are and How You Fit," "Strategic Management," "Positioning: The Reason for Being," "The Tools of Marketing," and "Putting It All Together."

803. Fairbrook, Paul. *Public Relations & Merchandising: A Handbook for College and University Food Services.* Stockton, CA: Colman Publishers, 1984. 352 p.
> This is a handbook for college and university foodservice managers. It is designed as both a guide and reference manual for improving public relations, marketing, and merchandising for a successful foodservice program. Chapters cover various types of communication and promotion from new student orientation to public relations throughout the year. Numerous examples of successful menus and posters that may be freely copied and adapted for use are included.

804. Feltenstein, Tom, and Lachmuth, Joe. *Restaurant Profits Through Advertising and Promotion: The Indispensable Plan.* Boston: CBI Publishing Co., 1983. 137 p.
> A marketing executive who served both McDonald's and Burger King presents the principles and practices of neighborhood restaurant marketing. All suggestions can be carried out by a limited staff and with a small budget. Situation analysis charts help pinpoint strengths and weaknesses. Chapters cover goal setting, advertising, promotion, and numerous other subjects from motivating employees to special markets.

805. Fisher, William P., ed. *Creative Marketing for the Foodservice Industry: A Practitioner's Handbook.* New York: Wiley, 1982. 296 p.
> Written for the smaller restaurateur, this is a very practical manual on marketing and promoting foodservice businesses. Each chapter is written by a different professional; they emphasize how-to ideas. Topics covered include market research, marketing both a new and an old restaurant, attracting group business, using the menu as a marketing tool,

merchandising new menu items and beverages, choosing an advertising agency, advertising in print, and public relations.

806. Fochs, Arnold, comp. *Prize Winning Ads Used by Nightclubs, Cafes, Drive-ins, Hotels/Motels.* Duluth, MN: A. J. Publishing Co., 1975?. 208 p.
This is a collection of advertisements for restaurants that were judged by the Minnesota Society of Local Advertisers at a meeting in 1975. Many of the ads can be used by other restaurants. Well over 200 are reproduced in black and white.

807. Gottlieb, Leon. *Foodservice/Hospitality Advertising & Promotion.* Indianapolis, IN: Bobbs-Merrill Educational Publishing, 1982. 363 p.
Gottlieb looks at every aspect of promotion and advertising as they apply to the field. He covers the objectives of advertising, print and media ads, promotions, premiums, publicity and related subjects such as public relations, complaints, and advertising agencies. The book is a text with chapter goals and summary questions provided. An appendix introduces the reader to market research.

808. Greene, Melvyn. *Marketing Hotels and Restaurants into the 90s: A Systematic Approach to Increasing Sales.* 2d ed. Westport, CT: AVI Publishing Co., 1987. 287 p.
Written in Britain but with principles applicable internationally, this book deals with marketing in the hotel and restaurant field. Greene looks at the future of hotels and deals with such subjects as main aspects of successful marketing, redefining markets, market segmentation, and sales action plans. Various forms of advertising and selling techniques are also discussed.

809. Hart, Christopher, and Troy, David. *Strategic Hotel/Motel Marketing.* rev. ed. East Lansing, MI: Educational Institute of the American Hotel & Motel Association, 1986. 319 p.
This is a text on marketing principles and planning. It covers basic concepts, analysis, advertising, and other tools of marketing, as well as the marketing plan and growth strategies. Case studies and present and future trends are included.

810. Hertzson, David. *Hotel-Motel Marketing.* Hotel-Motel Management Series. Indianapolis, IN: Bobbs-Merrill Educational Publishing, 1971. 198 p.
Designed as a text on marketing in the lodging industry, this book includes chapters on the role of marketing in the industry, organizing a sales department, planning a marketing program and establishing a salable product through various types of marketing analysis. In addition, there are chapters on various techniques of selling and advertising, publicity and promotion. Chapters on the development of room and food sales and the convention market are also included.

811. Johnson, Eugene M.; Scheuing, Eberhard E.; and Gaida, Kathleen A. *Profitable Service Marketing.* Homewood, IL: Dow Jones-Irwin, 1986. 303 p.
The authors present an application of marketing ideas and practices to the service industry. The book is divided into three parts: part one deals with both economic environment and consumer behavior; part two covers marketing research, planning, organization, implementation, and control; and part three, "The Service Mix," includes new service development, advertising, sales, promotion, distribution, and pricing. Emphasis throughout is on evolution and the necessity for flexibility and innovation in the service industries.

812. Kahrl, William L. *Foodservice Productivity and Profit Ideabook: With Appendix of Ideas from Operators.* Edited by Jule Wilkinson. Boston: Cahners Books, 1975. 233 p.
This is a practical book for improving productivity. Suggestions are made for improvements ranging from the most simple to the most sweeping. Section one helps provide the measurements needed to check productivity. Section two and section three deal with improvements that any operation can make with minor investment funding. Section four

and section five deal with areas such as site, location, decor, and remodeling costs where major changes are contemplated. The appendix includes suggestions from restaurant operators.

813. Koehl, Albert E. *How to Make Advertising Pay for Hotels, Motels, and Restaurants.* New York: Ahrens Publishing Co., 1960. 138 p.
This book is designed to help owners and managers plan effective advertising and promotion programs. Koehl has specialized in hotel advertising for many years. In this book, he covers media selection, agencies, advertising copy, banquet sales, and many other subjects and problems specific to advertising in this field. Somewhat dated, but still useful.

814. Kolb, Patricia Moore, ed. *Soup & Salad Bars.* Photographs by Don Kushnick. Boston: CBI Publishing Co., 1981. 56 p.
This is a guide to merchandising soups and salads. All items presented were developed in the test kitchen of *Restaurant Business Magazine.* Along with sections on the effective and profitable use of soup and salad bars, there are both soups and salads in "Before," "With," and "After" categories as accompaniments to other meals.

815. Kreul, Lee M.; Dennington, Lloyd J.; and Lohr, Judi. *Digest of Current Lodging Industry Market Research Studies. Vol. II.* s.l.: s.n., 1985. 92 p.
Like the first digest published in 1983, the purpose is to synthesize the findings of various research marketing studies. Thirty-nine research studies were used as the basis for this digest. Ten general questions about the lodging market such as "How Reservations Are Made" are answered using the data from the thirty-nine studies, in tables and charts. Each table identifies, by number, which studies the data were taken from. The studies are listed in the bibliography by the name of the study; size and identification of the sampled segment are given, as well as by and for whom it was prepared.

816. Laine, Steven, and Laine, Iris. *Promotion in Foodservice.* New York: McGraw-Hill, 1972. 202 p.
This is a textbook on the basics of promotion of products and services in the foodservice industry. The goals and aims of promotion are discussed and its subdivisions such as advertising, public relations, and publicity. Promotion is covered for all types of foodservices both commercial and institutional.

817. Lovelock, Christopher H. *Services Marketing: Text, Cases, & Readings.* Englewood Cliffs, NJ: Prentice-Hall, 1984. 492 p.
The author feels that service industries, including airlines, hotels, hospitals, restaurants, and banking, differ from manufacturing businesses and require different marketing tactics and strategies. Each section of the book begins with an overview of the subject and concludes with cases and readings.

818. Mayo, Edward J., Jr., and Jarvis, Lance P. *The Psychology of Leisure Travel: Effective Marketing and Selling of Travel Services.* Boston: CBI Publishing Co., 1981. 281 p.
This book was written to help those in the travel industry—airlines, hotels, car rental companies, and travel agents—understand the psychological reasons of the consumer-traveler. Instead of looking at demographics such as age, income, and education, the author focuses on the individual traveler's behavior. Chapters cover perception of travel, learning, personality, motivation, attitudes, and group influences. Five case studies are included in the appendix.

819. Nathan, Theodore Reade. *Hotelmanship: A Guide to Hospitality Industry Marketing and Management.* Englewood Cliffs, NJ: Institute for Business Planning, 1982. 347 p.
This book covers hotel marketing and management. The author's dynamic approach fits well with his philosophy that "Hotelmanship requires a combination of sound business principles and showmanship." Drawing from long experience, Nathan presents aggressive

techniques for promotion and advertising. He shows how to attract the convention and banquet trade and gives suggestions for improving operations as well as general policies for success.

820. National Restaurant Association. *The Dinner House Market.* Chicago, 1978. 34 leaves 15 p.
This is a summary of the findings of a study on the dinner house customer. Dinner house is defined as an upscale tableservice restaurant which typically does not serve breakfast and derives most of its sales from recreational dining. Part one contains data on customer spending and eating habits at dinner houses versus all restaurants. Part two looks at the dinner house market as it differs from the general restaurant market and examines the particular segment it attracts. Information is in tabular format and based on surveys in which 10,000 families kept diaries of restaurant visits for two-week periods.

821. National Restaurant Association. *Market Research for the Restaurateur: A Do-It-Yourself Handbook for Market Research.* Washington, DC, 1981. 118 p.
The National Restaurant Association provides a do-it-yourself guide to market research. It is intended to assist owners and managers in using established research techniques without having special training in statistics or mathematics. Chapters cover marketing research, sales records use, how to use customer comment cards, analyzing trading area, evaluating customer perceptions, and how to conduct a competitive analysis.

822. National Restaurant Association. *Promotions 83: What's Possible, What's Popular and What's Profitable.* Washington, DC, 1983. 76 p.
This is an edited transcript of the National Restaurant Association's Conference on promotions held in 1983. Several case studies are included with speeches given by industry experts.

823. National Restaurant Association, Research and Information Services Department. *Consumer Attitude and Behavior Study: Consumer Restaurant Behavior: A View Based on Occasion Segmentation.* Washington, DC, 1984?. 74 p.
Traditional market research has relied on demographic characteristics to describe target markets. But this type of research is ineffective in the restaurant industry where choice of restaurant is based on the occasion. This novel study was done to develop descriptions of the basic occasions for eating out. Seven restaurant occasions and their percentage of total restaurant occasions were identified: fast and inexpensive, 16 percent; familiar ground, 12 percent; convenience, 12 percent; business or social obligation, 13 percent; family meal, 16 percent; special night out, 15 percent; and social fun, 18 percent.

824. National Restaurant Association, Research and Information Services Department. *Foodservice Numbers: A Statistical Digest for the Foodservice Industry.* Washington, DC, 1986. 107 p.
This is a digest of National Restaurant Association statistical information from 1970–84. The book is divided into six sections: "Industry Food and Beverage Sales and Purchases," "Consumer Research Highlights," "Characteristics of the Restaurant Occasion," "Restaurant Operations," "Industry Trends," and "Major Economic Indicators." The second section is of special interest, giving highlights of research on consumer preferences, expectations, and nutritional concerns as well as why, where, and how often various types of people eat out.

825. Nykiel, Ronald A. *Marketing in the Hospitality Industry.* New York: Van Nostrand Reinhold Co., 1983. 240 p.
This basic text covers segmentation, consumer preferences, channels of distribution, marketing strategy, and total marketing planning as well as key marketing methodologies such as advertising, promotions, packaging, and pricing.

826. Reid, Robert D. *Foodservice and Restaurant Marketing.* New York: Van Nostrand Reinhold Co., 1983. 312 p.

This book is aimed at the foodservice manager and is designed to help him implement effective marketing in the 1980s. It provides an overview of basic marketing and explains strategic planning, marketing information systems, market segmentation, consumer behavior, menu planning, and pricing, as well as internal and external advertising and promotion.

827. Seltz, David D. *Food Service Marketing and Promotion.* New York: Lebhar-Friedman Books, 1977. 202 p.

Emphasizing the importance of a marketing plan, this book gives practical advice on on-premise and off-premise promotions, advertising, public relations, and special promotions such as children's events and group sales.

828. Stein, Bob. *Marketing in Action for Hotels—Motels—Restaurants.* New York: Ahrens Publishing Co., 1971. 191 p.

Stein defines marketing as the complete function of selling food and lodging to the consumer. After an introduction to the lodging and restaurant industries, he also gives an introduction to the phenomenon of marketing. He then deals with each industry separately giving a historical perspective followed by chapters on marketing, research and analysis, and budgeting.

829. Taylor, Derek. *Hotel and Catering Sales Promotion.* London: Iliffe Books, 1964. 180 p.

This basic text on marketing for the hotel industry does its best to be practical and avoid jargon. Selling, advertising, and public relations are discussed as the three major ingredients of sales promotion. Chapters get down to the specifics such as sales records and procedures, selling by telephone, banquet sales, hotel advertising, and so on. Case studies are provided in the final section.

830. Taylor, Derek. *How to Sell Banquets: The Key to Conference and Function Promotion.* 2d ed. Boston: CBI Publishing Co., 1981. 195 p.

As the title clearly indicates, this book is about marketing hotel banquets. It deals with promotional materials, sales training, entertaining, and advertising. Sample letters and a chapter covering the problem patron are included. The book has a very practical approach.

831. Wenzel, George Leonard. *How to Build Volume.* Austin, TX, 1971. 160 p.

This is a guide to motivation, merchandising, and advertising in the restaurant field. The pricing guidelines and such are long out of date, but the general advice and examples of advertising are still useful.

Menu Planning and Design

832. Atkinson, Alta B. *Volume Feeding Menu Selector*. Compiled and edited by Eulalia Blair. Boston: Cahners Books, 1971. 185 p.

> Designed to help in menu planning, this book is made up of 120 charts of menu items. There are ten for each month of the year. Instead of giving a calendar of prepared menus, items are arranged in four vertical columns: Meat, Poultry, Seafood, and Miscellaneous. These are crossed by four horizontal columns titled Appetizer, Entree, Vegetable, and Salad and Dessert. Thus, it is easy to select items that compliment each other while putting together a menu to fit specific needs or preferences.

833. Dardarian, Leo. *Put Profit on the Menu*. New York: Ahrens Publishing Co., 1959. 96 p.

> Dardarian looks at the menu as a catalog of items, a contract to deliver the items, a work order, and an investment determinant. In addition, the menu is a purchase order because it states the raw materials needed and a private newspaper because it communicates the operator's personality. Using these categories, the author goes on to discuss kinds of menus, menu structure, consistency, and other aspects of an effective menu.

834. Eckstein, Eleanor F. *Menu Planning*. 3d ed. Westport, CT: AVI Publishing Co., 1983. 463 p.

> This book presents the theoretical framework necessary for good menu planning. Section one covers consumer, worker, and management considerations as well as meal and menu patterns. Section two has chapters on various types of institutions including hospitals; nursing and retirement homes; and school, college, and industrial cafeterias as well as a chapter on menu planning for restaurant customers. Section three includes computers, model selection, data collection, programming, and interfacing. Section four gives basic information on food customs and preferences of some fifteen ethnic groups as well as vegetarians and fruitarians.

835. Fellman, Leonard F. *Merchandising by Design: Developing Effective Menus & Wine Lists*. New York: Chain Store Age Publishing Corp., 1981. 136 p.

> This short book combines menu design and wine list design into one work. It lacks the color illustrations found in many menu design books but includes good information on design and some black-and-white photographs. It covers the importance of design and color in menus, controlling costs of reproduction and the impact of language and words. Menus for special occasions are covered. The section on wine lists includes historical information of wine lists, planning and wording the list, and directions on proper service of wine.

836. Hoke, Ann. *Restaurant Menu Planning*. rev. ed. Evanston, IL: John Willy, Inc., 1964. 339 p.

> This book is based on a series of lectures given at the Hotel Administration School of Cornell. Each menu item is covered. The idea is to make the menu attractive, interesting, and profitable. Proper merchandising is emphasized. In this revised edition, a chapter has been added to help avoid monotony in luncheon menus by using a chart system.

837. Kahrl, William L. *Menu Planning, Merchandising.* Managing for Profit Series. New York: Chain Store Publishing Corp., 1978. 83 p.
One of the series done by Kahrl in which each manual deals with a specific problem area common to all segments of the industry, offering solutions and serving as a training aid, this volume gives advice on making an attractive and profitable menu. It deals with both content and style and also covers on-location and off-location merchandising.

838. Kasavana, Michael L., and Smith, Donald I. *Menu Engineering: A Practical Guide to Menu Analysis.* Lansing, MI: Hospitality Publications, Inc., 1982. 138 p.
This is a marketing-oriented approach to the evaluation of current and future menu pricing, design, and content decisions. It presents a model for menu planning that uses customer demand, customer preference, and item contribution margin to determine the best menu for a given restaurant. The menu engineering process is designed to present an accurate summary of the menu's marketing power by concentration on customer demand, menu mix analysis and item contribution margin. Chapters cover the concept and procedures of menu engineering. A self-correcting problem set for students is also included.

839. Kotschevar, Lendal Henry. *Management by Menu.* 2d ed. Dubuque, IA: W. C. Brown; Chicago: National Institute for the Foodservice Industry, 1987. 364 p.
Like the first edition, this updated edition presents the menu as the central theme controlling most other foodservice functions. It is still the only book that ties the menu in with management principles. Among other subjects, it covers menu planning, analysis, pricing, and merchandising.

840. Kreck, Lothar A. *Menus: Analysis and Planning.* 2d ed. Boston: Van Nostrand Reinhold Co., 1984. 277 p.
Kreck provides a thorough look at menus, illustrating concepts, techniques, special marketing approaches, and cost/price relationships. Chapters discuss the history of menus, pricing, measuring menu effectiveness, analysis of menus, improving menus, accuracy in language and wine lists. Many full-page examples are given.

841. Miller, Jack E. *Menu Pricing.* A Cahners Special Report. Boston: Cahners Books International, 1976. 24 p.
A short-page pamphlet that discusses menu pricing concepts and methods. Miller compares seven pricing methods and advocates one adapted from the Texas Restaurant Association system. Brief sections are also presented on price increases, volume increases, and menu strategies.

842. Miller, Jack E. *Menu Pricing and Strategy.* 2d ed. New York: Van Nostrand Reinhold Co., 1987. 170 p.
This new edition provides a choice of strategies for menu pricing and development. Calculations for figuring breakeven points, minimum sales points, and the like are fully explained. It shows how to design menus for different types of restaurants and determines prices. Various menu marketing techniques such as coupons are covered. It also includes sample menus and a menu self-evaluation. Provides both text and discussion of the "U. S. Government Guidelines for Accuracy in Menu Language."

843. National Restaurant Association. *Accuracy in Menus.* Washington, DC, 1985. 9 p.
A short pamphlet giving guidelines for truthful representation on menus as understood by the National Restaurant Association. Short sections discuss representation of quantity, quality, price, brand name, product identification and origin, merchandising terms, means of preservation, food preparation, verbal and visual presentation, and dietary or nutritional claims. The position statement of the National Restaurant Association on "Accuracy in Menu Offerings" is included.

844. National Restaurant Association. *Great American Menus Selected from Winners of the Menu Idea Exchange of the National Restaurant Association.* Chicago, 1964. 137 p.

Selected from the winners of the Menu Idea Exchange of the National Restaurant Association, this book reproduces exact replicas of about thirty of the 336 menus that were entered in the exchange. Winners were selected for excellence in appearance, merchandising power, ease of reading, content, and originality. Three menus appear in each of the following categories: "Nationality and Regional Cuisine Restaurants," "Specialty Restaurants," "Atmosphere Restaurants," "Table Service Dining Rooms or Restaurants," "Supper Clubs," "Combination Counter and Table Service Operations," "Drive-Ins and Coffee Houses," "Snack Bars," "Specialty Houses," and "Children's Menus."

845. National Restaurant Association. *A Nutrition Guide for the Restaurateur.* Washington, DC, 1986. 72 p.

This brief handbook reviews the basic information on nutrition so restaurant managers can adapt and plan menus that appeal to the nutrition-conscious consumer. Chapters include salt and sodium, fat and cholesterol, calories and weight control, and fiber. The last chapter covers marketing ideas. Each chapter has an appendix of facts in chart format.

846. Radice, Judi, and Hess, Diane. *Menu Design.* Locust Valley, NY: PBC International, Inc., 1985. 250 p.

This is a collection of color photographs of over 200 menus by well-known designers. Menus by Milton Glaser, David Bartels, and Wood Pirtle are included. The book is organized by type of menu including theme menu, ethnic, fine dining, regional, specialty, children's, and informal. Chapters are included on techniques of menu design and interviews with top designers.

847. Radice, Judi, and National Restaurant Association. *Menu Design 2: Marketing the Restaurant Through Graphics.* New York: PBC International Inc., 1987. 256 p.

By the author of *Menu Design,* this second book is an all new collection of over 200 menus showing exceptional design qualities. Each menu is superbly photographed in color and carefully described. The restaurant's name and location are included along with the names of the designers and specifications of size, paper and printer. Chapters cover techniques of design, theme menus, ethnic dining, catering and special feasts, hotel menus, institutional menus, specialty menus, and children's menus.

848. Restaurant Business, Inc. *Menu Planning and Foods Merchandising.* Hotel-Motel Management Series. Indianapolis, IN: Bobbs-Merrill Educational Publishing, 1971. 145 p.

This book begins with techniques for identifying and understanding the customer. Costs, pricing, and purchasing are covered. The main thrust of the book is on menu planning. The cyclical menu, ethnic menu, and time-block menu, among others, are discussed. A "Menu Medley" gives eighteen examples of actual menus. A glossary for menu writers includes pronunciation guides for foreign terms.

849. Scanlon, Nancy Loman. *Marketing by Menu.* New York: Van Nostrand Reinhold Co., 1985. 174 p.

The author includes menu format and the principles of design as well as menu content in this guide to professional menu planning. Recipe cards, cost cards, balanced selections, pricing, and profitable offerings are discussed as are basics such as purchasing and production. Many examples of good menu designs are included.

850. Seaberg, Albin G. *Menu Design, Merchandising and Marketing.* 3d ed. New York: Van Nostrand Reinhold Co., 1983. 319 p.

Seaberg says the menu is written and produced to sell. With this in mind, he discusses the menu from all angles. He deals with general considerations such as menu copy, color, and type selection; special menus such as children's and roomservice menus; and specific aspects such as appetizers and salads. Other chapters deal with subjects less often covered, such as merchandising low calorie items and "What Americans Can Learn from Foreign Menus." There are many example menus.

851. Sherwood, Karen. *Nutrition and Foodservice.* National Restaurant Association Current Issues Report. Washington, DC: National Restaurant Association, 1985. 12 p.

This is the first of a series of Current Issues Reports published by the National Restaurant Association. This one provides an analysis of the interest of consumers in nutrition and diet, how eating habits are changing, and the effect this is having on the foodservice industry and what restaurateurs can do in response to this trend. Included in the report are the dietary guidelines for Americans developed by the USDA's Health and Human Services.

852. U.S. Department of Agriculture, Food and Nutrition Division, Nutrition and Technical Services Division. *Menu Planning Guide for School Food Service.* rev. ed. Program Aid no. 1260. Washington DC: Government Printing Office, 1983. 97 p.

This government document covers the philosophy and principles of good menu planning, federal regulations, menu planning methods, and promotion of good nutrition as they relate to school foodservice. Chapters include "Lunch Requirements, Recommendations, and Policies"; "The Basics of Menu Planning"; "How to Vary Portions for Various Age/Grade Groups"; "Planning Breakfasts"; "Merchandising the School Lunch and Breakfast"; and "Nutrition Education and Menu Planning."

Miscellaneous

853. De Groot, Roy Andries. *In Search of the Perfect Meal: A Collection of the Best Food Writing of Roy Andries de Groot.* Selected by Lorna J. Sass. New York: St. Martin's Press, 1986. 411 p.
> A collection of forty-four essays by the famous gastronome. Many of these originally appeared in *Cuisine, Esquire,* and *The Chicago Tribune.* Two were never before published; some include favorite recipes.

854. Food and Nutrition Board, Commission on Life Sciences, National Research Council. *What Is America Eating?: Proceedings of a Symposium.* Washington, DC: National Academy Press, 1986. 173 p.
> This is the published proceedings of the 1984 Food and Nutrition Board Symposium held at the National Academy of Sciences. It includes twelve symposium presentations in four sections. The first section reviews eating patterns and health in the United States. The second discusses motivations for food selection. The third covers the nutritional consequences of eating trends, and the fourth discusses nutrition programs policy and research.

855. National Restaurant Association. *National Restaurant Association Annual Report.* Washington, DC. (Annual)
> Similar to company annual reports, this is a glossy publication reviewing the activity of the National Restaurant Association over the last year. Many photographs are included.

856. Society for the Advancement of Food Service Research. *Proceeding of the Conference.* West Lafayette, IN. (Annual)
> Each annual conference centers on a different topic. Some from past years have been *2000—A Food Service Odyssey* and *Image Economics.*

Periodicals

857. *Airline, Ship & Catering ONBOARD SERVICES Magazine.* Miami Springs, FL: Onboard Services. (9/year)
This is the official publication of Inflight Food Services Association, Marine Hotel, Catering & Duty Free Association, and IFCA. It covers foodservice management of domestic and international airlines, ships, railroads, catering firms, and duty free interests, as well as ship chandlers and other suppliers to the travel industry. Formerly called *Airline & Travel Food Service.*

858. *American Automatic Merchandiser.* Cleveland, OH: Harcourt Brace Jovanovich. (13/year)
This is the trade journal serving the merchandise vending, coffee service, and foodservice segment of the industry. Each issue has about six to ten articles. Regular columns include "Coffee Service Corner," "Foodservice Corner," "Convention Calendar," and industry news. A special issue called the "Blue Book Directory" is published in late August of each year.

859. *Annals of Tourism Research.* Elmsford, NY: Pergamon Journals, Inc. (Quarterly)
This is an international, refereed journal that focuses on academic perspectives of tourism, particularly the development of theoretical constructs. Each issue has from five to ten articles which emphasize the theoretical aspects of tourism. In addition, each issue includes reports on current research, review of new books, and brief annotations of new publications and journal articles of interest to tourism researchers. Contributors to the journal are scholars from around the world.

860. *Art Culinaire: The International Magazine in Good Taste.* Atlanta, GA: Culinaire Inc. 1986–. (Quarterly)
This quarterly journal features recipes for fine food beautifully served. Articles cover chefs, seasonal recipes, and garnishing. Each issue is bound in boards and is lavishly illustrated.

861. *Catering Today.* Santa Claus, IN: Pro Tech Publishing and Communications, Inc. (Monthly)
This is the trade journal that focuses specifically on the catering segment of the industry. Information on equipment, recipes, training, computers, and book reviews are included.

862. *Club Management.* St. Louis, MO: Commerce Publishing Co. (Monthly)
Subtitled the *National Magazine of Clubdom,* this is the official journal of the Club Managers Association of America. In addition to articles on club management, it also carries association news articles, reports on specific clubs and club managers, and announcements of new positions. One issue each spring is the official transcript of the association's conference.

863. *The Consultant.* Seattle, WA: The Foodservice Consultants Society International. (Quarterly)
This magazine is aimed specifically at the professional foodservice consultant; articles cover sanitation, equipment, new cooking techniques such as cook-freeze, industry trends, and design. Regular columns include association news, book reviews, and industry news.

864. *Convention World.* Stamford, CN: Bayard Publications, Inc. (6/year)
This is a trade journal for association meeting planners. The July/August issue is a directory of major association conventions planned for the next 15 years.

865. *Cooking for Profit.* Fond du Lac, WI: Metanoia Corporation. (Monthly)
This is a trade journal that emphasizes cooking for the profit segment of the industry. Regular columns include energy management, equipment analysis, equipment buyers' guide, purchasing, employee relations, recipes from chefs, and a profile of a restaurateur.

866. *Cornell Hotel and Restaurant Administration Quarterly.* Ithaca, NY: Cornell University, School of Hotel Administration. (Quarterly)
This is the most important journal in the industry; it is published at the Cornell School of Hotel and Restaurant Administration. Full-length feature articles are scholarly studies from researchers in the hospitality field. All articles are double-blind reviewed. In addition, each issue also includes news items related to the industry. "Educators' Forum" is a special issue published in August of each year.

867. *Executive Housekeeping Today.* Columbus, OH: Zimmerman Public Relations, Inc. (Monthly)
This is the official magazine of the National Executive Housekeepers Association. Articles cover topics on safe use of chemical cleaners, personnel management, pest control, and handling specialized cleaning problems. Association news and new products are regular columns.

868. *FBQ: Food Broker Quarterly.* Washington, DC: National Food Brokers Association. (Quarterly)
This is the official publication of the National Food Brokers Association.

869. *FIU Hospitality Review.* Miami, FL: Florida International University. (Biannual)
Each issue of this scholarly journal from the Florida International University School of Hospitality Management contains about ten articles written primarily by faculty members from hospitality schools from around the country. Emphasis is on hotel and restaurant management education, but there are also articles of interest to the whole industry.

870. *Food Management.* Cleveland, OH: Harcourt Brace Jovanovich. (Monthly)
This monthly trade journal focuses on management in the nonprofit segment of the foodservice industry. It includes articles about foodservice in healthcare facilities, schools, colleges, and business and industry. Each issue has two to three long articles on timely topics, as well as regular columns that focus on the four areas of nonprofit foodservice: schools, hospitals, colleges, and businesses. Several quantity recipes are included in each issue. Each spring, the journal has a "Presidents' Forum" which features the leaders of the five major foodservice associations.

871. *Foodservice Equipment & Supplies Specialist.* Newton, MA: Cahners Publishing Company. (Monthly)
This is the trade journal for equipment manufacturers and suppliers. Regular columns include "Industry News," "Industry Trends," "Products & Literature," and "Association News." In addition, each issue has full-length articles on equipment topics. Annual feature articles are "The 100 Giants of Distribution," "Consultant and Chain Giants," "The FE&S Industry Forecast," and the "Product Knowledge Handbook" which is a catalog of products by category. Every February a special issue is published called "The Buyers

Guide;" it is a comprehensive industry sourcebook with manufacturer sources for more than 500 products.

872. *Foodservice Product News.* New York: Young/Conway Publications, Inc. (Monthly)
This is a tabloid-size trade journal that reviews new food products and equipment.

873. *Gallup Annual Report on Eating Out.* Princeton, NJ: The Gallup Organization. 1985–. (Annual)
This annual publication pulls together statistics from the *Gallup Monthly Report on Eating Out.* It is divided into sections such as "Customer Demographics" and "New Menu Items."

874. *Gallup Monthly Report on Eating Out.* Princeton, NJ: The Gallup Organization. (Monthly)
This monthly newsletter includes extensive statistical charts on food trends. Each issue is only a few pages long but is packed with facts.

875. *Gourmet.* Beverly Hills, CA: Conde Nast Publications, Inc. (Monthly)
Subtitled The Magazine of Good Living, this is probably the most well-known food magazine published. Besides publishing about food and cookery, it also includes articles about travel.

876. *Hospital Food & Nutrition Focus.* Frederick, MD: Aspen Publishers, Inc. (Monthly)
An eight-page newsletter tracking trends, legislation, and other current information for the hospital dietitian and foodservice manager.

877. *Hospitality Education and Research Journal.* University Park, PA: Council on Hotel Restaurant and Institutional Education, (Biannual)
This is the main journal in hospitality education. Articles emphasis empirical investigation and theoretical analysis. All full-length articles are refereed by members of the editorial board and other experts. Each issue contains about five lengthy articles and a section called "Viewpoints and Commentary" which has rejoinders, commentaries, and rebuttals on earlier articles. Occasionally there is a section called "Research Notes" which has brief reports on current research projects.

878. *Hospitality Law.* Madison, WI: Magna Publishing, Inc. (Monthly)
This monthly publication explores legal problems and implications of topics such as overbooking, cancellations, insurance, and liquor liability. Each issue is about eight pages in length.

879. *Hotel and Motel Management.* Cleveland, OH: Harcourt Brace Jovanovich. (17/year)
Called the Newspaper for the Lodging Industry, this tabloid-size magazine is the best source for tracking company activity in the industry. Also included are articles on trends and issues before the industry such as tax reform, automation, and all-suite hotels. Indexed in *Business Periodicals Index* and *Business Index.*

880. *Hotel & Resort Industry.* New York: Coastal Communications Corporation. (Monthly)
Subtitled The Magazine for Lodging Management—Hotels, Resorts, Motor Hotels, this is one of the best trade journals in the lodging industry. Articles are longer and more substantial than are those in most trade journals. Emphasis is on management for the first class or luxury hotel and resort. Special issues include an annual economic forecast issue in December and semiannual franchise issues.

881. *Hotels and Restaurants International.* Newton, MA: Cahners Publishing Company. (Monthly)
> This trade journal covers industry news and features of major hotels and restaurants from around the world. Each issue has from six to ten articles. One article in each issue focuses on a worldwide chain. Other articles cover interior design, foodservice, computer technology, and stories on famous hoteliers or restaurateurs. The December issue is "The Worldwide Buyers Guide" which lists sources for buyers from all over the world. Indexed in *Business Index* and *Food Science & Technology Abstracts.*

882. *The HSMAI Marketing Review.* Washington, DC: Hotel Sales & Marketing Association. (Quarterly)
> This journal centers on increasing sales in hotels. Each issue carries about a dozen signed articles; each is three to five pages long.

883. *Innkeeping World.* Seattle, WA: Innkeeping World. (10/year)
> A newsletter that carries articles and interviews on managing, marketing, guest, and staff relations. No photographs or illustrations are included.

884. *Institutional Distribution.* New York: Bill Communications, Inc. (14/year)
> This is the trade journal for the food distributor that services the institutional segment of the industry.

885. *International Journal of Hospitality Management.* Elmsford, NY: Pergamon Journals Inc. (Quarterly)
> This journal is supported by the International Association of Hotel Management Schools, whose membership is derived from colleges in eight European countries. Each issue has four to eight articles which are refereed by experts in the field. In addition to the full-length research articles, there is a section called "Reviews and Features" which includes research notes and book reviews.

886. *Journal of Foodservice Systems.* Westport, CT: Food & Nutrition Press, Inc. (Quarterly)
> This is the official publication of the Society of Foodservice Systems Professionals. It is a refereed journal that publishes about six articles each issue which emphasize research, methodology, and case histories in foodservice systems analysis, design, implementation, and management.

887. *Journal of Travel Research.* Boulder, CO: Business Research Division. (Quarterly)
> This quarterly publication of the Travel and Tourism Research Association publishes articles on new techniques, creative views, generalizations about travel research thought and practice and synthesis of travel research material. Articles are blind reviewed by members of the editorial board. Each issue has from six to twelve research articles, an annotated list of new publications in a section called "Travel Research Bookshelf," and a few critical reviews of new books in the field.

888. *KARAS Executive Report for Foodservice Decision Makers.* New York: Restaurant Business, Inc. (50/year)
> This is a newsletter that tracks corporate changes, legislation, and other financial and newsworthy items in the industry. Each issue is four pages long.

889. *Lodging.* New York: American Hotel Association Directory Corporation. (11/year)
> This is the official publication of the American Hotel & Motel Association. In addition to news of the association and information on association meetings, the journal includes indepth articles on marketing, franchising, management, and design for hotels and motels. The April issue is a directory of products and services for the industry.

890. *Lodging Hospitality.* Cleveland, OH: Penton Publishing, Inc. (Monthly)
This is an excellent trade journal in the lodging segment. Articles are written primarily by the editorial staff. Each issue includes five lengthy articles on marketing, foodservice, amenities, computers, interior design, housekeeping, etc. Frequently articles focus on one of the big hotel chains and reviews their management and marketing techniques. In addition, there are numerous columns such as "Equipment At Work," "Economic Outlook," and "Marketwatch."

891. *Meeting News.* New York: Gralla Publications. (16/year)
This tabloid-size trade journal includes practical articles and news for meeting planners. One of the most useful sections is the site selection articles that review facilities, hotels, convention centers, and attractions in selected cities and states. The January issue is a directory of sites, suppliers, and services in the industry.

892. *Meetings & Conventions.* Cherry Hill, NJ: Business Publications Division of Murdoch Magazines. (Monthly)
This monthly trade journal includes longer articles on trends and issues in the meeting industry. Regular columns include "Planner's Portfolio," which includes helpful, practical ideas, and "Area Guides," which reviews facilities and activities available in convention cities. The annual "Gavel" issue in March is an international directory of hotels, resorts, conference centers, speakers, consultants, etc.

893. *Military Clubs & Recreation.* Alexandria, VA: Club Executive, Inc. (Monthly)
Subtitled Reaching Club and Recreation Personnel around the World, this is the official publication of the International Military Club Executives Association.

894. *NASFT Showcase.* New York: National Association for the Specialty Food Trade, Inc. (Bimonthly)
The purpose of this association journal is to promote specialty foods and related products. It is the official publication of the National Association for the Speciality Food Trade.

895. *The National Culinary Review.* St. Augustine, FL: American Culinary Federation, Inc. (Monthly)
This is the official magazine of the American Culinary Federation. As such, it carries association news and articles on cooking and menu planning with some recipes.

896. *Nation's Restaurant News.* New York: Lebhar-Friedman, Inc. (Weekly)
Regular scanning of this tabloid-size magazine is the best way to keep informed on the news and events in the restaurant industry. Mergers and acquisitions, new menu items, and marketing techniques and food trends are all closely tracked.

897. *Pizza Today.* Santa Claus, IN: ProTech Publishing and Communications, Inc. (Monthly)
This is a monthly trade journal specifically for pizza restaurateurs. Each issue features a pizza maker of the month, recipes, ingredients, and promotion ideas and reviews of new equipment. A regular column, "Resources," is a directory of suppliers and professional services for the pizza industry. Each year the magazine ranks the top pizza chains and independent restaurants.

898. *Resort & Hotel Management.* Solana Beach, CA: Source Communications, Inc. (8/year)
This journal includes brief articles on equipment, management, and design for resort hotels and many short columns including a "Software Review" and book reviews. The Spring issue is a "Buyer's Guide."

899. *Restaurant/Hotel Design International.* New York: Bill Communications, Inc. (10/year)
This trade journal focuses on the interior and exterior design of restaurants and hotels. Each issue carries approximately seven articles about new or remodeled facilities. In addition, there is a regular column "Solutions," which discusses design problems. Other regular columns are "On-Site," "Facilities," and "Marketplace." Lavishly illustrated. Formerly entitled *Restaurant Design* and *Restaurant and Hotel Design.*

900. *Restaurant Business.* New York: Bill Communications, Inc. (18/year)
This is one of the best trade journals in the restaurant field. Issued every three weeks, each issue has a major cover story article and several other feature articles which cover trends in the industry or focus on specific chains. Regular columns include "Menu Ideas" (with recipes) and "Drafts, Carafes & Spirits." In addition, there is information on mergers and acquisitions, marketing ideas, trade quotes, and new equipment.

901. *Restaurant Hospitality.* Cleveland, OH: Penton Publishing, Inc. (Monthly)
This is an excellent trade journal in the restaurant segment of the industry. It emphasizes management techniques for profitable, efficient, and comfortable restaurants. Most articles are written by the editorial staff of the journal; each issue includes about seven long articles and many columns such as "Food Trends," "Business Barometer," "Equipment Report," "Interior Design," and "Tabletop Design." There are many special issues; the most important ones are "RH 500" in June, "Top 100 Chains" in August, and "Forecast" in December.

902. *Restaurant Management.* Cleveland, OH: Electrical Information Publications, Inc. (Monthly)
Formerly entitled *Independent Restaurants,* this journal emphasizes management and marketing information to assist independent restaurateurs. Each issue has a cover article and three to four other long articles, one of which focuses on an independent restaurateur. Other articles cover menu planning ideas, bar business, and food trends. Short columns cover sanitation, marketing, personnel management, decor, computers, etc.

903. *Restaurant News.* Anaheim, CA: HANI Publications. (Irregular)
Subtitled The Voice of and for All Facets of the Foodservice Industry, this is a newspaper for owners, operators, managers, chefs, purchasing agents, dietitians, and foodservice executives.

904. *Restaurants & Institutions.* Denver, CO: Cahners Publishing Company. (Bi-weekly)
This trade journal services all aspects of foodservice, both profit and nonprofit segments. Emphasis is on high volume units; all articles are written by the staff. Each issue has about thirty articles; columns cover chains, independents, institutions, equipment, food, and beverage service. Special issues include "Buyers' Guide" in March, "Trends" in May, "R&I 400" in July, and "Tastes of America" in December.

905. *Restaurants USA.* Washington, DC: National Restaurant Association. (11/year)
Published by the National Restaurant Association, this journal's major value is the extensive statistical reports it publishes in the "Foodservice Trends" and "Crest (Consumer Report on Eating Share Trends) Reports." In addition, each issue has articles on managing and marketing restaurants and reports on current trends such as drive-thru restaurants, franchising, etc.

906. *School Food Service Journal.* Englewood, CO: American School Food Service Association. (11/year)
This association journal is aimed at the practicing school foodservice manager, not at researchers in the field. Association news is thoroughly covered; many articles focus on ideas from local schools. Over the last year, there has been a series of articles written by various food industry groups that review the history of foods. Quantity recipes appropriate for schools are also included.

907. *School Food Service Research Review.* Denver, CO: American School Food Service Association. (2/year)

This is the refereed journal from the American School Food Service Association. It is designed to disseminate research findings and other relevant information applicable to school foodservice in the areas of foodservice facilities, food quality and production, management, program evaluation, nutrition standards, and nutrition education. The journal also includes book reviews and abstracts of articles from other journals of interest to school foodservice professionals.

908. *Successful Meetings.* New York: Bill Communications, Inc. (Monthly)

This trade journal is subtitled The Authority on Meetings and Incentive Travel Management. Special quarterly issue sections cover "Incentive Travel" and "Travel/Transportation." Each issue includes about three features and numerous columns such as "Trade Show Trends" and "What's New in Sites." Also indepth site reports on states are included. The February issue is a "Facilities Directory" which lists hotels, convention centers, and meeting services.

909. *Tourism Management.* Guildford, England: Butterworth Scientific, Ltd. (Quarterly)

This quarterly journal publishes scholarly articles on tourism planning and development. The scope is international; full-length research reports, short articles, and reports of projects in development are included. Articles are refereed before publication.

910. *Vending Times.* New York: Vending Times, Inc. (Monthly)

Subtitled The National Newspaper of Vending, Feeding, and Recreational Services, this tabloid-sized magazine covers the news and trends in vending of food and music and games.

911. *Vintage.* New York: Vintage Ventures, Inc. (6/year)

Originally this magazine covered only wine, but now it has expanded to be a magazine of food, wine, and gracious living. It includes articles on specialty cooking, spices and herbs, cheeses, and many recipes, all beautifully illustrated. Reviews of wines are still included.

FOREIGN

912. *Asian Hotelkeeper and Catering Times.* Hong Kong: Thomson Press Hong Kong, Limited. (6/year)

This journal is aimed specifically at hoteliers and restaurateurs with international chains located in Asia or the Pacific area. Articles cover topics such as wines of different areas of the world, economic conditions of cities and areas in the East, and news of chains and people.

913. *Australia Hotelier.* Darlinghurst, Australia: Laurie Cottier Productions Pty. Ltd.

A journal specifically for hotel managers in Australia.

914. *BC Hotelman.* North Vancouver, BC: Naylor Communications Ltd. (6/year)

A trade magazine specifically for hoteliers of British Columbia.

915. *Canadian Hotel & Restaurant.* Toronto, ON: Maclean Hunter Ltd. (Monthly)

Subtitled The Magazine of Foodservice and Lodging Management, this journal provides news to the hospitality industry in Canada.

916. *Foodservice and Hospitality.* Toronto, ON: Kostuch Communications Ltd. (Monthly)
Subtitled Canada's Hospitality Business Magazine, this journal tracks trends and news of the hospitality industry in Canada.

917. *Hotel & Catering News.* Hong Kong: Thomson Press Hong Kong, Limited. (Biweekly)
A newsletter that comes as part of the *Asian Hotelkeeper and Catering Times.*

918. *Ontario Innkeeper.* Toronto, ON: Naylor Communications Ltd. (6/year)
This is the official publication of the Ontario Hotel & Motel Association.

919. *Prairie Hotelman.* Winnipeg, MB: Naylor Communications, Ltd. (6/year)
This trade journal on the hotel industry covers Manitoba, Saskatchewah, and Alberta.

STATE AND REGIONAL

920. *Amenities.* Atlanta, GA: Georgia Hospitality & Travel Association, Inc.
This is the official publication of the Georgia Hospitality & Travel Association.

921. *The Appetizer.* Des Moines, IA: Iowa Restaurant and Beverage Association. (Monthly)
The official publication of the Iowa Restaurant and Beverage Association.

922. *Arkansas Hospitality.* Little Rock, AR: Arkansas Lodging Association.
This is the official publication of the Arkansas Lodging Association.

923. *California Inntouch.* Sacramento, CA: Naylor Publications Inc.
This is the official publication of the California Hotel & Motel Association.

924. *The Culinarian.* San Francisco, CA: Chefs Association of the Pacific Coast, Inc. (Monthly)
This is the official publication of the Chefs Association of the Pacific Coast. Each issue has an article by the association president, one by the contributing editor, an article on wine, and one on purveyors.

925. *Empire State Food Service News.* Skaneateles, NY: Empire State Food Service News, Inc. (Monthly)
This newspaper provides coverage of the industry for the major cities in New York: Buffalo, Rochester, Syracuse, Binghamton, Watertown, Utica-Rome, and Albany.

926. *Florida Hotel & Motel Journal.* Tallahassee, FL: Accommodations, Inc. (subsidiary of Florida Hotel & Motel Association). (Monthly)
The official publication of the Florida Hotel & Motel Association.

729. *Food & Beverage Impact.* Raleigh, NC: North Carolina Restaurant Association. (Monthly)
The official publication of the North Carolina Restaurant Association.

928. *The Food & Beverage Journal.* Tiburon, CA: The Food & Beverage Journal. (Monthly)
A trade newspaper for the food and beverage professional of northern California and northern Nevada.

929. *Food & Service.* Austin, TX: Texas Restaurant Association. (10/year)
The official publication of the Texas Restaurant Association.

930. *Foodservice Metro.* New York: Metropolitan Restaurant News, Inc. (Monthly)
> The trade journal serving New York, New Jersey, Connecticut, and the Philadelphia area.

931. *Hawaii Foodservice News.* Honolulu, HA: Nicholas Publishing Company. (Monthly)
> Subtitled The Official Voice of Hawaii's Foodservice Industry, this newsletter is the official publication of Hawaii Restaurant Association, Food Service Executives Association, Chefs de Cuisine Association of Hawaii, Professional Cooks of Hawaii, National Association of Catering Exccutives-Hawaii, International Military Club Executives Association, and Club Managers Association of America.

932. *Hawaii Hospitality.* Honolulu, HA: Trade Publishing Company. (Quarterly)
> This is the official magazine of the Hawaii Hotel Association.

933. *Hawaii Hotel & Restaurant Purchasing Directory.* Honolulu, HA: Trade Publishing Company. (Annual)
> This annual publication lists companies serving hotels and restaurants in Hawaii, arranged by product, each entry name, address, telephone and a list of products.

934. *Hospitality Scene.* Minneapolis, MN: Bolger Publications, Inc. (10/year)
> This trade journal is designed for owners, managers, and purchasing agents in the hospitality industry. Although not the official association publication, the Upper Midwest Hospitality Association and the Upper Midwest Chef's Society are frequent contributing organizations.

935. *Hotel & Motel Journal.* Tallahassee, FL: Accommodations, Inc.
> This is the official publication of the Florida Hotel & Motel Association.

936. *Indiana Beverage Journal.* Indianapolis, IN: Indiana Beverage Life. (Monthly)
> This journal tracks trends in beverage consumption, both alcoholic and nonalcoholic. It also provides information on news, laws, and regulations related to the beverage industry.

937. *KRAReview.* Louisville, KY: Kentucky Restaurant Association, Inc. (Monthly)
> The official publication of the Kentucky Restaurant Association.

938. *Michigan Lodging.* Detroit, MI: Metropolitan Detroit Magazine, Inc.
> This is the official publication of the Michigan Lodging Association.

939. *Michigan Restaurateur.* Birmingham, MI: Michigan Restaurant Association. (Bimonthly)
> Subtitled The Official Voice of the Michigan Food Service & Hospitality Industry, this is the official publication of the Michigan Restaurant Association. Formerly entitled *Michigan Hospitality.*

940. *The Missouri Restaurant.* Kansas City, MO: Missouri Restaurant Association. (10/year)
> The official publication of the Missouri Restaurant Association.

941. *The Napa Valley Newsletter.* St. Helena, CA: The Napa Valley Vinterners Association. (Irregular)

942. *O. E. C. A. News* Orange, CA: Orange Empire Chef's Association. (Monthly)
> The official publication of the Chefs and Cooks in Orange County, California.

943. *Ohio Restaurant Journal.* Columbus, OH: Ohio Restaurant Association. (Bimonthly)
> The official publication of the Ohio Restaurant Association, this is available to members of the association only.

944. *Pacific N.W. Restaurateur.* Seattle, WA: Restaurant Association of the State of Washington. (Monthly)
> This is the official newsletter of the Restaurant Association of the State of Washington.

945. *Restaurateur.* Vienna, VA: Restaurant Association of Metropolitan Washington. (Monthly)
> The official publication of the Restaurant Association of Metropolitan Washington.

946. *Rochester Lodging.* Rochester, MN: Kahler Corporations, Rochester Lodging Group. (6/year?)
> Published for guests and friends of the Rochester Lodging properties.

947. *The Server Pennsylvania.* Pittsburgh, PA: Business Communications, Inc. (Monthly)
> Covers food, beverage, and lodging management in Pennsylvania.

948. *SFSN: Southeast Food Service News.* Atlanta, GA: Southeast Food Service News. (Monthly)
> A newspaper serving the foodservice market in Alabama, Florida, Georgia, Louisiana, Mississippi, North Carolina, South Carolina, Tennessee, and Virginia.

949. *Shelby's Southwest Foodservice.* Garland, TX: Shelby's Southwest Foodservice. (Monthly)
> A trade newspaper serving restaurants, vendors, distributors, caterers, brokers, schools, hospitals, prison feeding, nursing homes, in-plant feeding, military feeding, and airlines in Arkansas, Colorado, Kansas, Louisiana, New Mexico, Oklahoma, Texas, and western Tennessee.

950. *Southwest Hotel-Motel Review.* San Antonio, TX: Hotel Review Company, Inc. (Monthly)
> This is the official publication of the Texas Hotel & Motel Association.

951. *Today's Restaurant Manager.* Minneapolis, MN: Royce Publications. (Monthly)
> Subtitled For Minnesota Food Service Decision Makers, this trade journal was formerly entitled *Restaurant Shopper Magazine.*

952. *Western Foodservice.* New York: Young/Conway Publications, Inc. (Monthly)
> A trade journal for the western states.

953. *The Wisconsin Restaurateur.* Madison, WI: Wisconsin Restaurant Association. (11/year)
> Subtitled Promotion, Protection, Improvement of the Food Service Industry, this is the official publication of the Wisconsin Restaurant Association.

954. *Yankee Food Service.* Weymouth, MA: Griffin Publishing Co., Inc. (Monthly)
> This is a trade newspaper service for the New England region.

Personnel Management and Training

955. Baird, Shirley Chaska, and Sylvester, Joan. *Role Delineation and Verification for Entry-Level Positions in Foodservice Systems Management.* Chicago: American Dietetic Association, 1983. 134 p.
   The results of a study conducted by the American Dietetic Association. This book contains performance responsibility statements, knowledge statements, and a correlation of the two for the entry-level positions of registered dietitian and dietetic technician. Statements for the two positions are presented side by side for comparison.

956. Boella, M. J. *Personnel Management in the Hotel and Catering Industry.* 3d ed. Hutchinson Catering and Hotel Management Books. London: Hutchinson, 1983. 268 p.
   This book explains all basic aspects of personnel work. It is aimed at both students and those already in the field. Chapters cover background to personnel management, personnel policies, job descriptions, recruitment, selection, appointment, appraisal, training, management development, job evaluation, wages and salaries, incentives, fringe benefits, labor turnover and termination, industrial relations, laws, planning, records and statistics, and labor costs.

957. Bryan, John R. *Managing Restaurant Personnel: A Handbook for Food Service Operators.* New York: Chain Store Age Books, 1974. 184 p.
   This book offers very practical information on employee training and efficiency. The goal is to improve cost control through employee training and to improve policy communication through forms and written standards. Seven job manuals from restaurant owner-supervisor to dishwasher outline the duties of each position. Twenty-six forms that can be adapted to individual operations are also included.

958. Brymer, Robert A. *Stress Management for the Hospitality Manager.* Washington, DC: National Restaurant Association, 1984. 23 p.
   This is a short pamphlet designed to help the manager understand stress. It discusses both management and employee stress and teaches how to recognize the causes and reactions to it. Methods for the efficient control of stress are also included.

959. Condon, Thomas J. *"Fire Me & I'll Sue!": A Manager's Survival Guide to Employee Rights.* rev. ed. New York: Modern Business Reports, 1986. 252 p.
   Although not aimed specifically at the hospitality industry, this manual is very useful for hoteliers and restaurateurs. In nonlegal language, it explains employer's as well as employee's rights. Condon suggests how to remove legal traps from hiring and evaluation procedures and how to conduct a confrontation session and an exit interview. Leading cases from all fifty states and an appendix of forms, documents, and record keeping devices enhance the value of the book.

960. Costello, Thomas. *Gut-Level Management: Developing People Skills for Foodservice Managers.* Edited by Jacqueline Carter. Apsot, CA: Gut-Level Publishing, 1986. 151 p.

Costello defines a gut-level manager as one who works with each employee creating an individual action plan for each. Because this type of management cannot be outlined in steps, this book collects experiences the author has had in dealing with people in a foodservice setting. His goal is to help others develop this type of management skill.

961. Dahmer, Sondra J., and Kahl, Kurt W. *The Waiter and Waitress Training Manual.* 2d ed. New York: Van Nostrand Reinhold Co., 1982. 109 p.

In six chapters, the authors cover the major responsibilities and techniques of good service. Detailed instructions are given for initiating service, serving the meal, and serving wine and cocktails. There is a chapter on types of service including French, Russian, English, and American, as well as banquet and buffet service. Other chapters discuss the general qualifications for waiter and waitress and such additional subjects as dining room preparation and station assignments. Questions and projects accompany each chapter. There is a glossary and a quiz at the end of the book.

962. Daschler, John P., and Ninemeier, Jack D. *Supervision in the Hospitality Industry.* East Lansing, MI: Educational Institute of the American Hotel & Motel Association, 1984. 332 p.

This is an application of basic supervisory principles to hospitality operations. Part one gives background information and explains the responsibilities of the supervisor and his role in various aspects of the operation. Part two covers the supervisor in personnel administration including training, evaluation, and salary administration. Part three discusses communications, motivational techniques, the disciplinary process, and related skills. Part four includes working with unions, labor control systems, and management development.

963. Deveau, Jack, and Penraat, Jaap. *One of These Days We Must Do Something about Training: About Training in Hotels, Motels and Restaurants.* New York: Visual Programming, 1967. 127 p.

The author examines the training problems in the lodging industry and restaurant industry. He recommends the use of programmed instruction. Chapters discuss choosing and creating programs and the use of teaching machines. A descriptive catalog lists various programs available.

964. Elliott, Travis. *Capsule Chats with Restaurant Operators.* Austin, TX: Texas Restaurant Association, 1955. 167 p.

A compilation of fifty-two brief two- to six-page essays on various employee/employer problems in the restaurant industry, written by the management consultant for the Texas Restaurant Association. Originally published as weekly letters, they are informal, conversational, and often humorous. They have titles such as "Is Your Business Running You?", "Training vs. Blundering," and "What Does Supervision Mean?"

965. Faulkner, Elizabeth, and Hall, Chester G. *How to Invest in People: A Workbook for Foodservice Operators.* Chicago: National Restaurant Association, 1983?. 32 p.

A workbook to help employers design and implement a career ladder, structure for employee promotion. The book shows how to review current personnel policies, how to design a career ladder, and how to make it work. It provides a way to review the system after six months and presents various case studies.

966. Forrest, Lewis C., and Ninemeier, Jack D. *Training for the Hospitality Industry: Techniques to Improve Job Performance.* East Lansing, MI: Educational Institute of the American Hotel & Motel Association, 1983. 354 p.

Training is a problem in the lodging and foodservice industries because they are very labor-intensive fields that utilize large numbers of unskilled or semiskilled workers. This results in low productivity and high turnover rates. To combat these problems, Forrest outlines a framework for training including recruiting and selecting employees, initial training, assessing when job performance can be improved by training or other work-improvement approaches.

967. Gale, Ken, and Odgers, Peter. *Hotel and Catering, Supervision.* The M&E Hotel, Catering, and Tourism Series. Plymouth, England: Macdonald and Evans, 1984. 273 p.

This textbook was written to meet the curricular needs in the British BTEC Certificate and Diploma courses in hotel and catering supervision. It covers communication, human relations, supervisory studies, personnel practice and procedures, and commercial and economic aspects of supervision.

968. Gilbert, Edith. *Tabletop: The Right Way: An Information and Training Guide for the Professional in the Hospitality Industry.* rev. ed. Charlevoix, MI: Jetíquette, 1980. 54 p.

This manual presents all aspects of proper table setting and various types of service. Flatware, china, and napkins are discussed. Seventeen steps to smooth service are given as well as are explanations of American, French, and Russian service.

969. Harris, Ellen Adeline. *Professional Restaurant Service.* The McGraw-Hill Foundation Series. Toronto, ON: McGraw-Hill Co. of Canada, Ltd., 1966. 99 p.

Designed to be a training guide for waiters and waitresses, this book covers personal appearance, taking orders, types of table services, fountain service, legal rights, and responsibilities. A glossary of terms is also included.

970. Hartland, Robert W. *Responding to Unionization Efforts: A Guide to Assist Foodservice Owners and Managers in Overcoming Unionization Attempts.* Washington, DC: National Restaurant Association, 1984. 31 p.

This is a pamphlet designed to help management overcome unionization attempts. Stage one covers positive relationships with employees as well as "no solicitation" rules and proper security of employee lists. Stage two gives early warning signs. Stage three tells how to mobilize management, gather data about the union, and get your position heard. Stage four discusses how to deal with union representatives.

971. Heffner, Van V. *Serving Alcohol with Care: A Manual for Managers* and *Serving Alcohol with Care: A Manual for Servers.* East Lansing, MI: Educational Institute of the American Hotel & Motel Association, 1985. 61 p.

This is a program for groups and individual training intended to enhance proper responsibility in the serving of alcohol. The manager's handbook gives complete guidance for running a training seminar. Discussion questions, activities, and some quiz questions are included. The manual for servers is the text. A separate package of examinations with electronically scored answer sheets is included when the program is ordered. These will be graded by the Educational Institute. Subjects cover identifying responsibilities, understanding alcohol, defining and recognizing intoxication, monitoring alcohol consumption, and intervening.

972. Hiemstra, Stephen J. *Analysis and Future Needs of Human Resources Used in the Lodging Industry.* West Lafayette, IN: Restaurant, Hotel & Institutional Management Department, Purdue University, 1987. 87 p.

This is the second part of a study conducted by Purdue University for the American Hotel and Motel Association on employment trends in the lodging industry. It is a detailed analysis of statistical data gathered from 113 individual hotels randomly selected from AH&MA members. The objective was to understand the factors affecting supply and demand for labor. Efficiency, wage rates, and labor turnover were studied. Projections for total industry employment based on historical time-series data are made.

973. Hornsey, Timothy, and Dann, David. *Manpower Management in the Hotel and Catering Industry*. London: Batsford Academic and Educational, 1984. 158 p.

This is a basic text for British students studying for HCIMA degrees or higher TEC qualifications in hotel and catering management. The book gives an overview of the subject and special emphasis on working in cross-cultural situations.

974. Hospital Research and Educational Trust. *On-the-Job Training: A Practical Guide for Food Service Supervisors*. Chicago, 1975. 96 p.

Based on "Job Instruction Training" (JIT) methods, this manual is a practical guide for setting up and running training programs. Each step is carefully presented. Chapters cover preparing, conducting, and evaluating a JIT lesson. A final chapter includes blank forms for job descriptions, training schedules, and other forms.

975. Ingle, Sud, and Ingle, Nima. *Quality Circles in Service Industries: Comprehensive Guidelines for Increased Productivity and Efficiency*. Englewood Cliffs, NJ: Prentice-Hall, 1983. 353 p.

Quality circle is a system that draws managers and employees together to solve problems. This book discusses the use of quality circles and implementation for increased efficiency in service industries. The book is divided into sections on theory, process, implementation, and applications. Guidelines are included for writing a leader's handbook. Emphasis is on applications in government and health care organizations and large retail businesses, but restaurants and motels are also covered.

976. Ireland, Richard C. *The Waitress Training Resource Manual*. 2d ed. The Professional Waitress Series. Wheaton, IL: Hospitality Institute, 1974. 335 p.

This is a loose-leaf manual that begins with a section for the trainer giving instructions on how to train and how to setup a training program. This is followed by units for the employee covering an overview of foodservice, personal skills, duties and responsibilities, understanding the customer, and selling in the restaurant. Each unit includes programmed self-instruction frames that refer back to the text for testing and reinforcement.

977. Knoll, Anne Powell. *Food Service Management: A Human Relations Approach*. New York: McGraw-Hill, 1976. 200 p.

A text of management principles and methods presented covering planning and organizing a foodservice operation, how to manage and direct one, and information on personnel, quality control, production, and cost. There is a chapter on the future of the profession. Techniques that improve efficiency and also enhance sensitivity and skill in human relations problem solving are emphasized. Case studies are included.

978. Laventhol & Horwath, comps. *Executive Compensation and Benefits in the Foodservice Industry*. Washington, DC: National Restaurant Association; Philadelphia, PA: Laventhol & Horwath. (Triennial)

This 1985 issue is the third national study of executive compensation conducted in cooperation with Laventhol & Horwath by the National Restaurant Association. Compensation and benefits are presented for some twenty individual positions from chief executive officer to head bartender. There is a section on vacation and supplemental compensation as well. Questionnaire and profile of contributors is included.

979. Lundberg, Donald E., and Armatas, James P. *The Management of People in Hotels, Restaurants, and Clubs*. 4th ed. Dubuque, IA: W. C. Brown Co., 1980. 368 p.

This is a personnel management text aimed at the management student or supervisor who is not specifically training for personnel positions. It gives the basics of motivation, morale, job analysis, selection, appraisal, and training. It also includes chapters on behavior modification theory techniques of group leadership, wage/salary administration, and labor relations.

980. Magurn, J. Philip. *A Manual of Staff Management in the Hotel and Catering Industry.* London: Heinemann, 1977. 336 p.
This is a manual for the manager with a slightly British slant. Magurn discusses in detail how to recruit and keep staff, staff discipline, and staff relations.

981. Martin, William B. *Restaurant Servers Guide: A Fifty-Minute Program: A Step-by-Step Resource to Increase Your Success and Income as a Restaurant Server.* Edited by Michael Crisp. Los Altos, CA: Crisp Publications, Inc., 1986. 57 p.
This booklet is designed to teach servers basic customer relations and selling techniques. It is a self-paced training tool that aims at improving attitude and communication skills rather than at teaching the steps of basic serving.

982. McDermott, Albert L., and Glasgow, Frederick J. *Federal Wage & Hour Standards for the Hotel-Motel and Restaurant Industries.* Washington, DC: American Hotel & Motel Association, 1981–. (Loose-leaf)
Increased minimum wage requirements, overtime penalty pay, and record-keeping requirements of the federal labor laws and regulations have an important impact on the hospitality industry. Failure to comply can result in litigation and substantial liability. McDermott explains how these problems can be minimized by adapting appropriate management and personnel policies. This book discusses how Federal Fair Labor Standards Act (FLSA) and its various amendments, the Equal Pay Act, the Age Discrimination in Employment Act, and the Federal Wage Garnishment Law apply to hotels, motels, and restaurants.

983. McIntosh, Robert W. *Employee Management Standards.* The L. J. Minor Foodservice Standards Series, vol. 4. Westport, CT: AVI Publishing Co., 1984. 194 p.
McIntosh has written a very thorough text on personnel management in the foodservice industry. He covers communication skills, selection and hiring, training, motivation, and legal issues. Also included is a selected list of job descriptions.

984. Miller, Jack E., and Porter, Mary. *Supervision in the Hospitality Industry.* New York: Wiley, 1985. 347 p.
This text provides a basic introduction to the roles and responsibilities of the supervisor. Chapters cover necessary skills, attitudes, and abilities; communications; performance-based objectives; staff selection; orientation and training; evaluation; delegation; motivation; and discipline.

985. Morgan, William J., Jr. *Hospitality Personnel Management.* Boston: CBI Publishing Co., 1979. 226 p.
This textbook is aimed at the university-level student who is training to become a manager or first-line supervisor in a hotel or restaurant. Emphasis is placed on the personnel problems that are unique to hospitality organizations. Chapters cover employee selection and placement, managing human behavior, and labor relations.

986. National Restaurant Association. *Building Excellence: Selecting, Motivating and Retaining a Professional Foodservice Staff: Selected Articles from NRA News.* Washington, DC, 1985. 52 p.
This is a collection of sixteen articles from the *NRA News* on selecting, motivating, and retaining good employees. Articles appear in the following categories: "Making the Most of Each Employee Group," "Cultivating Greatness," "Motivation, Retention & Employee Incentives," and "Case Studies."

987. National Restaurant Association. *Designing an Employee Incentive Campaign: A Do-It-Yourself Handbook.* Washington, DC, 1984. 35 p.
A short handbook with worksheets for developing an incentive program for a restaurant. Chapters cover questions such as "What is an incentive campaign?"; "Are they cost effective?"; and "Does my restaurant need an incentive campaign?" The steps of implement-

ing, monitoring, and evaluating a campaign are given, and eight examples illustrating the steps are included.

988. National Restaurant Association. *The Facts about AIDS.* National Restaurant Association Current Issues Report. Washington, DC, 1985. 9 p.
This pamphlet reviews the facts about Acquired Immune Deficiency Syndrome (AIDS) and proposes steps that restaurateurs and foodservice managers are to take to deal with panic from customers and employees. It outlines the rights of employees to work. Excerpts from the Center for Disease Control Guidelines and a list of references are included.

989. National Restaurant Association. *Foodservice and the Labor Shortage.* National Restaurant Association Current Issues Report. Washington, DC, 1986. 10 p.
This report summarizes information about employees in the industry from a study conducted by Arthur D. Little, Inc. It presents comparisons with other industries, reports on the condition of employment, estimates the labor supply, and lists some of the industry's responses to the current shortages. The last section gives steps the National Restaurant Association will take to improve the situation.

990. National Restaurant Association. *Foodservice and the Older Worker.* National Restaurant Association Current Issues Report. Washington, DC, 1984. 10 p.
Older workers, those between the ages of sixty-five and sixty-nine, represent a potential answer to the current labor shortage in the foodservice industry. This pamphlet compiles statistics and factual information about these workers and how to recruit and hire them.

991. National Restaurant Association. *A Foodservice Operator's Guide to Benefit Plans for Hourly Wage Employees.* Washington, DC, 1982. 46 p.
This is a survey of benefits covering nearly 300 restaurant companies. Information is presented on sixteen benefits offered to hourly, primarily nonsupervisory employees. Graphs show the percent of respondents that provide each benefit and breakdown various benefits by number of units, sales volume, type of restaurant, and number of nonexempt employees.

992. National Restaurant Association. *Management Hospitality Guide for Cafeteria Restaurants.* Hospitality Project. Washington, DC, 198-?. 271 p. (With audio cassettes and slides)
This loose-leaf is one of three available in the Hospitality Project Series to help restaurateurs improve service by effectively training employees to use standards. This volume centers on the cafeteria segment. Included with the loose-leaf is a step-by-step training guide, an employee's workbook, a cassette tape and slides, and material that can be duplicated to hand out.

993. National Restaurant Association. *Management Hospitality Guide for Fast-Food Restaurants.* Hospitality Project. Washington, DC, 198-?. 271 p. (With audio cassettes and slides)
This loose-leaf is one of three available in the Hospitality Project Series to help restaurateurs improve service by effectively training employees to use standards. This volume centers on the fast food segment. Included with the loose-leaf is a step-by-step training guide, an employee's workbook, a cassette tape and slides, and material that can be duplicated to handout.

994. National Restaurant Association. *Management Hospitality Guide for Full-Service Restaurants.* Hospitality Project. Washington, DC, 198-?. 271 p. (With audio cassettes and slides)
This loose-leaf is set up as a do-it-yourself project to initiate standards to ensure good service in a full-service restaurant. Topics covered include training skills, hiring, and new employee orientation. Included with the loose-leaf is an *Employee Hospitality Manual* and masters to duplicate, audio cassettes, and slides.

995. National Restaurant Association. *The Success of Our Restaurant Depends on You!* Washington, DC, 1982. 18 p.
This is a payroll stuffer program intended for increasing employee satisfaction and morale. It contains designs for coupons for nine categories of workers. These are to be completed on the back with offers from local businesses (i.e., free movie admissions, bowling, etc.). Suggestions for types of special offers and a large poster for promotion of the program are included.

996. National Restaurant Association, Human Resources Department. *The First Day: A Checklist for Employee Orientation.* Washington, DC, 1981. 8 p.
This is a checklist of all the things that should be covered in restaurant orientation. The list gives over 150 items to help organize an orientation program. Basics about the establishment's goals, expectations, standards, policies, and fringe benefits are all covered.

997. Ninemeier, Jack D., and The Dietary Managers Association. *Managing Foodservice Operations: A Systems Approach for Healthcare and Institutions.* Hillside, IL: Dietary Managers Association, 1985. 442 p.
This book is a direct result of a role delineation study which identified ten distinct job responsibilities of dietary managers. It presents basic information on how to be effective in these ten areas.

998. Ross, Lynne Nannen. *Work Simplification in Food Service: Individualized Instruction.* Ames, IA: Iowa State University Press, 1972. 124 p.
Based on time and motion study methods, eight principles are presented as the basis for work simplification techniques. This is an individualized instruction manual that the employee can study independently. It can also be coordinated with 100 slides available through Iowa State University Press.

999. Schachter, Victor, and von Seeburg, Susan. *AIDS: A Manager's Guide.* New York: Executive Enterprises Publications, 1986. 71 p.
Although not written specifically for the foodservice industry this booklet addresses one of the major concerns of restaurateurs: employing individuals with AIDS (Acquired Immune Deficiency Syndrome). It identifies the key legal issues and how managers can respond to AIDS. Chapters cover medical facts about the disease, state laws related to AIDS (i.e., equal employment opportunity, tort claims, and legal protection for employees), and practical strategies for managers. One chapter is a set of questions and answers on AIDS issues. The appendix includes a sample policy and a key case.

1000. Ser-Vo-Tel Institute. *Customer/Employee Relationships.* Edited by Donald D. Todd and Joanne O'Haver. Foodservice Career Education Series, FS09. Boston: CBI Publishing Co., 1974. 120 p.
This is one of a series of short, basic texts. At a very simple level, the whole relationship between patrons and service personnel is discussed in a light style with many cartoon illustrations. Each chapter ends with a learning experience section which includes suggestions for projects such as observing at a local restaurant, and interviewing patrons and servers.

1001. Stokes, Arch. *The Collective Bargaining Handbook for Hotels, Restaurants, and Institutions.* Stokes Employee Relations Series. Boston: CBI Publishing Co., 1981. 363 p.
Stokes is an authority on labor relations laws in the hospitality industry. This book explains these laws in everyday English so a collective bargaining agreement can be crafted that is in compliance with the various laws and regulations and yet establishes good relations with the union. Stokes covers federal labor laws and the National Labor Relations Board; he describes the major unions which represent hospitality employees and the main topics covered in a labor agreement. He also outlines how to prepare for and negotiate a contract and how to deal with grievances, strikes, and picketing. Sample agreements are included in the appendices.

1002. Stokes, Arch. *The Equal Opportunity Handbook for Hotels, Restaurants, and Institutions.* Stokes Employee Relations Series. Boston: CBI Publishing Co., 1979. 283 p.

This is one of the Stokes Employee Relations Series. Stokes, a lawyer, explains the equal employment law and gives examples. After an introduction that covers the history and development of public accommodations and equal employment opportunity laws, the book covers jurisdiction, procedures, and administration; discrimination; the employment process; affirmative equal opportunity programs; and defense.

1003. Stowers, Sharon Lee. *Institutional Food Service and Nutritional Care.* 2d ed. Edited by Lori J. Stone. Newton Highlands, MA: Educational Planning Services, 1981. 195 p.

This is a collection of thirty-one inservice programs for foodservice employees designed to help hospital employees with little or no formal nutrition education understand the basic reason for foodservice procedures. Part one covers foodservice; part two covers nutritional care. Each program takes from fifteen to thirty minutes to present; all utilize readily available equipment.

1004. Sweeney, Neil R. *Managing People: Techniques for Food Service Operators.* New York: Chain Store Age Books, 1976. 198 p.

Written in a popular style, the author emphasizes the time and money saving advantages of training staff. Chapters cover selection, motivation, training, communication, planning and delegating, handling problems, working with minorities, and building a team spirit. Each chapter ends with a set of questions and answers.

1005. Tourism Education Corporation. *A Hospitality Industry Guide for Writing and Using Task Unit Job Descriptions.* Boston: CBI Publishing Co., 1976. 248 p.

The Task Unit Job Description contains specific job information on all requirements and aspects of a job. This guide shows how the TUJD can be used for training and supervision, restructuring, organization, job classification, performance appraisal, and other aspects of job evaluation and efficiency. There is also a discussion of job analysis and writing standard task procedures.

1006. Welch, John. *A Task Unit Concept for On-the-Job Training in Food Service.* Columbia, MO: University of Missouri, Extension Division, 1966. 118 p.

This is an application of industry-type training methods to foodservices. Welch not only presents the concepts but shows how to apply them. The systems approach to training is explained. A functional analysis of the foodservice industry is included as is an explanation of task identification, job instruction methods, and other elements necessary for use in actual situations.

1007. Wenzel, George Leonard. *Motivation Training Manual.* Austin, TX: Wenzel Associates, 1970. 272 p.

Wenzel presents a method of training which uses the principle of reinforcement and basic emotional needs. He demonstrates how prompt reinforcement can produce highly motivated restaurant employees. This is one of the classic studies on motivation in the industry.

1008. Whyte, William Foote. *Human Relations in the Restaurant Industry.* New York: McGraw-Hill, 1948. 378 p.

Through help from the National Restaurant Association, this was the first research report on human problems in the restaurant industry. The study was done during World War II and concentrates on human relations. Topics included in the volume are "From Kitchen to Customer," which concentrates on food production; "The Restaurant as a Social System," which covers interaction of employees including unionization; "Human Elements in Supervision," which deals with employer-employee interaction; and a conclusion. This is a classic in the field of restaurant research and is still in print.

1009. Witzky, Herbert K. *The Labor-Management Relations Handbook for Hotels, Motels, Restaurants, and Institutions.* Boston: Cahners Books, 1975. 257 p.

The author writes from the management point of view. In this book, he emphasizes methods, procedures, and strategies that have been used successfully in labor relations. He helps the manager understand how unions organize and grow, the anatomy of a strike, collective bargaining, and effective grievance handling and gives many other useful guidelines. He lists ten pitfalls to avoid in labor relations and discusses the principles of negotiation. His aim is to teach management how to be successful when dealing with labor issues and problems.

1010. Zabka, John R. *Personnel Management and Human Relations.* Hotel-Motel Management Series. Indianapolis, IN: Bobbs-Merrill, 1971. 216 p.

This book covers the basics of personnel management with emphasis on the triple process of organization, communication, and motivation. Many aspects of personnel are covered including job analysis and job evaluation, recruiting, interviewing orientation, training developing supervisors, and records administration, among others.

1011. Zuker, Elaina, and Maher, Barbara. *Coaching and Counseling Skills for Managers* (sound recording). New York: American Management Associations, 1983. 125 p.

A set of six cassettes to help managers deal with personnel. Subjects include "Coaching and Counseling as Management Tools," "Understanding the Employee's Point of View," "Setting the Stage for Managerial Coaching and Counseling," "Coaching for Current Job Performance," "Counseling for Career Development," "Helping the Employee with Personal Problems," "Eliminating Sexism and Discrimination," "The Manager as Mentor," and "Summary and Review." Designed to be used with a workbook.

Real Estate Sale and Investment

1012. Crystler, Julia. *Situation Analysis Workbook.* Edited by Karen Newton. Washington, DC: Hotel Sales and Management Association International Foundation; East Lansing, MI: Educational Institute of American Hotel & Motel Association. 1983. 135 p.

Situation analysis is "the determination, through systematic research of a property's current market position and projected opportunities for promotion." This workbook is a guide to conducting an analysis. Chapters cover the elements of good research, product analysis, market analysis, competition analysis, market segmentation, evaluation, and the marketing plan. Appendices give interviewing and questionnaire tips and a five-year statement of objectives.

1013. Daniels, P. W. *Service Industries: A Geographical Appraisal.* London: Methuen, 1985. 322 p.

This book examines the geographical consequences of growth in the service industry in the past twenty-five years. The effect upon metropolitan, regional, and local development in North America and western Europe is discussed, as well as locational dynamics of producer and consumer services, public policies, and the effect of new technology on the geography of services.

1014. Gee, Chuck Y. *Resort Development and Management: For Operators, Developers and Investors.* East Lansing, MI: Educational Institute of the American Hotel & Motel Association, 1981. 345 p.

This book is intended for developers and investors as well as for students and operators of resorts. It presents management principles and methods as well as discussing resort planning, development, marketing, and finance.

1015. Rushmore, Stephen. *Hotels, Motels and Restaurants: Valuations and Market Studies.* Chicago: American Institute of Real Estate Appraisers, 1983. 280 p.

This book is designed as a guide to appraisers wishing to specialize in hotels and restaurants. It presents the procedures for gathering and processing data about market value and other information. Case studies and hypothetical properties are used to demonstrate market analysis techniques. Chapters cover growth of the industry, demand for accommodations, supply of accommodations, hotels and motels as investments, market value and the valuation process, projecting income and expenses, and valuations and market studies for restaurants.

1016. Schnidman, Frank, ed. *The Approval Process: Recreation and Resort Development Experience.* Washington, DC: Urban Land Institute and Lincoln Institute of Land Policy, 1983. 43 p.
Schnidman discusses the effect of the approval process and related government environmental requirements on developers. Case studies on four large-scale recreational development projects are presented: Northstar at Tahoe; Glenbrook, Nevada; The Pelican Bay Community; PGA National. Each of these projects was in some way innovative.

1017. Sicherman, Irving. *The Investment in the Lodging Business.* Scranton, PA: ATZMI Books, 1977. 546 p.
An analysis of the principle factors involved in making an investment in the lodging business. The book is a result of the bad investment climate that prevailed in the late 1970s. It seeks to define the necessary conditions for attracting outside capital and questions the trend of growth through management contracts. Emphasis is on cash flow, management expertise, full disclosure, and communication.

1018. Stefanelli, John M. *The Sale and Purchase of Restaurants.* New York: Wiley, 1985. 237 p.
This is a book for the professional wishing to buy or sell an existing foodservice operation. Part one is for the seller; it discusses assets, real estate, and good will as well as prices and terms. Part two is from the buyer's perspective and covers financial analysis, assets and liabilities, market surveys, cash investment, and purchase price and terms. Part three discusses sales strategy, purchase strategy, financing alternatives, and the closing process.

1019. Taylor, Arlie L. *Motor Hotel Development Guide.* Dallas, TX: Hospitality Media, 1981. 302 p.
A loose-leaf binder guide for both developers and major investors in new lodging ventures. All aspects of development are covered including site selection, loan package, construction bids, ground breaking, supplies, equipment, landscaping, and many other subjects. Guidelines, checklists, worksheets, and instruction sheets for documents such as "Land Survey Agreements" are provided for every step of the development process. Twenty-six appendices list suppliers.

1020. Thompson, John S. *Site Selection.* New York: Chain Store Publishing Corp., 1982. 220 p.
This is a guide to site location research for all types of retail stores, including restaurants. Thompson puts special emphasis on volume expectation. He provides chapters on general methodology, analytical tools, store location research for single stores and various retail types, a simplified guide to store location research, and accuracy of volume estimate.

Reference Sources

ALMANACS AND HANDBOOKS

1021. Chalmers, Irena; Glaser, Milton; and Friends. *Great American Food Almanac.* New York: Harper & Row, 1986. 240 p.
> This is a fun-filled compendium of food facts, anecdotes, stories, trivia, trends, and recipes, all lavishly illustrated with photographs, cartoons, tables, and charts. Chapters cover important people, eating habits, food markets, eating out and eating in trends, cooking schools, agribusiness, aquabusiness, foodservice, food on video, cottage industry, and predictions.

BIBLIOGRAPHIES

1022. Beck, Leonard N. *Two Loaf-Givers: Or a Tour Through the Gastronomic Libraries of Katherine Golden Bitting and Elizabeth Robins Pennell.* Washington, DC: Library of Congress, 1984. 223 p.
> An examination of the historic cookbooks found in the Bitting and Pennel Libraries. The first chapter deals with Bartolomeo Plantina, the author of the first cookbook. Other chapters cover Renaissance gastronomy, and English, French, and "modern" cuisine.

1023. Borsenik, Frank D. *Literature of the Lodging Market; An Annotated Bibliography.* Bureau of Business and Economic Research, Michigan State University. Occasional paper. East Lansing, MI: Bureau of Business and Economic Research, Michigan State University, 1966. 213 p.
> An annotated bibliography of books, articles, and research reports on the lodging industry and the traveling public, it covers the period from 1946–1965. Summaries of the developments in the industry based on this literature are included at the end of the book with references back to relevant articles. Both bibliography and summaries are arranged by census region. Many charts and tables are also included to facilitate comparisons between regions and years.

1024. Brown, James W., and Brown, Shirley N. *Before You Go to Great Britain: A Resource Directory and Planning Guide.* Hamden, CT: Library Professional Publications, 1986. 201 p.
> This is an annotated directory to travel books, guidebooks, directories, and periodicals, as well as organizations, tour and travel companies, and audiovisual material pertaining to travel in Great Britain.

1025. Bylund, Horace Bruce; Hostetter, Robert S.; and Tomlinson, William L. *Consumer Behavior: An Annotated Bibliography with Special Emphasis on Food.* University Park, PA: Pennsylvania State University, 1962. 220 p.
> The bibliography annotates articles published between 1955 and 1959. Organized under the following headings: Methodology; Advertising and/or Merchandising; Cognitive and Affective Factors; Consumer Choice, Acceptance, and Preference; Marketing Research and

Consumption; Diet, Nutrition, etc. Articles that could logically fall in more than one category are listed in each appropriate one but annotated in only one. A book list accompanies each section for more comprehensive background reading.

1026. Cornell University, School of Hotel Administration. *Subject Catalog of the Library*. Boston: G.K. Hall, 1981. 2 vols.
> The catalog cards of the Library of the Cornell School of Hotel Administration are photographically reproduced in reduced size in this multi-volume work. The Hotel School at Cornell first opened in 1950, and since then the library has concentrated on building an extensive collection in the hospitality field. Nearly 20,000 books are represented in this collection, all cataloged by *Anglo American Cataloging Rules* (2d ed). Some of the library's special collections are not included in this list. Arrangement is alphabetical by subject heading. No author or title cards are included. All books are 1981 imprints or older.

1027. Culinary Institute of America. *Culinary Learning Resources Catalog*. Hyde Park, NY, 1985? (Loose-leaf)
> The Culinary Institute of America produces a wide variety of audiovisual materials to teach cooking and foodservice techniques. This catalog is a selected list of programs that can be purchased, previewed, or leased from them. Each entry includes a description of the program, time, instructor, and order number. In addition to cooking topics, there are programs on tableservice and sanitation. Most programs are video tapes; some are also available in slide-tape format.

1028. Gay, Jeanne. *Travel & Tourism Bibliography and Resource Handbook*. Santa Cruz, CA: Travel & Tourism Press, 1981. 3 vols.
> This is a very comprehensive bibliography of travel books and special articles arranged by continent, country, region, and then state. Citations are very brief and includes title, author, date, and publisher. No annotations are included.

1029. Goeldner, Charles R., and Dicke, Karen. *Bibliography of Tourism and Travel Research Studies, Reports, and Articles*. Boulder, CO: Business Research Division, Graduate School of Business Administration, University of Colorado, 1980. 9 vols.
> This is the fifth edition of the bibliography, and it provides references on travel, recreation, and tourism. Items listed include studies, surveys, statistical abstracts, fact books, articles, and similar publications related to the travel industry of the world. There are nine volumes in the set. Each volume covers a different topic which is in turn divided into narrower topics. Most of the references are to books, but some journal articles are included. All references are to pre-1980 publications.

1030. Hospitality Valuation Services, Inc., comps. *Hospitality Bibliography*. New York, 1986?. 119 p.
> Over 250 books and nearly 100 periodical articles have been cited in this bibliography. It is divided into two major sections: books and journal articles. Each section is arranged alphabetically by title. The book section includes a brief annotation with each entry. A subject index provides access to the two major sections. Publishers' addresses are also provided.

1031. Kleinman, Rhonda H., and Kleinman, Allan M., comps. *The International Cookery Index*. Neal-Schuman Cookery Index Series, no. 1. New York: Neal-Schuman Publishers, Inc., 1987. 230 p.
> This is an index to over 25,000 recipes from fifty-one English-language cookbooks that contain recipes from around the world. All books indexed are currently in print and available in the U.S. The index provides access by name of well-known dishes (i.e., sauerbraten), major ingredients, preparations (i.e., jellied or pickled), and nationality or cuisine. Under each nationality entry, there is a list of major books on that cuisine.

1032. Lück, Erich. *Bibliography of Dictionaries and Vocabularies on Food, Nutrition, and Cookery.* FSTA Reference Series, no. 4. Frankfurt, Germany: International Food Information Service, 1985. 139 p.
This bibliography lists the latest editions of books, leaflets, standards, and other independent publications, but not scientific or technical articles or scientific books. Entries are grouped by subject according to the FSTA (Food Science and Technology Abstracts) classification system. With few exceptions, all publications are later than 1960. Code numbers facilitate finding through author and subject indexes.

1033. National Restaurant Association. *Foodservice Library: A Comprehensive Catalog of Foodservice Publications.* Washington, DC, 1984. 108 p.
Over 500 books and audiovisual materials are listed in this bibliography. Each entry includes bibliographic information, ISBN, price, short description, and a list of chapters. National Restaurant Association publications are omitted because they are listed in a separate publications list. Indexes to authors and titles are included.

1034. United States, General Accounting Office. *Food: Reports, Legislation, and Information Sources: A Guide.* Washington, DC: Government Printing Office, 1978. 239 p.
This bibliography lists over 500 citations and abstracts to food-related documents of the federal government issued from July 1973 to September 1977. Topics covered include feeding programs, food safety, nutrition, food production, farm marketing and distribution, price supports, food aid, trade policy, population control, and food policy.

DICTIONARIES

1035. Bickel, Walter. *Hering's Dictionary of Classical and Modern Cookery and Practical Reference Manual for the Hotel, Restaurant and Catering Trade.* 6th rev. ed. Giessen, Germany: Fachbuchverlag Pfannenberg, 1980. 852 p.
Originally compiled by Richard Hering. This is a very comprehensive dictionary of English, French, German, Italian, and Spanish culinary terms. Over 16,000 entries are included arranged into standard menu categories: hors d'oeuvres, sauces, soups, eggs, fish, garnishes, main dishes, vegetables, salads, and sweets. Definitions are complete enough to be used as recipes by experienced chefs.

1036. Club Managers Association of America. *Expense and Payroll Dictionary for Clubs.* Washington, DC, 1967. 61 p.
A reference work for use in connection with the *Uniform System of Accounts for Clubs* (2d revised edition, 1967). It is divided into "Expense Dictionary" and "Payroll Dictionary." Entries are arranged alphabetically by item, and subclassification is given to show where and to what departmental expense each item belongs, i.e., Egg Beaters—Food—Utensils.

1037. Dahl, Crete. *Food & Menu Dictionary.* rev. ed. Edited by Jule Wilkinson. Chicago: Institutions/Volume Feeding Magazine, 1972. 135 p.
Defines over 2,000 terms commonly found on menus and in food preparation. Definitions are short and concise. Foreign words include a pronunciation guide. Entries are included from all menu categories as well as for beverages and some terms describing preparation, equipment, and service.

1038. Epstein, Becky Sue, and Klein, Hilary Dole. *Substituting Ingredients: A Cooking Reference Book.* Charlotte, NC: East Woods Press, 1986. 127 p.
This book lists over 350 ingredients that can be used as substitutes in recipes. The called for item is followed in each section by a list of possible substitutes. Chapters include baking ingredients; condiments; dairy products; fruits and nuts; general cooking; herbs, spices, and flavorings; meat, fish, and poultry; and vegetables. There also are chapters on measurement equivalents, formulas for home-made cleaners, and instructions on how to compensate for putting in too much of some ingredient.

1039. Farrell, Kenneth T. *Spices, Condiments, and Seasonings.* Westport, CT: AVI Publishing Co., 1985. 415 p.
This is a very thorough reference book on spices and seasonings. The major portion of the book is a listing of fifty spices, culinary herbs, and spice blends. Each entry includes common and botanical name, family, history, sources, characteristics, extractives, federal specifications, composition and nutritional data, and household and commercial uses. Also included is a brief history of spices; information on how extractives of spices are made and used; and formulas for condiments, sauces, and meat seasonings.

1040. *Funk & Wagnalls Cook's and Diner's Dictionary: A Lexicon of Food, Wine, and Culinary Terms.* New York: Funk & Wagnalls, 1968. 274 p.
This dictionary defines and gives pronunciation and derivation to cooking and food terms. No recipes are included. Some black-and-white sketches illustrate the terms.

1041. Hotel Sales Management Association. *Glossary of Hotel/Motel Terms: As Pertains to the Buyer-Seller Relationship.* Egg Harbor, NJ: 1970. 14 p.
This is a short glossary of buyer-seller terms for such subjects as room accommodations, reservations, food plans, banquets, and functions as well as meeting rooms and equipment. Its aim is to help avoid misunderstandings in the buyer-seller relationship.

1042. Igoe, Robert S. *Dictionary of Food Ingredients.* New York: Van Nostrand Reinhold Co., 1983. 173 p.
The major portion of this dictionary is an alphabetical list of ingredients found in food. Each entry includes function, properties, and applications. Chemical formulations and usage levels are also included if relevant. The book has a section defining the categories of ingredients such as emulsifiers, preservatives, and sweeteners. An excellent bibliography is also included.

1043. Knight, John Barton. *Knight's Foodservice Dictionary.* Edited by Charles A. Salter. New York: Van Nostrand Reinhold Co., 1987. 393 p.
This comprehensive dictionary gives short, concise definitions of basic ingredients and preparation methods, accounting and cost control terms, equipment, management and marketing concepts, nutrition, sanitation, and safety terms. Some foreign terms are included also. Cross-references to related terms are printed in bold type.

1044. Krohn, Norman Odya. *Menu Mystique: The Diner's Guide to Fine Food & Drink.* Middle Village, NY: Jonathan David Publishing, 1983. 404 p.
This book compiles and translates foreign phrases found on restaurant menus. Thousands of terms from many languages (including English) are defined. In addition, entries include language and cross-references to other terms.

1045. McClane, A. J. *The Encyclopedia of Fish Cookery.* Photographs by Arie DeZanger. New York: Holt, Rinehart and Winston, 1977. 511 p.
Set up as an encyclopedia, this book defines and describes hundreds of varieties of fish. It lists to which family of fish it belongs, where it is found, size and weight, and, in some cases, includes recipes. Many entries are illustrated with color photographs.

1046. Metelka, Charles J., ed. *The Dictionary of Tourism.* 2d ed. Wheaton, IL: Merton House Travel & Tourism Publishing, 1986. 116 p.
A dictionary of some 2,000 frequently used terms in the field of tourism, both in the industry and in academic study of the subject. Many trade associations are included and some slang terms. Short one- to four-line definitions are given for each term.

1047. Morton, Ian Douglas, and Morton, Chloe, comps. *Elsevier's Dictionary of Food Science and Technology: In Four Languages.* Amsterdam, The Netherlands: Elsevier Scientific Publishing Company, 1977. 207 p.
This is a multilingual dictionary of food science terms. The main body of the book is a list of terms in English with French, Spanish, and German equivalents. Three indexes follow which cross-reference the terms by each of the non-English languages.

1048. Riely, Elizabeth. *The Chef's Companion: A Concise Dictionary of Culinary Terms.* Illustrated by David Miller. New York: Van Nostrand Reinhold Co., 1986. 215 p.

This dictionary of over 3,000 culinary terms includes oriental, Middle Eastern, and Latin American food terms. There are entries for cooking terms, styles, and equipment as well as foods and spices, sauces, garnishes, and beverages. Cross-references are in boldface type.

1049. Simon, André L., and Howe, Robin. *A Dictionary of Gastronomy.* New York: McGraw-Hill, 1970. 400 p.

This is a dictionary of foods and cooking terms and techniques. Entries include a definition and brief historical background. Some entries include recipes as well. Color photographs and black-and-white diagrams illustrate the entries. This work is not as extensive as *The New Larousse Gastronomique,* but is excellent in its own right.

1050. Smith, Henry. *Classical Recipes of the World: With Occasions for Their Use and Master Culinary Guide.* London: Practical Press, 1954. 631 p.

This is a dictionary of historical recipes with interesting facts and explanations about the origin and meaning of dish names. French-English and English-French dictionaries of culinary terms and a dictionary of food names in five languages are included. Though many of these recipes from classical times are still usable, the book will be most valuable for writing correct and consistent menus.

1051. Voegele, Marguerite C., and Woolley, Grace H. *Menu Dictionary: Multilingual.* Illustrated by Paula Hoffman. New York: Ahrens Publishing Co., 1961. 318 p.

Over 5,000 menu terms from English, French, German, Italian, and Spanish dishes are defined in this small handy dictionary. Beside each word a letter denoting language is given; this is followed by a brief definition. No pronunciations are given.

DIRECTORIES

1052. Atcom, Inc., Publishers. *Hospitality & Foodservice Management Directory.* New York, 1985– . (Annual)

A directory to management companies which operate hospitality and foodservice businesses through management contracts with passive investors. Each entry gives a quick profile and lists types of properties managed, total numbers, special services, fees, future plans, and the year the company was founded.

1053. Council on Hotel, Restaurant, Institutional Education. *U.S. and International Directory of Schools.* Washington, DC, 1972–. (Annual)

Arranged alphabetically by state, this is a directory of schools which offer degrees in hospitality. It includes schools that are not members of the Council on Hotel, Restaurant, and Institutional Education as well as those that are members. The book is arranged by state or country. Within each state, schools are arranged by level (baccalaureate degree granting colleges, community and junior colleges, secondary school). Each entry includes school, department name, address, telephone, contact person, degrees and a brief description of the program. Some overseas schools are included.

1054. CSG Information Services. *Directory of Country Clubs.* Chicago: Lebhar-Friedman, Inc. (Annual)

This is the most comprehensive directory of country clubs available. It includes 4,000 country clubs with foodservice operators.

1055. Elster, Robert J., ed. *Trade Shows and Professional Exhibits Directory.* Detroit, MI: Gale Research Co., 1985. 549 p.

This directory lists over 2,000 exhibitions, trade shows, and association conventions at which there are direct sales and trade contracts through displays of products and services. The main section is arranged by broad topic; each entry includes address, phone number, exhibit manager, attendance, audience, number of exhibits, price, principle exhibits, and special features. The dates and locations of the shows from 1985 to 1988 are listed also. Indexes include keywords in show name, geographic, chronological, organization, and subject.

1056. Frank, Robyn C., ed. *Directory of Food and Nutrition Information Services and Resources.* Phoenix, AZ: Oryx Press, 1984. 287 p.

This book is a gold mine of information on the food industry; it is both a directory and a bibliography. Included are organizations and universities, databases, software, journals, abstracts and indexes, and a list of key reference materials.

1057. Geffen, Alice M., and Berglie, Carole. *Food Festival!: The Ultimate Guidebook to America's Best Regional Food Celebrations.* New York: Pantheon Books, 1986. 271 p.

A sampling of some of the many specialty food festivals across the country is presented in this book, arranged by season of the year. The emphasis is on local specialties festivals in small towns. Each of the fifty-eight entries describes the festival and gives directions, dates, cost, etc. They each also include a few recipes; there are 130 recipes in all and a recipe index. Festivals represented include expected regional foods such as the Maine Lobster Festival in Winter Harbor, Maine, and such unusual ones as the Persimmon Festival in Mitchell, Indiana.

1058. Hudman, Lloyd E., ed. *Directory of Tourism Education Programs: Guide to Programs in Aviation, Hospitality, and Tourism.* Wheaton, IL: Merton House Publishing Co., 1981. 107 p.

Over 350 two- and four-year college programs in aviation; hotel, motel, and restaurant management; and travel and tourism are listed in this directory. Entries include name, address, emphasis, degrees offered, contact person, and name of department.

1059. International Society of Restaurant Association Executives. *ISRAE Roster.* s.l.: s.n., 1985. 14 p.

This directory gives names, addresses, and phone numbers of restaurant associations in all states, Washington DC, and Canada. It also includes names of officers, board of directors, and executive committee for the ISRAE.

1060. National Restaurant Association. *Who's Who in the Foodservice Industry.* Washington, DC, 1984–. (Annual)

A directory of the National Restaurant Association members arranged alphabetically by state, city, and then by name of restaurant. An alphabetical index by the name of member's restaurants is found in the back. Association officers and a calendar of National Restaurant Association events are also included. This publication continues *Who's Who in the Restaurant Industry.*

1061. Norris, John, and Norris, Joann. *Amusement Parks: An American Guidebook.* Jefferson, NC: McFarland & Company, Inc., Publishers, 1986. 116 p.

This guidebook gives a brief history of U.S. amusement parks and provides an alphabetical guide to them by state. Each entry includes a brief description, address, prices, hours, season, and best days to attend. There is also a note in most entries about other sites of interest in the area. An appendix includes names and addresses of more parks for which information was not available.

1062. Ruff, Ann, and West, Austin, comps. *Cookoff!: Including the Blue-Ribbon Recipes from Texas' Most Famous Food Festivals.* Texas Monthly Guides. Austin, TX: Texas Monthly Press, 1986. 195 p.

This is a guide to thirty-five food festivals in Texas and a collection of their prize-winning recipes. The festivals section gives a description of the event, location, date, and address as well as a phone number for further information. The recipe collection includes over ninety recipes. Each recipe is accompanied by the name of its creator and the festival for which it was prepared. Some county fair winning recipes are included for variety.

1063. Sullivan, John E. *Directory of Foreign Government Tourist Offices.* Chicago: Travel Insider, 1981. 23 p.

This is a list of foreign government tourist offices and other information sources for overseas travelers. Addresses and phone numbers are provided for head and branch offices in the United States and Canada. Sources are given for over 100 countries.

1064. Woodman, Julie G. *IFMA Encyclopedia of World Foodservice Markets.* Chicago: International Foodservice Manufacturers Association, 1978. 130 p.

This directory of overseas foodservice markets is aimed at the American manufacturer seeking overseas sales. It provides extensive information on each country including basic country information such as population, language, and industry data; U.S. and overseas contacts; major market consultants; chains; suppliers; trade shows; associations; and publications. Statistical charts are included for major countries. The book is arranged by regions of the world and includes introductory information on foodservice markets of the world, for each region and for some countries.

DIRECTORIES OF HOTELS, RESORTS, INNS, AND B&BS

1065. American Hotel & Motel Association. *Directory of Hotel and Motel Systems.* New York: American Hotel Association Directory Corp. (Annual)

Lists alphabetically all hotel and motel systems operating three or more hotels or motels in the United States and many foreign countries. Each entry includes address and phone number of executive offices and the names of major executives. Individual hotels and motels are listed by name, with location and number of rooms. Total number of properties and rooms for each system are given at the end of each citation. A list of systems ranked by number of rooms is included.

1066. American Hotel Association Directory Corp. *OAG Travel Planner, Hotel & Motel Red Book.* Oak Brook, IL: Official Airline Guides, Inc. 1886–. (Quarterly)

This directory lists all members in the American Hotel & Motel Association plus nonmembers who apply for a listing. As such, it is very comprehensive and includes over 12,000 hotels and motels across the U.S. and Canada. The main section is arranged by state; the address, telephone, credit cards accepted, and rates are given for each hotel. In addition, each hotel is categorized by location, such as airport, expressway, downtown, resort, or suburban, and by meal plan. Special sections list airport hotels, meeting hotels, resort and condominiums, and international hotels.

1067. Andrews, Peter. *Inns of the Mid-Atlantic and the South.* Photographed by George W. Gardner. Classic Country Inns of America, vol. 2. Los Angeles: Knapp Press, 1978. 155 p.

Twenty inns are featured in this book. All are beautifully photographed to illustrate their guest rooms, dining areas, lobbies, and exteriors. The author has written a description of each which includes its history and special features. A chart in the back of the book gives the address, telephone, size, seasons, and prices for each inn.

1068. Barnes, Rik, and Barnes, Nancy. *Complete Guide to American Bed and Breakfast.* 2d ed. Gretna, LA: Pelican Publishing Co., 1988. 632 p.

Over 1,700 bed and breakfast inns are included in this directory. Each entry includes name; address; telephone; innkeeper; rates; and policies on credit cards, children, pets, etc. The directory is arranged by state with a black-and-white map of each state showing locations of the inns. Ink sketches of exteriors of some of the inns enhance the volume. An appendix lists organizations by state which can be contacted for reservations.

1069. Belote, Julianne. *Guide to the Recommended Country Inns of the West Coast: California, Oregon, Washington.* Illustrated by Olive Metcalf. Chester, CT: Globe Pequot Press, 1986. 394 p.

The author has personally visited and selected 186 inns which offer unique accommodations; some are bed and breakfast places, others are small inns and hotels. The guide is arranged by state; California is subdivided into geographic divisions. Within these divisions, inns are arranged alphabetically. Each inn receives a two-page write up and a chart of information including innkeeper's name, address, number of rooms, rates, seasons, facilities, and local attractions. Line drawings are provided for each entry.

1070. Chambers, Andrea. *Dream Resorts: 25 Exclusive and Unique American Hotels, Inns, Lodges, and Spas.* New York: Clark N. Potter, 1983. 204 p.

This is a highly selective list of resorts in the U.S. Each resort is described in a five-page essay that includes history of the resort, description of special rooms and lists of celebrity patrons. A summary page describes the premises, the rooms, meals, directions for getting there, prices, and side trips available in the area. Full-color photographs of each resort are included.

1071. Chesler, Bernice. *Bed & Breakfast Coast to Coast.* Lexington, MA: Stephen Greene Press, 1986. 416 p.

This directory lists over 200 B&B reservation services that can place travelers in bed and breakfast accommodations. Arranged by state, each entry includes name of the reservation service, address, telephone number and hours, type of accommodations available, other services (such as airport pick-up), settings of B&Bs, descriptions of hosts, breakfast and reservation policies, and rates.

1072. Crosette, Barbara, ed. *America's Wonderful Little Hotels and Inns.* New York: Congdon & Weed, 1980– . (Annual?)

Based upon recommendations from travelers, this book describes over 400 small hotels and inns. Each hotel is special in some way and reflects the area it is in. Entries include name, address, telephone, number of rooms, prices, credit cards accepted, and manager or innkeeper. The descriptive paragraphs are written by visitors and are signed. The book is arranged by regions with indexes by state and inn name. A report form is included so the reader can submit information on an inn for the next edition.

1073. Davis, William, ed. *The World's Best Business Hotels.* London: Hotel Guides International, 1985. 572 p.

This is an international guide to 550 hotels that provide the services needed by business travelers. Arranged alphabetically by country and then by city, each entry includes a descriptive paragraph and a chart listing location, personal and business services available, restaurants and foodservice, cost, credit card policy, the author's rating, and an ink sketch of the hotel.

1074. Gardner, Roberta Homan. *The Great Lakes, a Guide to the Inns of Illinois, Indiana, Ohio, Minnesota, Michigan, and Wisconsin.* Photographs by George Gardner. Country Inns of America. New York: Holt, Rinehart and Winston, 1981. 96 p.

A descriptive guide to thirty-two inns selected for excellence of food, ambiance, historical interest, and other attractive features, lavishly illustrated with photographs. The text is usually one page, giving a description of the inn and its charms. Address, prices, season, directions, and other information are given in a separate space on the same page for convenience.

1075. Gardner, Roberta Homan. *New York and Mid-Atlantic: A Guide to the Inns of New York, New Jersey, Pennsylvania, Maryland, and Virginia.* Photographs by George W. Gardner. Country Inns of America. New York: Henry Holt and Company, 1986. 120 p.

> Forty-two inns of New York, Pennsylvania, New Jersey, Maryland, and Virginia are photographed and described in this directory. The book is arranged by state; each entry includes a description noting special features such as special food or furnishings. Factual information is included in a box at the bottom of each page listing address, telephone, innkeeper, rate level, seasons, restaurant service, policies on children and pets, and amenities. The photographs are outstanding. This is a revision of *New York and Mid-Atlantic* by Peter Andrews and Tracy Ecclesine, 1980.

1076. Gardner, Roberta Homan; Black, Naomi; and Berger, Terry. *The East Coast Bed & Breakfast Guide: New England and the Mid-Atlantic.* Photographs by George W. Gardner. New York: Prentice-Hall, 1986. 160 p.

> This is a selective guide to 119 bed and breakfast accommodations in New England and the mid-Atlantic states. It is divided into two parts: B&Bs in the cities covering Boston, New York, Philadelphia, Baltimore, and Washington, DC; and B&Bs in the country covering the states of Maine, New Hampshire, Vermont, Massachusetts, Rhode Island, Connecticut, New York, Pennsylvania, New Jersey, Delaware, and Maryland. Each entry includes full-color photographs; a brief paragraph; address or agency representing the home; number of rooms; rates; seasons opened; and policies on children, pets, and smoking.

1077. Hale-Wehmann, Kenneth, ed. *Best Places to Stay in America's Cities.* Boston: Harvard Common Press, 1986. 404 p.

> This is a guide to unusual hotels, inns, and bed and breakfast places. Descriptions and recommendations are given for about 250 lodgings in forty cities. Entries include addresses and prices for single and double occupancy as well as several paragraphs of description.

1078. *Hotel & Travel Index.* New York: Ziff-Davis Publishing, 1951–. (Quarterly)

> Published quarterly, this is the most comprehensive and up-to-date directory of hotels available. It includes listings of hotels, motels, and resorts worldwide; over 36,000 hotels are listed. Arrangement is geographical by country, state, and city. Entries are very concise and include number of rooms, rates, appointed hotel representatives, manager, address, telephone, 800 number, cable number, a code denoting automated airline reservation system, and codes for credit cards accepted. Many advertisements are included that have additional information. Over 250 city maps are also included.

1079. Lamy, Marge. *Cross Country Ski Inns of the Eastern U.S. and Canada.* Photographs by George W. Gardner. Lexington, MA: Stephen Greene Press, 1986. 124 p.

> A guide to twenty-six inns in the North East and Canada (especially New York, New Hampshire, and Vermont) where good cross-country skiing is available. Articles describe ambiance and interesting local attractions as well as accommodations and food. At the end of the book, a separate section gives basic information on each inn, giving directions, rates, accommodations, winter facilities available, address, and season.

1080. Lanier, Pamela. *Elegant Small Hotels: A Connoisseur's Guide.* Santa Fe, NM: John Muir Publishing, 1986. 128 p.

> Over 100 hotels have been chosen for this directory. By "small," the author means less than 200 rooms; by "elegant," she means outstanding in decor and furnishings, providing services such as conference rooms and spas, and with excellent restaurants. Each entry includes a written description and a chart of basic facts such as address, the telephone number, number of rooms, services and amenities, and restaurants. A black-and-white photograph of a guest room is provided for each hotel. The directory is arranged by state.

1081. Lawliss, Chuck. *Great Resorts of America.* New York: Holt, Rinehart and Winston, 1983. 158 p.

Of the more than 400 resorts in the U.S., the author has selected twenty-eight to feature in this book. Each is described and photographed to help the reader picture its qualities and history. All resorts included have been personally visited by the author. Addresses, rates, credit cards accepted, and special facilities available are listed in an appendix.

1082. Pyle, Susan Newhof, and Pyle, Stephen J. *Michigan's Town & Country Inns.* 2d ed. Ann Arbor, MI: University of Michigan Press, 1987. 232 p.

This directory lists seventy-five guest houses and inns located all over Michigan. All of these are unusual, old-fashioned places with atmosphere and charm. Divided by sections of the state, each short entry includes a brief write up on the interesting features of the place and a list of basic information such as number of rooms, rates, and season. Entries are generally accompanied by one outside and one inside black-and-white photograph.

1083. Redtree Associates, comps. *America's Meeting Places.* New York: Facts on File, 1984. 277 p.

This is a directory of over 400 locations for meetings and conferences in America. Entries are listed by state and include information on meeting rooms, largest banquet possible, discounts, peak season, and other information pertinent to conference planners. The name of the contact person is also included. Appendices list entries in ten specific categories such as "Meeting Places in the Country," "Meeting Places in the Mountains," "Meeting Places of Historic Interest," etc.

1084. Rundback, Betty Revits, and Kramer, Nancy. *Bed & Breakfast USA: A Guide to Tourist Homes and Guest Houses.* Edited by Sandra W. Soule. New York: E. P. Dutton. (Annual)

This is an annually published guide to over 600 bed and breakfast places arranged by state and city. Each entry includes name; address; telephone number; hosts' names; number of rooms and number of people sharing a bath; price and season opened; whether breakfast is available; and policies on children, pets, smoking, and drinking. This factual information is accompanied by a descriptive paragraph. Also included are chapters on how to start a B&B, how to start a reservation system, and B&B recipes.

1085. Simpson, Norman T. *Bed and Breakfast American Style—1986.* A Harper Colophon Book. New York: Harper & Row, 1985. 438 p.

This book includes descriptions of 435 unusual accommodations all over the United States, Canada, Mexico, and even including one from New Zealand. Descriptions are a full-page long and include information about the hotel, rooms, location, and food as well as careful directions for finding the places. The index in the back lists the accommodations by state and town and includes the room rates.

1086. Simpson, Norman T. *Country Inns and Back Roads: Britain and Ireland.* 4th ed. New York: Harper & Row, 1986. 317 p.

Simpson, the acknowledged expert on out-of-the-way places, provides a guide to Scotland, Wales, and Northern Ireland as well as England and Ireland in this volume of a series that covers North America and Continental Europe. As always, one-page narrative essays give a feel for the atmosphere of the inn; and basic information such as location, number of rooms, and dining facilities are included in italics at the end of the entry. Rates are given in the index. Emphasis is on quaint and colorful castles, inns, and bed and breakfast guesthouses.

1087. Simpson, Norman T. *Country Inns and Back Roads. [North America].* Berkshire Traveller Travel Shelf. Stockbridge, MA: Berkshire Traveller Press. (Annual)

This is the most well-known directory to unusual, off-the-beaten path inns and B&Bs available. Each inn is described by the author and illustrated with a line drawing. Factual information and directions are included in italics at the end of each article.

1088. Stern, Steven B. *Guide to the Great Resorts of the World.* Englewood Cliffs, NJ: Prentice-Hall, 1985. 243 p.

Stern presents a guide to truly luxurious accommodations throughout the world. It is for those who seek the very best in comfort, facilities, food, and fun. In part one, he gives guidance on planning, booking, and preparing for a resort vacation as well as selecting a resort hotel. Part two, "The Great Resorts of the World," gives short descriptions of his choice of the best resorts in the United States, the Caribbean, Bahamas, Bermuda, South America, Mexico, Hawaii, the South Pacific, the Far East, and Europe. Appendices include 1985/86 price lists.

1089. Turner, Richard, ed. *Who's Who in the Lodging Industry.* New York: American Hotel & Motel Association, 1987. 304 p.

This directory lists individuals, property-companies, and consultants-purveyors in the hotel industry. The largest section is the alphabetical listing of individuals. Each entry includes name, position, business address, and telephone number. Over 15,000 people are listed. The property-company listing includes all hotel properties that are members of AH&MA; about 3,000 hotels are included. Entries include name of hotel, address, telephone number, and manager's name. The consultant-purveyors section is similar.

1090. Zellers, Margaret. *Caribbean, The Inn Way.* Southport, CT: Geomedi Productions, 1981. 208 p.

This is a guide to nearly 150 inns located in thirty Caribbean locations. Zellers, the travel editor of *Signature Magazine* and author of other travel guides, gives short descriptions of each small inn or hotel. Directions and special notes are given for each as are address, phone number, and number of rooms. Specific rates are not included. The 1978 edition was published under the title *The Inn Way...the Caribbean.*

DIRECTORIES OF RESTAURANTS

1091. *Aspen-Snowmass Epicure: A Menu Guide to the Better Restaurants in Aspen-Snowmass.* Seattle, WA: Peanut Butter Publishing. (Irregular)

This is one of a series of booklets that are collections of actual reproductions of menus from selected restaurants from major cities in the U.S. This book covers the Aspen-Snowmass area. In addition to a menu, basic information on location, hours, phone number, reservations, and credit cards is included.

1092. *Baltimore Epicure: A Menu Guide to Baltimore's Finest Restaurants.* Seattle, WA: Peanut Butter Publishing. (Irregular)

This is one of a series of booklets that are collections of actual reproductions of menus from selected restaurants from major cities in the U.S. This book covers the Baltimore area. In addition to a menu, basic information on location, hours, phone number, reservations, and credit cards is included.

1093. Benenson, Edward H. *The Benenson Restaurant Guide, 1986: Edward H. Benenson.* Edited by Burton Hobson. New York: Sterling, 1986. 192 p.

This is a guidebook that rates selected restaurants in all states and most major cities in the United States. There are also entries for Canada. Food, wine, service, and ambiance are rated on a scale of one to ten. Symbols and abbreviations tell hours, days open, meal served, price range, reservation, and dress code policies. A sentence or two of comment accompanies each entry. Intended as a guide to very fine dining, the entries come from members of gourmet societies. There are over 300 new entries in the 1986 edition.

1094. *The Best Restaurants in America.* New York: Simon and Schuster, 1985. 448 p.

Based on surveys conducted by East-West Network, Inc., the publishers of in-flight magazines for the airlines, this is a compilation of the best restaurants recommended by various readers based on over 100,000 survey responses. Restaurants in twenty-eight cities are rated by a four-star system on food, service, ambiance, and price. Entries include a short paragraph of comments on food and decor.

1095. Christopher, Robert, and Christopher, Ellen. *America's Favorite Restaurants & Inns: From Budget to Luxury.* 7th ed. Drawings by Richard A. Craig. Milford, CT: Travel Discoveries, 1980. 1,024 p.
This state-by-state directory of hotels, motels, and restaurants identifies low priced food and lodging businesses. The book begins with a description of the franchises so the entries under each state can be brief. Entries include address, phone number, and a price range code. For privately owned establishments, a fuller description is included. For chains, the reader is referred to the descriptions in the front of the book.

1096. Cronk, Loren Kennett, comp. and ed. *Guide to Natural Food Restaurants.* Illustrated by Lisa Free. Nicasio, CA: Daystar Publishing Co., 1983. 208 p.
This directory lists over 500 restaurants which serve natural food. Arranged by state, each entry includes address; telephone number; directions from highway; whether they serve Lacto-ovo vegetarian, vegetarian, or macrobiotic meals; size; prices; and a description written by the restaurant.

1097. CSG Information Services. *Directory of Chain Restaurant Operators.* Chicago: Lebhar-Friedman, Inc. (Annual)
This directory contains detailed information on 3,000 chain restaurants. In addition to the directory information, it gives sales, number of stores, and various other useful financial facts.

1098. CSG Information Services. *Directory of High Volume Independent Restaurants.* Chicago: Lebhar-Friedman, Inc. (Annual)
Nearly 6,000 one- or two-unit independent restaurants are listed in this directory which makes it the most comprehensive directory available. Each entry includes name, address, telephone, type of restaurant or foodservice operation, type of menu, number of meals served, number of seats, average checks, number of units, key executives and buyers, and year founded. The directory is arranged by state and city.

1099. *Egon Ronay's Guinness Pub Guide.* London: Egon Ronay Organisation. (Annual)
The Egon Ronay Organisation has published various restaurant guides. This is a guide to bar food and accommodations in pubs in England (with a separate section on London), Scotland, Wales, the Channel Islands, and the Isle of Man. Pubs with actual restaurants are not included. Entries list two typical dishes and describe accommodations as well as ambiance. Beers on draft are also listed.

1100. *Houston Epicure: A Menu Guide to the Houston Area's Finest Restaurants.* Seattle, WA: Peanut Butter Publishing. (Irregular)
This is one of a series of booklets that are collections of actual reproductions of menus from selected restaurants from major cities in the U.S. This one covers the Houston area. In addition to a menu, basic information on location, hours, phone number, reservations, and credit cards is included.

1101. *The Indianapolis Dining Guide.* Indianapolis, IN: Dining Guide Publications. (Annual)
A collection of menus with current prices from many Indianapolis restaurants. Information on location, hours, specialties, banquet facilities, and the like as well as brief descriptions of the restaurants are included above each menu. Simplified location maps in the back are keyed to the menus. A cuisine guide helps find restaurants by food type. Some short articles are also included on subjects such as celebrating wine and lunch places in Indianapolis.

1102. Kaplan, Donald, and Bellink, Alan. *Classic Diners of the Northeast.* Photographs by John Bean. Boston: Faber and Faber, 1980. 160 p.

This is a reprint of the 1980 *Diners of the Northeast.* By "diner," the authors mean the authentic "trolley car"-style place with counter, stools, and grill in full view. Most write ups include small black-and-white photographs of diners and owners along with descriptions and menu recommendations. About seventy diners in the following eight states are included: Connecticut, Maine, Massachusetts, New Hampshire, New Jersey, New York, Rhode Island, and Vermont.

1103. Lesberg, Sandy. *Sandy Lesberg's One Hundred Great Restaurants of America.* New York: Crown, 1981. 224 p.

The author has selected 100 restaurants to feature in this combination directory and cookbook. It is arranged by region and state. Each selected restaurant is described, and a characteristic recipe selected by the chef is included. Attractive line drawings of the restaurants enhance the descriptions. In the back of the book, there is a directory of over 400 restaurants also recommended by the author.

1104. MacNeice, Jill, et al. *Roadside Food: Good Home-Style Cooking Across America.* Photographs by LeRoy Woodson, Jr. New York: Stewart, Tabori & Chang, 1986. 160 p.

This is a collection of photographs and essays about good authentic roadside restaurants throughout America. Twenty-three restaurants are featured. They vary from hamburger and hotdog places to lobster and fish restaurants. Doughnut shops, rib and gumbo diners, and Mexican-style places appear. A list of addresses is included.

1105. Mariani, John F. *Eating Out: Fearless Dining in Ethnic Restaurants.* New York: Quill, 1985. 228 p.

Written in a light-hearted, amusing style, Mariani explains every step of dining out from making reservations to paying the bill. He explains the dishes and types of service in ethnic restaurants including French, Italian, Spanish, Japanese, Chinese, Asian, Russian, East European, African, Indian, Mexican, and American. A list of foods and dishes for each ethnic group is included.

1106. Mariani, John F., ed. *Mariani's Coast to Coast Dining Guide.* New York: Times Books, 1986. 866 p.

A guide to restaurants in fifty cities, each city is done by a local expert. Atmosphere, style, and menu specialties are given in short paragraphs along with locational information and price range. A wide range of price and cuisine are represented in this list of over 1,500 restaurants.

1107. Millstead, Kenneth L., ed. *American Road Guide, East: A Complete Interstate Guide to Popular Restaurants, Motels, and Diesel Fuel Gas Stations.* Roseville, MI: Leisure Leads, 1980. 160 p.

A guide to restaurants and motels on interstate highways east of the Mississippi River, over 4,000 places to eat and sleep at 1,330 exits in thirty-one states are included. The book is arranged alphabetically by state. Each page shows a length of highway map with dotted lines leading from exits to a series of symbols for various chains of restaurants and motels. No written information or evaluation of the places is given.

1108. *Minneapolis-St. Paul Epicure: A Menu Guide to the Better Restaurants in Minneapolis & St. Paul.* Seattle, WA: Peanut Butter Publishing. (Irregular)

This is one of a series of booklets that are collections of actual reproductions of menus from selected restaurants from major cities in the U.S. This one covers the Minneapolis-St. Paul area. In addition to a menu, basic information on location, hours, phone number, reservations, and credit cards is included.

1109. Muscatine, Doris. *A Cook's Tour of San Francisco; The Best Restaurants and Their Recipes.* Illustrated by Carolyn Cather. New York: Scribner, 1963. 370 p.
This is a guide to about seventy good restaurants in San Francisco. Each entry includes a lengthy description of food and ambiance plus several recipes. The introduction describes the culinary world of San Francisco in general. Restaurants are divided by ethnic food with entries also appearing under "Family Style," "Old-style San Francisco," "Elegant," "Off-Beat Places," and "Steak and Chicken Houses." There is a directory of restaurants and an index of recipes.

1110. Pritikin, Nathan, and Pritikin, Ilene. *The Official Pritikin Guide to Restaurant Eating.* Indianapolis, IN: Bobbs-Merrill, 1984. 210 p.
This is a guide to following the Pritikin diet while eating out. This well-known health diet is low in fat, cholesterol, and protein while emphasizing carbohydrates especially as found in fruits, vegetables, and whole grains. The book includes a guide to restaurants in the United States where specifically Pritikin meals can be obtained as well as instructs the reader in how to maintain the diet while eating out in a variety of settings.

1111. Rodriguez, Barbara, and Miller, Tom. *The Interstate Gourmet: Texas and the Southwest.* Edited by Neal Weiner and David Schwartz. New York: Summit Books, 1986. 232 p.
Another volume of this exit-by-exit guide to local restaurants along interstate highways. Arizona, New Mexico, Oklahoma, and Texas are included. Sections are divided by state and arranged by interstate and exit number in numerical order.

1112. Stern, Jane, and Stern, Michael. *Goodfood.* New York: Alfred A. Knopf, 1983. 460 p.
This is a guide to authentic regional food in the U.S. arranged by states within regions. Name, address, phone number, hours, and price range are printed above a one- or two-page article on nearly 400 restaurants. Articles give a feel for the character as well as the cuisine of each establishment. The writers have visited all the places they recommend and are sticklers for true authenticity. Therefore, regional restaurants outside their proper regions are not included. Some fascinating places and some little-known specialties have been discovered. There is a map locating restaurants at the beginning of each section.

1113. Stern, Jane, and Stern, Michael. *Roadfood and Goodfood: Jane and Michael Stern's Coast-to-Coast Restaurant Guide.* New York: Alfred A. Knopf, 1986. 561 p.
An updated and expanded combination of the Sterns' two previous books on restaurants in the United States, *Goodfood* and *Roadfood.* Only places serving authentic regional food are included here. Restaurants are listed by state within seven regions: New England, mid-Atlantic, mid-South, Deep South, Midwest, Southwest, and West. A guide at the front of each regional section lists restaurants by area specialty as well. Each entry includes a chatty essay about the restaurant, the authors' reaction to it, and the selections they liked best. The address, phone number, and hours and approximate price range are also included.

1114. *Sun Valley-Ketchum Epicure: A Menu Guide to the Better Restaurants in Sun Valley-Ketchum.* Seattle, WA: Peanut Butter Publishing. (Irregular)
This is one of a series of booklets that are collections of actual reproductions of menus from selected restaurants from major cities in the U.S. This one covers restaurants in Sun Valley-Ketchum. In addition to a menu, basic information on location, hours, phone number, reservations, and credit cards is included.

1115. *Vail Epicure: A Menu Guide to the Better Restaurants in Vail.* Seattle, WA: Peanut Butter Publishing. (Irregular)
This is one of a series of booklets that are collections of actual reproductions of menus from selected restaurants from major cities in the U.S. This book covers the Vail, Colorado area. In addition to a menu, basic information on location, hours, phone number, reservations, and credit cards is included.

1116. Weiner, Neal O., and Schwartz, David. *The Interstate Gourmet: Midwest.* New York: Summit Books, 1986. 287 p.

> This is a guide to good local restaurants within easy driving distance of midwestern interstate highways. Entries are arranged by highway and exit number. No chains are included. Each entry has a chatty description of the place and good directions. It is aimed at travelers with time to stop and enjoy local food in the low to medium price range. Editions are also available for mid-Atlantic, California and the Pacific Northwest, Southeast, and New England areas.

ENCYCLOPEDIAS

1117. Coyle, L. Patrick. *The World Encyclopedia of Food.* Photography by Bobbi Mapstone. Drawings by Shoshnah Dubiner and Erika Oller. New York: Facts on File, 1982. 790 p.

> Written for the general reader, this encyclopedia includes quick, basic information on foods and beverages. Some cooking techniques are also described. Articles include description of the food, where it is eaten or drunk, and what it tastes like. Some historical information is also given. Numerous black-and-white illustrations enhance the book.

1118. Ensminger, Audrey H. et al. *Foods & Nutrition Encyclopedia.* Clovis, CA: Pegus Press, 1983. 2 vols. 2,415 p.

> This two-volume encyclopedia covers virtually everything about food and nutrition for consumers and professionals. Over 2,800 entries covering historical topics, brief definitions of terms, and full encyclopedia-type entries on many foods, nutrition, and health topics. Black-and-white illustrations and charts are included. A full "Food Composition Table" is included in volume one.

1119. Gancel, Joseph. *Gancel's Culinary Encyclopedia of Modern Cooking.* 13th rev ed. New York: Radio City Bookstore, 1977. 503 p.

> This pocket-size book was written to help waiters understand the menu so that they could explain dishes to their customers. It contains a wealth of information in a very concise and handy format. Organized by menu categories, 8,000 terms, many of them French, are briefly defined. These definitions can serve as recipes for experienced chefs and cooks.

1120. Lang, Jenifer Harvey. *Tastings—The Best from Ketchup to Caviar: Thirty-One Pantry Basics & How They Rate with the Experts.* New York: Crown, 1986. 332 p.

> Lang rates some thirty-one items by taste. Using methods of professional tasting and participants well known in the food world, the author rates selected grain products, dairy products, condiments, canned foods, herbs and spices, beverages, baking goods, sweets, and luxury foods. Ratings are listed in order of preference, and comments are included. Brand names are given. Chapters also include brief information on history and production of the various items and some recipes.

1121. Montagné, Prosper. *The New Larousse Gastronomique: The Encyclopedia of Food, Wine & Cookery.* Edited by Charlotte Turgeon. Translated by Marion Hunter. New York: Crown Publishers, 1977. 1,064 p.

> This is the most comprehensive encyclopedia available. It covers the history of food, cooking, and eating habits in concise articles arranged in alphabetical order. Many of the entries include recipes, so it can serve as an extensive cookbook as well as an encyclopedia of food facts. Numerous color and black-and-white photographs and diagrams are included.

1122. Woodman, Julie G. *IFMA Encyclopedia of the Foodservice Industry.* 5th ed. Chicago: International Foodservice Manufacturers Association, 1985. 275 p.

> This is an extensive reference book that lists food, equipment, and supply companies; brokers; chain restaurant executives; publishers; market researchers; association executives; consultants; government agencies; libraries; HRI faculty; and advertising agencies. Also

included are articles and statistical charts on trends, size and segment of the foodservice market, food consumed away from home, and many other timely topics.

FOOD COMPOSITION TABLES

1123. Adams, Catherine F. *Handbook of the Nutritional Value of Foods: In Common Units.* New York: Dover Publications, 1986. 284 p.
This handbook provides calories and nutrients of food in household measures and market units. It is an unabridged and unaltered reproduction of Agricultural Handbook No. 456, *Nutritive Value of American Foods: In Common Units,* 1975.

1124. Bowes, Anna De Planter. *Bowes and Church's Food Values of Portions Commonly Used.* 14th ed. Revised by Jean A. T. Pennington and Helen Nichols Church. Philadelphia, PA: Lippincott, 1985. 257 p.
Designed as a quick reference for the nutritional value of foods. The main table, "Nutrient Contents of Food," lists almost every common food and beverage by name, description, brand name, and serving portion. Items are arranged in general categories (i.e., meats, etc.). Each entry has twenty-nine headings, ten more than the last edition. Water and cholesterol content and a number of new vitamin and mineral entries are now included. Amino acids are now in a supplementary table in the back where other substances of nutritional concern, such as caffeine, are also found. There is a straight alphabetical index by food item.

1125. *Composition of Foods.* Agricultural Handbook, no. 8. Washington, DC: U.S. Department of Agriculture, Human Nutrition Information Service, 1976–. (Loose-leaf)
Since 1896, the U.S. Department of Agriculture has compiled nutrition composition tables. This new edition is a major revision which will greatly expand the access to the information available on food composition. Instead of a slim, one-volume book, it is being issued in the following parts: "Dairy and Egg Products"; "Spices and Herbs"; "Baby Foods"; "Fats and Oils"; "Poultry Products"; "Soups, Sauces and Gravies"; "Sausages and Luncheon Meats"; "Breakfast Cereal"; "Fruits and Fruit Juices"; "Pork Products"; "Vegetables and Vegetable Products"; "Nut and Seed Products"; "Beef Products"; "Beverages"; and "Legumes and Legume Products." Other sections will be published in the future.

1126. Leveille, Gilbert A.; Zabik, Mary Ellen; and Morgan, Karen J. *Nutrients in Foods.* Cambridge, MA: Nutrition Guild, 1983. 291 p.
The nutrient composition of over 2,700 foods is listed in chart format. All dietary nutrients essential for growth and maintenance are included. Crude and dietary fiber (P/S ratio) is also included. Data in this book comes from the Michigan State University *Nutrient Data Bank;* most of the data is taken from USDA Handbook no. 8, *Composition of Foods.* The appendices include caffeine content and alcohol content of selected foods.

INDEXES

1127. Bohnet, Gerald V., ed. *The Travel and Tourism Index.* Laie, HI: Business Division, Brigham Young University—Hawaii Campus. 1984–. (Quarterly)
This is a new index published by Brigham Young University, Hawaii Campus. It indexes periodicals, newsletters, and bulletins related to the travel field. It does include some very important journals not indexed elsewhere and so is a good supplement.

1128. *Business Index [Microform].* Belmont, CA: Information Access Co., 1979–. (Monthly)
Produced on microfilm, this tool indexes hundreds of English-language business periodicals. Because it is published on microfilm, each monthly issue cumulates all the references for the past five years. The coverage of hospitality journals is very good,

although not as extensive as the *Lodging and Restaurant Index.* (Available online through Dialog as Trade and Industry Index.)

1129. *Business Periodicals Index.* New York: H. W. Wilson Co., 1958–. (Monthly)
This monthly publication indexes the major journals in the business field including several important journals in the hospitality fields. It is useful in identifying journal articles related to the hotel and restaurant industries published in general business periodicals. It is arranged by subject with full reference to each article included in each citation. Journal titles are abbreviated and in italics followed by volume number, page numbers and date of the periodical. In the front of each issue is a key to the periodical abbreviations. Available online through Wilsonline.

1130. The Consortium of Hospitality Research Information Services. *Lodging and Restaurant Index.* Judith M. Nixon, ed. West Lafayette, IN: The Restaurant, Hotel, and Institutional Management Institute, Purdue University, 1985–. (Quarterly)
This is the most comprehensive periodical index available in the hospitality industries. It indexes twenty-nine journals under subject headings developed especially for the industry. Each entry includes title, author, and bibliographic citation. Important articles are starred. The consortium plans to expand the scope in future years by adding additional titles and possibly other media.

1131. *Food Service Research Abstracts.* Fort Wayne, IN: Society for the Advancement of Food Service Research, 1966–. (Annual)
This is an index to current and recently completed research in foodservice. Arranged by university or research institution, most of the references are to theses.

1132. Hamilton, Malcolm. *Travel Index: A Guide to Books and Articles, 1985–86.* Phoenix, AZ: Oryx Press, 1988. 237 p.
This extensive bibliography includes magazine articles and books on travel published between 1985 and 1986. Divided into three sections, the first indexes articles from twenty-six popular magazines including *Better Homes & Gardens, Consumer Reports, Travel & Leisure,* and *National Geographic.* Articles are indexed by subject and geographic location. Part two briefly annotates books noted or reviewed in library reviewing journals and travel sections of eleven major newspapers. Books are listed by subject and geographic location. Part three lists travel newsletters and magazines by subject and location.

1133. *Leisure, Recreation and Tourism Abstracts.* Farnham Royal, England: International and World Leisure and Recreation Association, 1981–. (Quarterly)
This quarterly publication indexes and abstracts (or summarizes) journal articles from around the world related to tourism. It continues *Rural Recreation and Tourism Abstracts* (1976–1981). The abstracts in each issue are arranged by a broad subject classification. Author and detailed subject indexes are in the back of each issue. (Available online through Dialog as part of CAB Abstracts or on BRS.)

1134. National Agriculture Library, U.S. Department of Agriculture. *Food and Nutrition Quarterly Index.* Phoenix, AZ: Oryx Press, 1985–88. (Quarterly)
Compiled from data provided by the National Agriculture Library from their AGRICOLA database, this is an annotated index to books, periodical articles, and audiovisual materials on food, human nutrition, and foodservice management. It continues *Food and Nutrition Bibliography.* Annotations are arranged by broad subject categories with author, title, and subject indexes included in the back. Four journals from the restaurant industry are indexed. (Available online through Dialog and BRS.)

1135. National Agricultural Library, U.S. Department of Agriculture. *Food and Nutrition Bibliography*. Phoenix, AZ: Oryx Press, 1980–84. (Annual)

This continues *Food and Nutrition Information and Educational Materials Center Catalog.* It includes annotations of books, journal articles, and audiovisual materials related to food, human nutrition, and foodservice management. The entries are taken from the National Agricultural Library's AGRICOLA database. Volume eleven, the latest available, includes entries added to the database covering the 1980 acquisitions. For more current indexing see *Food and Nutrition Quarterly Index.* (Available online as the AGRICOLA through Dialog and BRS.)

1136. National Restaurant Association. *Information Service Abstracts*. Washington, DC. (Weekly)

This weekly publication reproduces selected abstracts from the computer files of the National Restaurant Association. Each issue is from twelve to twenty pages and is arranged by broad topics: "Trends," "Studies/Surveys," "Features," "Advertising," "Government Relations," "Management," "NRA News," "Upcoming Events." Thirteen journals and newsletters are reviewed for the publication.

1137. Oaksford, Margaret J. *Bibliography of Hotel and Restaurant Administration and Related Subjects*. Ithaca, NY: School of Hotel Administration, Cornell University. 1951–1987. (Annual)

This was the major index in the hotel and restaurant industry, published annually since the 1950s. It indexed books, pamphlets, and periodical articles. The index is arranged by subjects relevant to the field; a full bibliographic citation is given with each entry. The index ceased with journals published during 1985. Starting in 1987 Cornell School of Hotel Administration, Purdue University and University of Wisconsin-Stout have been working together on the *Lodging and Restaurant Index.*

1138. *Predicasts F & S Index United States*. Cleveland, OH: Predicasts, Inc., 1959?- . (Weekly)

This indexes hundreds of English-language business journals and newspapers. It is divided into two sections: "Industries and Products" and "Companies." The product section is arranged by SIC Codes (Standard Industrial Classification Codes). An alphabetical guide to products and their SIC numbers is listed in the front of each issue. The company section is arranged alphabetically by company name. (Available online through Dialog and BRS.)

1139. Torgeson, Kathryn W., and Weinstein, Sylvia J. *The Garland Recipe Index*. Garland Reference Library of the Humanities, vol. 414. New York: Garland Publishing, 1984. 314 p.

This is an index to recipes in nearly fifty well-known cookbooks. The cookbooks chosen were based upon Mimi Sheraton's list of basic cookbooks published in the August 15, 1981 issue of *New York Times.* Recipes are indexed by name, principle ingredient, and cooking style. If the recipe is of ethnic origin, that is noted also.

STATISTICS

1140. American Hotel & Motel Association, and Peat, Marwick, Mitchell & Co. *Hospitality Industry Compensation Survey 1985*. New York, 1985. 75 p.

The results of the twelfth Salary and Benefits Survey conducted in early 1985 by AH&MA are presented here, showing salaries paid for hotel and motel management positions throughout the United States. This report includes a list and descriptions of positions surveyed, demographics by region, room size, and food and beverage revenues as well as pay data presented by position and region.

1141. Food Service Marketing. *Gallup Survey: The National Poll of Patron Preferences Prejudices, and Trends.* Madison, WI: 1966–75. (Biennial)

These five booklets are collected reprints of the Gallup Survey articles that appeared each month in *Food Service Magazine* and *Food Services Marketing.* Each volume covers two years, beginning with January 1966. Surveys cover many aspects of restaurant and food service. Titles include "The Nations Most Desired Desserts," "Pollsters Learn Why Customers Don't Come Back," and "The Take-Out Marathon." Although the information is quite old now, this is a convenient source for historical comparisons. Continued by *Gallup Surveys of Opinions toward Food Service.*

1142. Food Service Marketing. *Gallup Surveys of Opinions toward Food Service.* Madison, WI, 1976?

Reprinted from *Food Service Marketing,* January 1974 through December 1976. See annotation under previous title *Gallup Survey: The National Poll of Patron Preferences, Prejudices, and Trends.*

1143. Hiemstra, Stephen J., and Kreul, Lee M. *Manpower Resources and Trends in the Lodging Industry: Past and Future.* New York: American Hotel & Motel Association, 1986. 53 p.

This is a study prepared for the American Hotel & Motel Association assessing projected manpower needs of the lodging industry. Charts and statistics present past trends and make projections to the year 2000. Trends covered include number of establishments, number of rooms, and other industry trends related to employment. In addition, factors affecting demand and supply of labor are included such as economic growth and labor productivity. Implications for the individual lodging operator and other conclusions are provided.

1144. Horwath & Horwath International. *Worldwide Lodging Industry.* New York, 1975–. (Annual)

This work compiles statistics from all over the world on various aspects of the lodging industry. It begins with an overall analysis of the present state of the worldwide industry. The data are then presented for the five regions: Africa, Europe, Asia and Australia, North America, and Latin America. The statistics on over a dozen subjects are presented for each region including market data, comparison of sales and profitability, occupancy, and food and beverage statistics. Each area includes a short section giving the highlights of the survey for that region, a general profile of the typical contributor, and currency conversion tables.

1145. Kreul, Lee M., and Lohr, Judi. *A Digest of Current Lodging Industry Market Research Studies.* s.l.: s.n., 1983. 95 p.

Phase one of this study shows the results of a survey by the authors of the American Hotel & Motel Association members asking their degree of interest in thirty-two commonly asked questions. Phase two is a synthesis and analysis of currently available studies on nine questions chosen as a result of this survey. These include "Average Length of Guest Stay," "How Reservations Are Made," "Who Selects the Hotel/Motel," "Who Makes the Reservations," "Lead Time in Making Reservations," "Factors Influencing the Hotel Selection," "What Media Is Most Effective on a Local Basis for Hotels," "Effectiveness of Contests/Special Promotions," and "Importance of Fire and Crime Security in Hotel Selection."

1146. Market Facts, Inc. *Patronage of Fast-Food/Drive-In Carry-Out Restaurants and Consumer Behavior on Selected Topics.* Chicago, 1975. 30 p.

This statistical survey was conducted by Market Facts for the National Restaurant Association in 1975. The survey sought to determine how frequently people visit fast food restaurants, what food and beverages they order, who in the family is most influential in choice of restaurant, where food is consumed and perception of price.

1147. McGowan, Sandra. *The Restaurant and Institutional Food Service Industry*. Business Opportunity Report, GA-039R. Stamford, CT: Business Communications Co., 1985. 97 p.

This is a comprehensive report on the foodservice industry with detailed analyses of the commercial and institutional market. Sales are shown from the past five years and forecasts for the next five. Most types of restaurants and institutions are covered. Statistics and analysis appear on marketing, distribution, the effects of changing demographic and socioeconomic factors, and the impact of emerging technologies on the food industry. This report was prepared for a special project; price is $1,250.00.

1148. National Restaurant Association. *Consumer Attitude and Behavior Study: Consumer Expectations with Regard to Dining at Atmosphere Restaurants.* Washington, DC, 1983. 118 p.

This is a report on a survey conducted by the National Restaurant Association to determine what factors are most important to patrons at an atmospheric restaurant. The objectives of the study were to determine what patrons want in terms of food, service, and atmosphere. Many statistical tables and charts are included.

1149. National Restaurant Association. *Consumer Attitude and Behavior Study: Consumer Expectations with Regard to Dining at Family Restaurants.* Washington, DC, 1983. 121 p.

This is one of three reports on what consumers want and expect in restaurants. This one centers on family restaurants. Specific areas of research were food, service, atmosphere, and general patron attitudes. Results are reported in statistical charts and tables.

1150. National Restaurant Association. *Consumer Attitude and Behavior Study: Consumer Expectations with Regard to Dining at Fast Food Restaurants.* Washington, DC, 1983. 118 p.

This is a report on a survey conducted by the National Restaurant Association to determine what factors are most important to patrons at a fast food restaurant. Fast food restaurants are defined as ones which are primarily self-service, offer carryout as well as eat-in service and are inexpensive. The objectives of the study were to determine what patrons want in terms of food, service, and atmosphere. Many statistical tables and charts are included.

1151. National Restaurant Association. *Foodservice Sales Panorama: Featuring Foodservice Industry Food and Drink Sales, 1970–1980.* Washington, DC, 1981. 47 p.

A report bringing together statistics on foodservice industry sales, purchases and unit numbers from 1970–1979. The overall summary and analysis is followed by forty-four detailed tables presenting various aspects of industry sales and other data.

1152. National Restaurant Association. *Meal Consumption Behavior.* Washington, DC, 1985. 81 p.

This is a presentation of the statistical results of a survey conducted by the National Restaurant Association on individual meal consumption behavior. The results include information from 14,255 individuals concerning where their meals were prepared and what meals were skipped. Information is tabulated by age, sex, and income.

1153. National Restaurant Association. *The Restaurant Industry in 1990.* National Restaurant Association Current Issues Report. Washington, DC, 1985. 16 p.

The Delphi technique, which uses opened questions and seeks a consensus from a group of experts, was used to forecast the future of the restaurant industry. The results are grouped into six categories: "The Economy," "Consumers," "Federal Legislation," "Labor Market," "Industry Structure," and "Foodservice Technology."

1154. National Restaurant Association and Laventhol & Horwath. *Restaurant Industry Operations Report for the United States.* Washington, DC, (Annual)

Based on over 700 questionnaires from restaurants, this report provides financial operating results of all types of restaurants from full service to fast food. Data are presented in charts based on type of restaurant, location, affiliation, years of operation, sales volume, and menu theme. The operating results are expressed as amounts per seat and ratios to total sales. Medium, upper, and lower quantiles are reported. A worksheet is included so a restaurant can compare its operation with the industry. Continues *Restaurant Operations.*

1155. National Restaurant Association, Research and Information Services Department. *Consumer Attitude and Behavior Study: Consumer Behavior and Attitudes towards Fast Food and Moderately Priced Family Restaurants.* Washington, DC, 1987. 125 p.

This is a report of the results of a survey conducted between September and October 1986. The purpose of the survey was to ascertain frequency, motive, and satisfaction of consumers patronizing fast food and family restaurants. Summaries and detailed tables are provided.

1156. National Restaurant Association, Research and Information Services Department. *Consumer Attitude and Behavior Study: Consumer Nutrition Concerns and Restaurant Choices.* Washington, DC, 1986. 2 vols.

This is the report of results from a survey conducted in February and March 1986. The survey was done to find out how health and nutrition attitudes influence restaurant and menu choices. Volume one provides a general overview of results and presents tables and charts on the traditional weight conscious, health conscious, and uncommitted consumer. Volume two provides more details and breaks down data by demographic characteristics such as age, sex, and income.

1157. National Restaurant Association, Research and Information Services Department. *Consumer Attitude and Behavior Study: Consumer Preferences for Ethnic Food in Restaurants.* Washington, DC, 1984. 86 p.

This is one of three reports on what consumers want and expect in restaurants. This one centers on ethnic restaurants. Specific areas of research were food, service, atmosphere, and general patron attitudes. Results are reported in statistical charts and tables.

1158. National Restaurant Association, Research Department. *Consumer Attitude and Behavior Study: Consumer Preferences for New Restaurant Concepts—1986.* Washington, DC, 1986. 120 p.

This is the second survey of consumer attitudes toward new types of restaurants. Over 2,000 people were interviewed by telephone. Consumers were asked what specialty restaurants they had patronized and what their attitude was toward those they had not patronized. Full statistics are given. Many types of specialty restaurants are included: bakery items, pizza, barbecue, pasta, hot dogs, hamburgers, ice cream, oriental fast food, diet or lite menu items, freshly baked cookies, gourmet, ready-to-eat take-out foods, chicken, spicy, Cajun-style cooking, display cooking, mesquite grilling, sushi, and sashimi.

1159. National Restaurant Association, Research and Information Services Department. *Consumer Attitude and Behavior Study: Consumer Reactions to and Use of Restaurant Promotions.* Washington, DC, 1982. 170 p.

The results of a National Restaurant Association survey of consumers is compiled in this publication. The purpose of the study was to identify consumer use and acceptance of promotions such as cents-off coupons, two-for-one deals, premiums, and games. Specifically the survey centered on who uses promotions, the frequency of use of various types of promotions, how consumers find out about promotions, and whether they attract new or repeat business. The survey also sought to ascertain consumer attitudes to promotions.

1160. National Restaurant Association, Research and Information Services Department. *Consumer Attitude and Behavior Study: How Consumers Make the Decision to Eat Out.* Washington, DC, 1982. 202 p.
The objectives of this study conducted in November 1981 include finding out where the decision to eat out is made, who influences it, and how far in advance it is made. Why consumers eat at particular types of restaurants and what factors are important when selecting one were also questions under study. Tables and summaries present data collected on the consumer decision-making process for fast food, family, and atmosphere restaurants.

1161. National Restaurant Association, Research and Information Services Department. *Consumer Attitude and Behavior Study: The Take Out Market.* Washington, DC, 1986. 140 p.
This is a consumer study; its purpose was to determine who purchases take-out meals, when, where, and why they are purchased as well as what is purchased. General attitudes toward take-out food were also surveyed. Data were obtained from a mailing to 1,000 households in April and May 1985. A summary is given. More detailed results are presented in tabular form, and the questionnaire is included.

1162. Opinion Research Corporation. *The Lodging Industry's Image: How the Adults and Teenagers View Hotels and Motels as Employers and Overall.* Princeton, NJ, 197?-. 77 p.
This is the results of a research study completed in 1969 for the American Hotel & Motel Association. Emphasis was on finding the industry's image both in general and as an employer. Interviews were conducted among 994 adults and 622 teenagers. A summary of the study is given as well as a detailed breakdown of the findings. The conclusion is that the general image is quite favorable, but the image of the industry as an employer needs some improvement.

1163. Pannell, Kerr, Forster. *Trends in the Hotel Industry (USA ed.).* New York, 1980-. (Annual)
This is a statistical review of trends in the lodging industry which continues *Trends in the Hotel-Motel Business.* The book is based on financial and operating data collected from 1,000 hotels and motels in the U.S. Overall statistics for the industry are presented first then broken down by region. Charts and figures appear on such subjects as payroll, occupancy rates, and comparative results of operations. These are followed by detailed statistics for specific sections of the industry: transient hotels, resort hotels, motels with restaurants, and motels without restaurants.

1164. Sandler, Mel. *Hotel/Motel Wage Rates and Other Payroll Costs for Major U.S. Cities.* New York: American Hotel & Motel Association, 1986. 43 p.
Data in this survey is taken from union contracts of hotels and motels in various major cities. Hourly wages by city are presented for seventeen job classifications. Other sections include benefits such as holiday clauses, vacations, pensions, health, and welfare; banquet arrangements; probationary period; jury duty; funeral pay; schedule posting requirements; shift differential; reporting pay; and other provisions. Sources of the data are listed.

1165. Sinclair, Valerie, ed. *The 1987 Gallup Annual Report on Eating Out.* Princeton, NJ: Gallup Organization, 1985-. (Annual)
Based on the extensive interviews and surveys conducted by the Gallup Organization, this annual statistical report summarizes food trends and customer service preferences in statistical charts. Sections include "Customer Demographics," "New Menu Items," "Beverages," "Take Out," "Menus," "Service," "Customer Motivation," "Ethnic Groups," and "Pricing."

1166. Technomic Consultants. *IFMA's 1984 Dynamics of the Chain Restaurant Market.* Chicago, 1984. 2 vols.
Prepared annually by Technomic Consultants, this publication is an interpretation and analysis of information gathered in their market survey. The top 100 restaurant companies and their chains are tracked statistically. Volume one includes an executive

overview and a look at the top 100 companies presented by types of chains. Industrial trends and outlook are also included. Volume two presents detailed profiles of the 185 restaurant chains from the top 100 companies by name, including headquarters, locations, menu specialty, three-year sales figures, average volume per unit, and number of units.

1167. U.S. Travel Data Center. *The...Economic Review of Travel in America.* Washington, DC, 1980–. (Annual)
This report reviews the economic characteristics of travel, the development in the U.S. travel industry, and the effect of recent economic changes in travel and tourism. It covers American and foreign travel in the U.S. Chapters cover travel industry trends, travel price inflation, employment in the industry, energy used by travelers, international travel trends, and region travel patterns.

1168. U.S. Travel Data Center. *The Impact of Travel on State Economies.* Washington, DC, 1974–. (Annual)
This is a statistical report of the economic impact of travel which uses the TEIM (Travel Economic Impact Model). It includes expenditures, employment, payroll, business receipts, and tax revenue generated by travel away from home in the U.S. The data in this report are estimates only.

1169. U.S. Travel Data Center. *National Travel Survey Quarterly Report.* Washington, DC, 1974–. (Quarterly)
See entry 1170.

1170. U.S. Travel Data Center. *National Travel Survey Full Year Report.* Washington, DC, 1974–. (Annual)
Since 1979, the U.S. Travel Data Center has conducted a monthly National Travel Survey. The results of these surveys are published quarterly with annual summaries. The statistical charts provide marketers and researchers with data on the major travel trends in the U.S. Regular tables include mode of transportation, purpose of trip, vacation travel, weekend travel, and hotel/motel lodging. Questionnaire and methodology are included.

1171. U.S. Travel Data Center. *Survey of State Travel Offices.* Washington, DC, 1973–. (Annual)
This report is the result of a mail survey sent to all state and territorial travel offices. The results are charted and cover general administration, advertising, budget, general promotion, press and public relations, research, and welcome centers.

1172. U.S. Travel Data Center, and Business Research Division, University of Colorado. *Tourism's Top Twenty: Fast Facts on Travel and Tourism.* Special Studies in Travel Economy and Marketing. Washington, DC, 1980. 86 p.
This compilation of facts, figures, and statistics on travel and tourism covers both the U.S. and the world. It provides a ranking of the "top twenty" in advertising, airlines, attractions, world travel, hotels and resorts, recreation, and visitors to cities and states. There are eighty-one tables; each cites the source of the statistics. Addresses for the sources are included in the back of the publication.

1173. Van Dress, Michael G. *The Foodservice Industry: Structure, Organization, and Use of Food, Equipment, and Supplies.* Statistical Bulletin, USDA, Economic Research Service, no. 690. Washington, DC: Government Printing Office, 1982. 154 p.
The primary objectives of the research studies reported here were to obtain information on industry structure and organization, the quantity of food received and use of foodservice equipment and nonfood supplies. Statistics are provided on number of establishments, divided by type of food served and type and size of business. Within these classifications information is given on product movement, equipment and supplies, and other selected subjects such as workers, cost components, and energy.

1174. Waters, Somerset R. *Travel Industry World Yearbook: The Big Picture.* Edited by Thomas Bridges. New York: Child & Waters, 1983–. (Annual)

This continues *The Big Picture* which has been published annually for thirty years. It records what is happening in world tourism for the purpose of recording the changes in tourism as a clue to the trends of the future. Many statistical charts are included, but the author has also provided written essays on each subject. Topics covered include economic and political influences; travel trends by states, regions of the world, and by industry sectors; and a world overview.

Security Management

1175. Axler, Bruce H. *Security for Hotels, Motels, and Restaurants.* His Focus on...the Hospitality Industry. Indianapolis, IN: ITT Educational Publishing, 1974. 114 p.
> Another book in Axler's series, this one covers security management. It lists the most common security problems: high-risk employees, counterfeit money and bad credit cards, and employee theft. He outlines a program that can be implemented in restaurants and hotels by managers without specialized security training.

1176. Burstein, Harvey. *Hotel Security Management.* 2d ed. New York: Praeger, 1985. 176 p.
> The goal of this book is the development of management's role in security. It presents a variety of security problems and suggests possible solutions. The book opens with an introduction to security and the hotel industry. This is followed by chapters on physical security, administrative and operational security, protection department, guests, and emergencies. This edition includes new developments for security and new problems posed by computers in the industry.

1177. Burstein, Harvey. *Management of Hotel and Motel Security.* Occupational Safety and Health, no. 5. New York: M. Dekker, 1980. 200 p.
> This is a book intended for security directors rather than a detailed plan for security operations. It deals with the general problems and various solutions found in the field and covers the relationship between security and other members of the management. Besides an introduction on the role and objectives of security, chapters cover the purpose of a security department and descriptions of the position of the security director/manager and property security directors/managers.

1178. Buzby, Walter J., II, and Paine, David. *Hotel & Motel Security Management.* Boston: Butterworth Publishers, 1976. 247 p.
> Detailed information is given here on security organization and practice. Chapters deal with guests; rooms; public areas; food and beverage; housekeeping; parking; and such specific problems as fraud, fire, bomb threats, and organized crime. Appendices give laws relating to hotels and motels in both the United States and Canada.

1179. Curtis, Bob. *Food Service Security: Internal Control.* New York: Chain Store Age Books, 1975. 222 p.
> Curtis deals frankly with the problem of employee dishonesty. He explains the basic safeguards including cash register, supply, and accounting controls. He also includes some very illuminating sections on subjects such as spotting a high-risk employee, employee theft methods, investigating techniques, and keeping your employees honest.

1180. Ellis, Raymond C., Jr., and the Security Committee of American Hotel & Motel Association. *Security and Loss Prevention Management.* East Lansing, MI: Educational Institute of the American Hotel & Motel Association, 1986. 285 p.

This text is designed to help in the development of a security program and also to inform employees about security concerns. The nine chapters address various security issues such as security programs, equipment, procedures covering guest concerns, responsibilities for guests' assets and funds, emergency management, and safety. A guide to OSHA regulations is included. Appendices include sample room postings and some court cases.

1181. Hughes, Denis. *Guide to Hotel Security.* Aldershot, Hants, England: Gower, 1984. 152 p.

This is a British publication designed to acquaint the hotel manager with the basics of hotel security. It covers the organization of a security department, building, security, rooms, property, food and drink security, housekeeping, fire, and even terrorism and disasters. An appendix gives laws related to hotels in the United Kingdom.

1182. National Restaurant Association. *Safety Operations Manual.* Washington, DC, 1981. (Loose-leaf)

This is a loose-leaf manual providing information about the possible components of a safety program. It covers elements of safety programs, statistics, insurance, security, emergencies and catastrophes, first aid, OSHA, fire prevention and protection, self-inspection programs, and sources of assistance. One section, Safety Program, is empty. It is intended to be filled by the reader with the policies, objectives, and activities of one's own program. Very basic information as well as some poster examples and checklists are provided.

1183. *Restaurant & Bar Security.* Boston: Butterworth Publishers, 1974. 104 p.

This book gives a concise picture of many of the problems and possible solutions for losses and theft in the restaurant business. Part one, on the back of the house, covers general precautions as well as specifics such as waste, storage and accountability, employee theft, methods of stealing, problem of fire, and security information sources. Part two, on the front of the house, deals with theft from the bar; theft that involves guests; and losses from fire, robbery, and burglary. There are chapters on methods of protection and carry-out operations.

1184. Service, J. Gregory. *Security for Hotels and Motels: A Perspective on Liabilities.* Springfield, IL: C.C. Thomas, 1986. 108 p.

The author, a lawyer, examines liability in lodging, using references to actual court decisions. Chapters cover liability for employee actions, negligence in hiring, policy considerations, contract security, control of persons entering, theft of hotel property, key control, parking areas, licensing arrangement liability, alcoholic beverage sale, and fire safety.

Tourism and Travel

1185. Association Internationale d'Experts Scientifiques du Tourisme. *Tendances Evolutives de la Demande Touristique (Trends of Tourist Demand).* St-Gall, Switzerland, 1985. vol. 26. 124 p.

This is a collection of the basic reports and some special reports of the thirty-fifth AIEST (Association Internationale d'Experts Scientifiques du Tourisme) Congress. Some of these reports are in French and German without translation. Reports in English include "The Consequences of Growing Ecological Consciousness, and Changing Socio-Cultural Needs on Tourism Policy"; "Monitoring Behavioral Changes through National Guest Surveys"; "Swiss and Austrian Experience"; "Marketing Adaptation to the Changing Trends in Tourist Behavior"; and "Trends of Tourist Demand."

1186. Chamberlin, Eric Russell. *The Idea of England.* New York: Thames and Hudson, 1986. 240 p.

A look at England based on accounts of travelers from Medieval times to the present. Emphasis is placed on those writers who are trying to give a portrait of the country and not just descriptions. The book is divided into three parts: "They Set Out," covering early pilgrims and travelers, "The Imposition of Form," which is primarily on the eighteenth century; and "New World," about present-day travelers. This is a scholarly but interesting book with beautiful illustrations.

1187. Curran, Patrick J. T. *Principles and Procedures of Tour Management.* Boston: CBI Publishing Co., 1978. 152 p.

This is a handbook for the beginning tour manager. It provides practical guidance to pretour preparations, basic tour management procedures, and some of the pros and cons of the profession. It also covers specifics such as tipping and luggage as well as reconfirmation and hotel procedures.

1188. Dearing, James W. *Home Exchanging: The Complete Sourcebook for Travelers at Home and Abroad.* Charlotte, NC: East Woods Press, 1986. 192 p.

This book explains the process of home exchanging as a means of international travel. It also discusses effective advertising and provides a reference guide to assist the exchanger in making contacts. Chapters cover the steps of exchanging, when to use an agency catalog, and preswap worries. Appendices list agencies, newspapers, colleges, international associations, and other sources where exchangers can be located.

1189. Edgell, David L. *International Trade in Tourism: A Manual for Managers and Executives.* Washington, DC: U.S. Department of Commerce, U.S. Travel and Tourism Administration, 1985. 40 p.

This is a short general guide to the concerns of U.S. tourism policy, published by the Department of Commerce. Chapters discuss international tourism as a commercial and economic activity as well as its political and sociocultural aspects. Projections through the year 2000 are included.

1190. Hensher, David A., and Dalvi, Quasim, eds. *Determinants of Travel Choice.* Praeger Special Studies. New York: Praeger, 1978. 394 p.

This is a thorough study of travel choice which examines the literature and lays groundwork for future study. Each chapter is authored separately by experts. The economic, behavioral, and psychological reasons for travel are analyzed. Also covered are the valuation of journey and destination choice and travel attributes, travel choices for recreational journeys, and time budgets.

1191. Jackle, John A. *The Tourist: Travel in Twentieth-Century North America.* Lincoln, NE: University of Nebraska Press, 1985. 382 p.

This is a historic survey of the travel and tourist industry in the U.S. and Canada in this century since the advent of the private car up to present time. The author covers the growth of vacation parks, accommodations, restaurants and fast food chains, and campgrounds.

1192. Kaul, Raghu Nath. *Dynamics of Tourism: A Trilogy.* New Delhi, India: Sterling, 1985. Vols. 1–3. 711 p.

Volume one, *The Phenomenon,* deals with the fundamental nature of tourism, its development through history, and the role and objectives of various aspects of the industry. Volume two, *Accommodation,* and volume three, *Transportation and Marketing,* discuss the interaction of these major factors and give specifics on planning and marketing. Together these three volumes give an extensive theoretical and practical coverage to the subject of tourism.

1193. Lundberg, Donald E. *International Travel and Tourism.* New York: Wiley, 1985. 254 p.

Written originally as a text for classes in travel management, this book presents statistical information and brief general travel information on most areas of the world. There are specific chapters on Canada, Alaska, Mexico, and United Kingdom. Other countries are presented in chapters on their regions such as Western Europe, Eastern Europe and the USSR, the Caribbean Region, South and Central America, and the Pacific Basin. There is a light touch to the style that makes it easier to read than many such works. General information about the travel industry is also included, but emphasis is on country information.

1194. Lundberg, Donald E. *The Tourist Business.* 5th ed. New York: Van Nostrand Reinhold Co., 1985. 252 p.

Now in its fifth edition, this book is a standard in the field. It covers all the various businesses that make up the tourism industry: travel agencies, tour operators, hotels, restaurants, airlines, rental car agencies, and tourist attractions. How these interrelate and affect one another is the focus of the book. It also addresses the social and economic impacts of tourism and addresses the strategies for developing a tourist attraction. Case studies of Club Med, Disney World, and the Rockresorts are used to illustrate marketing strategies. Special attention is given to travel agency business.

1195. Manning, Robert E. *Studies in Outdoor Recreation: Search and Research for Satisfaction.* Corvallis, OR: Oregon State University Press, 1986. 166 p.

A review and synthesis of research on outdoor recreation, this represents one of the first efforts to integrate the diverse studies in this field. Chapters cover social and descriptive aspects, camping capacity, density, motivation, recreation opportunity, and managing outdoor recreation in both planning and action.

1196. McIntosh, Robert W., and Goeldner, Charles R. *Tourism: Principles, Practices, Philosophies.* 5th ed. New York: Wiley, 1986. 564 p.

This is a college text on the basics of tourism. It is arranged in five parts and covers tourism's nature, history, and organization; motivation for travel; supply, demand, economics, and development of tourism; marketing and research; and tourism practices and prospects. The appendix includes a good list of information sources in the field.

1197. Mill, Robert Christie, and Morrison, Alastair M. *The Tourism System: An Introductory Text.* Englewood Cliffs, NJ: Prentice-Hall, 1985. 457 p.
The authors see tourism as a system rather than an industry. They divide it into four parts: "Market," "Travel," "Destination," and "Marketing." Within these major areas, chapters discuss specifics such as motivation, promotion, development, and regulation of tourism. Each section concludes with readings summarizing the overall theme. These are usually symposium papers and the like. It is a thorough analysis of tourism with many statistics and charts but with no illustrations.

1198. Murphy, Peter E. *Tourism: A Community Approach.* New York: Methuen, 1986. 200 p.
Murphy examines tourism from the viewpoint of the destination areas. He focuses on an ecological approach to development and planning which would encourage local initiative in development. Issues of accessibility, economics, social, and cultural aspects are covered. Final section discusses planned tourism as a community industry.

1199. Owen, John D. *The Price of Leisure: An Economic Analysis of the Demand for Leisure Time.* Montreal, PQ: McGill-Queen's University Press, 1969. 169 p.
Owen gives an economic analysis of the demand for leisure time and presents data on its growth from 1900–1961. He provides an analysis of commercial recreation in the United States for the same period. The study includes empirical models and statistical results as well as suggestions for further research.

1200. Payne, Daniel H. *A Guide to Resort Time Sharing.* eastern ed. Norfolk, VA: Donning, Co., 1983. 337 p.
Time sharing is a method of purchasing an apartment for a specified period of time each year. It can then be used for vacations or exchanged for a period of time at another resort. The author of this book has personally visited the timeshare resorts in the East and describes them in this directory. In addition, he describes the local region of the resort and gives directions to locate it.

1201. Pearce, Douglas. *Tourism Today: A Geographical Analysis.* Essex, England: Longman Scientific & Technical; New York: Wiley, 1987. 229 p.
This is a scholarly work that looks at the geographical methods of analyzing tourism. Pearce examines both the origin and the destination of tourist travel. Topics included are tourism models, motivation for travel, tourist flow internationally and domestically, study of destinations, and spatial structure of tourism.

1202. Phillips, Ralph G., and Webster, Susan. *Group Travel Operating Procedures.* New York: Van Nostrand Reinhold Co., 1983. 163 p.
The authors explain their system that assists travel agents in handling group travel effectively. Chapters describe preparing and selling the group package; processing reservations; invoicing; working with hotels, airlines, and ground operators; finalization; escorting; and reconciling of bills and adjustments.

1203. Reilly, Robert T. *Handbook of Professional Tour Management.* Wheaton, IL: Merton House Publishing Co., 1982. 138 p.
Reilly gives detailed information on tour management. He explains the skills and qualifications that make a good tour manager and provides many useful tips.

1204. Ritchie, J. R. Brent, and Goeldner, Charles R., eds. *Travel, Tourism, and Hospitality Research: A Handbook for Managers and Researchers.* New York: Wiley, 1987. 516 p.
This handbook by selected experts in various aspects of travel and tourism research, aimed at managers and beginning researchers, gives an overview of available research as well as fundamental concepts and methods. Intended primarily as a reference book or seminar text, it is divided into eight parts: "A Managerial Perspective," "Fundamentals of Tourism Research," "National, Regional, and Municipal Perspectives," "Some Disciplin-

ary Perspectives," "An Industry Sector Perspective," "Assessing the Impacts of Tourism," "Data Collection Methods of Particular Relevance," and "Special Marketing Applications."

1205. Rosenow, John E., and Pulsipher, Gerreld L. *Tourism, the Good, the Bad, and the Ugly.* Edited by Kathryn Collura. Lincoln, NE: Century Three Press, 1979. 264 p.

This book is on tourism's role in helping to preserve and enhance America's heritage and environment. The authors discuss a "new tourism" that will not spoil the very attractions being visited. Along with covering various places for tourism, this book discusses the limits of tourism, energy and its relationship to the new tourism, and the future of tourism in the U.S.

1206. Seth, Pran Nath. *Successful Tourism Management.* New Delhi, India: Sterling, 1985. 338 p.

This is an introduction to management and marketing in tourism. Chapters cover planning and development as well. Seth is an officer of the Department of Tourism in India and has included several chapters on tourism in India and other parts of Asia.

1207. *The Sierra Club Guides to the National Parks of the East and Middle West.* New York: Stewart, Tabori, & Chang, 1986. 395 p.

The first of five regional guides planned to cover all forty-eight national parks. The history, animals, plant life, and points of interest are presented for each park. Up-to-date information on facilities, trails, and sites is included along with excellent new maps. This volume describes Acadia, Biscayne, Everglades, Great Smoky Mountains, Hot Springs, Isle Royale, Mammoth Cave, Shenandoah, Virgin Islands, and Voyageurs national parks.

1208. U.S. Travel Data Center. *Special Studies in Travel Economics and Marketing: Impact of Foreign Visitors on State Economies, 1983.* Washington DC, 1985. 23 p.

This study was conducted by the U.S. Travel Data center and is the first objective estimate of the number of foreign travelers in individual states based upon large-scale surveys of foreign visitors. The text covers two topics: "Foreign Visitor Expenditures in the U.S." and "Economic Impact of Foreign Visitors Expenditures in the U.S." Appendices include methodologies, impact model, and additional statistical charts.

1209. U.S. Travel Data Center. *U.S. Market for Package Tours.* Special Studies in Travel Economics and Marketing. Washington, DC, 1984. 44 p.

The objective of this study was to determine the major characteristics of package tour purchasers and to determine the potential market for tour package travel. Statistics were gathered during 1981 and 1982 by the U.S. Travel Data Center. Statistical tables of the survey are included in the appendix.

1210. World Tourism Organization. *Methodologies for Carrying Out Sample Surveys on Tourism.* Statistical Methods and Techniques, C.3.1. Madrid, Spain: 1983. 91 p.

This is a handbook intended for national tourism administrations in developing countries. The approach is concrete and concise. It is aimed at producing a very basic statistical survey. Chapters cover how to conduct a sample survey, elements of planning sample surveys, sample surveys for holiday departures and holiday movements, monthly survey of hotel occupancy, road and rail survey of return movements from holidays, and survey of tourist generating and hosting bodies.

Appendix A:
Associations

STATE ASSOCIATIONS

Alabama

Alabama Hotel & Motel Association
660 Adams Avenue
Montgomery, AL 36014
205-263-3407
Alabama Restaurant & Foodservice
Association
2100 Data Drive, Suite 207
Birmingham, AL 35224
205-988-9880

Alaska

Alaska Cabaret, Hotel & Restaurant
Association
P.O. Box 10-4839
Anchorage, AK 99510
907-263-2800
Alaska Hotel & Motel Association
P.O. Box 104900
Anchorage, AK 99510
907-563-7977

Arizona

Arizona Hotel & Motel Association
3003 North Central, # 1204
Phoenix, AZ 85012
602-264-6081
Arizona Restaurant Association
112 North Central, Suite 417
Phoenix, AZ 85004
602-285-3256

Southern Arizona Restaurant Association
465 West St. Mary's Road, Suite 300
Tuscon, AZ 85705
602-791-9106

California

California Hotel & Motel Association
P.O. Box 160405
Sacramento, CA 95816
916-444-5780
California Restaurant Association
3780 Wilshire Blvd., Suite 600
Los Angeles, CA 90010
213-384-1200

Colorado

Colorado-Wyoming Hotel & Motel
Association
999 18th Street, Suite 1240
Denver, CO 80202
303-297-8335
Colorado-Wyoming Restaurant
Association
899 Logan Street, Suite 300
Denver, CO 80203
303-830-2972

Connecticut

Connecticut Hotel & Motel Association
179 Allyn Street, Suite 212
Hartford, CT 06103
203-522-0747

Connecticut Restaurant Association
19 Wallingford Road
Cheshire, CT 06410
203-271-2151

Delaware

Delaware Hotel-Motel Association
P.O. Box 2192
Wilmington, DE 19899
302-594-3121
Delaware Restaurant Association
325 E. Main Street, Suite 300
P.O. Box 7838
Newark, DE 19714
302-366-8565

District of Columbia

Hotel Association of Washington, DC
1219 Connecticut Avenue, N.W.
Washington, DC 20036
202-833-3350

Florida

Florida Hotel & Motel Association
P.O. Box 1529
Tallahassee, FL 32302
904-224-2888
Florida Restaurant Association
2441 Hollywood Blvd.
Hollywood, FL 33020
305-921-6300

Hawaii

Hawaii Hotel Association
2270 Kalakaua Avenue, Suite 1103
Honolulu, HI 96815
808-923-0407
Hawaii Restaurant Association
657 Kapiolani Blvd.
Honolulu, HI 96813
808-536-9105

Idaho

Idaho Innkeepers Association
P.O. Box 8212
Boise, ID 83707
208-362-2637
Idaho Restaurant & Beverage Association
P.O. Box 1594
Boise, ID 83701
208-345-9830

Illinois

Hotel-Motel Association of Illinois
27 East Monroe Street, Suite 700
Chicago, IL 60603
312-346-3135
Illinois Restaurant Association
350 West Ontario
Chicago, IL 60610
312-372-6200

Indiana

Indiana Hotel & Motel Association
310 North Alabama, Suite A-100
Indianapolis, IN 46204
317-636-6059
Indiana Restaurant Association
2120 North Meridian Street
Indianpolis, IN 46202
317-924-5106

Iowa

Iowa Lodging Association
515 28th Street
Des Moines, IA 50312
515-283-2000
Iowa Restaurant & Beverage Association
415 Shops Building
Des Moines, IA 50309
515-282-8304

Kansas

Kansas Lodging Association
810 Merchants Tower
Topeka, KS 66612
913-233-9344

Kansas Restaurant Association
359 South Hydraulic
Wichita, KS 67211
316-267-8383

Kentucky

Kentucky Hotel & Motel Association
6802 Windhurst Road
Louisville, KY 40207
502-454-0052
Kentucky Restaurant Association
422 Executive Park
Louisville, KY 40207
502-896-0464

Louisiana

Louisiana Hotel & Motel Association
330 Exchange Alley
New Orleans, LA 70130
504-525-9326
Louisiana Restaurant Association
2800 Veterans Blvd., Suite 160
Metairie, LA 70002
504-831-7788

Maine

Maine Innkeepers Association
142 Free Street
Portland, ME 04101
207-773-7670
Maine Restaurant Association
5 Wade Street
P.O. Box 5060
Augusta, ME 04330
207-623-2178

Maryland

Maryland Hotel-Motel Association
P.O. Box 209
Severna Park, MD 21146
301-647-7880
Restaurant Association of Maryland
Suburbia Building, Suite 305
5602 Baltimore National Pike
Baltimore, MD 21228
301-788-6400

Massachusetts

Massachusetts Hotel & Motel Association
20 Park Plaza, Suite 831
Boston, MA 02116
617-482-4414
Massachusetts Restaurant Association
11 Lakeside Office Park, 607 North
Avenue
Wakefield, MA 01880
617-245-8411

Michigan

Michigan Lodging Association
30161 Southfield Road, Suite 322
Southfield, MI 48076
313-645-5850
Michigan Restaurant Association
215 S. Washington Street, Suite D
Lansing, MI 48933
517-484-2444

Minnesota

Minnesota Hotel & Motor Hotel
Association
871 Jefferson Avenue
St. Paul, MN 55102
612-222-7401
Minnesota Restaurant Association
871 Jefferson Avenue
St. Paul, MN 55102
612-222-7401

Mississippi

Mississippi Hotel & Motel Association
5135 Galaxie Drive, Suite 504E
Jackson, MS 39206
601-981-1160
Mississippi Restaurant Association
P.O. Box 16395
Jackson, MS 39236
601-982-4281

Missouri

Missouri Hotel & Motel Association
119 Madison Street
Jefferson City, MO 65101
314-636-2107

Missouri Restaurant Association
P.O. Box 10277
Kansas City, MO 64111
816-753-5222

Montana

Montana Innkeepers Association
P.O. Box 6276
Helena, MT 59604
406-449-8408
Montana Restaurant Association
P.O. Box 1193
Great Falls, MT 59403
406-761-6370

Nebraska

Nebraska Lodging Association
1640 Woodmen Tower
Omaha, NE 68102
402-341-1717
Nebraska Restaurant Association
1220 Lincoln Benefit Building
Lincoln, NE 68508
402-475-4647

Nevada

Nevada Hotel & Motel Association
3017 West Charleston Blvd., Suite 50
Las Vegas, NV 89102
702-878-9272
Nevada Restaurant Association
3017 West Charleston Blvd., Suite 50
Las Vegas, NV 89102
702-878-2313

New Hampshire

New Hampshire Hospitality Association
15 Pleasant Street, # 14
P.O. Box 1175
Concord, NH 03301
603-228-9585

New Jersey

New Jersey Hotel-Motel Association
826 West State Street
Trenton, NJ 08618
609-599-9000
New Jersey Restaurant Association
853 Kearny Avenue
Kearny, NJ 07032
201-997-8800

New Mexico

New Mexico Hotel & Motel Association
2161 Candelero Street
P.O. Box 4665
Santa Fe, NM 87502
505-982-9625
New Mexico Restaurant Association
2130 San Mateo Blvd., N.E., Suite C
Albuquerque, NM 87110
505-268-2474

New York

New York State Hotel & Motel
    Association
505 Eighth Avenue
New York, NY 10018
212-564-2300
New York State Restaurant Association
505 Eighth Avenue, 7th floor
New York, NY 10018
212-714-1330

North Carolina

North Carolina Hotel & Motel
    Association
5 West Harget 1100
P.O. Box 2598
Raleigh, NC 27602
919-821-1435
North Carolina Restaurant Association
P.O. Box 6528
Raleigh, NC 27628
919-782-5022

North Dakota

North Dakota Hospitality Association
P.O. Box 428
Bismarck, ND 58502
701-223-3313

Ohio

Ohio Hotel & Motel Association
50 West Broad Street, Suite 3140
Columbus, OH 43215
614-224-9843
Ohio Restaurant Association
490 City Park Avenue, Suite 200
Columbus, OH 43215
614-228-0522

Oklahoma

Oklahoma Hotel & Motel Association
8612 South Kentucky
Oklahoma City, OK 73159
405-685-5429
Oklahoma Restaurant Association
3800 North Portland
Oklahoma City, OK 73112
405-942-8181

Oregon

Oregon Lodging Association
12724 S.E. Stark Street
Portland, OR 97233
503-255-5135
Oregon Restaurant & Hospitality
Association
3724 N.E. Broadway
Portland, OR 97232
503-249-0974

Pennsylvania

Pennsylvania Restaurant Association
501 North Front Street, Suite 200
Harrisburg, PA 17101
717-232-4433
Pennsylvania Travel Council
21 North Fourth Street
Harrisburg, PA 17101
717-232-8880

Rhode Island

Rhode Island Hospitality Association
P.O. Box 7415
Cumberland, RI 02864
401-334-3180

South Carolina

South Carolina Hotel & Motel
Association
1338 Main Street, Suite 507
Columbia, SC 29201
803-252-0004
South Carolina Restaurant Association
Barringer Building, Suite 510
1338 Main Street
Columbia, SC 29201
803-254-3906

South Dakota

South Dakota Inn Keepers Association
809 West Avenue, North
Sioux Falls, SD 57104
605-331-4194
South Dakota Restaurant Association
805½ South Main Avenue
Sioux Falls, SD 57101
605-361-7227

Tennessee

Tennessee Hotel & Motel Association
644 West Iris Drive
Nashville, TN 37204
615-385-9770
Tennessee Restaurant Association
229 Court Square
P.O. Box 1029
Franklin, TN 37065
615-790-2703

Texas

Texas Hotel & Motel Association
8602 Crownhill Blvd.
San Antonio, TX 78209
512-828-3566

Texas Restaurant Association
P.O. Box 1429
Austin, TX 78767
512-444-6543

Utah

Utah Hotel & Motel Association
#9 Exchange Place, Suite 715
Salt Lake City, UT 84111
801-359-0104
Utah Restaurant Association
141 West Haven Avenue, Suite 2
Salt Lake City, UT 84115
801-487-4821

Vermont

Vermont Lodging & Restaurant
Association
100 State Street
P.O. Box 9
Montpelier, VT 05602
802-229-0062

Virginia

Restaurant Association of Metropolitan
Washington
7926 Jones Branch Drive, #530
McLean, VA 22102
703-356-1315
Virginia Hotel & Motel Association
300 West Franklin Street
Richmond, VA 23220
804-648-4895
Virginia Restaurant Association
2101 Libbie Avenue
Richmond, VA 23230
804-288-3065

Washington

Restaurant Association of the State of
Washington
722 Securities Building
Seattle, WA 98101
206-682-6174
Washington State Lodging Association
497 Tyee Avenue
Olympia, WA 98502
206-754-0655

West Virginia

West Virginia Hotel & Motel Association
P.O. Box 1946
Charleston, WV 25327
304-342-1169
West Virginia Restaurant Association
P.O. Box 2391
Charleston, WV 25328
304-342-6511

Wisconsin

Wisconsin Innkeepers Association
509 W. Wisconsin Avenue, Suite 619
Milwaukee, WI 53203
414-217-2851
Wisconsin Restaurant Association
122 West Washington Avenue
Madison, WI 53703
608-251-3663

Wyoming

See Colorado-Wyoming Hotel & Motel
Association
Colorado-Wyoming Restaurant
Association

NATIONAL AND INTERNATIONAL ASSOCIATIONS

American Bed & Breakfast Association
16 Villiage Green
Crofton, MD 21114
301-261-0180
American Correctional Food Services
277 East 6100, South
Salt Lake City, UT 84107
801-268-3000

American Culinary Federation
P. O. Box 3466
St. Augustine, FL 32084
904-824-4468
American Dietetic Association
208 South LaSalle, Suite 1100
Chicago, IL 60604
312-899-4855

American Dinner Theater Institute
Box 367
Cockeyville, MD 21030
301-771-0367

American Gas Association
1515 Wilson Blvd.
Arlington, VA 22209

American Hotel & Motel Association
1201 New York Avenue, N.W.
Washington, DC, 20005
202-289-3100

American Institute of Food Distributors
28-12 Broadway
Fair Lawn, NJ 07410
201-791-5570

American Institutions Food Service
Association
277 East 6100, South
Salt Lake City, UT 84107
801-268-3000

American School Food Service
Association
5600 Quebec Street, 300B
Englewood, CO 80222
303-757-8555

American Society for Hospital Food
Service Administrators
840 North Lake Shore Drive
Chicago, IL 60611
312-280-6416

American Society of Associations
Executives
1575 Eye Street, N.W.
Washington, DC, 20005
202-626-ASAE

American Society of Travel Agents, Inc.
1101 Ring Street
P. O. Box 23992
Washington, DC, 42314
703-739-2782

American Truck Stop Operators
Association
P. O. Box 14126
North Palm Beach, FL 33408
305-848-9999

Association of Group Travel Executives
320 East 58th Street
New York, NY 10022
212-938-0033

Association of Independent Meeting
Planners
1012 Atlantic Avenue
Atlantic City, NJ 08401
609-347-8683

Canadian Restaurant and Foodservice
Association
80 Bloor Street, Suite 1201
Toronto, ON Canada M5S2V
416-923-8416

Chefs de Cuisine Association
235 West 46th Street, Suite 329
New York, NY 10036
212-245-7173

Club Managers Association of America
7615 Winterberry Place
Bethesda, MD 20817
202-229-3600

Commercial Food Equipment Service
Association
60 Revere Drive, Suite 500
Northbrook, IL 60062
312-480-9080

Convention Liaison Council
1575 Eye Street, N.W. Suite 1200
Washington, DC, 20005
202-626-2764

Council on Hotel, Restaurant &
Institutional Education
Human Development Bldg., Rm.
5-208
University Park, PA 16802
814-863-0586

Education Foundation of the National
Restaurant Association
20 North Wacker Drive, Suite 2620
Chicago, IL 60606
312-782-1703

Exposition Service Contractors
Association
1516 South Pontius Avenue
Los Angeles, CA 90025
213-478-0215

Food Equipment Manufacturers
Association
111 East Wacker Drive, Suite 600
Chicago, IL 60601
312-644-6610

Food Marketing Institute
1750 K Street, N.W.
Washington, DC, 20006
202-452-8444

Foodservice & Lodging Institute
1919 Pennsylvania Avenue, N.W.,
#504
Washington, DC, 20006
202-659-9060

Foodservice Consultants Society
International
12345 30th Avenue N.E., Suite H
Seattle, WA 98125
206-367-3274

Foodservice Equipment Distributors
Association
332 South Michigan Avenue, 1840
Chicago, IL 60604
312-427-9605

Foundation for International Meetings
1726 M Street, N.W., Suite 1002
Washington, DC, 20036
202-457-0909
Hotel and Motel Brokers
10920 Ambassadors Drive
Kansas City, MO 64153
816-891-7070
Hotel Employees & Restaurant
  Employees International Union
120 East 4th Street
Cincinnati, OH 45202
513-621-0300
Hotel Sales and Marketing Association
  International
1300 L Street, N.W., Suite 800
Washington, DC 20005
202-789-0089
In-Flight Food Service Association
304 West Liberty Street, Suite 301
Louisville, KY 40202
502-583-3783
Institute of Food Technologists
221 North LaSalle Street
Chicago, IL 60601
312-782-8424
International Association of Conference
  Centers
45 Progress Parkway
Maraly Heights, MO 13604
314-469-9093
International Association of Convention
  and Visitor Bureaus
1802 Woodfield Drive
Savoy, IL 61874
217-359-8881
International Association of Hospitality
  Accountants
Box 27649
Austin, TX 78755
512-346-5680
International Chefs Association
P.O. Box 1889
New York, NY 10116
201-825-8455
International Council of Hotel/Motel
  Management Company
888 Seventh Avenue
New York, NY 10106
212-265-4506
International Council of Hotel,
  Restaurant & Institutional
  Education
311 First Street, N.W.
Washington, DC, 20001
International Exhibitors Association
5103-13 Backlick Road
Annandale, VA 22003
703-941-3725

International Foodservice Distributors
  Association
201 Park Washington Court
Falls Church, VA 22046
703-532-9400
International Foodservice Editorial
  Council
82 Osborne Lane
East Hampton, NY 11937
516-324-2725
International Food Service Executives
  Association
3017 West Charleston Blvd., #50
Las Vegas, NV 89102
702-878-2029
International Foodservice Manufacturers
  Association
321 North Clark Street, Suite 2900
Chicago, IL 60610
312-644-8989
International Franchise Association
1350 New York Street, Suite 900
Washington, DC, 20005
202-628-8000
International Hotel Association
89, rue du Faubourg-Saint-Honore
F-75008
Paris, France
International Hotel, Catering and Duty
  Free Association
5000 Van Nuys Blvd., Suite 400
Sherman Oaks, CA 91403
818-995-7338
International Military Clubs Executive
  Association
1438 Duke Street
Alexandria, VA 22314
703-548-0093
International Society of Hotel Association
  Executives
P.O. Box 1529
Tallahassee, FL 32302
612-222-7401
Marine Hotel, Catering and Duty Free
  Association
5000 Van Nuys Blvd., Suite 400
Sherman Oaks, CA 91403
818-995-7338
Marketing Agents for Food Service
  Industry
111 East Wacker Drive, Suite 600
Chicago, IL 60601
312-644-6610
Meeting Planners International
1950 Stemmons Freeway
Dallas, TX 75207
214-746-5222

Multi-Unit Food Service Operators
425 Park Avenue
New York, NY 10022
212-371-9400

National Association for Concessionaires
35 East Wacker Drive, Suite 1849
Chicago, IL 60601
312-236-3858

National Association of Black Hospitality
Professionals
Box 5443
Plainfield, NJ 07060
201-753-7856

National Association of Catering
Executives
2500 Wilshire Blvd., Suite 603
Los Angeles, CA 90057
213-483-6223

National Association of College &
University Food Services
1405 South Harrison Road, Suite 303
Manly Miles Building, Michigan State
University
East Lansing, MI 48824
517-332-2494

National Association of Convenience
Stores
1605 King Street
Alexandria, VA 22314
703-684-3600

National Association of Exposition
Managers
334 East Garfield Road
Box 377
Aurora, OH 44202
216-562-8255

National Association of Food Equipment
Manufacturers
111 East Wacker Drive, Suite 600
Chicago, IL 60601
312-644-6610

National Association of Pizza Operators
P.O. Box 114
Santa Claus, IN 47579
812-544-2608

National Association of Restaurant
Managers
2849 East North Lane
Phoenix, AZ 85028
602-482-6705

National Association of Truck Stop
Operators
1199 North Fairfax Street, Suite 801
Alexandria, VA 22313
703-549-2100

National Automatic Merchandising
Association
20 North Wacker Drive, Suite 3500
Chicago, IL 60606
312-346-0370

National Bartenders Association
1377 K Street N.W., #67
Washington, DC, 20005
800-227-8637

National Club Association
1625 Eye Street, N.W., Suite 609
Washington, DC, 20006
202-296-3426

National Executive Housekeepers
Association
1001 Eastwind Drive, Suite 301
Westerville, OH 43081
614-895-7166

National Food Brokers Association
1010 Massachusetts Avenue, N.W.
Washington, DC, 20001
202-789-2844

National Food Distributors Association
111 East Wacker Drive, Suite 600
Chicago, IL 60601
312-644-6610

National Food Processors Association
1401 New York Avenue, N.W.
Washington, DC, 20005
202-639-5900

National Food Service Association
P. O. Box 1932
Columbus, OH 43216
614-262-3346

National Institutional Food Distributors
P.O. Box 724945
Atlanta, GA 30339
404-952-0871

National Licensed Beverage Association
309 North Washington
Alexandria, VA 22314
703-683-6633

National Prepared Frozen Food
Association
99 West Hawthorne Avenue
Valley Stream, NY 11508
516-825-3000

National Restaurant Association
311 First Street, N.W.
Washington, DC, 20001
800-424-5156

National Sanitation Foundation
3475 Plymouth Road
P.O. Box 1468
Ann Arbor, MI 48105
313-769-8010

National Single Service Food Association
5775 Peachtree-Dunwoodry Road,
   Suite 500D
Atlanta, GA 30342

Pacific Area Travel Association
1 Montgomery Street Telesis, Suite
   1750
San Francisco, CA 94104
415-986-4646

Preferred Hotels Association
1901 South Meyers Road, Suite 220
Oakbrook Terrace, IL 60148
312-953-0404

Professional Convention Management
   Association
100 Vestavia Office Park, Suite 220
Birmingham, AL 35216
205-823-7262

Roundtable for Women in Foodservice
145 West First Street, Suite A
Tustin, CA 92680
714-838-1662

Society for Foodservice Management
304 West Liberty Street, Suite 301
Louisville, KY 40202
502-583-3783

Society for Foodservice Systems
40 ITM
760 Transfer Road
St Paul, MN 55114
612-646-7077

Society for the Advancement of
   Foodservice Research
304 West Liberty Street, Suite 301
Louisville, KY 40202
502-583-3783

Society of Incentive Travel Executives
271 Madison Avenue, Suite 904
New York, NY 10016
212-889-9340

Sommelier Society of America
35 West 36th Street
New York, NY 10016
212-686-7435

Tourist House Association of America
Box 355-A
R.D.2
Greentown, PA 18426

Trade Show Bureau
8 Beach Road
East Orleans, MA 02643
617-240-0177

Travel & Tourism Research Association
Box 8066
Foothill Station
Salt Lake City, UT 84108
801-581-3351

Travel Industry Association of America
1133 21st Street, N.W.
2 Lafayette Center
Washington, DC 20036
202-293-1433

Vatel Club
250 West 57th Street, Room 2231
New York, NY 10019
212-246-9397

Wine & Spirits Wholesalers of America
1023 15th Street, N.W., 4th Floor
Washington, DC 20005
202-371-WSWA

Wine Institute
165 Post Street
San Francisco, CA 94108
415-986-0878

Appendix B:
Hotel, Restaurant, and
Foodservice College Programs

Alaska Pacific University
    4101 University Drive   \
    Anchorage, AK 99508
Andrews University
    Food Distribution and Management
    Berrien Springs, MI 49104
Appalachian State University
    Department of Home Economics
    Boone, NC 28608
    704-262-3120
Arizona State University
    Department of Family Resources and
        Human Development
    Tempe, AZ 85287
    602-965-7731
Arkansas Tech University
    Hotel, Restaurant Management
    Tucker Hall 11D
    Russellville, AR 72801
    501-968-0607
Ashland College
    School of Business Administration
    Miller Hall
    Ashland, OH 44805
    419-289-4142
Auburn University
    School of Home Economics, Nutrition,
        and Foods
    360 Spidle Hall
    Auburn, AL 36849
    205-826-4261
Ball State University
    Department of Home Economics
    Muncie, IN 47306
    317-285-5931

Barber-Scotia College
    Hospitality Department
    145 Cabarrus Avenue
    Concord, NC 28025
    704-786-5171
Boston University
    Metro College, Hotel & Food
        Administration
    808 Commonwealth Avenue
    Boston, MA 02215
    617-353-3261
Bowling Green State University
    Department of Home Economics
    Johnston Hall
    Bowling Green, OH 43403
    419-372-2026
Brigham Young University
    Food Systems Administration
    2218 SFLC
    Provo, UT 84602
Brooklyn College
    Department of Health and Nutrition
        Sciences
    Bedford Avenue and Avenue H
    Brooklyn, NY 11210
    718-780-5026
Bryant College
    Hotel, Restaurant, and Institutional
        Management
    Smithfield, RI 02917
    401-231-1200
California Polytechnic State University
    Food Science/ Nutrition Deparment
    San Luis Obispo, CA 93407
    805-546-2377

California State Polytechnic University
    School of Hotel, Restaurant, and
        Travel Management
    3801 West Temple
    Pomona, CA 91768
    714-598-4235
California State University, Chico
    School of Home Economics
    117 Glenn Hall
    Chico, CA 95929
    916-895-6805
California State University, Fresno
    Department of Enology, Food Science,
        and Nutrition
    Fresno, CA 93740
    209-294-2164
California State University, Long Beach
    Department of Home Economics
    1250 Bellfolower Road
    Long Beach, CA 90840
    213-498-4485
California State University, Los Angeles
    Department of Family Studies and
        Consumer Science
    5151 State University Drive
    Los Angeles, CA 90032
    213-224-3682
California State University, Northridge
    Department of Home Economics
    18111 Nordhoff Street
    Northridge, CA 91330
    818-885-3051
Campbell University
    Foodservice Management
    Buies Creek, NC 27506
Central Michigan University
    Hospitality Services Administration
    100 Smith Hall
    Mt. Pleasant, MI 48859
    517-774-3701
Central Missouri State University
    Home Economics—Applied Sciences
        and Technology
    250 Grinstead
    Warrensburg, MO 64093
    816-429-4362
Chicago State University
    Hotel and Restaurant Management
    95th and King Drive
    Chicago, IL 60628
    312-995-3978
College of Boca Raton
    3601 North Military Trail
    Boca Raton, FL 33431
College of Mount St. Joseph on the Ohio
    Foodservice Management
    Mount St. Joseph, OH 45051

College of St. Scholastica
    Foodservice Management
    Duluth, MN 55811
Colorado State University
    Restaurant Management
    Gifford Building
    Fort Collins, CO 80523
Cornell University
    School of Hotel Administration
    Statler Hall
    Ithaca, NY 14853
    607-256-4990
Culinary School of Kendall College
    2408 Orrington Avenue
    Evanston, IL 60201
    312-866-1314
Drexel University
    Foodservice Systems Management
    Department of Nutrition & Food
        Sciences
    Philadelphia, PA 19103
East Carolina University
    Food, Nutrition, and Institutional
        Management
    School of Home Economics
    Greenville, NC 27334
East Stroudsburg State College
    Department of Hotel & Resort
        Management
    East Stroudsburg, PA 18301
    717-424-3511
Eastern Michigan University
    Dietetics
    Roosevelt Hall
    Ypsilanti, MI 48197
El Centro College—DCCCD
    Food and Hospitality Services Institute
    Main at Lamar
    Dallas, TX 75202
    214-746-2202
Fairleigh Dickinson University
    Hotel-Restaurant Management
    180 Fairview Avenue
    Rutherford, NJ 07070
    201-460-5362
Fairmont State College
    Foodservice Management
    Home Economics
    Fairmont, WV 26554
Ferris State College
    FoodService—Hospitality Management
    Hospitality Management
    Big Rapids, MI 49307
    616-796-0461
Florida International University
    School of Hospitality Management
    Tamiami Campus
    Miami, FL 33199
    305-554-5291

Florida State University
Hospitality Administration
225 William Johnston Building
Tallahassee, FL 32306
904-644-4787

Framingham State College
State Street, Hemenway Hall
Framingham, MA 01701

George Washington University
817 23rd Street, N.W.
Washington, DC 20052
202-676-7071

Georgia State University
Hotel, Restaurant, and Travel
Administration
College of Public and Urban Affairs
Atlanta, GA 30303
404-658-3512

Glassboro State College
Department of Home Economics
Westby Building
Glassboro, NJ 08028
609-863-7042

Golden Gate University
Hotel, Restaurant, and Institutional
Management
534 Mission Street
San Francisco, CA 94105
415-442-7215

Hampton University
Human Ecology Deparment
Hampton, VA 23668
804-727-5469

Herbert H. Lehman College
Department of Health Services,
Dietetics, Food, & Nutrition
Bedford Park Blvd., West
Bronx, NY 10468
212-960-8775

Hofstra University
School of Business
Hempstead Turnpike
Hempstead, NY 11550
516-560-5015

Howard University
Foodservice Administration
2400 6th Street, N.W.
Washington, DC 20059

Hunter College
Nutritional and Food Science Program
425 East 25th Street
New York, NY 10010
212-481-7590

Huston-Tillotson College
Hospitality Management
1820 East 8th Street
Austin, TX 78702
512-476-7421

Immaculata College
Foodservice Management
Immaculata, PA 19345

Indiana University of Pennsylvania
10 Ackerman Hall
Indiana, PA 15701

Iowa State University
Hotel, Restaurant, and Institutional
Management
11 MacKay Hall
Ames, IA 50011

James Madison University
Hotel and Restaurant Management
Harrisonburg, VA 22807
703-568-6694

Jefferson Community College
Business Division, Culinary Arts
Department
109 East Broadway
Louisville, KY 40202
502-584-0181

Johnson & Wales College
Culinary Arts Division
One Washington Avenue
Providence, RI 02905
401-456-1192

Kansas State University
Dietetics, Restaurant, & Institutional
Management
104 Justin Hall
Manhattan, KS 66506
913-532-5521

Kent State University
School of Family and Consumer
Studies
Nixson Hall
Kent, OH 44242
216-672-2197

Lake Michigan College
Foodservice Management
2755 East Napier Avenue
Benton Harbor, MI 49022

Loma Linda University
Food Systems Management
11234 Anderson
Loma Linda, CA 92354

Mankato State University
Home Economics, Food, and
Nutrition
Box 44
Mankato, MN 56001

Mansfield State College
Foodservice/Dietetics
Home Economics Department
Mansfield, PA 16933

Marshall University
Foodservice Management
Huntington, WV 25701

Mercyhurst College
    Hotel and Restaurant Management
    Slenwood Hills
    Erie, PA 16546
    814-825-0333
Messiah College
    Home Economics Department
    Grantham, PA 17027
Miami University
    Food Management, Home Economics
    260 McGuffey Hall
    Oxford, OH 45056
Michigan State University
    School of Hotel, Restaurant, and
        Institutional Management
    425 Eppley Center
    East Lansing, MI 48824
    517-355-5080
Mississippi State University
    Department of Home Economics
    P.O. Drawer HE
    Mississippi State, MS 39762
    601-325-3820
Montana State University
    Department of Home Economics
    122 Herrick Hall
    Bozeman, MT 59717
    406-994-5004
Montclair State College
    Department of Home Economics
    Upper Montclair, NJ 07043
    210-893-5291
Moorhead State University
    Institutional Foods Laboratory
    UPO Box 708
    Moorehead, KY 40351
    606-783-2280
Mundelein College
    Department of Home Economics
    6363 North Sheridan Road
    Chicago, IL 60660
    312-262-8100
New Hampshire College
    Culinary Arts, Hotel—Restaurant
        Management
    2500 North River Road
    Manchester, NH 03104
    603-668-2211
New Mexico Highlands University
    Division of Business & Economics
    Las Vegas, NM 87701
    505-425-7511
New York University
    Department of Home Economics and
        Nutrition
    239 Green Street, Rm. 537 East Bldg.
    New York, NY 10003
    212-998-5580

Nicholls State University
    Food Distribution and Management
    Thibodaux, LA 70301
North Carolina Wesleyan College
    Wesleyan College Station
    Rocky Mount, NC 27801
North Dakota State University
    Food and Nutrition
    P.O. Box 5057
    Fargo, ND 58105
    701-237-7474
Northern Arizona University
    School of Health Professions
    CU Box 6003
    Flagstaff, AZ 86011
    602-523-6174
Northern Arizona University
    School of Hotel and Restaurant
        Management
    Box 15066
    Flagstaff, AZ 86011
    602-523-2845
Northern Illinois University
    Department of Home Economics
    Dekalb, IL 60115
Ohio State University
    Department of Human Nutrition and
        Food Management
    265 Campbell Hall
    Columbus, OH 43210
    614-422-4485
Oklahoma State University
    Food, Nutrition, and Institution
        Administration
    Stillwater, OK 74078
    405-624-5039
Oregon State Universtiy
    Hotel, Restaurant, and Tourism
        Management
    Bexell Hall
    Corvallis, OR 97331
    503-754-3693
Pennsylvania State University
    Hotel, Restaurant, and Institutional
        Mangement
    20 Henderson Building
    University Park, PA 16802
    814-865-1736
Plattsburgh State University
    College of Arts and Sciences
    Ward Hall
    Plattsburgh, NY 12901
    518-564-4170
Potomac State College
    Food Management
    Keyser, WV 26726

Pratt Institute
  Department of Nutrition & Dietetics
  200 Willoughby Avenue
  Brooklyn, NY 11205
  718-636-3586
Purdue University
  Restaurant, Hotel & Institutional
    Management
  106 Stone Hall
  West Lafayette, IN 47907
  317-494-4643
Purdue University at Indianapolis
  Restaurant and Hotel Management
  799 West Michigan Avenue
  Indianapolis, IN 46202
  317-264-8772
Queens College
  Department of Home Economics
  65-30 Kissena Blvd.
  Flushing, NY 11367
  718-520-7219
Rochester Institute of Technology
  Food, Hotel, and Tourism
    Management
  1 Long Memorial Drive
  Rochester, NY 14623
  716-475-2867
Rosary College
  Department of Home Economics
  7900 West Division Street
  River Forest, IL 60305
  312-366-2490
Saint Leo College
  Restaurant Management—Business
    Administration Division
  P.O. Box 2067
  Saint Leo, FL 33574
  904-588-8309
San Diego State University
  School of Family Studies and
    Consumer Sciences
  FSCS Building
  San Diego, CA 92182
  619-265-3704
San Jose State University
  Department of Nutrition and Food
    Sciences
  San Jose, CA 95192
Shepherd College
  Division of Business
  Shepardstown, WV 25443
  304-876-2511
Siena Heights College
  Hotel, Restaurant, and Institutional
    Management
  1247 East Siena Heights Drive
  Adrian, MI 49221
  517-263-0731

Southern Arkansas University
  Hotel, Restaurant Management
  P.O. Box 3048
  Camden, AR 71701
Southern Illinois University
  Foods Nutrition Department
  Quigley Hall
  Carbondale, IL 62901
Southwest State University
  HRA Division
  Marshall, MN 56258
  507-537-7380
Southwest Texas State University
  Home Economics Department
  San Marcos, TX 78666
  512-245-2483
St. Thomas University
  16400 N.W. 32nd Avenue
  Miami, FL 33054
St. Vincent College
  Foodservice Management
  Latrobe, PA 15650
State University College at Buffalo
  Department of Nutrition and Food
    Science
  1300 Elmwood Avenue
  Buffalo, NY 14222
  716-878-4333
State University of New York—Oneonta
  Department of Home Economics
  Oneonta, NY 13820
  607-431-2704
Syracuse University
  Department of Human Nutrition
  200 Slocum Hall
  Syracuse, NY 13210
Texas Tech University
  Restaurant, Hotel, and Institutional
    Management
  Box 4170
  Lubbock, TX 79409
  806-742-3068
Tiffin University
  Hotel and Restaurant Management
    Program
  155 Miami Street
  Tiffin, OH 44883
  419-447-6442
Transylvania University
  Hotel, Restaurant, & Tourism
    Management
  MFA Building, 300 North Broadway
  Lexington, KY 40508
  606-333-8249
Tuskegee Institute
  Home Economics and Food
    Administration
  Tuskegee, AL 36088
  205-727-8331

University of Akron
  Food Distribution and Management
  302 East Buchtel Avenue
  Akron, OH 44325
University of Alaska
  Travel Industry Management
  School of Management
  Fairbanks, AK 99701
  907-474-6528
University of Arizona
  Department of Nutrition and Food
    Science
  Tucson, AZ 85721
  602-621-1449
University of California—Berkeley
  Department of Nutritional Sciences
  119 Morgan Hall
  Berkeley, CA 94720
  415-642-4090
University of California—Davis
  Dietetics Foodservice Management
  Department of Nutrition
  Davis, CA 95616
University of Denver
  School of Hotel & Restaurant
    Management
  Denver, CO 80208
  303-871-4271
University of Georgia
  Foodservice Management
  Dawson Hall
  Athens, GA 30602
University of Hawaii—Manoa
  School of Travel Industry Management
  2560 Campus Road
  Honolulu, HI 96822
  808-948-8946
University of Houston—University Park
  Conrad N. Hilton College of Hotel &
    Restaurant Management
  4800 Calhoun
  Houston, TX 77004
  713-749-2482
University of Illinois
  Foods and Nutrition
  386 Bevier Hall
  905 South Goodwin
  Urbana, IL 61801
  217-333-1324
University of Kentucky
  Restaurant Managment Program
  205 Erickson Hall
  Lexington, KY 40506
  606-257-3705
University of Maryland: College Park
  Department of Food, Nutrition, and
    Institutional Admin.
  College Park, MD 20742
  301-454-5289

University of Maryland: Eastern Shore
  Department of Hotel and Restaurant
    Management
  Room 409, Somerset Hall
  Princess Anne, MD 21853
  301-651-2200
University of Massachusetts
  Department of Hotel, Restaurant and
    Travel Administration
  Flint Lab
  Amherst, MA 01003
  413-545-2535
University of Minnesota Tech College
  Division of HRI Management
  Crookston, MN 56716
  218-281-6510
University of Minnesota—Twin Cities
  Hospitality and Foodservice
    Management
  1334 Eckles Avenue
  St. Paul, MN 55108
University of Missouri
  Food Science and Nutrition
  Building T-14, Room 118
  Columbia, MO 65211
  314-882-4113
University of Nebraska—Lincoln
  Human Nutrition & Foodservice
    Management
  202 Ruth Leverton Hall
  Lincoln, NE 68583
  402-472-2925
University of Nevada—Las Vegas
  College of Hotel Administration
  5400 Maryland Pkwy
  Las Vegas, NV 89154
  702-734-3230
University of New Hampshire
  Hotel Administration
  Whittemore School of Business
  Durham, NH 03824
  603-862-3303
University of New Haven
  School of Hotel, Restaurant, and
    Tourism Administration
  233 Harugari Hall
  300 Orange Avenue
  West Haven, CT 06516
  203-932-7362
University of New Orleans
  School of Hotel, Restaurant, and
    Tourism Administration
  New Orleans, LA 70148
  504-286-6385
University of North Carolina
  Food-Nutrition-Foodservices
  School of Home Economics
  Greensboro, NC 27412

University of Rhode Island
  Food & Nutritional Sciences
  College of Home Economics
  Kingston, RI 02881
University of San Francisco
  McLaren College of Business
  Golden Gate Avenue
  San Francisco, CA 94117
  415-666-6771
University of South Carolina
  Hotel, Restaurant, & Tourism
    Administration
  College of Applied Professional
    Sciences
  Columbia, SC 29208
  803-777-6665
University of Southern Mississippi
  Institution Administration
  Southern Station, Box 10025
  Hattiesburg, MS 39406
  601-266-4680
University of Southwestern Louisiana
  School of Home Economics
  USL P.O. Box 40399
  Lafayette, LA 70504
  318-231-6644
University of Tennessee
  Tourism, Food, and Lodging
    Administration
  220 CHE
  Knoxville, TN 37996
  615-974-5445
University of the Pacific
  3601 Pacific Avenue
  Stockton, CA 95211
University of Toledo
  Community & Technical College
  2 Bancroft Street
  Toledo, OH 43606
University of Vermont
  Human Nutrition and Foods
  Terrill Hall
  Burlington, VT 05405
  802-656-3374
University of Wisconsin—Madison
  Department of Food Science
  Babcock Hall
  1605 Linden Drive
  Madison, WI 53706
  608-263-1967
University of Wisconsin—Stout
  School of Home Economics
  Home Economics Building
  Menomonie, WI 54751
  715-232-2137
US International University
  Foodservice Industry Management
  10455 Pomerado Road
  San Diego, CA 92131

Virginia Polytechnic & State University
  Hotel, Restaurant, and Institutional
    Management
  Hillcrest Hall
  Blacksburg, VA 24061
  703-961-5515
Virginia State University
  Hotel-Restaurant Management
  School of Business, Box 427
  Petersburg, VA 23805
  804-520-6389
Washington State University
  Hotel and Restaurant Administration
  245 Todd Hall
  Pullman, WA 99164
  509-335-5766
Weber State College
  Foodservice Management
  Ogden, UT 84408
West Virginia University
  HRIM
  Institute, WV 25112
Western Illinois University
  Home Economics Department
  KH 204
  Macomb, IL 61455
  309-298-1085
Western Kentucky University
  Food, Nutrition, and Institutional
    Management
  Academic Complex
  Bowling Green, KY 42101
  502-745-4352
Western Michigan University
  Foodservice Administration
  Kalamazoo, MI 49008
Western States University
  111 North State College Blvd.
  Fullerton, CA 92631
  714-738-1000
Widener University
  The School of Hotel and Restaurant
    Management
  P.O. Box 7139
  Concord Pike
  Wilmington, DE 19803
  302-478-3000
Winthrop College
  School of Conservation Science and
    Allied Professions
  200 Thurmond Hall
  Rock Hill, SC 29733
  803-323-2101
Youngstown State University
  Food & Nutrition/Dietetics
  410 Wick Avenue
  Youngstown, OH 44555

Author Index

Numbers refer to citation numbers, not to page numbers.

Title Index

Numbers refer to citation numbers, not to page numbers.

Subject Index